The historical meanings of work

The historical meanings of work

Edited by

PATRICK JOYCE

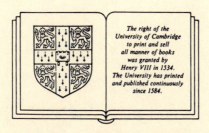

The right of the University of Cambridge to print and sell all manner of books was granted by Henry VIII in 1534. The University has printed and published continuously since 1584.

CAMBRIDGE UNIVERSITY PRESS

Cambridge
New York   New Rochelle
Melbourne   Sydney

Published by the Press Syndicate of the University of Cambridge
The Pitt Building, Trumpington Street, Cambridge CB2 1RP
32 East 57th Street, New York, NY 10022, USA
10 Stamford Road, Oakleigh, Melbourne 3166, Australia

First published 1987

First paperback edition 1989

Printed in Great Britain by
Redwood Burn Ltd, Trowbridge, Wiltshire

British Library cataloguing in publication data

The historical meanings of work.
1. Work – History
I. Joyce, Patrick, 1945–
306'.36'0903   HD6955

Library of Congress cataloguing in publication data

The historical meanings of work.
Bibliography.
Includes index.
1. Work.   2. Leisure.   3. Work ethic.   I. Joyce,
Patrick.
HD4904.H54   1987   306'.36   87–788

ISBN 0 521 30897 6 hard covers
ISBN 0 521 36686 0 paperback

Contents

For Roisin

1

The historical meanings of work: an introduction

PATRICK JOYCE

At a time when work and its future is under intense discussion the time is ripe for consideration of the history of work. In Britain this is all the more pressing as present public debate is laden with presuppositions about past work, mostly of dubious historical validity. Present concerns are interwoven with visions of work in such a way as to create mythological pasts for political purposes, whether those of the left or right; as for instance, that of the disappearing past of the supposedly 'traditional' working class, or the would-be renascent past of the 'Victorian values' of self-help and entrepreneurship. Such representations of work dissolve under closer historical scrutiny, yet in themselves they evince the intensely subjective and ideological nature of work. In their turn, they will become a part of the history of work. Hitherto, that history has in fact had relatively little to say about these quite central aspects of work, aspects that may be broadly described as the meanings of work. This volume is concerned with those meanings, with work as a cultural activity, rather than simply an economic one, and with the discourses with which this activity has been invested in the past. In a preliminary way and from a diversity of approaches and problems, this collection may be regarded as mapping out some of the ground for a new history of work.

Responses to current economic change in Britain and the industrial West have highlighted the meanings of work in other senses too. The variety of economic strategies involved in people's handling of recession, and the perceptions of work involved in these processes, have shifted our understanding of work as being primarily located in paid employment. They have put into question what we mean by 'work'; a matter approached frontally by Moorhouse in this volume. In whatever domain 'work' is situated, what emerges from this collection points firmly to the significance of work as a social construct. It also points to the need for looking beyond the realm of the economic and of production if work is to be understood. Production is inexplicable without an understanding of

I

reproduction, both in its limited sense as the reproduction of labour power and its larger sense as the reproduction of society itself. Work is thus approached in its broader contexts, in which the political and social are inseparable from the economic. From this vantage these historians' essays clearly converge with and complement new approaches to work emerging in other disciplines.[1] Before considering the historical themes raised by this volume it is necessary to say something about the contributions of anthropology and sociology to our understanding of work and its meanings. This account will be followed by a treatment of what historians have had to say on these matters, before the explorations of the individual contributions are considered. As with these essays, the tone of this introduction will be exploratory. Rather than the usual survey of the field of study, I shall attempt a synthesis of different approaches, of necessity in a tentative and speculative fashion.

I

Anthropology reminds us that in other cultures 'work' is embedded in a variety of structures from which it takes its organisation and meaning. This degree of connectedness with the spheres of kinship, religion, politics, and so on, is less marked in our own kind of society. This degree of disjunction is of course historical and ideological. Godelier has pointed to the emergence in the West of the idea of 'work in general', work separate from its individual forms and from these structural locations, so that it is seen as a discrete activity in a distinct 'economic' realm.[2] We may look to the late eighteenth century for this separation out of the 'economic': yet, working in complex ways with this current and reminding us of the cultural connectedness of work in the West too, there has been the transformation of words investing work from connotations of pain and degradation to words denoting dignity and the transformation of nature and man's being. These major transformations point to the need for an historical anthropology or an anthropological history of work. These we do not yet have.

Godelier's aphorism, that the division of labour is the result of the social hierarchy and not its cause, alerts us to the rich possibilities of anthropological approaches. The major figures in economic anthropology, scholars like Sahlins, Firth, Godelier and Geertz, provide foundations upon which to build, but a more focussed and historically-aware anthropology of work is elusive. Wallman's recent collection of essays is useful,[3] yet it still appears the case that few anthropologists are anthropologists of work *per se*. There has also been a tendency to ignore the societies in which anthropologists are themselves based. When work in industrial societies is considered there tends to be a concentration upon aspects akin to non-industrial ones, upon crofting and fishing, say, rather than engineering or textiles. This is not without its value however: as the historical unevenness of industrialisation in the West itself is increasingly perceived, and the consequent plurality of sources of livelihood and inter-relation of household and work is understood, so these approaches have proved revealing.[4] There are other currents that are also of value, for instance work based on folklore studies,[5] and the well-established ethno-graphical tradition linking employment and community through the study of socialisation into work.[6]

Recent initiatives in Britain promise however to redress this failure to direct anthropological insight upon industrial society. The collection of Roberts, Finnegan and Gallie breaks not only with established notions of industrial society but also with the models of economic rationality that to a large extent underpin them.[7] Instead of the idea of economic growth, of the convergence of industrial societies upon a single model, and the social homogenisation of the workforce, there is a new attention to divergence and heterogeneity. It should perhaps be noted here that for rather longer than has been the case among sociologists and anthropologists, historians have been aware of the profound unevenness of capitalist, industrial de-velopment in the West.[8] Instead of the shibboleths of mainstream econ-omic theory – a calculating economic 'rationality' operating in a perfect market of standard products – there is also a welcome attention to ordi-nary people's agency and to subjective economic rationalities. The lessons learned in the anthropological study of non-Western society exhibit their relevance for an understanding of our own economies. There is for instance Geertz's account of the 'efficiency' of the economic practices of the bazaar, which are based upon the 'rationality' of investing time to create relationships of trust and understanding so as to minimise risks in an environment where the product is not a standard one.[9] The collection challenges established economics by reformulating labour market theory to take account of what may be termed a 'social economics', a recognition that the labour market is ordered by institutions and values emerging in particular conjunctures, and must be understood in relation to factors such as ethnicity, community, gender and household. In particular there is the basic recognition that the 'non-economic' has a critical role in the 'economic' and that values are socially constructed.

This sort of ethnographic approach to economics is still developing. In the collection under discussion there is a valuable attention to people's own attitudes to work and the 'work ethic' – although the historical dimension of this is lacking[10] – but the theoretical claims of new approaches are still somewhat tentative and under-elaborated.[11] None the less, the central recognition that economies are human creations, and are thus also moral and political, is of great importance. It emerges too in other studies, such as that of Gudeman,[12] which not only recognises that models of livelihood are culturally produced but begins to unearth the historical processes involved. Gudeman considers the emergence of the dominant Western model of the economy as a separate sphere of instrumental and practical action in the course of the eighteenth and early nineteenth centuries.

This kind of approach is much needed, as the study of valuations of work and economies still tends to be conducted in terms of hardy old perennials of very dubious historical validity, none of which is hoarier than the Protestant work ethic. Anthony's book *The Ideology of Work* still tends to be cited.[13] It is highly impressionistic, dealing in a kind of vulgar Weberianism several times removed from Weber's own attempt at understanding the meanings of work. The critical study of 'the work ethic' (this volume makes plain how illusory it is to think of a single, monolithic ethic), especially in its contextualised and particular manifestations such as the Victorian 'gospel of work', must be acknowledged as a serious gap in the historical literature.[14] The absence of critical consideration means that even when a monolithic work ethic is criticised Weberian stereotypes still tend to rule by default. This is the case with Rose's recent *Re-Working the Work Ethic*[15] where the Protestant ethic serves as a straw man which it is absurdly easy to topple. Rose's concern is to show that real behaviour was something like the inverse of the Weberian stereotype. The result is that the historical analysis is distorted, predicated as it is upon the illusory opposite of an illusory paradigm: many historians would object strongly to Rose's judgements that the British labour movement and British workers have been narrowly instrumental and sectionalist in their attitude to work, and that the industrial bourgeoisie has been sadly deficient in 'the industrial spirit'[16] (the latter judgement is part of the cant of our times and to this degree Rose may be given individual absolution). In more popular and propagandistic accounts of work values, a growing genre of which Robertson's *Future Work* is not untypical,[17] the historical judgements are even more cavalier. 'The Situation Now' is contrasted with a romantic vision of 'pre-industrial' times in which the holistic virtues of self-reliance and co-operation were practised within the charmed circle of free household production. Readers may turn to the essays of Berg and Rule in this volume to see how misleading such accounts are.

Propagandistic accounts also tend to exaggerate the novelty of recent developments, such as homeworking. This is so in large measure because they deal with very crude 'stage-model' notions of industrialisation, which are evolutionary or linear in character and predicated on the misleading idea that the phase of large-scale factory production has been the goal and defining characteristic of historical development up to the recent past. Industrialisation, itself an unsatisfactory term, took many routes. The present continues to go down many of the same ones, and departures that seem new are in fact reproductions of older avenues of change. Current, propagandistic accounts are in fact mythologies of work and need to be revealed for what they are. Historians need to reclaim this ground against a formidable array of academic, media and government views which, in the cases of past 'failure' (pre-eminently that of the entrepreneurial bourgeoisie) and future work, are rapidly hardening into a series of new orthodoxies.

Thus anthropological and ethnographic accounts of work have much to offer, even if they remain to be theoretically worked over and realised in terms of historical scholarship. They can be seen as attending to how in fact work is actually perceived and represented rather than being led uncritically by *a priori* theoretical assumptions. At the same time, the ideological and political processes by which meanings are constituted tend often to be a rather attenuated presence in much ethnographic work, given its frequent phenomenological assumptions. Theoretical ambition and historical perspective, if not anthropological insight, can however hardly be said to be lacking in perhaps the single most productive and influential strand within the sociology of work, namely the labour process approach. Braverman's recuperation of Marx has been seminal,[18] and has led to much elaboration and critique of the categories he has employed.[19] For Braverman the capitalist labour process involves the separation of thought and execution in work, direct capitalist control of work, primarily by de-skilling, together with the degradation of work and the homogenisation of the labour force. Reformulations have involved emphasising the recomposition of skill and its complex placement in industry, rather than its simple degradation.[20] They have also involved a consideration of modes of capitalist control other than de-skilling, for instance job design, and technologies that in themselves are never ideologically neutral.[21] The creation of internal labour markets which divide the labour force economically and ideologically have been examined, whether these operate by means of 'responsible autonomy' or bureaucratic emphasis on rule and procedure rather than direct control, or by internalising in the firm or sector ideological features of the external market.[22] Theories of labour market segmentation have indeed been a major outcome of the literature.[23]

Both from within and beyond the perspective of labour process approaches the exclusion of 'subjective' factors has been noted; the auton-

omous effect on the distribution and nature of work of factors such as
gender, race and class now being more widely acknowledged. Much of the
labour process literature has been rightly criticised for the exclusion of the
consciousness and agency of labour and capital, the labour process being
seen as the inexorable unfolding of capitalist rationality acting upon a
passive workforce. Instead of this static understanding, an omniscient
capital has been displaced by understandings of market structure and
market choices, and of the ideological and political presuppositions of
capital. There has similarly been an emphasis upon worker organisation
and resistance, and their role in shaping the division of labour. Many of
these advances are registered in the recent work of Burawoy,[24] and directed onwards to new, and to my mind especially fruitful, interpretations.
Burawoy moves the debate on from control and resistance to the creation
of consent, thereby greatly widening its scope. In his latest work he offers
valuable new theoretical perspectives on the labour process,[25] and, not
least, a firm historical context for his arguments, a virtue not always
present in the labour process literature.[26]

It is less the historical treatment offered that I am concerned with here,
or the general defence of the historical, political agency of the working
class, than aspects of Burawoy's general approach. In particular, Burawoy expands the conception of production beyond its purely formal
moment to include the ideological and political. The process of production is seen as having two distinct political moments: the labour process in
which the organisation of work is seen to be about the transformation of
social relations as well as nature; and the ideological and political
apparatus which regulates production relations, and which may, among
other aspects, involve the degree of state involvement. Both these aspects
are embraced by the notion of production or factory regime. Variations in
factory regime are held to be sufficient to explain the nature of working-
class politics. Even with such an expanded notion of production this does
not seem to me likely. However, despite some lack of clarity in the conceptual categories he employs, the thrust of Burawoy's approach has several
advantages over earlier ones. Burawoy takes up Marx's concept of commodity fetishism, emphasising that in production not only things are produced. Social relations are reproduced and this means the production of
ideas about these relations. In short, the labour process is rightly seen as
inherently about the production and mediations of meaning, though this
does not of course imply that it is only about this, and that 'economic' factors are of a secondary or purely 'cultural' character. This emphasis sup-
plants Braverman's understanding of the labour process as characterised
by the unity and separation of conception and execution. It emphasises a
relational understanding of the labour process. The advantage of switch-

ing from questions of domination to ones of the reproduction of social relations is clear. Not least of these advantages is that questions of change, and hence of history, are put at the top of the agenda.

The Braverman paradigm of control, as with classical Marxism, rests on the notion that capitalist social relations are inherently antagonistic. This antagonism becomes in much analysis a meta-historical category, a kind of intellectual strait-jacket. As Burawoy argues,[27] antagonism may be present at an abstract level but not at the level at which workers understand their interests. The interests that organise the daily life of workers are not irrevocably given but are reproduced in particular ways. We must therefore look to a theory of interests that permits us to investigate the conditions under which the interests of labour and capital may or may not be antagonistic. Leaving aside for one moment Burawoy's interpretation of the ideological terrain on which interests are organised, it is the understanding of the dimension of consent itself to which Burawoy has made a particularly important contribution.[28]

This dimension takes one directly into the question of the meanings of work, concerned as it is with the way in which workers bring significance and order to their experience of labour. It is a dimension that has tended to be underplayed by historians. In previous work I have explored the economic circumstances which lead to co-operation and compromise between capital and labour, features that in certain historical conjunctures of a fairly long-term nature can be very marked.[29] I have also considered the employment relation as far more than economic in character, in such a way as to examine the generation of co-operation and beyond it a more positive consent and commitment.[30] The drawbacks of conceiving of the employment relation as solely or even mainly antagonistic in form need to be emphasised. It is arguable that employment relations may be culturally structured in such a way as to be mainly reciprocal or even consensual in character.[31] There is a danger here that the category of consent may be over-emphasised, just as that of resistance before it, and that consent may be seen in too static and functionalist a way.[32] In Burawoy's work for example there is a tendency to view the strategies and games by which workers bring meaning to work as functional for capital: consent to rules becomes consent to capitalist production, whereas such 'game-playing' may be dysfunctional and lead to worker resistance. The emphasis on consent has immeasurably enlarged our understanding of the labour process, though it should be emphasised as well that the stick ought not to be lost sight of for concentration on the carrot.

The essays in this volume bear directly on the question of consent. Gray considers the outlook of early nineteenth-century textile workers on the employment relation and its subsequent reconstitution. McClelland takes up the substance of this reconstitution, looking at the relationship of nascent market ideologies and workers' own representations. This relationship involved workers in making sense of new values and circumstances in terms of older notions: the aspiration to co-operation with employers was integrated in a market ideology which yet operated in the context of employers' paternalist strategies and language,[33] and so can be seen as reconstituting older notions, though not necessarily 'paternalist' ones, of the trade as a community of interests that Gray points to. McClelland also shows how the language of the trade served to underpin the union and resistance to employers at the same time as it meshed with market ideology, so achieving a similar integration of old and new. This realisation of the interrelation of co-operation and conflict points back to Burawoy's more satisfactory emphasis on the ideological ground on which interests are actually organised, to the historical conditions which determine which characteristic of the capital–labour equation will be most marked.

A critique of Burawoy's particular theory of interests need not detain us here. Again it is a matter of an individual work serving to introduce a wider range of issues. His concentration on what he takes to be the ideological masking of profit and of the power relations inherent in production (what he calls the 'obscuring and securing of surplus value') is germane to any study of the meanings of work: it emphasises the importance of the workings of ideology. More particularly, it opens up the question of the particular sites in which work ideologies are generated and developed. Burawoy's emphasis tends to be on work and the workplace but it is more likely that the extra-work situation is primarily important. One thinks here of such matters as the legitimation and ideological neutering of ideas of private property, technology and the market, or the social construction of knowledge involved in ideologies legitimating notions of management as a distinct sphere involving special claims to competence and efficiency, and so to power. The growth of such ideologies from the later nineteenth century, involving the eclipse of popular conceptions of labour as creative, is a subject that has yet to receive adequate historical treatment. The site of such ideologies is as likely to be in the media, in education, in the family or the state, as in the work situation itself, though it should be said that ideologies legitimating work depend for their full effect on the articulation of these different spheres with work arrangements and experience.[34] The often autonomous operation of gender considerations upon the sphere of production is a specially clear example of the dangers of production-centred explorations.

These dangers are particularly evident in the area of class. In Britain the influence of recession and changes in working-class politics in the 1980s are once again bringing Marxist notations of class under scrutiny. From neo-

Weberian positions much theoretical Marxism is criticised for its failure to produce a theory of action and of interests.[35] Structural location in the capitalist market is seen as creating sets of potential interests. Which interests are taken up depends on how they are seen in relation to other individuals and groups. Collective social identities are the crucial link between social structure and social action. Interests depend for their realisation on the creation of such social identities. Sociologists have been chided for assuming such identities arise mainly from production and paid work, in the process ignoring non-work areas of life, and especially the spheres of consumption and the home. There is much of value in these strictures: a good deal of Marxist theory assumes that the working class is already constituted in production as an historical class acting according to its imagined interests. And this goes for recent studies too, such as Wright's claim that other classes have a contradictory class location but the working class a determinate one.[36]

Such criticisms of Marxist positions from neo-Weberian perspectives are however sweeping. Although remaining insistently production-centred,[37] Burawoy can be seen as searching for a theory of interests in a way analogous to that of the neo-Weberians (and of course the analysis from the question of consent immediately challenges the notion that the labour process automatically produces class 'for itself'). As is not infrequently the case in these matters Marxist positions are presented in rather a stereotyped fashion. Gramscian and structuralist positions are set to one side, and the contributions of historians to our understanding of class are forgotten. Whether based in production or market location both sets of assumptions about class often tend to pay little attention in practice to how class and the social order are actually represented, to the symbolic and ideological forms of this representation, and to the media in which representations are formed. Class is very importantly a symbolic construct, verbal and non-verbal, rhetorical and ritual. Historians are turning with increasing urgency to questions of class discourse and language itself.[38] This work seems likely to link the economic and political, and production and consumption, in new ways, ways that emphasise the force of symbolic representations, and their role in constructing and mediating social interests and action.

This is not a literature review, but it would be wrong to leave readers with the impression that labour process approaches have been the only or the main influence operating within the sociology of work, or indeed that sociology and anthropology are the only disciplines that have contributed to this field. This collection of essays has something to say about temporal components of work, but very little about spatial ones. In this critical area a revitalised socio-historical geography has made a considerable impact in

recent years. The work of geographers like Gregory and Thrift has produced significant insights into our understanding of space, ideology and
the meanings of work.[39] In sociological terms the foregoing discussion of
anthropological approaches to work indicated a British sociology newly
sensitised to questions of work ideologies and values.[40] In breaking with
the earlier problematic of 'industrial society' theory, it should not be forgotten that this earlier body of literature provided work of outstanding
value, most of it critical of such theory if at the same time fixed within its
terms of argument.[41] The research initiative sponsored by the British
Economic and Social Research Council,[42] to which the Roberts, Finnegan
and Gallie collection is related, promises to further shift research towards
interdisciplinary activity. Unfortunately, historical work is something of a
poor relation in this initiative, consigned as it often is to the limbo of 'context'. None the less, recent works of considerable quality, such as those of
Gallie and Sabel,[43] leave considerable scope for historical determinations.
There is also a more general convergence of historical and sociological
approaches, traced for example in Whipp's survey of the literature on
communities and labour markets.[44] Aside from the important general recognition that communities and markets are closely linked, common
themes begin to emerge as does the awareness of the social construction of
workplace and community, itself part of a new awareness of what constitutes production and reproduction. It is to the role of historical work in
these new developments that I now wish to turn.

II

The lineage of the social history of work in Britain is somewhat convol-
uted, and this account can only be schematic.[45] Progenitors can be traced
into the 1960s in terms of 'labour history' and its broadening out as a
reaction to 'economic history'. Teleological models of economic growth
and modernisation were challenged, as was a mechanical Marxism. E. P.
Thompson was a seminal figure in this movement towards 'culture', and
toward the understanding of work as a site of active cultural agency
rather than passive adaptation. The continuing influence of Thompson
has been criticised in terms of his lack of an adequate economic account of
industrialisation in which to situate the role of culture in class formation.
It is indeed still the case that we lack an adequate historical account of that
complex series of changes subsumed under the misleading heading of 'the
industrial revolution'. The privileged existence of 'culture' has also been
criticised, more recently in terms of a lack of attention to the processes
whereby culture is produced, especially to the role of language and
ideology.[46]

The effect of Thompson's work was to leave many questions unsettled, especially those concerning subsequent class development and the role of change in the structure of work. In the 1970s and subsequently the 'labour aristocracy' debate, arising from another founding father of social history, E. J. Hobsbawm, has proved to be a central area in which these questions were pursued. The debate moved from economistic evaluations of work and rather static and idealised notions of class in Hobsbawm and Foster, to more subtle readings of the ideological effects of work and leisure in Gray and Crossick, and to a closer attention to the labour process in other work.[47] Of late the influence of labour process approaches has in fact been marked, whether in Reid's work on sectionalism in the workforce, Melling on structures of authority in industry, or Zeitlin on the role of the state and in his and Sabel's critique of received notions of industrialisation.[48] Some of this work has tended to be rather narrow, as if the labour process offered the keys of the castle. There has tended to be an avoidance of cultural and ideological aspects. None the less, our understanding of the economic and institutional factors shaping the division of labour has been greatly advanced, and so our understanding of the whole process of industrialisation. In terms of work ideologies and values, the considerable contribution of historical studies of leisure to our understanding of work should also be accounted in this reckoning of historical approaches.[49]

From the late 1970s there has been a much closer interest in how 'work', 'labour' and 'employment' are in fact culturally defined. Again, the perception of economic recession and industrial restructuring has been important, posing new questions about class relations and alignments, and about new experiences of work and worklessness. As in other disciplines the influence of feminist approaches has been of the first importance, signalling from its own perspective the characteristic shift from production to social reproduction. The recruitment and reproduction of classes and workforces, also of capital, becomes as important to our understanding as the internal structuring of the labour process. Many of these new concerns are reflected in this collection of essays. The influences are of course more varied, and the range of historians wider, than this rather anglo-centric account can convey. Typical developments may be seen in studies of proto-industrialisation and the links between waged and unwaged work, and between work, family, market and community. They are also apparent in studies of the relationship between industrial and 'pre-industrial' work, and important dimensions of work such as time.[50]

A particularly fine examination of the relationship between work, home and community is Segalen's *Love and Power in the Peasant Family*.[51] This work also raises important aspects of the social construc-

tion of work and its meanings. In showing how meanings are mediated between the public sphere and the private sphere of peasant marriage, it
draws a very necessary distinction between what people said and what
they did. This distinction between discourse and practice is apparent in
the public face of male authority and the mutuality of man and wife that
marked marriage and work practices. However, one should not draw too
marked a distinction between 'discourse' and 'practice'. As Segalen so
amply shows the 'practices' and material arrangements of everyday life
were themselves richly symbolic in character. They composed their own
symbolic discourse, the character of which it is important to stress was
highly ambivalent and polysemic. Thus, in attempting to understand the
meanings of work one should not conceive of symbolic discourse in this
sense as an epiphenomenon of underlying 'economic' processes. Segalen
indicates the interrelation of the two, without approaching meanings as
solely resolvable by 'linguistic' or symbolic modes of analysis. Rather,
'discourse' is a term that may embrace different levels; seen as 'symbolic
practice' it is simultaneously material and cultural, a way of doing things
and saying things.[52] In turn, symbolic practice may be seen as making up
codes or languages, call them what one may. The term 'ideology' may be
applied to these. However, this kind of reading of discourse is removed
from and superior to connotations that word often has, whether 'ideology' is seen as the representation of 'interests',[53] or as imposed consciousness. What is perhaps needed is a deconstruction of the term ideology, as
indeed of 'consciousness', including the notion of 'class consciousness'.[54]
In this volume, one is not searching for the labour process in context, but
aiming to dispense with the category of 'context' altogether: as with any
other human activity, work cannot be understood unless it is seen as inseparable from the discursive fields of which it is an integral part. In short,
in considering the meanings of work one is in the area of the meaning of
meaning.

In this respect I can again only be schematic, doing little more than summoning up influences which, acknowledged or unacknowledged, have
been powerful. These influences have a marked Parisian character: post-
structuralist emphases on the deconstruction of texts and on their agency
have been influential. But there have been many tributaries feeding the
recognition of the social construction of reality. Among other influences,
semiology, hermeneutics, the sociology of knowledge and certain kinds of
cultural anthropology relate with one another to produce a rich harvest of
insights, one historians have yet to draw amply upon. The subjectivism of
some of these approaches, apparent in many phenomenological and ethnographic positions, also their lack of attention to matters of power,
history and social relations, is properly criticised from within the Marxist

tradition, in which Gramsci's probing of ideology and power has been of particular moment. The work of Foucault on the construction of knowledge, and on the relations of knowledge and power, has served as something of a bridge between the different traditions. More overtly political influences have also been at work: feminism has responded to these intellectual currents but figured independently as well in emphasising the cultural derivation and power of meanings. In political terms, at least in Britain, the power of right-wing ideology and its successful appropriation of ideological motifs such as 'freedom' and 'nation' has sensitised many to the social construction of meaning.

In all this it should not be thought that historical work has been a passive recipient of these widespread intellectual influences. The characteristic *Past and Present* fusion of history and anthropology has issued in work on invented traditions, especially Hobsbawm's account of the seminal 1870–1914 period.[55] In Britain, much of the emphasis of the History Workshop movement in the 1980s has been toward the study of representations; towards an understanding of myth, memory and power. In Britain too, there has been an increasing play between history and the field of cultural studies, especially around the idea of 'popular culture', with its own characteristic mélange of many of the intellectual currents mentioned here. Historians are also beginning to learn much from students of the primary medium of culture, namely language. Socio-linguistics, and the related study of dimensions of communication such as orality and print, often have more to offer history than the decontextualised and often anti-historical operation of some semiological approaches. As well as language in its sense of bodies of ideological discourse (as with 'the language of Chartism' or 'the discourse of the French Revolution')[56] there is a new attention to language *qua* language; its history, its dimensions, and its symbolic function as the source and object of discourse.[57]

More searching accounts of the historical meanings of work are also beginning to appear. Not inappropriately it is social historians of France who have been particularly active. The debt to major British social historians is however as marked as French intellectual influences, whether it be to Thompson's recovery of meanings and experiences marginalised in the historical record, or Hobsbawm's work on the experience and outlook of artisans. Indeed, much of the discussion of the meanings and experience of work has centred on the crucial role of the artisans in European social history.[58] As with the previous generation of social historians, the new generation owes much to anthropological perspectives. Sewell has explored the interaction of politics and the workshop in France, looking at the ways in which discourses of work negotiated both political and economic change.[59] More recently Reddy has explored the language and values of the market, noting their penetration of the public sphere.[60] He poses very important questions about work, meanings and social relations, though his position does in fact reveal some of the drawbacks of this kind of approach, namely a tendency when emphasising the agency and reality of cultural factors to lose sight of structural ones. For Reddy the market tends to lack all objective form and necessity, and his workers exist in a cultural realm hermetically sealed from its operations (in this volume Berg and McClelland point to a more complex material and ideological relation of workers to the market and 'market culture'). None the less, his work is a vital contribution to a new area. The same can be said of the work of Sonenscher, especially his account of how the discourse of the Parisian *sans-culottes* cannot be read as an account of objective workplace relations but was developed to manage political exigencies.[61] This kind of subtle exploration and placing of the languages of work takes us directly into the themes of this collection.

III

These themes are diverse, as is the geographical and temporal scope of the volume. Given the novelty of the common theme and the state of research into it, a more unified approach is as yet hardly possible. Rather, these essays take up a number of the most important aspects of the area of study and indicate a range of directions for future work. The essays operate within their own fields of debate, and this is as it should be. Yet they all firmly establish the significance of the historical meanings of work. They establish the central fact that meanings *are* socially produced, a fact that needs to be reiterated. They show something of the processes involved, and they consider the dimension of historical change as central to these processes. The central theme of the volume, the production of meaning, is thus pursued in these ways, and in what follows I shall dwell in a little more detail upon them.

As Moorhouse's study of the post-1945 US hot-rod subculture establishes, meaning is not intrinsic to a particular piece of labour but has to be attached, learned and sustained. This occurs at the most fundamental levels at which work is given cognitive structure: as Whipp's essay on work and time shows, the actual media in which meanings are situated are themselves socially created. In the case of time, instead of the given nature of clock time, and dominant models of time–work discipline, what is evident is the plurality of time registers which are the outcome of social relations and historical change. The social production of meaning is evident in all the essays. In those of Gray and McClelland, for example, meanings are identified as the outcome of contending bodies of discourse, and of contending social groups and institutions. In turn, the examination of ideology itself can be pursued on a more adequate and rewarding level. Instead of ideology as a fixed and intrinsic realm of significance, as coherent bodies of discourse representative of fixed interests say, what becomes evident are the historically contingent processes of ideological formation.

The essays take one directly into questions of process around the issue of language, and this in several senses of that term. Sonenscher's essay on the *compagnonnages* of eighteenth- and early nineteenth-century France considers a dimension that deserves much wider attention. He points to the lack of French equivalents for the English terms 'skilled' and 'skill'. In French, the language of work classification was related more to the attributes of the worker and the qualities of work, the two being relatively indistinguishable. This points to the need for comparative, interlingual analyses of work's meanings. However, intralingual work has itself hardly begun, though Godelier has traced in a preliminary way the genesis and development of terms denoting work in French, and there is work on what may be termed the contextualised etymology of items like 'artisan' and 'mechanic' for eighteenth- and nineteenth-century England.[62]

Among the several senses of language which may be pursued in considering the processes whereby meanings are constituted I shall isolate three, albeit in a fairly arbitrary and *ad hoc* manner. The first of these may be described as the mode of communication, the material nature and social consequences of what have been termed the 'technologies' of communication. These may be described as the modes of speech, writing, print, and, somewhat loosely, 'electronic' means. The second sense may be called the forms of language. By this I simply wish to point to the wide variety of practices that can be regarded as making up distinct codes of meaning: the verbal and non-verbal, with emphasis on the latter; the literal and symbolic, with emphasis on the latter. Finally, I would point to more direct and explicit, and often 'imaginative', presentations of reality, aspects which have often been called 'representations'. The sense will be apparent in what follows. The three senses clearly overlap, though it may be of use to disaggregate them here.

Sonenscher's work alerts us to the matter of mode and technology of communication. He attends to the oral aspects of the culture in which his example of work is embedded. By so doing, he avoids anachronistic readings of the significance of the ritual of the *compagnonnages*. In cultures especially marked by oral modes of communication, the past is constituted in a particular way: less fixed by the media of writing and print, it is constantly adapted to the needs and perceptions of the present in a more radical fashion than in (say) 'print cultures'. The differences are of degree, but the past is even more a moveable feast in examples such as Sonens-cher's. By so attending to the consequences of communicative mode Son-enscher avoids models of cultural continuity and linear descent that have characterised previous interpretations of his example. Awareness of these consequences means that attention is shifted to the purpose of the ritual rather than to its content and the fact of its iteration. This recognition of the cultural consequences of modes of communication, a recognition pur-sued fruitfully in a range of disciplines,[63] is of wider significance than this individual case. Historians have in general neglected the problem, though in terms of the orality–print relationship alone it is of great significance, the two aspects in European culture having for many centuries been very closely related, orality itself continuing to extend its profound cultural consequences far into twentieth-century life. In a less overt way Rule's essay is also sensitive to the utilisation of a structure of myth and ritual to legitimate and maintain workers' notions of work; in this case the eighteenth-century artisan's use of the past to establish the notion of prop-erty in skill and hence to manage the daily business of work's present. If a history of work that is neither teleological nor anachronistic is to be writ-ten then attention to the modes of communication and their consequences is imperative. The way in which the past is made is of course only one among many such consequences.

These essays also take up the question of what I have termed forms of language. Sonenscher and Rule write on ritual. Berg's study of women's work in early industrialisation takes up Mary Douglas's work on the sym-bolic import of goods.[64] Goods are in a sense also a linguistic medium, as are gesture, dress, the built environment, and so on. In this case Berg points to the area of consumption and its ideological effects. So too does the essay of Moorhouse on his twentieth-century example. The eighteenth and the twentieth centuries thus show revealing and perhaps surprising correspondences. As Berg shows, from at least as early as the eighteenth century production and consumption were closely linked at the levels of both economic organisation and cultural meanings. As well as the link be-tween production and consumption, both essays show the importance of reading for non-verbal forms of language. Rule also indicates the import-ance of non-verbal modes: clothing, ritual and tools were all important in securing an historically important discourse of work.

The question of forms of communication leads into the matter of more distinctly imaginative representations, though these senses mesh with each other and with language in the sense of modes of communication. The interrelation of these different levels may be seen for example in Ludtke's study of photographic representations of work in Germany be-tween 1900 and 1940.[65] Here what may loosely be termed post-print technologies of communication, non-verbal communicative forms, and imaginative representations come together in an examination of visualisation as contested territory. Drawing partly on Foucault's work on visualisation and power, the capacity of images and icons to cut across as well as delimit social boundaries is noted. The central place of the visual in creating meanings of work in the twentieth century is apparent, though the iconography of work is of course of great significance long before this. It is a subject of great complexity, which can only be adverted to here, as indeed can the more general field of imaginative representations of work. None the less, several contributions in this volume do bear on the matter of representations, even if the issue is not approached as directly as in Ludtke's work.

This is apparent in Moorhouse's work on the hot-rod literature, in Gray's study of the languages of factory reform, and especially in Scott's essay on the role of gender in the discourse of nineteenth-century French political economy. As with Gray, Scott attends closely to the rhetorical as well as literal functions of discourse. She shows how important it is to examine the rhetorical aspects of supposedly non-imaginative forms of literature. In the discourse of political economy, images of sexuality, women, work and the social order were all deeply interlaced, especially around the rhetorical forms of the *femmes isolées* and the woman worker in manufacturing industry. This consideration of the substance out of which meanings are made already points to the intimate relation of language and ideology. It indicates a direct concern with ideology found in many of the essays presented here.

Gray's work in particular indicates the importance of examining the social processes underlying the constitution of the meanings of work. He considers the essential dimensions of the structure and development of local communities, of the state, and of industry. He also isolates the different groups involved, whether operatives, employers, intellectuals or state officials. More than this, he shows how these different groups are never monolithic. This echoes Scott's emphasis on the assonance and dissonance of different discourses, in the French case pointing to how the seeming dissimilarities of political economy, feminism, socialism and other currents may divulge marked similarities in the representation of sexuality and the social order. The difficult business of dissolving monolithic structures while discriminating the intersections of varied outlooks is indicated here. In substantive terms the two essays are also closely related. Scott shows the internal discursive workings of political economy: how, around the same time as in Britain, it established new canons of knowledge, and came into dominance partly by laying new claims to legitimacy as 'science' and partly by grafting morality onto economics. In both

Britain and France the family became the site of regulation, while the economy, with differing emphases however, became a sphere of self-regulation. Both essays form an essential ingredient for the kind of anthropological history of work mooted in an earlier section of this introduction; both are essential points of departure in examining the genesis of our own 'work ethics'.

Gray shows clearly how such 'ethics' or meanings are themselves the outcome of different social and ideological forces. He elicits the rhetorical devices employed (for example the honest yeoman or squire), and the different fields of imaginative life that were exploited (gothic romanticism, evangelical discourse). It is important to recognise that these resources were not merely expressive of some anterior reality but were themselves, as the foci of social forces and intellectual traditions, directly constitutive of historical change. One also sees in Gray other very important means by which discourses wax and wane, dominate or are marginalised: his essay begins to probe these means, whether they be the constitution and deployment of 'expert' opinion in the making of parliamentary commissions and reports, or the general promulgation of new ways of seeing factory labour present in fashion, journalism and fiction. More widely he indicates the historic significance of the factory reform question, inserting it into the changing outlook of the operatives, and the formation of the manufacturing interest and the liberal state.

He shows how discourses of work have, as often as not, to be located in extra-economic spheres. This question of locating the discourses of work reflects concerns in the sociological literature on work examined earlier in this introduction. Historians of British labour have seen how important the political realm is for the constitution of work ideologies (as have Sewell and Sonenscher in their work on French labour).[66] Behagg has shown how for the Birmingham trades of the early nineteenth century Chartism served to articulate workplace and community-based solidarities.[67] Subsequently, in the form of popular liberalism, political ideology served to facilitate new valuations of work in terms of the vaunting of the big employer, the marginalisation of the small master, as well as the idealisation of progress. Political liberalism served as the fount of ideas about progress that were very often transferred directly to the sphere of work in the form of notions of industrial advance and of the 'respectable artisan'.[68] Similar kinds of development have been noted for the Sheffield trades around the same time.[69] In many respects the 'labour aristocracy' debate as it has developed in Britain could be usefully transposed from the economic to the political key, especially to the context of public debate surrounding the issue of political reform. Recent work on mid-Victorian artisan 'respectability' suggests the usefulness of emphasising social context and social semantics.[70] Ideologies of work are political as well as 'economic': as Gray shows, they are constructed in terms of the operations of law and the state as well as politics, rather than with reference to economic factors alone.

The point is of wider relevance: discourses that seem of a particular character may prove on closer analysis to be elusive. The seemingly 'economic' may evaporate, but so too may the seemingly 'political'. This is a point made by Gray in criticism of Stedman Jones's account of the language of class in Chartism as primarily political in character.[71] When probed more deeply the language of Chartism begins to reveal a popular romanticism which is neither quite political nor quite economic in character. Rather, this powerful semantic resource proves on closer inspection to form a moral language capable of articulating both spheres, also one that shows the anachronism of the categories 'economic' and 'political'. In this volume Sonenscher also shows how the elusive discourses of work may be nailed down. Avoiding the anachronism of construing *compagnonnages* ritual as one aimed at the creation of solidarities against masters or in the face of geographical dispersal, he renders its broader function in terms of the management of labour and product markets, and the absence of legal rights and distinctions. In managing the world, ritual gives it meaning: symbols both do things and say things.

In considering the outcome of the language of factory reform Gray raises the matter not only of the constitution of work ideologies but also of their changing form. The industrial and political appropriations of the new, still-fragile dispensation of the mid nineteenth century were to be of direct consequence for at least half a century afterwards.[72] This understanding of change suggests how meanings are always selected, edited and changed; how they are always a matter of memory located in the interstices of social and political relationships. McClelland's account of workers' perceptions of work in north-east England is also centrally about these aspects. He shows how the language of the trade served as a matrix for the language of the union. In this selective re-working of tradition – a working class 'invention of tradition' – the discourse of trade union leaders was of pivotal importance. Dealing with the appropriation of earlier ethics of work, he also delineates the construction of a figure who was to be of the first moment in the class and political discourses of Britain, namely that of the male, skilled, head of household; the 'classic proletarian' who has come down to us from that time.

McClelland's subtle exploration of valuations of work serves to indicate just how poor is so much of the secondary literature on 'the work ethic'. He points briefly to aspects outside worker discourse that must be regarded as central to any account of the Victorian 'gospel of work', a gospel still promulgated today. McClelland considers the role of employers and their spokesmen, and of the intellectuals, in creating a set of injunctions to work which partook of the religious, economic, moral and political. There were of course powerful cross-currents in contemporary discourse. If Carlyle, say, might be conscripted in the cause of a moralised political economy, one should not forget the powerful critique of 'industrialism' issuing forth from the early Romantics onwards. If appropriated in different ways, this critique often made unlikely bedfellows of high tories and low socialists.[73] Carlyle, Ruskin and Morris were later joined by others in the pantheon of prophets, figures like Tolstoy, Emerson and Thoreau, whose influence is less discussed but which was of equal importance. The critique of capitalism and the market was of course inseparable from the injunctions to strive, above all to 'work', and in so doing to do the duty of life. If one searches for a British or English 'work ethic', illusory as the search is, then this moral conception of work, of which Marx is also a part, is as likely a candidate as the usually more favoured Smilesian gospel of self-help and social mobility.[74]

Until recently historians have paid surprisingly little attention to the substance of their own discipline, to memory and how it was and is made. In terms of workers' evaluations of work one major avenue into the question is the category of 'custom'. In showing the selective operation of memory McClelland deals with custom, as do a number of the other essays. They indicate how custom operates as a reworking of the past to meet present exigencies. Thus, 'tradition' and custom should not, as is often the case, be seen as fixed and immobile categories, or as socially conservative in their operation. Rather, custom may be innovative and adaptive. There is a real sense in which in the course of the nineteenth century customary evaluations of work were displaced or marginalised.[75] The development of a more centralised state, at local and national levels, the growth of a capitalist leisure market, and a greater degree of organisation in working-class life all contributed to this, as did the exigencies of time and space in the industrial town. At the discursive level, a process charted by Gray and McClelland, the language of the market and of the organised trade union tended to displace the language of custom from public discourse, as in part did that of the 'rational', autodidactic working man. As a generic and public part of popular culture custom was in many respects eclipsed and forced underground, though its persistence within British industry into the twentieth century has been marked.[76]

However, if we approach custom as a cultural activity characteristic of the less public realms of the workplace and the community, then I think we can begin to see how important it is as a means of workers' perceptions of work.[77] The tendency to sanctify as custom or precedent practices that may be of recent origin points to a process of invented pasts, invented tradition, that indeed goes on continually and is very much a part of the present. One example must suffice, that of contemporary unskilled and semi-skilled car workers in Britain who have taken over the language of the skilled as their own customary possession.[78]

Many aspects of this are apparent in these essays. Rule shows something of invented custom in the eighteenth century, and Whipp's consideration of time reveals how the historical time sense of pottery workers was highly selective in recalling long-ago strikes (chiefly victories) as seminal. The constitution of the memory of work was however often more deliberate and public than these examples suggest. Reddy has recently emphasised how important, and neglected, the rhetorical construction of social identities is. His example is taken from the dialect literature of French textile workers.[79] My own work on the hugely popular dialect literature of the northern industrial regions of England similarly points to the importance of work remembered, to the reality of 'mythological' work.[80] In two 'moments' of rhetorical self-creation textile workers in Lancashire and Yorkshire first utilised the mythology of the handloom weaver to manage the changes consequent upon factory mechanisation, and then, towards the end of the nineteenth century, elaborated a social identity as 'factory foaks'. The making of a *working* class is apparent, but work was related in a highly complex fashion to industry, region, nation and language. It was so not only in the case of textile workers: social identities formed around the 'pitman' and 'keelman' of the north-east were as important as the textile example. Indeed, across Europe and the USA, the mythologised work and worker of textiles and coalmining have been vastly important aspects of communal and class identity.[81]

The social production of meaning is but one of the themes to emerge in this volume. The other major ones may be itemised as follows: work and skill, work and gender, and work and time. In various disciplines 'skill' has been the subject of debates as to whether it is, primarily, objectively present or socially created. While the objective presence of skill cannot be gainsaid,[82] it is none the less always to some extent the case that it is culturally established and maintained. As Sonenscher's work indicates, the very presence of the concept of skill is a linguistic happening. Rule shows how the property of skill in the period of manufacture was at the centre of workers' self-evaluations, and hence at the centre of early nineteenth-century radical and labour movements. Conceptions of skill spilled far beyond the workplace to enter the vocabulary of a more generalised 'labour', with its own rights and dignity. McClelland takes up this theme directly in his account of late nineteenth-century proprietorial notions of skill. He indicates marked continuities in terms of the solidarities skill enabled and the social cleavages it emphasised; divisions between the skilled and unskilled, but also the crucial and intimate link between skill and gender seen in the extension of skill to embrace masculinity and patriarchy. As in the earlier period this nexus was central to labour and political movements. Gray also considers the importance of notions of the family economy, of patriarchy and of skill to the particular moral vision of work and social relations that he outlines for the textile operatives.[83] As work develops in this area it is fast becoming evident just how important conceptions of gender and the family were for workers' collective and industrial identity, and for their outlook on the social order. Aspects that have tended to be viewed in isolation, like skill, are seen to be inextricably linked to other dimensions (these internal patterns of connection are clearly evident in all the essays presented here).

The essays also point to neglected aspects of the study of skill. The links between skill (also work more generally) and national identity are important and little studied. Rule touches upon the connections of skill and patriotism, and McClelland on the ways in which the outlook of skilled workers might be related to ideological emphases on peace, freedom, and industrial and national advance. Again, a certain compartmentalisation is evident in the literature: skill has been traced in terms of radicalism and class, much less in terms of other sources of identity such as the nation (the same might be said of class and patriotism, categories that have tended wrongly to be seen as antithetical). As Moorhouse stresses in this volume, it is also possible to emphasise skill too much and mistake its provenance. The equation of work ethics with craft or professional job ethics has meant that many meanings have been ignored. Location, firm and product can all produce significance of a negative or positive sort. At all levels of skill, even the lowest, work may denote special meanings, such as those to do with rites of passage, with handling danger and with testing identity. Above all, it is the considerable subjectivity of proficiency at work which is apparent: workers in 'menial' jobs may attach the utmost significance to their work, to getting it done well and earning the respect of others.

The importance of the relationship between work and gender in this collection will already be amply evident in this introduction. Berg's work reminds us that the study of meaning is impossible without a close attention to what was actually going on in terms of the economy and the organisation of work: structural and cultural approaches are complementary. Interpretations of work will have to take full account of her assault on the notion of a 'great divide' between home and work in early industrialisation. A more complex and satisfying picture emerges which notes marked differentiation earlier, considerable continuity, but also elements of integration later on. In the light of her examination of community structures in relation to work organisation what is apparent is, again, the element of social cleavage, especially marked at a time held to be characterised by the solidarities of a plebeian 'moral economy'. Divisions between artisans and casual workers, between neighbouring communities, and particularly between men and women are evident. The latter became apparent at much the same time as Rule notes a growing gender and occupational exclusiveness among artisans.

While Rule and Berg chart the emergence of lower-class conceptions of gender roles and family relations, Scott and Gray consider the subsequent nineteenth-century reordering of gender relations from 'above'. In Scott's and Gray's essays a closer demarcation of the spheres of work and home is apparent, as are the related aspects of a reconstructed femininity and childhood. In a rather similar way in France and England political economy in its moral, familial guise served to orchestrate the hitherto discordant ensemble of voices making up discussions of work. A thoroughgoing analysis of the relationship between 'high' and 'low' in the major restructuring of gender relations seen in the mid nineteenth century has yet to be attempted. However, from the work already in hand, it is evident that representations from above worked with as well as against the grain of those coming from below. Gray points to one aspect of this subsequent reordering,[84] namely the relocation of ideas of property in labour and the right to a livelihood from the family economy to individual, skilled working men (though still as the head of a household). McClelland shows other aspects of how this came about and discusses its ramifications: the trade initiated, quite literally, a worker into being a man. The workshop was the school of masculinity. Skill as property became skill as patriarchy.

Work and time is considered in two aspects here: the construction of different time registers and perceptions charted by Whipp (considered presently); and the relationship between work and non-work time. Berg's nuanced picture of the relationship between work and home suggests that the demarcation of work and non-work time may, earlier on, be more marked than is sometimes imagined. The ideological elaboration of the distinction begins to gather a powerful pace in the nineteenth century. Gray's work is of relevance here. In certain kinds of discourse the factory is increasingly seen as a higher form of social organisation embodying order, discipline and regularity.[85] Ideas of regularity and punctuality are related to the idea of the standard working day and to the moral improvement made possible by shorter hours. Instead of the problem the factory becomes seen as the solution; or at least part of it, as coterminous with this idealisation of the factory the invented 'problem' of factory work is also displaced into the non-factory environment and seen as a matter of education, religion and 'leisure'. (The identification of non-work time as 'leisure' is of course an ideological construction, one of the many non-work time could and did take.) The factory becomes a sort of exemplar of non-work life; and, increasingly defined as 'leisure', that life becomes the site of contending discourses. This demarcation of separate spheres of work and non-work time is directly taken up by McClelland.[86] Satisfactions and needs were increasingly identified as coming out of non-work time. It is in this period, as McClelland observes, that the cult of family and home became established. Recent work on the 'mass leisure' of the late nineteenth and early twentieth centuries, in particular Bailey's brief but illuminating study of the comic art of the 1880s,[87] indicates how social values and identities were increasingly explored and defined in terms of leisure. Leisure as a democratic Utopia, a kingdom upon which all may enter, announced the pioneering of new, populist social identities that were to be of major significance in the twentieth century.

None the less, in Britain work still continued to be of major significance as the source of values.[88] There is a revulsion from work, but also a continuing obsession with it.[89] This complex movement has yet to be adequately examined. Whipp's essay is an important point of reference here: he indicates how, in continually constructing new registers of time in work, workers continually imbue their own work with new meaning. Any sharp dichotomy of work and non-work time and values seems out of the question, therefore, and does so from early on, as Berg's work suggests. It is also the case that in examining 'popular culture' work will have to be more closely attended to than has often been the case hitherto: the amount of attention given 'leisure' is surely disproportionate. In Moorhouse's essay many of these aspects are brought up to the recent past. He offers a vigorous and justified assault on the widely prevalent idea that work defined as paid labour is the major source of social identity in western, industrial societies. The life beyond work is seen as the principal source of identity and creativity. The earlier essays provide a context for this one, showing how the relations of work and time have for long been complex ones. Moorhouse's account itself provides just the nuanced reading of values called for earlier: instead of a dichotomous rendering of work and non-work time what is striking is the transferral into the area of leisure of values emanating elsewhere, especially from the world of work. The moral entrepreneurs he examines emphasised striving, mastery, the practical dreamer. In so doing the hot rodder took on something of the outlook of the independent artisan. The work ethic was transposed to leisure. Even as it was transcended, work still obsessed.

Moorhouse's essay shows how valuable detailed examination of particular aspects of work can be. He stakes out the ground for further investigation that would have to establish how the meanings he discusses were mediated by factors such as class, race, gender and occupation. These meanings would also have to be related to other sources of ideology, such as education and advertising, and to other ideological clusters that he touches upon such as 'the American way of life' and youth cults and youth culture. This volume as a whole points towards this expansive history of work. There are other themes within it than those discussed here. Among major ones not discussed so far are those of the market and of class. These, however, can most appropriately be treated in a somewhat more historical and less thematic fashion than has hitherto been the case.

This collection has no claims to comprehensiveness. It is mostly about industrial work and workers, chiefly male ones. The list of subjects left out would of course be a long one: among the most notable absences would certainly be some account of domestic service, domestic labour, agricultural work, and – particularly – of non-manual work. A connected account of historical developments over a period of some two hundred years is not possible. None the less, the foregoing account has registered particular historical shifts in the significance of the meanings of work. Others may be registered around the themes of class and the market, and some brief historiographical observations may be made.

A number of the essays suggest the necessity of rethinking some of the interpretations that are used to explain the history of work and broader historical developments. Whipp's account of the construction of time by workers, employers and managers offers a valuable critique of E. P. Thompson's seminal account of time, work discipline and industrial capitalism.[90] According to Thompson, in the process of industrialisation there is a linear progression from 'task' to clock time. Time is standardised and regularised, and in its 'commodified' form serves to integrate the worker, albeit with continuing resistance, into the routines of industrial capitalism. The Marx upon whom Thompson relies is akin to the Marx utilised by Braverman. There is a similar presumption of the omniscience of capitalist control. As Whipp shows, rather than any linear progression, time is constantly redefined. Rather than a unitary process of commodification, it is the plasticity of time that is apparent. Recent work on Japanese industrialisation also questions Thompson's paradigm, including the utility of the notion of 'task-based' time when applied to the English example.[91]

Whipp's interpretation highlights, and undermines, more widely prevalent notions of industrialisation. Despite Thompson's subtlety there is still the tendency to accept what may be dubbed 'big-bang' theories of industrialisation. Such models of before and after continue to be widely held whether the couplets be traditional and modern, custom and the market, pre-industrial and industrial, or plebeity and class (the list could be extended). These notions are increasingly under challenge: for instance, the factory and the steam-powered machine are now recognised to be less central to industrialisation than previously viewed.[92] In this volume, both Berg and Whipp explicitly contend with unilinear notions of economic development and the history of work.[93] These, and the other essays, begin to dissolve into more comprehensible and less anachronistic parts that whole series of changes known by the misnomer of 'the industrial revolution'. Dichotomous interpretations of industrialisation are approached not only by a consideration of time but also of the market and of class.

Berg's disaggregation of the household/non-household dualism directly takes up the notion that the market and custom, or 'moral economy', are polar opposites. As well as describing social cleavages created by the market, Berg also notes that kin and community networks need not always involve a code based on mutuality. On the one hand, the penetration of the capitalist market ruptured communities as well as creating solidarities within them. The customary defences of 'moral economy' were often fragile. On the other hand, the opposition of the capitalist market and moral economy is seen in many respects to be a false one. The two areas were joined in the organisation and management of consumption.[94] Interpreting consumption as social exchange and symbolic transaction Berg shows how it may loosen as well as strengthen community bonds. The experience of status and participation through consumption indicates how community and the market, custom and capitalism, do indeed walk hand in hand. The ramifications of this remain to be worked out. Berg does not directly approach the constitution and nature of systems of belief, and representations of the social order, contained within the moral economy of the poor.

Thompson's interpretation of moral economy has had and continues to have an immense influence on the writing of social history. There are however signs of a welcome questioning of what has now become something like a new orthodoxy. This questioning, and defence, of the notion of moral economy introduces some useful distinctions often blurred in the literature: later eighteenth-century workers had for long been involved in a market economy, one that was very much capitalist in character; if a moral economy set morally determined parameters to market forces this did not necessarily mean that workers were opposed to the capitalist market system *per se*.[95] As Berg indicates, as they were so intimately joined to it, this could hardly be the case.

Quite what workers' outlooks on the market were will remain unclear until we know more about how workers perceived work and economies, indeed whether they had any clear understanding of what we would term an 'economy'. As Snell has observed recently, Thompson's moral economy is extremely amorphous in character. We need to know not only about perceptions of economies but also about popular attitudes to matters like the poor law and settlement procedures.[96] Gray's work certainly takes us into the realm of perceptions of economies, showing the moral imperatives that underlay them in terms of the family economy, patriarchy, the integrity of communities and 'paternalist' interpretations of employment relationships. While we know something of how these operated in relation to particular expressions of the capitalist market imperative, we as yet know less about the quotidian realities of living a capitalist market that by the early nineteenth century had been long established. Clearly, custom or moral economy was a way of living the market and was not a resource sealed in hermetic opposition to it. A recognition of this might inform a reading of McClelland's essay here: the anti-capitalism of the first half of the nineteenth century which he adumbrates was certainly marked, but it may have been a response to particular crises or aspects of the system rather than to the market *tout court*. If this was the case then the break he notes around mid century would be less marked. For the earlier part of the century one also needs to note widely prevalent reciprocal notions of employment, and ideas of rightful profit, just markets and honest employers which these continued to carry; one also needs to know whether ideas of the right to the whole produce of labour were primarily intrinsic to the trade mentality or chiefly articulated by radical spokesmen. Be this as it may, McClelland's account of the later nineteenth century is exemplary in showing how workers' discourse cannot be read as sealed off from market categories. Acceptance of these was more than instrumental. Rather, McClelland's account of the interaction of union and market discourse is a fine example of the point stressed here that the market and workers' evaluations cannot be seen as dichotomous.

Attitudes to the market are inextricably linked to the category of 'custom'. My earlier comments on custom indicate how in popular culture it operates as a sanctioning or legitimating device. It thus has cognitive as well as instrumental dimensions. As indicated earlier, it may be regarded as carrying with it conceptions of present social behaviour and values which are themselves invented and adjusted with reference to imagined pasts. Looking at custom in these ways, as forming codes of symbolic meaning, has not been a feature of the historical literature, and it is difficult to trace the history of custom subsequent to the mid nineteenth century. Something of this history has been indicated in a speculative manner: its tenacity, its marginalisation in the public sphere, its subterranean currents. The history of work and its meanings would certainly have to be imbedded in the stream of custom, and integrated in its symbolic universes. Not that custom should be seen in isolation from the major currents of its time: for too long the history of popular culture has tended to be written in isolation from aspects such as 'high' culture, law, and state and nation. Penetrating the symbolic worlds in which meaning was created would involve taking account of the nineteenth-century explosion of print, and subsequent developments in structures of communication.[97] These brought with them new intersections of 'high' and 'low' discourse, new readings of the past, new ways of constructing meanings, and new meanings themselves – indeed among these new meanings was the social construction of class out of the customary discourse of moral economy. There are many items on the agenda of this interrogation of custom and its subsequent manifestations: among these would be the symbolic import of kin and neighbourhood networks (for example, 'penny capitalism', relations of credit, management of life-courses); the public ritual of towns, the nation and working-class organisations; the pivotal role of women in relation to consumption as well as production. Account would also have to be taken of the symbolic meaning of architecture and the internal arrangements of the home, of patterns of consumption, of speech and imaginative life.[98] The armoury of interpretation brought to bear on 'pre-industrial' popular culture needs to be directed at the industrial popular culture that we mistakenly think we know so well.[99] The history of work has to be about more than work alone.

Finally, there is the question of class. Instead of the 'before' and 'after' of 'plebeians' and 'working class' (the sudden annunciation of the proletariat as in Engels for instance), what emerges here is a more satisfactory blend of continuity and change. The foregoing discussion of skill has indicated how proprietorial evaluations were central to both early and later nineteenth-century popular labour and political movements (in the latter example, to popular liberalism as much as labour or socialist politics, there being no necessary connection between such evaluations and particular political parties). If the 'labour consciousness' Rule points to becomes later on a 'class consciousness' then the similarities are still striking: similar kinds of solidarities and differentiations were produced within the labouring populations as a whole. As we have seen, the late nineteenth-century outlook was evolved by a process of the selective appropriation of the earlier language of the trade. In this the discourse of union leaders was critical as they struggled to control the labour market, create a viable union structure, and reach an understanding with employers. In so doing they created a voice for labour that was to be of great moment, flowing beyond Liberalism into the twentieth-century Labour party. However, if an important voice, and in a sense the voice that won, it was not at all the only voice of class, nor necessarily the one that at the time shaped developments most powerfully. We need to know how our own outlook has edited out other popular visions of the social order. McClelland has however given us this major voice, and in so doing has also suggested new ways in which the history of trade unionism may be written. This essay also prompts the remark that the insights and conceptual apparatus applied in feminist scholarship to the gender roles of women might with equal success be applied to those of men. Of course, while continuities must be emphasised between different manifestations of class, McClelland shows clearly that the circumstances of his conjuncture marked new departures as well. The changed nature of capitalism, and the relationship of labour to the language of the market both represented a crucially new spiral in development in the mid nineteenth century.

McClelland in fact shows how in the subsequent period the new class identity in which trade and union combined was in itself fragile. It also set up lines of division within labour more broadly, whether between society men (themselves in sectionalist competition) and the non-unionist, or the very large category of the 'dependent'. The standing of the 'independent' and proud union man was always undermined by the culture of drink and of the 'rough', and by the squalor of housing conditions. This undermining might create solidarities between different ranks of labour in its turn, the pub serving to unite as well as dissolve common feeling, just as it is noticeable how the unskilled used the language of the skilled in contrasting their condition as bondsmen and as free. This imagery of dependence and independence, of bondsmen and free, has both an antique and a modern ring. It was invoked in the recent long and bitter miners' strike in Britain. If the key was different the tune was the same. Whether the future will bring a new tune remains to be seen.

This collection of essays shows something of how the languages of labour and more widely of work have evolved. In drawing connections between the different contributions one must acknowledge many difficulties of theory and empirical interpretation that remain when work is considered in the 'cultural' terms of reference urged here. The relationship between 'representations' or 'discourse' and 'practice', the role of structural and especially economic processes in the construction of meaning and the history of work; these are among matters touched on here. Solution, or at least detailed elucidation of these and other difficulties will have to wait upon more appropriate occasions than the present one, also upon the contributions of differing kinds of expertise and academic discipline. While acknowledging the difficulties, the attempt here has been to advocate a new and valuable way of seeing the history of work. In substantive terms the diverse contributions none the less serve well to present understandings of work that have left a powerful impression on our own century. We have lived through many of these meanings, and in the case of some of them we are living past them. In doing so, we ask new questions of the past, respecting its otherness yet summoning it to bear witness to our needs. These essays certainly ask such questions. It is to be hoped that they also begin to trace the forms of answers to them.

2

Mythical work: workshop production and the *compagnonnages* of eighteenth-century France

MICHAEL SONENSCHER

INTRODUCTION

The *compagnonnages* are a mystery. This is not, of course, an accident. An aura of mystery has been part of the history of the *compagnonnages* ever since their existence was revealed by the Doctors of the Faculty of Theology of the Sorbonne in 1655.[1] In that year, the Faculty issued a resolution condemning journeymen in five Parisian trades – tailors, shoemakers, hatters, saddlers and cutlers – for practising a heretical ceremony of initiation into what was termed the *devoir*. The *devoir* was, they stated, an informal and clandestine association of journeymen. In various forms, the pattern of association by initiation which characterised the *devoir* was a continuous part of the life of the French trades between the mid seventeenth and the mid nineteenth century.[2] Mystery was therefore, and perhaps paradoxically, something with which many journeymen were familiar. This is a study of its significance.

Mystery can be approached in two ways: as a veil concealing a more substantial reality, or as a performance which creates or recreates a reality which might otherwise not exist. The distinction is, of course, one of degree rather than kind. Yet, as will be shown, it is more helpful to approach the mysterious ceremonial of the *compagnonnages* from the latter point of view rather than the former. For the significance of mystery in the context of the *compagnonnages* lay in what journeymen sought to create, rather than in what they attempted to conceal. What they created was a complex world of ephemeral distinctions.

There were, as will be shown, good reasons why such distinctions mattered greatly in the everyday life of many eighteenth-century trades. There were also good reasons why they should be ephemeral. In a world in which the range of materials used in many trades, and the levels of competence required to manipulate them did not vary greatly, mystery supplied a vocabulary of distinction when legal rights did not. The ceremonial of the *compagnonnages* initially provided an informal counterpoint to the legal rights enjoyed by some journeymen. As these legal rights gradually disappeared, ritual enabled journeymen to create their own ephemeral hierarchies and distinctions to meet the complex schedules of the workshop economy. The golden age of the *compagnonnages*, which ran from the mid eighteenth century to the July Monarchy, coincided with a gradual redefinition of the relationship between the law and the trades.

This study is not, therefore, a study of the *compagnonnages* as a prefiguration of the modern labour movement.[3] Nor is it a study of the *compagnonnages* as vehicles of solidarity among journeymen.[4] Networks of association created by journeymen depended, of course, upon solidarities of a certain kind, but the creation of solidarity was not their primary purpose. Nor, it will be argued, were the *compagnonnages* an informal counterpart to the corporations to which master artisans belonged.[5] They flourished well after the abolition of the corporations in 1791 and their continued existence cannot be explained satisfactorily in terms of the mutations of an informal 'corporate idiom' of popular association. The emergence of the *compagnonnages* – and their relative ubiquity in the late eighteenth and early nineteenth centuries – was the product of three factors: the wide diffusion of a relatively limited range of skills in many urban trades; the very large number of towns in eighteenth-century France (larger than in any other territorial state in Europe at the time) in which they were practised; and the gradual erosion of those legal provisions which distinguished the formal rights of journeymen in some urban centres from others. This, rather than the more limited context of the corporate world, was the wider context in which the *compagnonnages* emerged. Their ceremonial was a commentary upon a world in which the work that people did was often very similar. The point, however, was to make it appear to be different.

I

Throughout the eighteenth century, journeymen's associations in France – as in the rest of Europe – existed on the margins of public life. Only in the first decade of the nineteenth century did their existence receive some form of positive acknowledgment. It was, however, an acknowledgment of a limited and confused kind. In 1821, Charles Evérat, a member of the *Société philanthropique de Paris*, recalled how, after the publication of Sir Frederick Morton Eden's *Inquiry into the State and Present Condition of the Poor*, the society had decided to investigate whether the French capital contained any associations similar to the English Friendly Societies upon which Eden had lavished such praise. A sub-committee of the society had been established in 1804 and, after three months' work, its president, the political economist Pierre Samuel Dupont de Nemours, reported the discovery of twenty-eight mutual aid societies, or *sociétés de prévoyance*.[6] He also stated that there were other types of society in existence in the capital, and mentioned that journeymen carpenters and joiners were known to belong to an association known as the *devoir* which could be found all over France.

As Evérat recalled, it had been impossible to discover anything more about the *devoir*.[7] He proceeded none the less to describe the internal organisation of this mysterious association. To become what was known as a *compagnon du devoir*, he said, an initiate was first required to have been a *Gavaud*, 'a term which means the same as the masonic word apprentice'.[8] One then passed to the rank of what was called a *Drille* and, after a further period, to that of *Renard*. From this grade one moved to the most prestigious of all ranks – that of *compagnon du devoir*. A *compagnon du devoir* was identified easily, Evérat claimed, by the long stave which he carried on his travels around the country on the celebrated *Tour de France*. Those on the lower grades of the hierarchy were allowed to bear only short batons. Finally, a *compagnon du devoir* was acquainted with a number of secret passwords, like the Freemasons.

Evérat's description of the *compagnonnages* was, of course, completely wrong. In 1839 something of their real identity emerged when the journeyman joiner Agricol Perdiguier published his *Livre du Compagnonnage*.[9] Instead of the quasi-masonic hierarchy of grades which Evérat had imagined, Perdiguier revealed that the *compagnonnages* consisted of three relatively distinct groupings, distinguished from one another by their insignia, their rituals and, most fundamentally, by their different origins in a mythical history which began on the site of Solomon's Temple. The first and, according to Perdiguier, most senior of the associations, or rites, were the *Enfants de Salomon*. They were the descendants of the stonecutters and masons who had constructed Solomon's Temple as described in the Book of Kings.[10] They were also called *gavots, compagnons étrangers, loups, renards* or, in the nineteenth century, *compagnons du devoir de liberté*.

The second rite consisted of the *Enfants de maître Jacques*, descended, it was said, from a master craftsman who had organised the construction of Solomon's Temple before leaving Judea to sail to France. They were also known as *compagnons du devoir, devoirants, compagnons passants* or *loups garous*. The third association was made up of the followers of another master craftsman, the *père Soubise*. He too had worked upon Solomon's Temple and had sailed to France with *maître Jacques*. After their arrival, there had been a quarrel and Soubise's allies had conspired to murder *maître Jacques* as he meditated, Christ-like, in the wilderness. The *Enfants du père Soubise* were also variously entitled *drilles, bons enfants,* or *compagnons passants.*

These, according to Perdiguier, were the three different rites to which journeymen in a number of trades belonged. It is a characterisation of the *compagnonnages* which has remained largely unchallenged, even though much of Perdiguier's description is as redolent of the early nineteenth-century fascination with mystery, clandestinity and secret societies as of anything to do with the history of informal association in the trades of early modern France.[11] This has been one reason why historians have had some difficulty in explaining the nature and function of the *compagnonnages*. Perdiguier's description has been taken at its face value and historical interpretation has consisted largely of attempts to graft the corpus of myth which he presented on to earlier, and arguably different, contexts.[12]

The assumption of continuity which has been the result of accepting Perdiguier's characterisation of the *compagnonnages* appears to beg a large number of questions. The possibility that journeymen in a certain number of apparently clearly identified trades could set off on their great peregrination around the kingdom, perform the same ceremonies, have the same adventures and conflicts, and belong to the same associations in 1780 as their counterparts had done in 1680, if not 1580 or earlier, induces an initial scepticism. It is not easy to accept that the *compagnonnages* were so highly structured and durable that Perdiguier, writing in the late 1830s, could describe a type of association that had existed in the same form for a hundred, or two hundred years or more.

This has not been the only difficulty. For many of the myths and ceremonies which Perdiguier described in 1839 undoubtedly existed, in somewhat different form, before the nineteenth century. This has presented historians with a more abiding problem. For it is not easy to see how the specific forms of ritual associated with the *compagnonnages* were related to the practical concerns of journeymen in the trades. There is no clear connection between the mythical exploits of *maître Jacques*, the *père Soubise*, the construction of Solomon's Temple and the daily preoccupations of journeymen attached to the *compagnonnages*. It is equally hard to understand the sense of the ritual involved in the elaborate ceremonies surrounding the *réception* of a new initiate, or the business of eating and drinking together in inns – where the innkeeper's wife (or widow) was designated as the journeymen's *mère* and often had a prominent role in the life of the association – or the distinctive ribbons and greetings used by *compagnons* of different rites. There is no obvious link between the performance of such ceremonies and the wider objectives which, it has been assumed, the *compagnonnages* were designed to meet.

These objectives have been defined either in terms of the imperatives of workshop production (and attendant conflicts between masters and journeymen), or in terms of the scale and ubiquity of journeymen's migrations (and the integrative functions of ritual). The two functions are not, in any sense, mutually exclusive. Widespread and protracted stoppages in the trades imply the existence of solidarities of some kind. Extensive networks of migration may have had their effects upon the supply of labour and the level of wages. To this extent it has been possible to offer an explanation of the *compagnonnages* which is consonant with prevailing assumptions about the workings of labour markets and the circumstances of journeymen as wage earners. Yet neither approach offers much of an explanation of what made the *compagnonnages* different from the other types of informal association established by journeymen in early modern Europe.[13] Nothing equivalent to the ritual and mythology of the *compagnonnages* can be found in Protestant England or Catholic Italy, while the German *Bruderschaften* had their own forms of ceremonial life.[14] Neglect of the distinctive ritual of the *compagnonnages* has made it difficult to find a way of simultaneously understanding their more exotic and mythical characteristics, as well as their more prosaic role in the organisation of journeymen's migrations in early modern France. As a result, the tendency – which is understandable – has been to emphasise either one aspect or another of these elusive associations.

Faced with such problems, an earlier generation of historians preferred to relegate the apparently intractable and inessential aspects of the ceremonial life of the *compagnonnages* to the rubric of the pre-history of the working class movement, welcoming their disappearance with relief as the movement reached a more recognisable maturity.[15] More recently, the emphasis has shifted away from teleological speculations of this kind and a more serious attempt has been made to understand the exotic penumbra of the *compagnonnages* in its own terms. Cynthia Truant and Jean Lecuir have argued that the ritual and ceremonial of journeymen's associations are best understood as rites of passage or mnemonic exercises whose function was to produce the internal solidarities which endowed the *compagnonnages* with their durability in space and over time.[16] Lecuir has also pointed out the similarities between the *compagnonnages* – particularly their ritual festivities and ornate public ceremonies – and other types of informal association which existed among young men in early modern France and which Natalie Davis, in particular, has examined with great subtlety.[17]

This is clearly the direction in which to proceed. It may however, have its own pitfalls. For it is all too easy to envisage a study of the *compagnon-nages* produced under the aegis of that nebulous concept 'popular cul-ture', where journeymen appear to be doomed forever to perform rituals or practise rites.[18] The rituals and rites in question had, however, a con-tent of their own and it is not clear how that content can be related to the concept of solidarity. This is because the term solidarity is itself problem-atic and has connotations whose relevance to the world of workshop pro-duction in the eighteenth century is debatable. Historians have tended, however, to assume that journeymen in the eighteenth-century trades faced conditions which, if smaller in scale, were analogous to those faced by industrial workers. The extravagance of the ritual of the *compagnon-nages* was therefore a corollorary to the obstacles to solidarity faced by itinerant individuals employed in dispersed, small-scale units of produc-tion. The absence of the solidarities induced by the environment of the fac-tory implicitly explains the additional effort required of those who worked in workshops. In this sense, ritual was a compensation for the absence of steam power and the assembly line. The anachronism and logi-cal incoherence of this approach to popular culture is clear.[19] It means that a closer examination of the ritual and ceremonial of the *compagnon-nages* informed by a less anachronistic understanding of the imperatives of the workshop is needed. It may then be possible to show that, to their agents, the performance of ritual meant something more complicated than the creation of solidarity. It offered instead a rich and flexible com-mentary upon similarities and inequalities among journeymen that were intrinsic to the life of the trades.

II

There are, as has been said, many indications that the distinctive features of the *compagnonnages* formed a long tradition. The rituals which Perdi-guier described in 1839 were very similar in form to those proscribed as heretical by the Faculty of Theology of the Sorbonne in 1655. In both accounts the aspiring initiate was led blindfold into an elaborately decor-ated room, turned around or otherwise made to feel anxious and dis-oriented, invited to respond to a number of commands and questions, and was baptised into the *devoir* after swearing an oath of allegiance to its pre-cepts. Similar continuities can be found in the insignia, the greetings and the songs performed by initiates.[20]

It is not easy to explain how these continuities occurred. It is true that accounts of the practices condemned by the Sorbonne in 1655 were published during the seventeenth and eighteenth centuries, so that the printed record may have contributed something to the survival of the ritual into the early nineteenth century.[21] Yet, as the ceremonies of initiation themselves indicate, the culture of the *compagnonnages* was a complex combination of oral and written elements. Although the procedures followed in the ceremony of initiation were very similar, minor differences of style and presentation affected each performance. Information acquired orally allowed members of different rites to recognise one another not only by their distinctively coloured ribbons, but by the words of greeting they used (a ritual known as *taupage*) and the songs they sang. There was, above all, no documentary evidence of the exploits of the mythical *maître Jacques*, whose presence in the life of the *compagnonnages* was certainly a durable one.[22] The stamp of his authority upon the identity of the rites was created by word of mouth rather than written evidence. This suggests that it may be necessary to account for the continuity of the *compagnonnages* outside the terms of reference of a model of linear descent. We need to explain why the stories were told rather than how they passed from one generation to the next.

It is well known that oral cultures generate a certain structural amnesia in the course of their transmission.[23] Yet historians continue to use the concept of custom as if it denoted an unchanging reality over long periods of time. The past, as it is constituted in oral cultures is, however, inherently unstable. Hatters in late nineteenth-century France fought bitterly to maintain a system of payment by the piece for the work of finishing and dressing hats. The system was, they claimed, best adapted to their customs and independence.[24] A hundred years earlier journeymen in the same trade had fought equally bitterly to prevent the introduction of the same system.[25]

As this example suggests, the form of the past embodied in spoken histories echoes the circumstances of the present. Payment by the piece in the late nineteenth century hatting trade was apparently sanctioned by a long tradition of independence, which, in fact, only came into existence after the Revolution. This adaptation of the past to conform to contemporary perceptions of the present suggests that instead of attempting to discover how a corpus of myth and ritual was passed from one generation to the next as an unvarying totality, it may be more helpful to think in terms of modifications, mutations and accretions to a loosely structured series of stories and ceremonies recognised by journeymen in different times and circumstances in ways which were themselves often very different. What, in other words, may be required is a disaggregation of the synthesis presented by Perdiguier in the early nineteenth century into a multiplicity of smaller dramas, told and retold across the passage of time, so that their reverberations underwent subtle shifts of key and emphasis as they echoed and re-echoed over the generations. This may make it possible to divest the mythology of the *compagnonnages* of its aura of timelessness.

More importantly, it may help to redefine the problem of continuity as a problem of agency rather than reception. For what needs explanation is not so much the content of the mythology, as its continued reiteration. The need, in other words, is to understand what made it necessary for journeymen to tell each other stories about the legendary exploits of *maître Jacques* and the mythical history of the *compagnonnages*. The recurrent re-enactment of the drama, rather than the content of the drama itself, may be the key to a closer understanding of other, more ordinary, dramas enacted in the eighteenth-century trades.

There is an initial clue as to how the work of disaggregation should be done in the founding myth itself. For each of the three rites associated with the *compagnonnages* claimed an ancestry reaching back to the site of Solomon's Temple. Yet it is impossible to identify a clear line of descent running from the *Enfants de Salomon* to the *Enfants de maître Jacques* and the *Enfants du père Soubise*. The genealogy is blurred and ambiguous, allowing each rite to claim precedence over the others in the hierarchy of descent.[26] In a curious way, the genealogy of the *compagnonnages* seems to be a claim upon precedence as much as an affirmation of continuity. The imprecision of the lineage – and the ensuing implication that tradition was itself a matter of competing claims – suggests that much of the ritual of the *compagnonnages* was linked to matters of precedence within the trades themselves. It may therefore be helpful to follow a procedure capable of revealing what these matters were, and how they were linked to the ritual of the *compagnonnages*. This procedure is best developed by a careful examination of an episode involving members of one of the rites of the *compagnonnages* towards the end of the eighteenth century.

The episode contains one of the fullest accounts of the ceremonial of the *compagnonnages* produced during the eighteenth century. It was the result of legal proceedings undertaken by the municipal authorities of the town of Troyes in 1782. The affair came to light when a nineteen-year-old journeyman leather dresser (*mégissier*) named Jacques Minder, acting under some pressure from his master, complained to the police authorities that he had been forced to spend thirty *livres* to be initiated into the *compagnons du devoir*.[27]

The ceremony had occurred on Sunday 25 August 1782. On that day, towards four in the afternoon, Minder had been in his room above his master's shop on the rue de la Grande Tannerie when a journeyman named Pierre Briand, known as *le Bordelais*, had come to find him. Briand took Minder to a nearby *cabaret*, where they found five other journeymen leather dressers drinking at a table. After three or four bottles of wine had been consumed, Minder was persuaded to become a *compagnon du devoir* and gave the *Bordelais* fifteen *livres*, promising to pay a further fifteen when he could. The seven journeymen went to buy what they termed their livery from a milliner and then proceeded to a second *cabaret* in the *faubourg de Croncels* kept by the *mère des compagnons du devoir*. There, in a room upstairs, Minder was initiated into the association, in a ceremony which, he later said, involved kneeling down to be baptised with wine, and swearing on his blood never to reveal what happened in assemblies of the rite.[28] He was then given a name. That chosen for him was *L'Aimable*. The six other journeymen then wrote something on a sheet of paper which he was asked to sign. When the ceremony was over the journeymen went down and presented a livery, consisting of a long ribbon or sash, to their *mère* to mark the occasion.

Minder spent the night at the inn and on the Monday morning he and the other journeymen went out to buy some more ribbons to prepare for the initiation of two more individuals. Several witnesses later described this as a very public affair. The journeymen paraded around the streets with their hats and coats garlanded with brightly coloured ribbons, making a point of passing workshops on the rue de la Grande Tannerie and adjoining alleys to encourage other members of their trade to join them. Ten of them were seen at 10 a.m. in the haberdasher's shop where they seemed to be a little drunk. They bought thirty ells of ribbon, explaining that it was needed for the purpose of receiving 'un de leurs du devoir', and that there would be further receptions at the end of the week, for which even more ribbon would be required.[29]

Monday was thus given over to ceremonial, food and wine, so that all the journeymen spent the night in the *cabaret*. On Tuesday morning some of them wanted to return to work, but came under pressure from the others to remain. There was an argument and a brief fight in which a journeyman was slightly injured. Minder, who owed the *compagnons* half the initiation fee, made his way back to work where, perhaps rather naively, he asked his master for an advance of fifteen *livres* on his wages. As a result, he was encouraged by his master to complain to the authorities.

The ensuing proceedings throw considerable light upon the combination of ritual and improvisation which, it is probable, was highly characteristic of the *compagnonnages*. When Pierre Briand, the journeyman known as *le Bordelais* who had been the main figure in organising the initiation ceremonies, heard of what had happened he decided to try and avoid criminal proceedings by joining the army. He approached a recruiting sergeant-major of the *Régiment de Brie* garrisoned in Troyes and asked to enlist. He explained rather disingenuously that he had been unaware that the *compagnonnages* were illegal in Troyes and hoped that by joining the army a blind eye would be turned to his offence.[30]

According to Briand the initiations into the *compagnonnage* had taken place because the association of *compagnons du devoir* in Troyes had become moribund. He had, he said, only just arrived in the town and had made the acquaintance of two journeymen known as *Vivarais* and *Mâconnais* in order to find work. *Vivarais* asked him whether he was a *compagnon du devoir*. He replied that he was.[31] Accordingly he and the only other two *compagnons du devoir* in the trade initiated five journeymen into the association. It was a costly procedure because none of the initiates could pay the customary thirty *livres* in full. The three journeymen were owed a total of fifty-four *livres* by the *aspirants* and were also involved in discussions over the settlement of a sum of thirty *livres* outstanding on the sixty *livres* which they had spent on food and drink in the inn run by their *mère*.

The journeymen's *mère*, a *cabaretière* named Briey, raised difficulties when attempts were made to negotiate over when the outstanding sum would be paid. She said too that she did not wish to be considered to be the *mère des compagnons du devoir* because she had not been given a formal title by the journeymen. It transpired that the formal title consisted of the papers of the *compagnons du devoir*. These papers were in the possession of another *cabaretière* named Marie Maître, who had an inn on the rue Dauphin. She admitted that she had been the *mère* of the *compagnons tanneurs* several years ago, but had decided to renounce the position in 1776 when, according to her, the *compagnonnages* had been prohibited. At that time the journeymen had owed her sixty *livres* and had left their papers with her in a small chest as security. The debt was never paid and the papers had been left in their chest until April 1782, when a number of journeymen had arrived and asked for a room. When it became evident that they were *compagnons du devoir* they were ordered to leave. This was why they had transferred their activities to the inn in the *faubourg de Croncels*.

The new venue was not a random choice. The journeymen's new *mere*, Marie Briey, had worked as a domestic servant for the *cabaretière* Marie Maître, before setting up in her own right when she married. She had, she said, initially suspected that the journeymen who invited her to become their *mère* were not genuine *compagnons du devoir* because, as she put it, they did not have a *maître Jacques*.[32]

The *maître Jacques* in question was, it was revealed, a figure painted on the chest containing the papers of the *compagnons du devoir*. A search of the *cabaret* on the rue Dauphin led to the discovery of the chest, upon whose cover were the figures of what the police officials described as three saints, with the figure in the middle representing Saint Jacques Pellerin (which was why the journeymen called it a *maître Jacques*). When the chest was opened it was found to contain nothing more than some cards and an empty notebook cover.

Four aspects of this sequence of events are immediately striking. The first is the content of the ceremonial of the *compagnonnages* and the familiarity of the journeymen responsible for the initiations with a corpus of ritual which was enacted in the time-honoured and traditional way. There are other examples of this attachment to correct procedure. A journeyman wheelwright drinking in an inn in the little town of Montereau near Paris in 1763 was heard to say that he was about to leave and regretted that there was no one to see him on his way in the prescribed manner. A journeyman mason offered to perform the honours. They gathered his possessions, bought some wine and prepared to escort him out on to the road, only to find, to their disgust, that the wheelwright had changed his mind and wanted to stay.[33]

In this, as in the ceremonies of initiation in Troyes, ritual was conducted on a small, almost intimate, scale. At the most, no more than a dozen individuals were involved in the events which took place in 1782 in Troyes. This too was by no means unusual. As will be shown, the rites of the *compagnonnages* belonged to a wider continuum of ceremonial performed by different groups of journeymen in a variety of circumstances. The relationship between the particularity of the rite and the general idiom of association is one of the keys to the identity of the *compagnonnages*. This will be easier to understand in the light of the two remaining features of the events in Troyes in 1782.

The third of these is the notable absence of secrecy surrounding much of what the journeymen did. They paraded openly around the town and had no inhibitions in announcing that their celebrations had been occasioned by the initiation of a number of new members to the *devoir*. Despite the aura of clandestinity surrounding the *compagnonnages*, their presence was highly visible and, on many occasions, extremely public.[34] It is clear therefore that the aura of clandestinity surrounding the *compagnonnages* – and their oaths of secrecy in particular – need careful consideration. Secrets are exclusive. Yet it is not immediately obvious who was excluded from the secrets of the *compagnonnages*.

Relations between the journeymen and master artisans in Troyes were hardly in keeping with what might have been expected of a clandestine association. This is the fourth aspect of the sequence of events which calls for comment. It is particularly striking that Jacques Minder was evidently unaware of any contradiction between taking an oath to keep the secrets

of the *compagnonnages* and approaching his master for an advance of fifteen *livres* to meet the costs of his initiation. There was one very obvious
reason why he did so. Master artisans had, in most cases, once been journeymen and, like many journeymen, had been members of one or other of
the rites of the *compagnonnages*. For them, the ceremonies of the rites
were no mystery.

It is not difficult to find examples of masters' continued involvement
with the *compagnonnages*. A journeyman stonecutter described how he
had been initiated into the *devoir* in Bordeaux on Ascension Day 1754 by
a master architect and two dozen current and former members of the
rite.[35] Masters were therefore likely to have been entirely conversant with
the rituals of the *compagnonnages*. A journeyman carpenter from Troyes
described how he had been approached by a *compagnon du devoir* in the
same trade in 1771 and asked the whereabouts of the *cayenne* (the inn
used by the *devoirants*). He explained that since it was the custom to
examine a newcomer on the mysteries of the *devoir*, he had performed
various exercises with the journeyman.[36] They had then retired for a meal
to a baker's shop where they found two master carpenters with whom
they ate sumptuously and resumed their exercises.[37] In 1774 the master
turners of Bordeaux complained that all their shops had been boycotted
by the *compagnons du devoir* when some masters revealed the secrets of
the rite in an attempt to put an end to the association.[38]

For many masters therefore, the secrecy of the *compagnonnages* was a
very open secret indeed. Surprisingly none of the historians of the *compagnonnages* appears to have been aware of this rather obvious fact. One
of its clearest implications is that, if the identity of the *compagnonnages*
was a mystery, it was a mystery which was most impenetrable to other
journeymen. This suggests that the *compagnonnages* are best situated primarily within a context informed by relationships among journeymen,
and only secondarily, and in a different sense, within one informed by relations between masters and journeymen. The problem then is to explain
the significance of ritual and clandestinity among journeymen in the
urban trades of eighteenth-century France.

III

In almost every detail the ceremonies performed by the *compagnons du
devoir* in Troyes in 1782 conform to the description of the ceremonies
condemned by the Faculty of Theology of the University of Paris in 1655
and the practices which Perdiguier revealed in 1839.[39] Thus, although the
parallels between the *compagnonnages* and the *associations de jeunesse*
of early modern France are striking, there were also clear differences be-

tween them. The ritual content of the practices followed by the *compagnonnages* was more highly structured, more uniform and more durable over time and place than the wide range of practices which can be catalogued under the rubric of *fêtes, fêtes baladoires, fêtes votives* and *charivaris*.[40] Although both kinds of practice might be said to have had a common source in the situation of young men (and young women), it is clear from the enduring content of the rituals of the *compagnonnages* that *their* practices derived more specifically from circumstances particular to the urban trades and the situation of those engaged in them.

The episode in Troyes suggests, however, that the number of *compagnons du devoir* who worked as leather dressers accounted for a relatively small proportion of the total employed in the trade. It is not possible to know how many journeymen worked in the leather trade in Troyes at this time. In 1787 there were thirty-three master tanners in the city, which suggests that a further sixty to a hundred journeymen were employed in the trade.[41] The majority of them were clearly not *compagnons du devoir*. Both the journeymen and the other witnesses called to give evidence in 1782 concurred in describing the association as small and almost defunct. The same image emerges from a further complaint about the rite four years later, in 1786. A journeyman tanner from Bonn in Germany reported that half a dozen 'compagnons chamoiseurs se disant du devoir', had demanded six *livres* from him if he wanted to work in the town. Another journeyman working in the same trade, but from Burgundy, had been told by nine *compagnons du devoir* seated in an inn that he and his company were not fit to sit at their table because they had refused to join the *devoir*.[42]

Encounters of this kind are indicative of the small scale of the world of informal association in the trades. There is no reason to suppose that the small number of *compagnons du devoir* working in the tanning and leather trades of Troyes was exceptional. Much of course depended upon the size of towns and the numbers employed in particular trades. Yet even in large cities like Lyons, Marseilles, Bordeaux or Nantes the surviving evidence reveals that the ordinary life of informal associations was maintained by groups of journeymen who could be counted more usually by the dozen or the score and only exceptionally by the hundred. In Bordeaux two series of registers confiscated from the *compagnons du devoir* in 1742 and 1761 provide some information about the size of the rite among journeymen locksmiths. The number of new arrivals to the city recorded by the *compagnons du devoir* was never more than half a dozen a month. At any one time the association appears to have had between thirty and seventy members.[43] In Nantes, fifty-six journeymen joiners and twenty-two saddlers took a solemn oath to renounce the *devoir* when it was prohibited by the municipal authorities in 1750.[44] Reports of the number of individuals present on occasions when the *compagnonnages* encountered the police authorities reveal gatherings of comparable magnitude. A funeral for a journeyman joiner in the parish of St Nizier in Lyons in 1764 was attended by some fifty joiners and a further thirty or forty journeymen locksmiths who were also *compagnons du devoir*.[45] Other occasions saw larger gatherings. In Bordeaux, over 300 journeymen carpenters were reported to have gathered at the inn kept by their *mère* on Saint Joseph's day, their trade holiday, and escorted her in pomp to mass at the Cordeliers church and back again.[46] At least 150 journeymen joiners arrived bearing bouquets of flowers to attend a high mass performed by three priests in honour of their trade patron, Saint Anne, in Bordeaux in 1788. The mass was followed by a huge banquet in an inn on the *allée* Boutant.[47]

The figure is substantial. Yet there were 126 master joiners or widows employing journeymen in Bordeaux in 1788.[48] If each master or widow employed only two or three individuals on average, it is likely that there were between 250 and 370 journeymen working in the city. There were at least as many journeymen in Bordeaux who were not *compagnons du devoir* as those who were. This does not mean that they were not involved in the *compagnonnages* at all. Others undoubtedly belonged to the *gavots* or *compagnons du devoir de liberté*, who had a substantial following among joiners and locksmiths in Bordeaux. Others too were not involved in any of the rites and were known derisively by those who were as *espontons*.

Membership of the *compagnonnages* varied widely from trade to trade. There is little trace of their ritual in the activities of journeymen employed in the luxury trades: among painters, decorators, gilders, sculptors on metal, marble polishers and sculptors, jewellers, gold and silversmiths, watchmakers, instrument makers, or high quality bronze or iron founders. There were, as will be shown, good reasons for this. Instead, the ceremonial life of the *compagnonnages* was most ubiquitous in the building, furniture and leather trades. Joiners, locksmiths, wheelwrights, harnessmakers, stonecutters and masons, carpenters and nail-makers were among the trades most usually associated with one or other of the rites. For the rites embraced more than one trade. *Gavots* were found among stonecutters, joiners and locksmiths. The *devoir* included journeymen from each of these three trades as well as another twenty-five to thirty others. A report sent by the mayor of Orléans to the Prefect of the Department of the Loiret in 1805 referred to associations among journeymen in thirty trades.[49] All were small in size. In most cases journeymen were associated with the *devoir*. In some trades, notably the carpenters, joiners and locksmiths, both *gavots* and *devoirants* had their supporters.

Schism and division were therefore intrinsic to the *compagnonnages*. The ambiguity of the founding myth was the mark of an inherent evasion of unity. Such attempts as were made to unite the different rites occurred only in the nineteenth century and owed everything to a later preoccupation with the common destiny of working people as a class. During the eighteenth century the life of the trades was informed by other preoccupations, whose most recurrent expression was the pitched ritual battle between members of rival rites. A fifteen-year-old boy described how one such battle, between joiners belonging to the *gavots* and the *devoirants*, was organised in Troyes in 1773. The two groups of journeymen gathered near the corn market towards nine in the morning. The *devoirants* approached the *gavots* and, in a formal way, offered to make their peace. The *gavots* rejected the invitation and announced their desire to fight.[50] The two groups then separated and made their way to the appointed place in the suburbs of Troyes where the fight was to take place. Both, of course, took good care to bring their staves.

The frequency of such battles or *rixes*, and the absence of any obvious connection between the occupations of the participants and divisions in the trades, is disconcerting, and has disconcerted many of the historians of the *compagnonnages*. Fights between members of different rites involved journeymen from a wide variety of different trades. Joiners assaulted locksmiths; hatters attacked wheelwrights; iron-founders fell upon harness-makers; shoemakers stoned building workers.[51] Such heterogeneity has perplexed and saddened historians predisposed to view the *compagnonnages* as a protean form of the modern labour movement. As a result, explanation has rapidly collapsed into anachronistic apology.

The difficulty evaporates as soon as it is recognised that it is impossible to explain the ritual fights of the *compagnonnages* as prefigurations of modern labour disputes or ascribe roles to their protagonists analogous to those occupied by blacklegs and strikers at the factory gates of nineteenth-century cities. Fights between members of rival rites, whether in the same trade or in entirely unconnected trades, were not fights about command of the workplace, the level of wages or the composition of the workforce. Like the open secret of the apparently mysterious ceremony of initiation itself, they were performed mainly for the benefit of other journeymen. The dramas played out in such brawls were played out not before an audience of apprehensive millowners, but an audience of journeymen and, in particular, journeymen in the *same rite*. Indirectly, they were also played out to an audience of master artisans, whose memories carried their own accounts of other brawls, in other places, when they too had been young. Prowess in combat was, in this sense, an entirely narcissistic, but immensely practical exercise. For victory in the immediate, physical, sense was also victory of a less tangible kind. It was a symbolic victory over other members of the same rite: a mark of distinction which represented a guarantee of an honoured place in the ceremonial life of the rite. Fighting a member of another rite in an entirely unrelated trade was a way of demonstrating prowess in one's own rite and one's own trade. As will be shown, there were good reasons why it was necessary, in certain trades, to demonstrate prowess of this kind.

The presence of the *compagnonnages* in the life of the trades was invariably partial. Their place was defined by the way in which those initiated into their rites were distinguished from those either outside the *compagnonnages* altogether, or those working in trades where they were not to be found. Journeymen were fully aware of the minutiae of the distinctions between different rites, and between trades associated with the *compagnonnages* and those which were not. A cabinet maker charged with membership of the *devoir* in Bordeaux in 1737 explained that he was not entitled to membership of the *devoir*, which was why journeymen joiners who were *compagnons* had attacked him.[52] A journeyman farrier involved in a dispute with a number of masters in 1776 in the same city stated that he did not belong to any of the rites because his trade was unattached to the *compagnonnages*.[53]

Journeymen farriers and shoemakers were among the members of a number of trades with no formal connection with the rites of the *compagnonnages*. This did not prevent them from conducting a ceremonial life of their own which had many similarities to the ritual of *devoirants* or *gavots*. Farriers in Paris frequented an inn near the Place Maubert in 1697 kept by their *mère*. Ninety years later, in 1786, the same inn remained a meeting place and lodging house for journeymen in the trade.[54] A group of journeymen farriers arrested in Chalon-sur-Saône in 1731 as they marched, singing and carrying a figure of a horseshoe struck in silver at the end of a stave, explained that they were practising the *devoir*.[55] Peripatetic journeymen tailors were known as *garçons de logis* and frequently borrowed the idiom of the *devoir*. A journeyman tailor in Nantes revealed his attitude to a requirement to register his name with the corporate authorities by stating that the name he had on the *Tour de France* was 'I don't give a fuck.'[56]

There were, in other words, many forms of informal association. Older, more settled journeymen frequented *chambrées*. A journeyman tailor in Lyons told his master that during the political disturbances there in the summer of 1790, a journeyman hatter had approached him to invite the members of the *chambrée* to which he belonged to join the hatters and other workers in their campaign against the municipality.[57] In Lille, as in many Northern French towns, the *compagnonnages* were unknown. Journeymen met in *estaminets* which were open only to those who paid for their upkeep.[58]

If *chambrées* and *estaminets* were the venues of other types of informal association in the trades, the most substantial and widespread alternative to the *compagnonnages* remained the confraternity. Journeymen in centres of textile production like Rouen, Amiens, Troyes and Nîmes all maintained their own separate and semi-legal confraternities for much of the eighteenth century.[59] More importantly, they remained the most usual form of association among journeymen in Paris until the last quarter of the eighteenth century.[60] As the *jurats* of Bordeaux explained in 1726, the *devoir* was not to be found in the capital. Confraternities of journeymen existed in at least thirty Parisian trades during the eighteenth century.[61] Unlike the *compagnonnages*, the confraternities were trade specific. This too, as will be shown, has a significant bearing on the identity of the *compagnonnages*.

For the moment, however, it is important to emphasise that the *compagnonnages* were only one component of a mosaic of informal association which existed among journeymen in the trades of urban France in the eighteenth century. Although each grouping may have been small, so that each particular form of association occupied only a limited position within a single trade, the variety of different types of association meant that it is probable that most journeymen were attached to some kind of informal collectivity at one time or another. The problem, of course, is to explain the differences between them and account for the bewildering variety of local inflections placed upon the general pattern of association.

Journeymen had their own explanations. A stonecutter arrested in Bordeaux in 1754 after a fight with two *gavots* explained that he had nothing in particular against non-members of the *devoir*, but could not tolerate them wearing the ribbons of the rite. He added that they were to be found usually in Burgundy and the Champagne.[62] It is possible that geographical differences of this kind had some relationship to the distribution of the various rites. As we have seen, there were very few *compagnons du devoir* in the leather trades of Troyes. A similar state of affairs appears to have existed among joiners and locksmiths. After a *compagnon du devoir* had been assaulted by a dozen journeymen joiners in Troyes in 1748, one of his assailants explained that the victim was a *compagnon du devoir* and had been ordered to leave the town by the other journeymen, who were all *gavots*.[63] The town was not one of the fifteen localities in which, according to a memorandum on the *compagnonnages* drawn up by the *jurats* of Bordeaux in 1726, the *devoir* was celebrated publicly or in secret. The list included three cities in eastern France – Chalons, Reims and Dijon – where the *devoir* existed. A further ten towns were noted as places in which members of the rite were prohibited from working (see map).[64]

The frequency of fights between members of rival rites suggests, however, that geographical affinities of this kind were more symbolic than real. The claims made by *gavots* and *devoirants* to exclusive control of particular towns were claims of precedence which went beyond the assertion of formally defined zones of influence. Variations in the spatial distribution of the rites were called regularly into question as journeymen laid claim to local priority in ways which embodied more subtle distinctions of definition and counter-definition than mere geographical difference.

A *devoirant*, for example, could be recognised if he was well mannered, worked well, paid his way and did no wrong to anyone, according to a stonecutter in Bordeaux in 1754.[65] Membership of the *devoir* implied friendship and mutual pleasure, a journeyman in the same trade explained in 1761.[66] *Gavots* had their own self-definitions. A journeyman joiner arrested in 1737 after a fight with a *compagnon du devoir* in Bordeaux stated that he was a *gavot*, which he said, meant that he was free to work where he chose. A second journeyman, asked to explain what the term meant, replied that it meant the freedom to find work wherever it could be found, without having to pay a customary fee.[67]

These definitions should not be taken to mean that *gavots* were indifferent to the ceremonial of the *compagnonnages*. A fight in Bordeaux in 1770 occurred when over 150 *gavots* – some of them joiners, others locksmiths, masons or stonecutters – who had attended the funeral of one of their members came upon a group of *compagnons du devoir* as they were escorting two other *gavots* about to leave Bordeaux and, as the phrase went, 'battre au champs'.[68] The *compagnons étrangers* or *gavots* were therefore more than non-members of the *devoir*. Although the word *gavot* had perjorative connotations of rusticity and was used in southern France to refer to migrants from remote rural areas of Haute Provence or even Spain, it also referred to a rite as distinct as the *devoir*.[69] Papers confiscated from the *gavots* of Mâcon in the mid eighteenth century reveal a ceremonial life as elaborate as that of the *devoir* and a clear sense of the geographical horizons of the association from the vantage point of the Burgundian town:

> Dans Lyon cette grande ville
> Nous avons des compagnons
> tous gavots plain de courrage
> qui soutiendront notre nom
> Vienne, Romans et Vallance
> Avignon faut le nommer
> nos compagnons d'assurance
> ils sont fort bien renommés.[70]

Towns associated with the *devoir* of
journeymen locksmiths (1726)

In Lyons joiners and locksmiths belonging to the two rites frequented different inns on virtually the same street.[71] Both *gavots* and *devoirants* performed the same elaborate ceremonies in ways which were at once distinct and, at the same time, a pastiche of those of the other rite. Each rite had its regular assemblies and elected officers. The locksmiths affiliated to the *gavots* met in the church of the *Recollets* to celebrate mass and present an offering on the first Sunday of every month and the principal trade holidays. Afterwards they adjourned to the nearby cloisters to discuss their affairs and settle their accounts.[72]

In many respects, mimesis was the hallmark of the *compagnonnages*. It was always, of course, more than mimesis. For the imitative ritual of the *compagnonnages* was designed to demonstrate, by a particular feat of prowess, the superiority of a particular rite or individual performer. Like the secret initiation which was not a secret, and the fights in which victory was won on one's own side, whether or not one defeated one's opponents, mimesis also involved meeting a hidden agenda. That agenda was set by the tension between proficiency in a trade and the vagaries of workshop production.

IV

There are no real French equivalents to the English terms 'skilled' and 'unskilled'. The usual terms – 'ouvrier qualifié', 'ouvrier professionel' and 'ouvrier specialisé' are relatively recent in origin and became current only in the years following the First World War.[73] Journeymen in the eighteenth century did not use a vocabulary which discriminated between different types of work in a general way. Instead they talked about work in a more personal way, so that the proficiency of the worker and the qualities of the work were relatively indistinguishable. The phrases which journeymen used most frequently to acknowledge respect for one another was 'le plus gros' or 'le plus fort'.[74] This ascription of the quality of work to the quality of the individual informed many of the exchanges which occurred when journeymen talked disparagingly about one another, and was particularly marked in arguments over the *compagnonnages*. Two Parisian locksmiths who had been engaged to work for a master locksmith in the little town of Auxerre in 1760 ostentatiously refused to have anything to do with the local *compagnons du devoir*. They were asked if they were *gavots*. One of them replied dismissively that he had never heard the term. The other said haughtily that they had been sent for from Paris and that the customs of the *compagnonnages* were fit only for apprentices. Anyone who resented their presence was free to try and do their work themselves.[75] The equation between apprentices, the *compagnonnages* and shoddy work was plain enough. Not surprisingly, the two journeymen were assaulted.

The difference between the various rites of the *compagnonnages* was measured in a similar way. After a brawl between a number of journeymen carpenters in Nantes in 1791, the municipal authorities received a long memorandum on behalf of the *compagnons du devoir* stating that the fight was an expression of 'les haines que les renards charpentiers portent aux vrais artistes compagnons du devoir'. Its author, a member of the National Guard of Richebourg and the cashier of the artillery works there, explained that he had done the *Tour de France* on foot himself and (in an evocation of the rhetoric of the Revolution) had come to admire the fraternity displayed by journeymen carpenters affiliated to the *devoir*. He proceeded to define the difference between a *compagnon du devoir* and a *renard*. Members of the former rite had a long practical and theoretical experience of architectural drawing. They were 'vrais artistes'. *Gavots* on the other hand, were utterly ignorant and only to be found in Nantes, where they were prepared to work for twenty to twenty-four *sous* a day, instead of the thirty *sous* paid to members of the *devoir*. A *gavot* was incapable of the most elementary building work.[76]

The opposition between *vrais artistes* and a despicable minority of incompetent individuals, willing to accept derisory rates for shoddy work, could not have been more complete. There is no reason to suppose that a *gavot* would not have made the same claims about the *devoirants*.[77] The identity of each rite, as of informal groupings of journeymen outside the *compagnonnages* was constituted by such comparisons, evaluations and assertions. A near riot by a crowd of sixty journeymen joiners attempting to find a German journeyman employed by a cabinet maker in Troyes in 1788 was caused, the authorities were told, by 'jalousie d'état' and an argument over whether Germans were better than French journeymen in the finer arts of joinery.[78]

Claims and counter claims of this kind could lead to ritual competitions between rival groups of journeymen and their respective champions. The *fer de gageur* was a competition widely enacted among journeymen farriers. Jean-Baptiste Varin, a Parisian journeyman known as *Le Petit Champagne* who had been arrested in 1745 for possession of a forged double *louis d'or* explained that it had been the prize he had won for a *fer de gageur*. He had been in a *cabaret* along with four other journeymen in the faubourg Saint-Germain. There had been a discussion of some kind and Varin became embroiled in an argument with a journeyman known as the *Auvergnat*. They traded challenges, and the following morning Varin arranged to have what was called a *lopin* – a small iron bar – sent to where the *Auvergnat* worked. The *lopin* contained a mark indicating how much the wager was to be: in this instance a single *louis d'or*. The *Auvergnat* responded with his own challenge. He had no desire, he said, to take on so small a wager. He had already lost two wagers for that amount during the past year and had no wish to compete for such trivial sums, particularly in Paris. He proposed a wager of six *louis* and, some days later, on the eve of Candlemass, sent a further *lopin* increasing the wager to forty-eight *livres*. His challenge was accepted and the competition took place at Neuilly outside Paris on the following day. Varin, *Le Petit Champagne*, did not have the money and borrowed two *louis* from a compatriot known as *Le Grand Champagne*. When the shoes were made, Varin was adjudged the winner by those present and was given the stake of ninety-six *livres*. He spent half of his winnings on a dinner for all those who had been present and returned the money he had borrowed, in the form of the forged double *louis*, to *Le Grand Champagne*.[79]

The sums of money involved in these trials of proficiency were relatively large. A competition between rival groups of journeymen locksmiths in Chalon-sur-Saône in 1775 ended in acrimony when the *compagnon du devoir* took flight, leaving the *compagnons de liberté* (or *gavots*) in possession of the 120 *livres* wagered on the competition.[80] Disaster was narrowly averted during a trial between rival groups of stonecutters over the sum of 720 *livres* in Bordeaux in 1774. The two contestants, one a *compagnon passant*, the other a *compagnon étranger*, challenged one another to execute two projects which each had devised. Each contestant was to work alone in a closely guarded room. The plans were exchanged and the contestants were locked away for almost three months. It was then discovered that one of the journeymen had executed the plan presented by his opponent, while the other had attempted to do them both. The *jurats* of Bordeaux were called upon to adjudicate. Prudently they decided that the competition was a dead-heat, returned the sums of money to the journeymen and offered to exhibit each contestant's work as an example to students in the school of architecture.[81] Honour was thus preserved, at least to the satisfaction of the municipal authorities if not the journeymen themselves. The rival rites continued to be involved in pitched battles on and around the site of Victor Louis' new theatre throughout the rest of the decade.

The money was the measure of the challenge rather than the prize to be won. The victor did not keep the money wagered on these feats of prowess but, as *Le Petit Champagne* did in 1745, spent it on food and drink with other members of the trade or rite. The ultimate challenge was a competition for the right to work in a particular town. A rite would, through its champion, compete for exclusive control of employment in Mâcon or Marseilles. Victory would become part of the orally transmitted annals of the rite. The great battle between *gavots* and *devoirants* fought at Tournus, near Mâcon in 1825 was a physical re-enactment of a competition (which, it was said, the *gavots* had lost) held in 1725.[82] The prize had been the right to work in the town for a hundred years.

Feats of prowess were demonstrations of superiority conducted in the mode of mimesis. Competitors made the same things, but made them better. Difference induced suspicion. A journeyman locksmith from Lyons who was also a *gavot* admitted that he had refused to work with a number of Germans, but denied that this was because they were *compagnons du devoir*. He pointed out that they were not members of any of the rites, but would not work with them because, not being able to understand what they were saying, he was afraid that they were mocking him.[83] Similarity, however, had its own dangers and made the need to assert distinction one of the characteristic ways in which journeymen talked about one another's work. A journeyman joiner named Louis Faroux who walked out on his master in Troyes in 1784 said that he had done so because a locksmith with whom he had been working had told another joiner that the door he had been making was shoddy. The talk had reached the master of the two joiners, who had boasted that Faroux had been caught at fault. Stung, Faroux made it clear that he would ensure that the master in question had to wait a long time for another journeyman.[84]

In a small way, the incident is an indication of why feats of prowess mattered so much to eighteenth-century journeymen. Talk about the quality of work was also talk about the quality of the individual. The ritual of the *compagnonnages* was also a form of talk about the qualities of individuals. Like the secret that was not entirely a secret, and the fights in which the mark of superiority was bestowed upon the victor by an audience situated metaphorically (and sometimes literally) behind his back, feats of proficiency in the trades were performed by men who shared more than they wished to acknowledge.

V

This is the key to an understanding of the *compagnonnages*. Although it makes good sense to argue that the *compagnonnages* cannot be understood 'as somehow prefiguring the movements which eventually issued in trade unions', it does not follow that they arose 'historically out of the particular social and cultural context' of the corporate world.[85] The divisions between different rites were not merely 'paradoxical', nor yet 'an outgrowth of an inherently divisive and exclusive corporate idiom', nor even a measure of the 'depth and intensity' of journeymen's participation in the 'values, the presuppositions and the general forms of old regime society'.[86] They may have been all these things, but explanations conducted at this level of abstraction explain very little.

The *compagnonnages* owed more to circumstances which were closer to the work which journeymen did than the 'particular social and cultural context' of the corporate world. The corporations were one of a number of quasi-public institutions upon which the administration of public finance was devolved from the mid sixteenth century onwards.[87] They were grafted piecemeal onto the trades during the sixteenth and seventeenth centuries for fiscal and commercial reasons. Corporate regulation was most elaborate in those trades, particularly the textile trades, producing for distant markets.[88] As a result, the geographical distribution of the trades and the geographical distribution of the corporations were never the same. Explanations of the *compagnonnages* in terms of the ubiquity of the corporate idiom is a conflation of Paris (where the *compagnonnages* were rarely present until the late eighteenth century) with the provinces (where many trades were never incorporated into *jurandes*) in a way which does justice to neither. The *compagnonnages* were created by journeymen for reasons which had more to do with work in the trades than with the place of corporations in French public life.

The ritual of the *compagnonnages* was a mechanism of selection and exclusion. It belonged to a world in which many people did the same thing, but some did it better than others. This, of course, was the point of the ritual. It is not difficult, in the light of this, to identify the reasons why it was necessary to make the point. There is an initial clue in the occupations of the journeymen involved in the ceremonies of the *compagnons du devoir* in Troyes in 1782 and 1786.[89] Some of them were called *compagnons mégissiers*; others were *compagnons tanneurs*; others still were *compagnons chamoiseurs*. All of them however, worked on the same materials (leather) and used the same range of implements. Too close an emphasis upon the diversity of the corporate world can lead to too little consideration of the relatively limited range of materials used in the eighteenth-century trades and the very substantial number of localities in which it was possible to work upon many of them.

There were some 286 'towns' with populations of over 5,000 inhabitants in France in 1794 and 292 in 1806. A total of 867 localities had populations of 2,000 inhabitants or more in 1806.[90] At this stage, it is impossible to know the range of occupations that they housed. To give one, entirely random example, the 1,103 *capitables* listed on the *capitation* roll of Anduze, in the Cévennes, in 1782 included two goldsmiths, nine wigmakers, eight farriers, nine locksmiths, twenty tanners, fifteen hatters, six harness or bridle makers, three carpenters, twenty-five masons, thir-

teen tailors, twenty-one joiners, coopers or casket makers, fifty-one shoemakers or cobblers, as well as a mass of peasant proprietors and an
assortment of weavers, framework knitters and ancillary textile
workers.[91] There is no reason to suppose that this range of occupations
was in any way typical, but there is no reason, equally, to suppose that the
arts of working with wood, leather and iron were not practised in some
way or another in most of the 800 or so localities qualified as towns (and
many more which were not) in France during the eighteenth century. The
rudiments of most trades were available to a large number of potential
practitioners. By any objective criterion, there was a vast pool of labour
available for most of the work done in most eighteenth-century trades.

The *compagnonnages* were, of course, most ubiquitous in those trades
in which the pool of labour was most substantial: among workers on
wood, stone, leather and metal, rather than glass, ceramics, gold, bronze,
marble or paint. The measure of skill in the eighteenth century was largely
a matter of materials and the kinds of familiarity and dexterity which
workers could be expected to have with them. There were, for example,
hatters who made woollen hats and hatters who made beaver hats. Wool
was cheap and widely available. Beaver was not, and was used almost entirely in Paris, Lyons and Marseilles.[92] This was why there was a difference between a hatter from Paris and a hatter from Reims or Auxerre.

Differences of this kind contributed a great deal to the diversity of the
work performed in the eighteenth-century trades. The names of the trades
have a very misleading precision and most historians of the *compagnonnages* have assumed that words like *menuisier* or *serrurier* meant something technically precise about the work done by members of such trades.
Journeymen locksmiths made springs for carriages, made or repaired the
wrought iron used on railings, staircases and shop signs, installed the
complicated clusters of needles and rods used in stocking frames, and also
made the metal clamps and hinges needed for doors and shutters. Some of
them actually made locks. Joiners made trellises as well as doors,
window-frames and staircases. They also made coach bodies, looms and
many different items of household furniture. Each type of work implied a
certain degree of specialised ability. Yet mastery of many of them was
relatively easy for those familiar with the basic techniques of working
with iron or wood. There was therefore no rigid correlation between the
nomenclature of the trades and the work which journeymen could do. A
farrier could be employed by a locksmith; a wheelwright or a turner by a
master joiner.

Not all journeymen could match the elaborate wrought iron produced
by Philippe Lamour for the place Stanislas in Nancy, or equal the mar-
quetry and ornate furniture made in the workshops belonging to Jean-

Henri Riesener or Louis Delanois.[93] There are, of course, many examples of their interest in the techniques of their trades. A *compagnon du devoir* arrested after a fight in Bordeaux in 1754 produced an account of his leisure activities that was such a model of propriety that it could only have been true. On trade holidays he went to mass in the morning and then to evensong and a sermon in the afternoon. Afterwards he would return home to practise technical drawing.[94] A journeyman carpenter admitted having attended an assembly of over a hundred other journeymen in Bordeaux in 1777, but stated that its only object had been for relaxation and instruction in the arts of their trade.[95] A Parisian journeyman carpenter was outraged when the professor of design whose course he was attending remarked that a book that the journeyman was reading must have been written by some penniless and ignorant worker. The journeyman retorted angrily that his professor had no talent and was incapable of doing anything more than drawing pretty pictures.[96] Yet work in many trades did not require rare abilities or esoteric techniques. The ritual of the *compagnonnages* – the initiatory ceremonies, the pitched battles, the feats of prowess in arts which too many of them could master – were an inverted acknowledgment of the wide dissemination of ordinary abilities. They made it possible to transform similarity into difference in a world in which too many people could do the same thing.

Opportunities to find work in the trades were not distributed uniformly over the surface of France. The geographical distribution of the urban trades remains largely unknown. There were, however, wide variations in the size of particular sectors of employment. There were as many master joiners (sixty-three) in Troyes (population less than 20,000) in 1776 as in Nîmes (population 35,000) which had only sixty-nine master joiners in 1769. Bordeaux (population 100,000) had only 141 master joiners in 1788, while Lyon had 216 for a comparable population in 1746 and Paris, with a population over five times as large in 1789 had more than 1,000 masters.[97]

Closer study of the geographical distribution of the urban trades will do much to explain the many patterns of journeymen's migrations. The phenomenon was undoubtedly very much greater than measurements based upon registers of hospital admissions or parish registers have indicated.[98] It is almost impossible to know whether the scale of migration was rising or falling during the eighteenth century, although the discrepancy between the rate of growth of the population as a whole and that of the urban population in particular suggests that it was rising. There were, as will be shown, institutional changes during the latter half of the eighteenth century which favoured geographical mobility.

Journeymen's migrations affected the trades in a number of ways. The absence of rigid technical divisions in the work carried out in trades associated most closely with the *compagnonnages* was reinforced by the scale of turnover of labour in the building, clothing and furnishing trades. Precise measurement of the phenomenon is not easy because the appropriate source material is very scarce. It is possible, however, to present an approximation of the scale of the turnover of labour in the case of one relatively typical trade: the locksmiths of Rouen. Between November 1782 and April 1791 (a total of 102 months) 1,086 journeymen locksmiths registered their names, ages and places of birth with the trade's corporate employment office (*bureau de placement*).[99] The monthly average of new arrivals to Rouen was therefore 10.65. Shortly before the introduction of the regulation requiring new arrivals to register, an enumeration of the total number of masters and journeymen working in the trade was made. The forty-six master locksmiths listed employed a total of 110 journeymen.[100] If the figure of 110 journeymen is taken as a constant over the entire eight and a half year period, so that the monthly average of new arrivals (10.65) was matched by an equivalent number of departures, some 10% of the labour force of the trade changed every month. After ten months the whole workforce of the trade would have been entirely different. In the space of eight and a half years, the entire labour force of the trade would have turned over no less than ten times.

These are, of course, deductions based upon the assumption that the aggregate size of the trade remained constant over the medium term. They are, however, limited solely to the inward and outward movement of journeymen to and from Rouen. The registers of the *bureau de placement* established by the locksmiths of Rouen do not record the times when journeymen moved from master to master *within* the city. Were it possible to ascertain the frequency of such movements, the magnitude of labour turnover at the level of the individual workshop would be substantially greater. All the evidence indicates (as one would expect) that journeymen moved from master to master more frequently than they moved from town to town. A list of seventeen journeymen joiners working for the twelve masters in the trade in the little town of Auxerre in 1786 discloses that only two journeymen had been working for the same master for over a year. Almost all the rest had been working in the same workshop for less than three months.[101] The registers of the *bureau de placement* established by the tailors of Rouen make it possible to produce more precise figures, for they record changes of employment within the city as well as the registration of new arrivals. There a total of 1,859 journeymen registered to find work on 4,903 occasions between 1778 and 1781. By linking successive records of registration it is possible to calculate that the average period of employment in the tailoring trade was no more than five weeks, while the median (i.e. the period of employment which was most frequent) was no more than fifteen days.[102]

These very high levels of labour turnover affected the circumstances of journeymen in a number of ways. They meant that the working environment changed very frequently and that a premium was attached to adaptability and flexibility. The connection between the rhetoric of the *compagnonnages*, the benefits of the *tour de France* and this structural characteristic of workshop production is obvious. 'Vrais artistes', who could claim mastery of a wide range of different types of work in the same trade – from making springs to making railings, for example – were most able to find work.

A further effect of the very high level of mobility of eighteenth-century journeymen was that there was a very substantial degree of medium-term uniformity in the level of wage-rates offered by master artisans in most trades and most towns. The relative stagnation of money wage rates during the eighteenth century in France was at once a reflection of the local uniformity of nominal rates within particular urban or regional labour pools and a result of the wider homogeneity of the range of abilities and skills needed in many eighteenth-century trades.[103] At the same time, however, the large number of master artisans in many of the principle urban trades meant that demand for labour was highly decentralised, erratic and subject to considerable short-term fluctuation. As a result, long-term wage stability could coexist with short-term fluctuations in the scale and frequency of the penumbra of cash advances, meals, non-monetary rights and other forms of irregular income which, to varying degrees, complemented the money wage. For just as journeymen required symbolically created inequalities in order to establish the porous barriers protecting their fragile claims to the work they did, master artisans required symbolically created inequalities to negotiate the uniformity of wage-rates intrinsic to the structural organisation of workshop production. Money alone did not determine whether a *boutique* would be recognised as *bonne* or not, or whether a piece of work would be finished on time. Interpersonal evaluation enabled master artisans to recognise feats of prowess for their own reasons. A petition presented by the *compagnons du devoir* of Auxerre, after some of them had been arrested in 1786 for assaulting a number of *gavots* explained that only a small minority of masters employed journeymen who were not attached to the *devoir*. Members of the rite had, they claimed, been disgusted by their brutality and would not work for them.[104] Master artisans, as much as journeymen, had their own reasons – in a world in which too many people earned similar sums of money – for identifying some journeymen as *les plus forts* and *les plus gros*. In circumstances in which work in most trades was geared to specific orders and precise schedules, it was little use to know that there were many potential candidates for employment in the longer term. The allocation of informal marks of esteem allowed masters greater control over the short-term availability of reliable workers and helped to ensure that work would be finished on time. The ritual of the *compagnonnages* echoed this complicity and ensured that many disputes in the trades took the form of charges and counter-charges of breach of contract.[105] Young men's feats of prowess were often the expression of older men's expectations and rivalries.

The high incidence of labour turnover placed a further constraint upon eighteenth-century journeymen. Just as the kind of work expected of them was never entirely the same, so the men with whom they worked were also subject to regular change. The relationship between a journeyman's age, experience, competence and seniority changed constantly in the passage from *boutique* to *boutique* and, more obviously, from town to town. A man of thirty who had been established for months or years in one *boutique* could find himself working as a newcomer alongside a seventeen or eighteen year old in another. The *premier compagnon* in one locality became the *dernier en ville* when he reached the next.

The elaborate, but impermanent, hierarchies created by the ceremonial of the *compagnonnages* were a symbolic counterpoint to the frequent inversions of age, seniority and precedence attendant upon a high level of labour turnover. Within the *cayenne* journeymen fined one another for virtually anything. Fines were paid into the common box and the funds were consumed on trade holidays. In this way, real differences were transcended by the equality created in what amounted to joking relationships. The papers of the locksmiths of Bordeaux list fines imposed during the first six months of 1758 for breaking the furniture, hitting another journeyman, talking about the *devoir* in public, working twice in the same shop, drawing a pistol indoors, taking a bottle of wine at an initiation, failing to collect money, finding work for an aspiring member of the *devoir* without permission, failing to attend an assembly and for having lost some of the association's property.[106] Although there were rules, it is clear that they were sufficiently imprecise to allow offences to be invented when the need arose. In a world which was turned upside down all too frequently, the equalities created by offences of which everyone was guilty at one time or another were a counterpart to the inequalities of age, ability and experience which itinerant journeymen encountered in the course of their peregrinations.

VI

The ritual of the *compagonnages* was re-enacted over so long a period
because it allowed journeymen to escape the anonymity of the market for
labour. To those outside the circle of the initiate, it created inequalities –
in a world where too many men had too much in common. To those
within the circle, it created equalities – in which differences of age, ability
and geographical origin might be suspended. If the content of the ritual
formed a counterpoint to the intrinsic similarities of much of the work in
the trades and the structural imperatives of the schedules of workshop
production, its form owed surprisingly little to the ceremonial of the corporations. The forms which Sewell has associated with the ubiquitous
corporate idiom were, rather, derived from three other institutions which
impinged more closely upon journeymen's experience: confraternities,
the courts and the army.

If the *compagnonnages* are to be characterised in an institutional sense,
it is more accurate to define them as counter-confraternities than counter-
corporations. Journeymen's confraternities were not the same as the *compagnonnages*. They were specific to particular trades and, for long
periods, enjoyed forms of legal recognition which were never given to the
compagnonnages. The first documented manifestations of the *compagnonnages* accompanied the elaboration of a body of formal prescription
which supplied journeymen in some of the major cities of sixteenth- and
seventeenth-century France with relatively substantial legal rights. There
was, in other words, a time when differences of a formal kind distinguished journeymen in certain localities and trades from one another.

The *compagnonnages* emerged when differences between journeymen
were sanctioned by the law. Of the five Parisian trades singled out by the
Doctors of the Sorbonne for their associations with the *devoir*, journeymen in three of them – shoemakers, hatters and cutlers – enjoyed rights of
some sort to preferential employment over migrants from the provinces. It
is possible that harness makers and tailors did so too, for there is evidence
that such rights existed in a number of other Parisian trades in the seventeenth century. Journeymen in all five trades were among many groups of
Parisian journeymen whose confraternities remained in existence until the
second half of the eighteenth century.[107] Members of confraternities were
usually journeymen who were settled in a trade and a city. The law
ensured that they had access to employment in preference to journeymen
from elsewhere. Article 20 of the statues of the Parisian shoemakers of
1573 made it clear that masters were permitted to employ *étrangers* only
when there were no *compagnons de Paris* seeking work.[108] Master cutlers
were prohibited, by their statutes of 1565, from employing more than

three journeymen at a time. Migrants from the provinces were required to leave the city and find work outside Paris and its suburbs if they were unable to find work under the terms of the provision.[109] Journeymen hatters, who had two confraternities in seventeenth-century Paris, took successful legal action against masters employing what they termed 'compagnons battans la semelle'. In 1700 a ruling by the *chambre de police* ordered master hatters to give preferential employment to Parisian journeymen provided that they did not attempt to raise their wages to levels higher than those paid to provincial journeymen.[110]

It is not difficult to equate 'compagnons battans la semelle' with the journeymen singled out by the Doctors of the Sorbonne in 1655 for their heretical ceremonies. These ceremonies, as of much else in the public ritual of the *compagnonnages*, were an adaptation of the ceremonial of established journeymen's confraternities. They were an assertion of identity by journeymen whose own peripatetic circumstances were not recognised by the law, and whose livelihoods were unprotected by the provisions which the law had made for the members of confraternities.

For much of the eighteenth century, older established journeymen in a number of trades, particularly in Paris (but also in Lyons, Marseilles, Bordeaux, Toulouse and Nantes) made considerable use of the law to define or defend the conditions in which they worked. Journeymen in the hatting trades of Paris, Lyons and Marseilles, for example, repeatedly engaged solicitors and barristers to bring legal actions in the *Parlements* against their masters over a wide variety of disputed questions throughout the eighteenth century. Disputes in the trades were conducted in the courts as frequently as they were conducted on the streets. The procedures and conventions of litigation were widely available and widely recognised. On one occasion, in 1783, journeymen hatters in Marseilles, who belonged to what had been a recognised confraternity, brought a legal action in the *Parlement* of Aix against the *compagnons du devoir*.[111]

It is not surprising, therefore, that many of the informal ceremonies of the *compagnonnages* were modelled on the procedures of the courts. As has been mentioned, fines were a regular part of the life of the *cayenne*. Disputes among members of the rites were settled by informal trials. Journeymen carpenters in Lyon were said in 1776 to have conducted mock judicial proceedings at their *cayenne* in the suburb of Vaise, wearing women's wigs to impersonate members of the legal profession.[112]

The idiom of the law, which was translated into informal trials and the more frequent fines and ceremonial admonitions observed by members of the *compagnonnages*, was complemented by an idiom of military provenance. When Pierre Briand, the journeyman known as *Le Bordelais*, approached an army officer to enlist in the *Régiment de Brie* in order to avoid prosecution for membership of the *compagnonnages* in Troyes in 1782, he was acknowledging a procedure followed by journeymen in many trades in the eighteenth century. The army in the eighteenth century was not very distant from civilian life.[113] It was, as to some degree (in the form of the Foreign Legion) it has remained, the last refuge for men without other resources. A significant number of the 1,086 journeymen locksmiths who registered to find work in Rouen between 1782 and 1791 were soldiers. Enlistment into the army did not prevent journeymen from practising their trades. Soldiers, of course, had their *noms de guerre* and it is not difficult to understand why single men in solitary circumstances should have had recourse to an idiom of military prowess to mark the difference between their own fragile claims to distinction and the anonymity of the poor.[114] *Devoirants* and *gavots* owed their baptisms and spectacular *sobriquets* to the presence of a military culture in the life of the trades. In some cases, a name may have been all there was between fellowship and the hospital.[115]

VII

The ritual of the *compagnonnages* emerged on the periphery of the corporate world. Its characteristic forms imitated the ceremonial performed by journeymen's confraternities, echoed rights sanctioned by the courts and transposed feats of military prowess to small workshops in suburban localities. The *compagnonnages* were created by journeymen from Bolbec and Bapaume, Laval or Largentière, rather than men who were settled in Bordeaux or Lyons, Paris or Toulouse. They were created by men who had little to expect and not much to inherit, but who also needed to work in order to live. As the formal distinctions which separated journeymen from Paris or the other major cities from those of the rest of France were gradually destroyed during the eighteenth century, the *compagnonnages* came into their own. Most of the incidents cited in this essay occurred during the second half of the eighteenth century. This is more than a result of the greater rate of survival of archival material. By the last quarter of the eighteenth century, shoemakers or hatters or cutlers in Paris (and journeymen in many other trades and cities) were no longer able to find recognition in the courts for their distinctive legal rights. A ruling by the *Conseil d'Etat* in 1775, for example, allowed master cutlers in Paris to employ as many journeymen as they saw fit.[116] As a result, differences which had been sanctioned by the courts gave way to differences which journeymen created among themselves. The golden age of the *compagnonnages*, which ran from roughly 1760 to 1830, was the product of this state of affairs. In a world divested of legal rights, symbolic distinction – the distinction created by ceremonies of initiation, physical fights and feats of prowess in particular trades – came into its own. Agricol Perdiguier, the source of so much information about the *compagnonnages* and so little about journeymen's confraternities and their relation to the law, was very much a child of his times.

3

Women's work, mechanisation and the early phases of industrialisation in England

MAXINE BERG

THE PREVAILING ASSUMPTION

The fundamental transformation of the meaning of work in the day to day lives of individuals and families is usually believed to have come with the reorganisation of production which separated the household from the workplace at some point during industrialisation. The separation in space between household and workplace became the foundation for the separation in conception between market activities and communities. Families were divided from the trades, consumption from production, women's activities from men's, and ultimately the ethos of mutuality and moral imperative from the ethos of the individual and market imperatives. The division between home and work is also associated with wider divisions between the 'private' and the 'public' spheres; the division has accounted for a sexual division of labour going far beyond original divisions rooted in biological reproduction and family life. It is a division which is fundamentally historical, and it carries with it the assumption of some past historical time when home and work were one and the same.

The historical meanings of work were in some way changed with the movement of work away from the home: it is therefore important to go back to those early stages of industrial capitalism when most production was carried out in the home, but the first phases of mechanisation and factory production were presenting new challenges. This chapter will thus focus on production conditions – workplace organisation, techniques of production and their community context – in eighteenth-century industry, especially in those industries which underwent significant expansion and transformation in the eighteenth century – textiles and metals.

Assumptions about the changes in the meaning of work no longer car-

ried on within the home and family setting have been particularly important in recent writing on gender divisions in the workforce. Most research
on women's current subordination in the workforce rests on the assumption of a fundamental historical transition in women's workforce participation and status in the eighteenth or early nineteenth century,
coterminous with the rise of industrial capitalism. This assumption per-
vades much Marxist-feminist analysis of women's work; it is at the core
of debates on patriarchy and capitalist production.[1] The search for an historical basis of subordination remains fundamental and has taken the
form of seeking a transition in production relations, in trade union and
class relations, in the role of the state and in ideology.[2]

The analysis of a historical transition in women's employment is a part
of larger debates on the transition from feudalism to capitalism, and the
transition in the labour process from handicraft and domestic manufacture to modern industry, the factory system and industrial capitalism. The
enormously complex and many-sided processes of change which mark the
transformation from a pre-industrial to an industrial world have been
studied by generations of historians trying to unravel the content and
timing of fundamental changes stretching from the late seventeenth to the
early twentieth centuries. Where, once, we spoke with some certainty of
an Industrial Revolution, concentrated within a relatively short fifty-year
period, our conception of industrialisation is now of a longer, more complex process. With this shift of focus, older certainties about the funda-
mentals of the transition to capitalism have been questioned, so that we can
no longer say just when capitalist social relations overcame feudal traditions,
or indeed what constituted the fundamental cause of transformation.[3]

Hence the search for the historical basis of the inequities faced by
women in the workplace has become one fraught with dead ends, wrong
turnings and an ever-receding destination. One result of this is an appeal
to ever more elastic terminology which becomes invested with explanatory value. Key concepts appealed to by Marxist feminists and other historians alike are the 'family-wage economy', or simply 'family economy'
and the 'family-household system'.[4] In fact these terms cover a variety of
meanings. The 'family-wage economy' was a unit made up of family members who worked for wages in the family interest. It succeeded the old
'family economy' of the household mode of production[5] yet the hold of
the family economy on behaviour, mentalities and social structures continued as long as all family members had some economic function.[6] Marxist feminists argue that this 'family economy' was overtaken by the
'family-household system', a combination of a household structure based
on the dependence of members on the paid labour of husbands or fathers
and the unpaid labour of the wife/mother in domestic tasks, and the ideol-

ogy of the family, 'the private sphere beyond the public realm of commerce and industry'. Developments in the mid nineteenth century forced
women into the domestic sphere and created the basis for a sexually-
segregated labour market.[7]

Whatever the stages of the transitions from family economy to family
wage economies and on to the family household system, there lies at the
heart of these debates the still more fundamental separation of home and
workplace. The belief that the historical separation of the workplace from
the home and personal life with the development of capitalism was
accountable for women's particular oppression was and still is much debated in Marxist-feminist literature.[8] But accounting for the socially constructed gender differences which lie deeply embedded in the sexual
division of labour has taken feminists far beyond the economy, production relations or Marxist economic categories into broader spheres of
ideology and social constructs. They have subsequently called for the
study of links between the organisation of production and gender divisions.[9] Nevertheless the history of waged and unwaged work has
remained a vital component of the analysis of these connections. And the
assumption of an earlier historical epoch where work and home life were
integrated underpins the general focus of much contemporary research on
women's subordination.

Throughout the current debate there exists consensus about the model
of a pre-capitalist system of production based on the family work unit,
which allowed women to combine their productive work with children
and housework. The transition to an industrial capitalism which separated production from the home to the workshop or factory is then said to
account for the declining opportunities for women. The timing of this
transition in England has been variously placed at points ranging from the
early eighteenth century to the mid nineteenth century,[10] and the focus lies
on differences in working conditions under the 'domestic system' and
those under the factory system.

The key historical questions about this transition were set in the 1920s
and 1930s by Lillian Knowles, Alice Clark, Dorothy George and Ivy
Pinchbeck. Alice Clark asked how economic development in the seventeenth and eighteenth centuries had affected the productivity and status of
women, and argued that their jobs were narrowed and their position
degraded with the 'triumph of capitalistic organisation' and the decline of
the household economy. Yet Lillian Knowles, Ivy Pinchbeck and Dorothy
George all found a vital and positive transition in the rise of the factory
system which took women out of the home to work, and they took pains
to debunk the idea of historical golden ages in the conditions of domestic
manufacture.[11]

The crucial questions debated by these historians were, first, what conditions prevailed for women under domestic manufacture? And, second, did the displacement of work away from the home to workshop or factory enhance or reduce their condition? Dorothy George blamed domestic manufacture for keeping wages low and for being largely dependent on the excessive labour of women and children.[12] Ivy Pinchbeck argued that the family industrial unit established a tradition of low wages which subsequently affected women's wage levels when they did enter the factory.[13] But Alice Clark argued that women in the seventeenth century had occupied an assured position whenever the 'system of family industry prevailed', and that the greater equality in their economic positions depended upon whether enterprises were carried on at home or elsewhere.[14]

This issue of women's work in domestic manufacture has never been resolved. It has remained crucial to assumptions underlying feminist debates, but in spite of raising the historical problem in the twenties and thirties, the work of these historians has not been followed up. Research on women's work, especially industrial work in the eighteenth century and early nineteenth century, remains very limited. Apart from what can be gleaned from a few general surveys, some substantial research on women in agriculture, and Keith Snell's very recent research on women's apprenticeship in the south of England, we know very little of women's working lives in this crucial historical period.[15] As Olwen Hufton has recently revealed in her survey on women's history,

We are thus carried into the realm of women and work and are confronted with a curious paradox. We all know that women in pre-industrial society worked ... Sense tells us that in the proto-industrial phase their role was crucial. They were the more numerous sector of the cheap labour force. Yet we have very little detailed modern research bearing on the nature and importance of their labour.[16]

Feminists are prepared to pronounce with confidence on the great transition from the household manufacture or domestic industry to the factory system, but as yet we know little of what this 'transition' really involved for women.

PROTO-INDUSTRIALISATION AND FAMILY LABOUR

If feminism has not in this country generated an economic history of women since the early classics, current trends in economic and social history have nevertheless made one possible. The recent debate over proto-industrialisation, whatever one's reservations over the concept, has revived interest in the eighteenth century, and has shifted the formerly agrarian focus of research on to the industrial activities of the countryside. The demographic orientation of the historians of proto-industrialisation did lead them to raise important questions about the family economy in the phase of transitional industrial expansion before full industrialisation. But it blinkered them in other respects, for few of these historians, at least until recently, have written about the place of women in proto-industrialisation in terms other than those of breeding and child rearing.[17] Some of the original contributions to the debate did, however, point out women's special role in the labour force. Hans Medick and David Levine argued that the new domestic industries thrived on cheap, infinitely expandable supplies of labour.[18] These industries increased the intensity of labour, and the productive effort of women and children contributed indispensably to the family subsistence wage. But this decisive marginal work effort in the family went underpaid. A large proportion of the labour time of these women and children went to merchant capitalists in the form of extra profit. Medick and Levine also credited proto-industrialisation with bringing about a transformation of the division of labour between the sexes, giving women a greater and more equal position in the labour force than hitherto. But this argument consigns to women a rather minor role in agriculture and indeed in the urban trades before proto-industrialisation. Other historians have, however, marshalled substantial evidence of just the reverse.[19]

Before we can pronounce on the implications of the separation of work from home, we must examine the conditions of domestic manufacture, and especially the place of women within this. The employment of women in the dispersed handicraft production of the seventeenth and eighteenth centuries may not have been novel, but the rapid expansion of these industries and their reliance on low-paid labour entailed higher proportions of female and child labour. Yet this reliance on women's labour and, more significantly, children's labour is now little remarked upon in reference to handicraft and even early factory industry. It was once singled out as the keynote of the system. Dorothy George devoted a chapter of her *England in Transition* to child labour, and argued strongly that the custom of child labour at an early age was deeply rooted in the domestic system, and was only seriously challenged with the coming of the factory system. 'What was new and revolutionary', she argued, 'was that for the first time toiling children were regarded as an outrage, not something to be admired ... it was the sense of something monstrous in the factory system which directed attention to the yet more monstrous exploitation of the labour of young children.'[20] Historians are only now returning to consider the place of this child labour. David Levine has argued recently that handicraft manufacture coincided with high fertility and high proportions of children in the population. The labour of children was an elastic resource, with children aged five to fourteen comprising one-sixth to one quarter of the total population. With the decline in the handicraft trades came a decline in the demand for female and child labour. The result was a sharp reversal in the rates of population increase; the age of first marriage for women rose. With the relocation of the workplace away from the family by the mid nineteenth century the family's material base was changed from a locus of production to one of reproduction and consumption. Women become identified with the domestic sphere, while sexuality and especially masculinity was related to work. Working class boys learned to labour 'as an expression of their masculinity'. Levine argued that it was the flow of wealth within the family that determined fertility, it was not until as late as the 1920s that wealth flowed from parents to children instead of the reverse, and that the imperatives of the family economy started to recede.[21]

THE FEMALE WORKFORCE AND INDUSTRIAL EMPLOYMENT IN EIGHTEENTH-CENTURY INDUSTRY

This chapter will now examine the case for a transition in the role of women in the industrial workforce in the eighteenth century. It will look at changes which took place within an industrial production still largely dominated by households and small workshops. The chapter will focus on those early changes in technology which defined the Industrial Revolution, and their implications for women's employment and skills, and compare the experiences of women workers in the textiles industries and metal trades. This mechanisation has come to be seen as synonymous with the demise of home based handicraft production. I will also raise the problem of community and work networks for women, but as evidence on this area is so very limited, I can do no more than to ask some questions. I will draw on a survey of present knowledge informed by economic analysis of labour markets, and I will pose questions of whether changes in work processes increased or reduced opportunities for women. My major work on only two of the most advanced sectors shows a diversity of experience that make generalisation very difficult.

Quantitative evidence about women in industrial occupations in the eighteenth century is non-existent. Conjecture is combined with broad estimates to convey an idea of a high proportion, but beyond this, there is little we can say with certainty. Occupational structure for the eighteenth century can be gleaned from contemporary estimates and recent revisions of these. Peter Lindert's new social tables are now fairly widely used in preference to the estimates of Gregory King (1688), Joseph Massie (1759) and Patrick Colquhoun (1811). His tables convey a sense of an occupational structure much more industrial than previously assumed. His estimates also show that though occupational structure was relatively stable before 1755, agriculture and manufacturing increased faster than average and, in the last half of the eighteenth century, manufacturing employment increased substantially, dominated by textiles. By his estimate, employment in textiles more than tripled in the second half of the eighteenth century.[22]

Occupations in eighteenth-century England

Commerce and Industry

King		Lindert	
Merchants & traders by sea (greater)	2,000	All commerce	135,333
Merchants & traders by sea (lesser)	8,000	Manufacturing trades	179,774
Shopkeepers & tradesmen	40,000	Mining	15,082
Artizans & handycrafts	60,000	Building trades	77,232
	110,000		407,421
			(excluding labourers)

Agriculture

King		Lindert	
Freeholders (greater)	40,000	All agriculture	241,373
Freeholders (lesser)	140,000		(excluding labourers)
Farmers	150,000		
	330,000		

There is, however, no certainty in these estimates; they come with high margins of error.[23] The tables are, furthermore, subject to the other serious reservation expressed by David Levine, that Lindert's analysis focusses on the occupations of men (they are based on male burial records) not those of women, youth and children, and also fails to account for the multiplicity of different activities by industrial and non-industrial workers.[24] Levine, nevertheless, chooses to use the tables as a base line indicator of economic activity. We may have doubts over the aggregate estimates, but they do give us a picture of a substantially industrial occupational structure in the eighteenth century. Though there are no figures, it is almost certainly the case, as Levine points out, that there was a substantial female and youthful industrial population.[25]

Conjectures on the employment structures of individual textile industries confirm this impression. Adrian Randall has calculated that in the West Country woollen industry in the period 1781–96, women accounted for higher proportionate numbers of workers than men, and children higher numbers than men.[26] As most of the women involved were spinners, there is no reason to think the ratio would be different for the industry in other parts of the country, at least before the spread of the spinning jenny. Spinning also provided the greatest employment in the linen industry, and this was again the employment of women.[27] Adam Smith calculated that in addition to flax growers and dressers, three or four spinners were necessary to keep one weaver in constant employment.[28] Women also predominated in the silk manufacture; Natalie Rothstein has estimated that in 1765 the proportion of women and children to men in the London silk trade was 1,400 to 100. Out of approximately 4,000 employed in Spitalfields, most were women and children.[29] When silk throwing started to move out of London to the home counties it was to tap an even larger female labour market in farming communities.[30] Lacemaking in the eighteenth century was almost exclusively a female trade.[31] Hand knitting occupied the hands of women, children and old men over many areas such as the dales of the West Riding even after the widespread use of framework knitting.[32] Framework knitting, though carried out early in the eighteenth century by men, relied heavily on the ancillary labour of women and children. Increasingly over the eighteenth century, once apprenticeship regulations were bypassed, women and children also worked the frames.

The knitter's wife was also one of his greatest industrial assets. When he worked on fancies and completed the whole article, she seamed and finished it. After he became a specialist at a single process on the frame, she supervised and assisted the younger children in winding the yarn and keeping the shuttles filled ... Occasionally women worked on the frame, but usually as an emergency measure, although after the 'long depression' many women kept their husband's frame busy far into the night in order to eke out the husband's income.[33]

The early factory cotton industry was also dominated by women's and children's labour. Most of the mills surveyed in 1816 were small scale and employed significantly more women than men, and roughly equal numbers of adults and children. The few large scale mills at the time employed roughly equal proportions of men and women; adults and children.[34] The textile industries formed the largest manufacturing sector in eighteenth-century England. On the evidence of these individual sectors, women dominated all its major manufactures. The other major eighteenth-century manufacturing industries were the leather trades and the metalworking industries. Women were employed in limited sections of the leather industries. They were widely employed in certain sectors of the metal trades, particularly in nailmaking, but also in a wide range of hardware trades. Employment data for eighteenth-century industries is not available, but some indication of the relative significance of the various eighteenth-century industries can be gleaned from estimates of the contribution of individual industries to increases in the national product.

Estimates of economic growth[35]
Value added in British industry (£m, current)

	1770	%	1801	%	1831	%
Cotton	0.6	(2.6)	9.2	(17.0)	25.3	(22.4)
Wool	7.0	(30.6)	10.1	(18.7)	15.9	(14.1)
Linen	1.9	(8.3)	2.6	(4.8)	5.0	(4.4)
Silk	1.0	(4.4)	2.0	(3.7)	5.8	(5.1)
Building	2.4	(10.5)	9.3	(17.2)	26.5	(23.5)
Iron	1.5	(6.6)	4.0	(7.4)	7.6	(6.7)
Copper	0.2	(0.9)	0.9	(1.7)	0.8	(0.7)
Beer	1.3	(5.7)	2.5	(4.6)	5.2	(4.6)
Leather	5.1	(22.3)	8.4	(15.5)	9.8	(8.7)
Soap	0.3	(1.3)	0.8	(1.5)	1.2	(1.1)
Candles	0.5	(2.2)	1.0	(1.8)	1.2	(1.1)
Coal	0.9	(4.4)	2.7	(5.0)	7.9	(7.0)
Paper	0.1	(0.4)	0.6	(1.1)	0.8	(0.7)
Total	22.8		54.1		113.0	

Though male occupations such as leathermaking, building, and coal were very important, the textile industries were clearly dominant, and mixed trades such as iron and brewing were also significant.

Another indication of the high potential figures for female employment can be recovered from the listings which survive of inhabitants for the two parishes of Cardington, Bedfordshire and Corfe Castle, Dorset.[36] Such detailed listings are rare, but these two examples form a source. They reveal high participation rates in both places in the eighteenth century, but experience in the nineteenth century diverged sharply. In the 1790s employment opportunities for women in spinning and knitting in Corfe Castle were respectable, but by 1851 had virtually disappeared with the contraction of cottage industry. In Cardington female employment in lacemaking was high and remained so through 1851. Indeed, activity rates for married women aged twenty to thirty-nine in Cardington in 1752 was a remarkable 82 per cent. In our own time a high rate for married women was 58 per cent, the figure for 1971, but this was for the narrower category of the age group forty-five to fifty-four, those without young children at home.[37]

The contraction of such opportunities with industrialisation would certainly confirm the argument of Eric Richards that the nineteenth century brought a great decline in women's industrial employment caused by a contraction in rural industry. Other research has shown a great decline not just in women's work, but in male employment and in village trades as a whole, a decline closely linked with the enclosure of the commons.[38]

A contraction of women's employment opportunities was reflected not only in this contraction of domestic industries, but also in a striking decline in the range of trades to which women were apprenticed in the eighteenth century. Keith Snell has drawn a rather remarkable picture of widespread female apprenticeship in the southern and eastern counties of England in the early half of the century. Thirty-four per cent of the apprenticeships he examined were for girls and these were appointed to as many as fifty-one trades, more than in the case of men. Many were apprenticed to the same trades as their fathers, and their premiums were comparable to those of boys. Girls apprenticed by the parish were further-more to be found in the widest range of occupations. By the nineteenth century the number of female apprentices had fallen, women were appren-ticed to less than half the trades that men were, and these were largely re-stricted to the household and clothing manufactures.[39]

This picture of widespread female employment across the trades in the pre-industrial and early industrial period fits with other pictures of the pre-industrial crafts in Europe.[40] The reasons suggested for the great con-traction after this are, however, difficult to reconcile. Alice Clark in 1919 accounted for it by the movement of manufacture and business out of the home. Keith Snell produces similar reasons. He argues that demographic conditions in the late seventeenth century to the eighteenth century favoured female employment. Low population pressure was combined with a high age of marriage and more single women. Between the late seventeenth century and the 1780s the age of first marriage for women fell from twenty-seven to twenty-four, and the proportion of women never marrying fell from 15 per cent to 7 per cent. But these demographic trends coincided with both the growing capitalisation of the trades which took work out of the framework of the family economy, and with a glutting of the trades in the early nineteenth century. Substantial male unemploy-ment meant the barring of female labour from many trades.

This perspective is also endorsed by research in the organisation of the trades. Where women earlier in the eighteenth century had belonged to many of the trade organisations, by its end and they were increasingly ex-cluded. In 1769 the Spitalfields silk weavers excluded women from higher-paid work, and in 1779 journeymen bookbinders excluded women from their union. The Stockport Hatmakers' society in 1808 declared strikes against women in the trade, and the Cotton Spinners' Union in 1829 excluded women. The handloom weavers refused to admit women to their unions, and in 1834 the London tailors struck work to drive women from the trade.[41]

There is, however, a substantial amount of evidence to indicate a rather more complex pre-industrial and proto-industrial experience than is allowed for in these analyses of the crucial transition in women's employment opportunities. First the pre-industrial experience was highly variable between industries and parts of the country. The women of fourteenth- and fifteenth-century Leiden may have occupied the trades in considerable numbers and status, but this was not necessarily the position in England. The experience of fourteenth-century Shrewsbury and sixteenth- and seventeenth-century Salisbury showed a clear sexual division of labour with women predominantly found in occupations associated with domestic labour, or in the 'casual menial end of the market, an area which may not have involved large numbers at any one time, but which must have given employment to a significant number of women at some stage during their life cycle'.[42] Though women may have worked across a wide range of trades, their roles were restricted; they rarely entered fully into the 'mysteries' of the craft, and capital, including tools and workshops, was bequeathed where possible to sons.[43] Women went on to only limited opportunities in eighteenth-century Oxford. They played only a small role as market traders even in the casual sectors, and this became even more circumscribed with gradual market deregulation, when many dealings moved to the male social world of the inn or public house.[44] There were expanding opportunities for women in the new ready-made clothing trades of mantua-making and millinery, but these trades were unregulated, and destined by the early nineteenth century to suffer flooded labour markets and sweating.[45]

If these cases would confirm a long-standing restricted and subordinate position for women workers, pre-dating any transition to industrial capitalism, the important position of the silk women of London provides the necessary exception. Women made up virtually the whole labour force of the silk industry in London at least until the end of the fifteenth century, and they carried out all procedures in the manufacture of narrow silks, ribbons, corses, and lace.[46] Broad silk weaving was introduced in Norwich from the sixteenth century, but its great expansion came with the Huguenots in 1685–7, when 100,000 arrived in the country and transformed the Spitalfields trade. The broad silk weavers from France brought a new division of labour where weaving was done by men, and winding, quilling and warping by women and children. Narrow silk weaving suffered a great decline in status, and the women occupied in the ancillary processes of broad silk weaving were low-paid workers whose job was also considered a suitable activity for workhouses and parish apprentice girls. This said, it was also true, however, that the silk women, though once exercising a monopoly over a luxury trade, had never held a guild status. In London itself they thus lacked the formal craft status and power of men in other trades; they also lacked the status given by the guilds in other major European towns engaged in silk manufacture.[47]

The decline of apprenticeship also forms a problematic divide, for though women were apprenticed, and took apprentices themselves, the meaning attached to this cannot be assumed to be the same as that for men. Recent research by Deborah Lantz on eighteenth-century Essex and Staffordshire, reveals that quite high proportions of girls were apprenticed; one-tenth to one-third of apprentices were girls, depending on the type of indenture. But the skill content and the training component of many of the trades to which they were apprenticed were modest, and for girls in particular a training in values and behaviour was as much a part of the purpose of apprenticeship as any industrial training.[48] There were orthodox indenture procedures and apprenticeship patterns in the London silk trade, but these did not lead to the foundation of a guild. Apprenticeship for girls was about maintenance and general training before marriage, while boys underwent systematic industrial training and entered a guild.[49]

Women did themselves take apprentices but in small numbers. Very small numbers were recorded for Wiltshire and Warwickshire in the seventeenth and eighteenth centuries; apprenticeship, moreover was predominantly recorded in the name of a couple, or of a husband alone.[50] In Oxford the number of widows taking apprentices varied from 0.2 per cent to as high as 8.5 per cent of the total apprenticeships taken out over the whole period 1601 to 1800.[51]

The argument for a reduction in female employment and job status with the contraction of domestic industry is problematic when placed against the substantial evidence of very limited opportunities in the pre-existing period. Pinning one's hopes for explanation to the vicissitudes of female apprenticeship is no more rewarding. Domestic industry, furthermore, poses its own special problems. On the one hand, the growth of the new consumer industries, the proto-industrial manufactures, was at the cost of guild-regulated urban trades. Women, as well as men, in traditional industries lost out in the regional and industrial restructuring of eighteenth-century industry, but the new putting-out industries were also predominantly employers of women. They did not, on the whole, require formal apprenticeships, so that entry for women was easier. But equally, the whole point of the relocation of industry from town to country was the search for cheap labour, and merchants found an infinitely expandable pool in the large numbers of spinsters as well as the wives and daughters of agricultural labourers, miners, cottagers and squatters in rural areas, and in the still small but rapidly expanding unincorporated towns or suburbs. Women proliferated in these industries to be sure, but because they were cheap labour. Women endured the time discipline imposed on such domestic industries by market dates, raw material delivery times and putting-out networks – a discipline greatly amplified by the intensification of labour through the driving down of piece rates.

The close relationship between this domestic manufacture and the family economy is accepted *prima facie* as the reason for high participation rates of women. Industry carried out at home supposedly allowed a flexible integration of productive and domestic labour; indeed feminists have recently argued that pre-capitalist manufacture, because it was centred on the home, was more compatible with child-bearing and rearing and in particular breast-feeding.[52] But this is speculation; the extent of any such compatibility depended on work, status, industry and the economic cycle.[53] The experience of a late eighteenth-century female nail-worker was not the same as that of a pottery worker or buttonmaker; the vagaries of international markets brought bouts of highly intensive labour followed by phases of unemployment. Though women were the most important part of the proto-industrial workforce, the intensity of labour from a woman with young children even if she was working at home was not likely to be high. It was the numbers of these women available for some work at less than subsistence wages, the numbers of their children who made some contribution to work, and especially the numbers of youths, who yielded both high labour intensity and high productivity, which made household manufacture so lucrative to merchants. It was the life cycle of the labour force as well as its supply that was crucial. The expansion of the unregulated domestic industries may have enhanced women's employment opportunities, but there is little evidence that they enhanced their job status or wages. The highest paid female workers of the eighteenth century were girls and young women who worked away from home in workshops in the hand weaving, calico printing and pottery trades, metal and hardware workshops and small jenny factories.[54]

WOMEN AND MECHANISATION

One important case made for a general exclusion of women from productive work in the eighteenth century, and their concentration in positions of low pay and low skill has been the differential effect of mechanisation in the eighteenth century upon women. Several historians have drawn attention to the existence of an eighteenth-century 'machinery question', a machinery question before the introduction of the big power technologies and large-scale factories of the nineteenth century. Clapham argued long ago that spinning machinery, knitting and lockworking implements had left women's hands idle and family earnings curtailed in an age of hunger and high prices.[55] Eric Jones argued more recently that mechanisation drove many of the handicraft districts into industrial oblivion, cutting deeply into the base of 'mother and daughter power' in the south and the east.[56] Adrian Randall has stressed that in the woollen industry, it was the first wave of mechanisation in the eighteenth century which had the most sweeping changes for workers, especially women.[57] But this decline in employment for women was by no means final. To argue so would be to ignore the extent to which industrialisation also involved the use of more, cheaper labour more intensively. Cheap women's labour, particularly in woollen and linen manufacture, was driven by mechanisation to even lower wage-levels, and became a source for new rural industries in lace, straw plait manufacture, glovemaking and shirt button making, boot and shoemaking, nailmaking and in the new urban sweated trades, especially in tailoring which flourished from the 1830s.

But the impact of technological change on women's employment cannot be assessed in the aggregate. It cannot be proved at the aggregate level that technological change creates either more or less employment. The issue needs to be examined at the level of the individual industries and individual innovations. Two fruitful industries for investigation and comparison in the eighteenth century are the textile industries and the metal trades. Both industries experienced substantial change in technology in the eighteenth century and we can examine in some detail the impact of technology on the division of labour and on women's productivity and employment.

Textiles

Hand spinning was the archetype of women's employment in the eighteenth century. The women who practised the trade right across the country were invariably among the lowest paid of workers. Eden in the 1790s found the earnings of the female domestic spinners of Essex, Norfolk, Oxfordshire, Leicestershire and Yorkshire ranged from 1s. 6d. to 3s. a week, while the women who worked in three Yorkshire factories at the time earned 4s. to 5s. a week. Julia Mann described the hand spinners as 'an unorganised mass of sweated labour'.[58]

In the linen industry in Scotland in 1751 it was argued that a good spinner producing 1½ spindles a week in twelve-hour days, 'can gain between

15 and 16d a week, but the price of corn at 3d a sack leaves a woman 1d a week for clothing, firing house rents, etc. Therefore she must starve.'[59] In spite of the low wages of spinners, constraints were felt in the supply of yarn, and three machines were invented which revolutionised spinning: Arkwright's water frame (1769), Hargreaves' jenny (1770) and Crompton's mule which came into use in the 1780s. All of these machines were used first in the cotton industry, but the jenny was soon introduced to the much larger woollen industry. The jenny was introduced among a range of new techniques in the woollen industry: scribbling and carding machinery, spinning machinery, the flying shuttle and the gig mill. All were introduced within a ten-year period to an industry which had previously known only one powered technique, its fulling mills. The jenny had an immediate, but differential impact on women workers. Randall explains that from 1781–96 to 1805 the number of women per cloth fell to 18 per cent of its former total; their job losses being due directly to the jenny and the slubbing billy.[60] The worst hit areas were agricultural and rural parishes. Eden described such an area where 'hand spinning has fallen into disuse ... and the poor from the great reduction in the price scarcely have the heart to earn the little that can be made'.

Resistance to the machine was proverbial and widespread. Jennies were destroyed across Lancashire in 1769, and there were famous riots around Blackburn in 1779, which Wadsworth and Mann described as a state of 'guerilla warfare'. Resistance in the West Country was widespread, and it was not until the early 1790s that the machine spread in any numbers in Wiltshire and Gloucestershire. A magistrate in Somerset in 1790 described how he was called in by two manufacturers to protect their property:

from the Depredations of a lawless Banditi of colliers and their wives, for the wives had lost their work to spinning engines ... they advanced at first with much Insolence, avowing their intention of cutting to pieces the Machinery introduced in the woollen manufacture; which they suppose, if generally adopted, will lessen the demand for manual labour. The women became clamorous. The men were open to conviction and after some Expostulation were induced to desist from their purpose and return peaceably home.[61]

But the impact of the jenny on women's employment was not clear cut. It was a great deal more damaging in agricultural areas than in textile centres.[62] The early jenny of twelve to twenty spindles was operated by women in the home. It was part of the domestic system, the machine of the poor. When it came to the Holmfirth district of Yorkshire in 1776 it was 'hailed as a prodigy'.

Every weaver learned to spin on the jenny, every clothier (or manufacturer) had more work in his house, and also kept a number of women spinning yarn for him in their cottages.[63]

In the context of fairly competitive yarn prices and little industrial concentration in the early Lancashire cotton industry, the machine benefited those who owned and operated the machines themselves. It was the cottage producers and those who ran small centralised workshops who reaped the first gains in efficiency from the jenny, and they did so until merchants and factors saw the gains to be had through setting up their own jenny factories.[64] Some women, mainly those in clothworking families clearly gained from the jenny. It increased their productivity in proportion to the number of spindles, and wages initially increased.

But as William Reddy has argued, the very design of the machine lent itself to large-scale production, and large jennies usually of sixty to eighty spindles were soon combined with machine carding and installed in the so called jenny factories. These jennies were still operated by women, but in going to the factories they had lost the entrepreneurial control of their own labour as well as early windfall gains to a male manufacturer. The women's wages fell; those who had been earning 8s. to 9s. a week on jennies of 24 spindles could now earn only from 4s. to 6s. The early jennies were part of the domestic system, the machines of the poor; the larger ones were in the hands of merchant manufacturers. As a contemporary petition proclaimed:

That the Jenneys are in the Hands of the Poor, and the Patent Machines are in the Hands of the Rich; and that the work is better manufactured by small Jenneys than by large ones.[65]

Most of the jennies introduced into the woollen industry, especially in the south west, made their entry in times of booming trade in the early 1790s. But levels of resistance depended on more than the trade cycle; they depended on a gestation period for fostering popular resentment, and on levels of community and trade organisations in a district.[66]

The jenny had quite devastating effects on women's employment in some areas; but for some textile families at least, the early jenny was a veritable 'women's technology'. Another major spinning technology, the water frame, relied from the outset on the labour of children and especially girls and young women. The spinning mule, however, which was to become the most efficient technique, rapidly became an enclave of male labour. This machine, too, started as a hand technology, used in small workshops within the framework of the domestic system. Before power was applied it required substantial physical strength, and male labour was employed. But the technique was not competitive with the jenny or water frames, run by low-wage female labour. After power was applied the machine still required substantial stamina and the continued attendance of a skilled operative; more significantly, substantial amounts of capital were required to buy or build the machine, and engineering skills were required to maintain and repair the machine. In spite of these obstacles, women could and did learn the skills and were quite widely used on the smaller mules even into the 1830s.[67] It was the Mule Spinners' Union, not the machine, which excluded women workers. It consistently struck over women workers from 1810, and in 1829 explicitly forbade women joining the union.

Silk throwing was carried out almost entirely by women before the introduction of throwing mills. Most of these worked in their own homes with simple throwing equipment made of wood. Though throwing mills existed from the first quarter of the eighteenth century, these began to replace home production significantly only from the later part of the century. Some throwers, mostly men with high earnings gained in putting work out, turned to building throwing mills employing over 100 workers, in rural areas close to the East End of London. The new machinery and skills also drew on women's and girls' labour, but now from the declining textile regions of Essex where high female unemployment and large numbers of workhouses provided a pool of cheap labour.[68]

The new spinning machinery undoubtedly destroyed a large source of casual female employment. But some women found more or less lucrative employment in the rationalised structures and mechanised processes introduced from the later eighteenth century.

Was women's experience in the weaving and finishing processes any different? Contrary to popular belief, hand weaving was not a skilled male pursuit, transposed to unskilled women workers only with the advent of the power loom and factory. It was widely practised by women, particularly in the silk industry, but also to a considerable extent in wool, linen and cotton. The techniques which threatened this employment were the Dutch engine or double engine loom, the Jacquard, the flying shuttle and the power loom.

In the silk industry, three quarters of the single hand weavers in Staffordshire and Warwickshire were women. Men played only a small part in the industry in Macclesfield, and it was there, in 1719, that women, boys and girls were the most violent assailants of ladies wearing calico gowns.[69] In Spitalfields, regulations against women weavers, other than widows or daughters supporting old parents, existed from early in the eighteenth century but these lapsed or were revived according to the demand for labour. Women used both single and double engine looms in the 1760s, to such an extent that this was a cause of the great hostility of male weavers in 1769. And women were again widely employed in weaving in the Napoleonic Wars.[70]

Across the silk, woollen and cotton industries there was the introduction of new weaving technologies particularly the broad loom, the Jacquard loom, the double engine loom and the Dutch loom. Judy Lown has shown that in Spitalfields women were mainly employed in plain or narrow silk weaving, while men worked the broad looms brought over from the continent for larger silk pieces, then on the Jacquard from the early nineteenth century for fancy work. Both the techniques and their products were regarded as more highly skilled, and women became associated with subsidiary roles in silk weaving and ribbon weaving.[71] But nevertheless, by the early nineteenth century, women were doing broad silk weaving from Macclesfield to Spitalfields.[72] Broad loom and Jacquard loom weaving, however, also brought new categories of employment. The drawboys and drawgirls were employed in fancy weaving to 'read' a pattern onto the cards, but this was considered menial labour. At the first opportunity (such as the edict in France in 1786, permitting women to weave) the drawgirls abandoned their arduous and undervalued employment and took to the loom. The effect of the shortage of ancillary labour was to hasten the development of the Jacquard system of automatic design control.[73]

The introduction of the double engine loom in Macclesfield in the 1730s was greeted with rioting female button workers. The Dutch engine loom was the occasion for separating the Coventry ribbon-weaving industry into a skilled male section using the new looms, and an unskilled female section using single hand looms. But this exclusion operated only until shortly after 1815 when the hold of larger manufacturers was challenged by small capitalists employing cheap labour, notably women on the machines.[74] Women weavers were common in the Yorkshire and the West Country woollen industry, though crisis years provided occasions for attempts to exclude them from the use of the more efficient double looms, if not from the trade itself. Over the course of the eighteenth century the double loom was increasingly worked by women, youths and apprentices in the west country. In the later 1790s women became weavers in large numbers, but by the early nineteenth century men displaced from scribbling and finishing processes turned in high proportions to the loom. Where, before mechanisation, 57 per cent of the male workforce went into weaving, by 1828 this was as high as 84 per cent.[75] But women were also a substantial part of the weaving workforce among the illegal weavers put to the flying shuttle or spring loom in the early loom shops. Several clothiers from Yorkshire and the West Country also reported to the 1806 Woollen Committee that women and girls were employed weaving, and wives and daughters as well as men used the loom in cottage industry.[76]

The experiences of the linen and cotton industries were no different.

When linen spinning passed out of the hands of female domestic spinners, these turned increasingly to hand weaving, and one-third of all the weavers in the south Scotland linen industry by the beginning of the nineteenth century were women and children. In the early cotton industry the divisions were to manifest themselves both in machinery, and in geography. Women were employed in the less skilled country branches of the trade using the ordinary hand loom, not in the urban smallware trade where master weavers used the Dutch loom in large workshops.[77] Women, children, Irish migrants and the aged were concentrated in the coarser, less skilled, branches of cotton weaving, and it was their jobs which were threatened by the new power looms, looms which paradoxically also drew on the labour of young women. Male craft workers weaving fine or figured cloth had nothing to fear from the machine until well into the second third of the nineteenth century.[78] The power loom, like the spinning jenny before it, did not set unskilled women against male craft workers. It set women against women, especially young women working in the shops or mills against older married women working at home.

Finishing processes in the cloth manufacture were frequently skilled male crafts, though girls and young women were widely employed as assistants, particularly in bleaching and calico printing. Boys apprenticed to the woollen manufacture were taught the highly skilled parts of the trade – dyeing, putting cloth into the fulling mill, and sorting wool only in the last two years of their apprenticeship. Girls and women performed most other processes in the manufacture, but rarely these ones.[79] New techniques introduced into finishing processes clearly affected male employment. The two techniques that fuelled the classic Luddite attacks, the gig mill and shearing frame, displaced six out of seven and three out of four men respectively.[80] But it was calico printing techniques which demonstrated the most remarkable gender typing of technological development. In this case more mechanised processes were bypassed and labour intensive technologies specifically developed along with an advanced division of labour in order to tap a female labour force. Four such technical innovations were developed over the second third of the eighteenth century. The first was 'picotage' or the patterning of printing blocks with pins or studs tapped into the blocks. This was delicate work, for one large block contained 63,000 pins, but it was a job done by women who earned 12s.–14s. a week after their apprenticeship. Another labour-intensive process introduced at the time was 'pencilling' or the hand-painting of patterns directly on to the cloth. This was performed by women who worked in long terraces of cottage-like workshops under the superintendence of 'mistresses'.

In the shop each woman had her piece suspended before her with a supply of hair pencils of different degrees of fineness according to the size of the object ... to be touched, and containing colour ... according to the pattern required ... a good workwoman might earn £2.00 a week, though it was likely most earned a lot less.

The style of patterns changed little from year to year. This laborious work was done by women, and so was regarded as an unskilled process which bypassed the employment of the highly paid craftsmen who engraved and used wooden printing blocks and, after 1760, copper plates. Copper-plate printing, introduced in 1760, followed by roller-printing in 1785, constituted the real technical improvements of the industry, but they required the use of highly-organised and highly-paid 'gentlemen journeymen', so that such manufacturers as Peel bypassed these and instead organised 'protofactories' using elementary labour-intensive techniques and extensive division of labour, along with special training and disciplining of workers. The scarcity, together with the very high status, of skilled calico printers was the main stimulus behind the attempts by entrepreneurs to look for alternative methods of production on which they could employ low-paid women and girls.[81]

The style of patterns changed little from year to year. This laborious work was done by women, and so was regarded as an unskilled process which bypassed the employment of the highly paid craftsmen who engraved and used wooden printing blocks and, after 1760, copper plates. Copper-plate printing, introduced in 1760, followed by roller-printing in 1785, constituted the real technical improvements of the industry, but they required the use of highly-organised and highly-paid 'gentlemen journeymen', so that such manufacturers as Peel bypassed these and instead organised 'protofactories' using elementary labour-intensive techniques and extensive division of labour, along with special training and disciplining of workers. The scarcity, together with the very high status, of skilled calico printers was the main stimulus behind the attempts by entrepreneurs to look for alternative methods of production on which they could employ low-paid women and girls.[81]

The metal trades

The industrial revolution is usually conceived of in terms of power-driven technologies and large-scale factories in the textile industries, and a transposition of work from male craftsmen to a female factory proletariat. However, as I have shown in the case of textile workers, many of the techniques introduced were developed initially on a small scale within the framework of the domestic system, and women had dominated the industry long before the appearance of power-driven machinery. The development of the metal trades was another important aspect of eighteenth- and early-nineteenth-century industrialisation. On the one hand, there were the classic puddling and blast-furnace technologies of iron processing; on the other, a range of new technologies in the working of metals, new technologies which, in the nineteenth century, would be associated with the engineering industry. In the eighteenth century the metal trades were much more diffuse and less specialised, producing goods ranging from swords, cutlery and agricultural implements to hardware goods, guns, tools, machinery and 'toys'.

Metals or small hardware goods and ornamental ware have usually been assumed the preserve of the male craftsman; on the face of it, not an unreasonable assumption given the historic association of the engineering industry with male workers, other than in wartime. Even in 1980, the engineering industry, while providing 13 per cent of total employment in Britain, afforded only 7 per cent of women's employment.[82] The male preponderance in metal-related industries perhaps goes back to the religious and mythical association of the armourer and the warrior – Hephaestus and Achilles. The forge historically conjured up images of strength, power and domination, and the very term engineering originally applied only to those in the military profession. Carlo Cipolla has pointed out how in the fourteenth century, the workmen who made the bells which tolled out the rhythms of peaceful village and town life also made the cannon that continually blasted apart the peace tolled by the bells. Seventeenth- and eighteenth-century developments in gun manufacture and in the great arsenals were technically interrelated with the early hardware and engineering trades. Sophistication in the technology of producing guns also entailed new forms of fighting. As Cipolla has argued, the whole art of gunnery produced a new type of warrior – cold-blooded and technically inclined – who in the middle of the fight had to stop, carry out a series of measurements and calculations; he was no longer the hot-blooded warrior of the old days.[83]

But women also worked in significant numbers across the metal trades – in large numbers in some, not at all in others. Technical change in the eighteenth century in these trades in contrast to textiles was almost entirely associated with the workshop and domestic manufacture. What did this high-productivity household and workshop manufacture mean for the women who worked in these trades?

First, innovation did not displace the household workshop. The earliest working equipment of the metal trades were anvil, hammer, file and grindstone. If we look specifically at the metal trades of Birmingham, major eighteenth-century innovations were the stamp, press and draw-bench, and the lathe. These tools, along with the division of labour certainly did combine to save time and effort. Shelbourne cited mixed metals and stamping machinery used with the divison of labour to produce cheap buttons. And there were besides, 'an infinity of smaller improvements which each workman has and keeps secret from the rest'. In Britain's Soho works, it was not just the skilled artisans who contributed to success but 'the number of ingenious mechanical contrivances they avail themselves of, by means of Water Mills, which much facilitates their work and saves a great portion of time and labour'. In Birmingham, machinery was, however, in the main hand operated, only supplemented in some cases by horse and water power. Steam power, though the most famous product of the town, was hardly ever used there before 1800, and by 1815 there were still only forty engines in the town.[84]

Evidence that the Birmingham toy trades made use of apprentices, non-apprenticed and women's and children's labour from the start in many of the processes makes it difficult to assess the impact of new technology on skills and the status and structure of the labour force. Apprenticeship and the sexual division of labour were not necessarily any index of changes in the labour process. Certainly the new technology did affect the division of labour in the trades. Contemporaries argued simultaneously that the techniques used in Birmingham did not reduce the skill or labour required in production processes, and that the new machinery allowed extensive use of child labour. Taylor and Garbett, for instance, reported that Birmingham machines reduced the manual labour and enabled boys to do men's work. Shelbourne cited a division of labour that made work so simple that 'five times in six, children of 6 or 8 years old do it as well as men'.[85] And Dean Tucker described the close connection between machinery and child labour in Birmingham: 'When a Man stamps on the metal Button by means of an Engine, a Child stands by him to place the Button in readiness to receive the Stamp, and to remove it when received and then to place another.'[86] But equally, the differentiation of existing trades and the proliferation of a whole number of new trades reflected changes in product as well as in processes. It is particularly difficult to gain any clear idea of the sexual division of labour in trades which displayed such varied industrial structures. It is said, however, that the adoption of machines for stamping and piercing extended the range of female employment especially for young girls.[87] And it was recognised that women's work was widespread in the japanning and the stamping and piercing trades. Girls were specifically requested in advertisements for button-piercers, annealers, and stoving and polishing work in the japanning trades. Another advertisement for button-burnishers in 1788 also sought 'a woman that has been used to looking over and carding plain, plated and gilted buttons, also a few women that have been used to grind steels, either at foot lathes or mill'.

The delicacy of the work in buttonmaking and piercing, as well as in the hand-painting of designs, was regarded as the special province of women and girls with their smaller hands and the deftness and concentration already acquired at household needlework. The lacquering and japanning trades required stove management and even in the nineteenth century it was women who worked in the trade. The small lacquering rooms in the brass trades, only twelve by fifteen feet and eleven feet high, characteristically contained a couple of iron plate stoves and five to six women workers.[88]

In the Black-Country trades there was no lighter alternative work open to women, and they worked beside the men in heavy industry – on the pit-bank, in the nail manufacture, and in the manufacture of chains, saddlery, harness and hollow ware. But in many of these trades, and in particular in nailmaking, they had long been degraded workers. The most noted women workers of the West Midlands trades were the nailers. Their subservience in this degraded and poverty-stricken trade reflected the wider subservience of their sex. William Hutton, on his travels in 1741, provided an exemplary male image of his workforce.

In some of these shops I observed one, or more females, stript of their upper garment, and not overcharged with their lower, wielding the hammer with all the grace of the sex. The beauties of their face were rather eclipsed by the smut of the anvil; or in poetical phrase, the tincture of the forge had taken possession of those lips, which might have been taken by the kiss. Struck with the novelty, I enquired, 'whether the ladies of this country shod horses?' but was answered, with a smile, 'they are nailers'. A fire without head, a nailer of a fair complexion, or one who despises the tankard, are equally rare among them.[89]

Yet certain women did have a knowledge of a wide range of trades. Many women carried on with their husbands' businesses after their death, and though they may have employed some journeymen they would themselves have had to have a great deal of practical experience and knowledge to make a success of running what were in the main small artisan businesses. These women ran the businesses not only where one might have expected women's work – as in toy, button and bucklemaking, and japanning. But widows and daughters also appeared in strength in the iron business, in plumbing and glazing, in the brass founding and pewtering trades, and among the hammer, anvil and edgetool making trades (see Appendix 1). A survey of *Aris's Gazette* from 1752 to 1790 indicates that women were taking over husbands' businesses or dealing with various problems which arose in the trades over a wide range of processes. Notices appeared over this whole period from nine female ironmongers, eight plumbers and glaziers, seven buttonmakers and seven bucklemakers, six watchmakers, five brass manufacturers and braziers, five toolmakers, and five chain and toymakers. There were notices from three women running ironworks, three female plateworkers, two nailworkers, two women running coalworks, as well as individual locksmiths, japanners, wireworkers, and file cutters[90] (see Appendix 2).

Women occupied an important place in the eighteenth-century Birmingham toy trades, as workers and employers. And though the evidence available does not indicate the extent to which there was a 'sexual division of labour' between individual trades and processes, it does indicate an economic and social subservience to men, for their wages were much lower, and they appear as tradeswomen and owners of business in their own right in effect only where they were continuing the business of a deceased husband or father. But we cannot deny the knowledge and expertise possessed by such women in these trades, for their businesses were mainly small-scale or at most medium-scale enterprises. And success for women as much as for men in these Birmingham trades was dependent on skill and on knowledge.

In the nineteenth century women were still employed over a wide range of processes in the Birmingham trades, but these were by-and-large concentrated in the newer, lighter or more unskilled branches. Women did the lacquering in the brass shops, japanning in the tin plateware manufacture, and barrel boring in the gun trade. In the button trade there was a division between the old and more skilled branches such as the metal and pearl button section which employed men, and the new covered and linen button section, which employed women. Men made high-class jewellery, and women and girls were left to the cheap end of the trade in gilt articles and chains. In stamping and piercing the tools were fitted into the press by male toolworkers who also attended to the condition of the tools in cutting the larger stamped work. But women worked even with the large presses, though girls were left to cut out smaller examples of the work. When women were employed in piercing and cutting-out work, they received only 8s.–12s. a week and girls got 6s.–8s.; while the toolmaker who superintended the work claimed 30s.–40s.

Surveys of education in Birmingham carried out in the mid nineteenth century found that while half the working girls surveyed were found in the button manufacture and service, the button trade was strictly subdivided by gender and age. In the pearl button manufacture, for example, men cut the pearl from shell then turned it on a lathe, women drilled holes and polished, boys filled edges and girls carded. In the metal button trade, little button girls from the age of nine were employed as 'putters-in', feeding the press with raw materials. They were paid at 1s. to 2s. 6d. a week, while women got 7s. to 10s. Women's and children's wages in the trade fell during the nineteenth century as mechanisation cheapened piece-work.[91]

It seems, on the basis of close study of the textile and the metal manufactures, that there is no straightforward case to be made for a great transition in women's role in the workplace in response to mechanisation. In the nineteenth century as before in the eighteenth women worked at a broad range of processes. In textiles attempts were made from early in the eighteenth century to exclude them from using more advanced techniques, and large numbers of women were indeed left behind by the revolution in technology to continue their traditional reliance on hand processes used at home. But the attempts at exclusion were rarely successful, for the market and profitability ultimately set the terms of industrial structure; while large numbers of women ultimately lost out on domestic employment in textiles, others were drawn in to use the new machines in workshops and factories, usually at lower wages than their male counterparts.

The metal industries tell a different, but related tale of widespread women's employment in both centuries. The new techniques only reinforced gender divisions there in the trades from early in the eighteenth century. The celebrated female nailworkers were sweated women workers by the mid eighteenth century, long before any mechanisation. But women's wages, working conditions and job status relative to those in the rest of the country did decline in the nineteenth century, not so much in response to mechanisation, however, as to a dramatic change in the fortunes of the Birmingham traders, from new growth sector to relatively declining industry. Cost-cutting rationalisation, not the windfall gains of a new industry, governed job opportunities for women as well as men.

THE ORGANISATION OF PRODUCTION AND WOMEN'S COMMUNITY NETWORKS

The difficulty of assigning a clear-cut transition in women's roles to the introduction of machinery also arises in examining the relationship between the organisation of production and women's trade organisation. It is difficult to uncover very much about the role of women in eighteenth-century trade societies. We occasionally uncover some evidence of female membership, but little else. And this evidence tells us nothing of the greater part of women's employment in those trades with no formal organisation or in the rural domestic industries. Traditional assumptions of low levels of worker organisation among dispersed rural labourers have been discounted by recent research which has demonstrated the high levels of organisation among country workers, not only in industrial disputes, but in food and enclosure riots. Research has shown bonds formed among agricultural, urban industrial and rural industrial workers. Protests against enclosure were frequently led by workers from the towns, or industrial workers squatting on the commons. Opposition to enclosure was strongest where open fields and rural industry coincided, and the decline of food rioting in areas of southern England has been attributed to the decline of the industrial communities themselves.

Women were an important section of these rural communities, and frequently played a leading part in local custom and protest; there is evidence that they led food riots, organised gleaning, mobbed poor-law officials and played an important part in instances of rough music or charivari and seasonal rites. There is little evidence indeed to tell us of their role in the details of organising production, though sense tells us that in largely female workforces, networks formed among women must have been vital in the training and recruitment of the labour force. Certainly in the woollen and worsted spinning, women acted as intermediaries, 'putting out yarn' to their neighbours.[92]

I have tried to demonstrate so far that the idea of a fundamental transformation in women's employment and skills with the separation of work and home rests on simple assumptions about pre-industrial and early industrial household production. Sexual divisions and hierarchy already present in many early-eighteenth-century household industries were sometimes reinforced even within the household by mechanisation. Or they could be reassembled in new ways by both mechanisation and outside workshop or factory production which in the process brought some, at least short-term, opportunities to some women. The implications of eighteenth-century mechanisation and reorganisation of production within and outside the home really cannot be assessed outside its context in growing and declining sectors, and competitive or monopolistic structures. The household economy as it has been understood is a myth. But dissected as a changing part of a dynamic process of industrial and capitalist growth or decline it can help to reveal undiscovered directions and possibilities.

Ahistorical assumptions of static structures and even a static past have entailed rather uninteresting unidirectional accounts of women's subordination. They have also reinforced the faithful rendering of the creed of community. Much has been written about the close community networks, the corporate identity, the plebeian culture and the moral economy of pre-industrial England, but the connections between the world of the local community and the world of work has been less frequently explored.[93] Kinship and community have been equated with notions of mutuality, but this has been assumed, not investigated. By extension, it has also been assumed that the cohesiveness of the local community and with this the social and organisational role of women was broken by the advance of capitalist competition and the market. Where once home and local community formed the location and framework of labour, its harmony and corporate identity were said to dissolve under the impact of population growth and migration, as well as the movement of production outside the home. But this assumption of close ties among workers, and especially among women needs to be examined anew; it is only one side of the story. For equally there were many divisions, and these divisions may well have been even greater before the late eighteenth century than they were to be after.

There are many strong arguments for the importance of community. Neighbourhood and community ties structured the work unit of the rural handicraft industries. The rural workforce was certainly not an unorganised one, in contrast to the urban, and in addition, as Chambers argued over twenty years ago, 'the values of the domestic worker were also the values of the society in which he lived'. It was the local communities which hid the Luddites and which in the East and West Midlands supported the resistance of their framework knitters and silk weavers to the advance of machinery.

Some of these community ties were based in agrarian relations, and several historians, including Keith Snell, J. M. Neeson, J. M. Martin and Pat Hudson, have recently argued for the close interdependence between common right and the structures and extent of domestic industry. They have also demonstrated how closely connected was the decline of rural manufacturing with enclosure. The destruction of one of the major institutions of community – common right – seemed to break the resilience of the handicraft sector. But as Keith Snell so cogently argues in his *Annals of the Labouring Poor*, other institutions came into play – notably the settlement provisions of the Old Poor Law. Outdated legal provisions on settlement rarely relevant at the time they were introduced in the seventeenth century, came into play in the later eighteenth century. They transformed a relatively mobile rural population in the early eighteenth century into the 'stay at home' agricultural labourer of the nineteenth century. The enforcement of these settlement laws ended the earlier ease in gaining settlements, forcing high proportions of the rural workforce to take their fathers' settlement. Snell argues that in the case of the artisan and proto-industrial trades, this perpetuated families practising certain trades in the same place over the generations. They developed familiarity with parochial issues stretching back in to their family history, 'creating a community and political consciousness which could never have existed to the same degree when up to sixty percent of village populations might disappear every twelve years through migration and low life expectancy'.[94]

The juxtaposition of community mentality versus individual action and of moral economy against the market is difficult to pursue in any clearcut manner in discussion of changing industrial work structures in the eighteenth century. There is certainly a new and strong tradition of research rekindling the debate on the moral economy, and now exploring this in industrial contexts. William Reddy has contrasted the 'language of the crowd' with the 'language of market culture', demonstrating the existence of a community of shared values and expectations, beliefs and attitudes among eighteenth- and early nineteenth-century textile workers. But gradually this language of the crowd began to recede. Market language, categories and culture became the public code, limiting industrial action and political behaviour to a narrow range of monetary calculations.[95] Applying this model plus Thompson's concept of the 'moral economy of the poor' to the West Country, Randall has also argued for the common basis of strikes and food riots in a strong community consensus. Trade consciousness was thus synonymous with community consciousness.[96] But the explanatory value of this sharp dichotomy between the area of moral imperatives and the market breaks down in areas undergoing industrial change. The dichotomy raises the thorny question of the definition of community.

There were divisions between artisans with a long and stable stake in the community or in the trade society, and casual outworkers in temporary residence. There were divisions created by the differential impact of international price fluctuations on neighbouring communities producing slightly different products. There were divisions inherent in the division of labour itself, especially the division between men and women workers. There was, in addition, no reason, as has been argued so cogently by Olivia Harris, why the existence of kin or community should imply a behaviour code based on mutuality, morality or custom.

Both the language of kinship and the way co-residence is represented, contain underlying assumptions about the exclusion of economic relations based on direct exchange and precise calculation, and the presence of other relations of generosity without calculation. This ideology ... should not, however, be confused with what relations actually obtain between kin and non kin ... The degree to which people exhibit such behaviour to each other is a matter for investigation rather than assumption.[97]

Community was not, furthermore, something simply associated with a pre-industrial past, something bound up with custom and common right and outside of interaction with the market. Nor was it external and unchanging in the way that community is often invoked against the market and industrialisation. Community and the custom to which it is related is, rather, a living product – it is not egalitarian nor is it free of relations of power and subordination. Divisions of interest within any one community may be marked, yet the 'interests of the community' be defined in terms of the group which at that moment wielded some authority.[98] Community was frequently invoked, for instance, when the livelihoods of skilled and craft workers were at stake; rarely when those of squatters, casual labourers and women were threatened. These people were regarded as mobile, anonymous, 'without community'. The creation of new products, the use of new techniques and access to a whole range of markets could form the basis for different types of community – such as existed in eighteenth-century Birmingham and its hinterland. Here, close family connections between town and country, and rural traditions of partible inheritance appear to have allowed the easy transmission of skills and capital. Industrial concentration and monopolisation of the market cut off the possibility of such flexible community structures in the West Country, and the textile community there became one entrenched in its own traditions, traditions which were, however, the artifact of fairly recent processes of monopoly and proletarianisation.

The imposition of a strict ditchotomy between the community and the market is particularly difficult when applied to women workers. Women have been traditionally identified with the idiom of mutuality of the family and the community. They are assumed to accept this code of behaviour, and the priority they give to family and home places them at a disadvantage in the labour market. They behave, in other words, like Chayanovian peasants, placing family before profitability, when male workers have 'learned the rules of the game' in operating the labour market to their best advantage. But just as Chayanov's peasant has been dissected and found to be mythical,[99] so must the sceptic question our traditional attitudes to identities and communities among women.[100] Bonds among women and female networks were closely tuned to the family life-cycle. The large youthful labour force of early industrial England made up predominantly of girls and young women cannot be assumed to have found its sole priorities and connections within the 'family economy' of married women and mothers. The changing historical divisions and networks created among working women with the impact of both the new industrial work opportunities and the industrial decline that characterised the eighteenth century need to be examined before historians can pronounce on women's identity with the values of the community.

Another arena where the dichotomy between custom and commerce breaks down is in the area of consumption. Women were central to informal popular protests on issues concerning consumption, in the food riots and in later protests over the adulteration of food. They carried over these traditions of protest in their role in enforcing moral codes of behaviour and sexual relations within their communities.[101] But they also organised consumption in a manner which brought the community and the market together.

Economics was at the basis of mutuality just as much as of the market. In eighteenth-century England the community consumption which Hans Medick had attached to E. P. Thompson's 'plebeian culture' was economic both in its manifestation and in its motivation. Time and especially money spent by the poor on cultural ritual, gifts, feasts and luxury consumer display were a form of 'social exchange', a means of strengthening bonds of neighbourhood and friendship.[102]

Anthropologists such as Mary Douglas have also treated consumer goods as an information system or means of communication. 'A household's expenditures on other people gives an idea of whether it is isolated or well involved.' Consumption, and particularly luxury consumption, convey the fine gradations of social class, age and hierarchy as well as cementing particular kinds of degrees of social relationship. Goods are 'the medium, less objects of desire than threads of a veil that disguises the social relations under it'.[103]

It can be argued that this consumer culture was very important to the community networks formed among women in the eighteenth century. The household production unit was also a unit of consumption. The consumer needs of the household had to be maintained and organised. To what extent was it women who organised household consumption, and indulged in private and social luxury consumption? We know this was the case in early-twentieth-century Europe. In London, wives' skills and tastes could do as much as husbands' wages to determine how comfortably their families lived. Among the Amsterdam seamstresses the first task of a married woman was housekeeping. She saved on the family budget by sewing clothes for her family, and tidiness became 'the most valued quality in housekeeping'.[104]

In eighteenth-century England too, there is at least indirect evidence to show that women organised a large proportion of household consumption. It is evident that many of the new consumer industries reproduced goods which women already made for household consumption. Women's hands were busied producing yarn, stockings and clothing for their families. They also took pride in their labour-intensive efforts to bypass the market and so to clothe their families better and with a smaller outlay of precious cash earnings.

In both England and Scotland most linen was made by private families for their own use. Though needlework and cooking had existed throughout the early modern period as the essential elements of housewifery performed by women, the demands made by these on women's time became more intensive and a higher degree of skill was called for as new lighter materials in grades of cotton and linen, and new furnishings and cooking implements, were introduced over the course of the eighteenth century. The amount and the variety of household consumption increased, and women's household tasks increased with this. A woman's labour-power was an important asset, but her consuming power for the household was also an asset of rising significance in the eighteenth century. It is no mere coincidence that many of the new domestic manufactures of the seventeenth and eighteenth centuries were also consumer industries catering to a mass market, and that their labour force was made up predominantly of women.[105]

It has been argued that the so-called 'home market' of the eighteenth century was largely a women's market. The consumer industries of the early Industrial Revolution were 'those in which women took the decision to consume: the cotton, woollen, linen and silk industries, the pottery industry, the cutlery industry, the Birmingham small trades'.[106] But discussions of consumption in the eighteenth century are thus far almost wholly tied to the evidence of inventories, and these have been left largely by those from established craftsmen or tradesmen backgrounds and middle incomes or higher. Such evidence cannot give us clues to labourers' consumption or the mass markets of the poor. What we have to say about the growth of consumption and the market consumer culture is thus tied to a relatively limited social group. It is also the case that, though social status and not just basic needs was behind much of this consumption, the character and composition of a range of consumer goods varied enormously between social groups.[107] The relationship of women to this consumer market would similarly take on this complexity of interaction with production and consumption. Among some social groups labour-intensive and costly home-production of commodities was valued more than the option to purchase those goods in the market. Both, however, were manifestations of consumption. Consumption reveals the great range of connections between the home and the market which the rise of market culture helped to create, rather than to destroy.

We can ask moreover to what extent women's organisation of this household consumption actually created a consumer culture centred on the market place. Household management was also dependent on a knowledge of the price, a knowledge acquired through long-term participation in the market, and through the information acquired in the networks formed among consumers, particularly women. It was this process of haggling and bargaining in the market, according to 'that sort of rough equality which though not exact, is sufficient for carrying on the business of common life' which Adam Smith argued actually determined the extent to which the value of commodities accorded with their price.[108]

The consumer culture did not contradict the household economies and production of early industrial artisans. It was but one part of household management. Similarly these proto-industrial workers and consumers were not obviously aware of any special distinction between the market and the moral economy. Many of the seasonal activities, rituals and customs were important sources of income in themselves, making it worthwhile leaving off waged work for one or more days at a time. Where waged work and household management intertwined, other time and money economies took their own priorities, and they frequently concerned female members of the workforce.

Community relations and networks were integrated into the priorities of workplace relations not just, as in earlier periods, because the household was both the unit of production and the unit of residence. In the early industrial economy of the eighteenth century, consumption was the activity which bound community and capitalism together. The new industries produced consumer goods; they transformed goods formerly produced (largely by women) within the household to meet basic needs into commodities to be sold on a world market. The new industries also tapped a women's labour force, a labour force which brought valuable skills and social networks. It was also a cheap labour force, bound as it was within the household. But the communities into which this capitalist production penetrated themselves became consumer and market communities. Social status and participation, custom and community continued to hold sway and to impinge upon work, but they did so in new ways, in ways expressed increasingly through consumption, by the individual, by the household and by the whole community.

The impact of custom and community on the workplace was not, however, a casualty of industrialisation; rather it took on other forms. Before we can understand the change which did come with the later phases of industrialisation we must understand the content and dynamics of custom as well as the household itself. Appeals by historians to pre-industrial social values, non-market behaviour, family subsistence economy and backward-sloping labour-supply curves are all inadequate. Certainly the behaviour and characteristics subsumed under these terms affected the rhythms of work, the division of labour, and the use and reception of new technology. But they were neither timeless nor homogeneous and as yet we know very little indeed about them. One important aspect of these characteristics during the early phases of industrialisation was the special integration of waged work, household subsistence and consumption, and community networks. It was women who filled the interstices of all these centres of activity. And it was the mixed character of women's household, waged and community work whose purpose above all others was to ensure the subsistence of their families, which made women workers so vulnerable to exploitation, and their labour such a lucrative source of profit to capitalists.

The idea of a transition in the eighteenth century from a community-based workforce where women may have played a prominent role to the more individualist, market-orientated, and, by association, more male labour force needs to be unravelled, and tested against the complex character of the contact between market and custom, individual and community which developed in the early industrial period. Clear-cut divisions are difficult to identify, and were they to emerge, may well have been caused by rather than eliminated by the processes of industrialisation.

CONCLUSION

The identification of a great transition in women's working lives with the advent of industrialisation seems on present evidence to be an impossible task. But perhaps it is after all a chimera of simplistic linear notions of Marxist historiography. Circular and cyclical ideas must be at least as germane to our understanding of industrialisation; the existence of a complex array of paths of development calls for a less deterministic history. This is particularly important in the study of women's work, where the parallels between women in eighteenth-century domestic industry, in the sweated homework of the nineteenth century, and in the new subcontracting proliferating today in metropolitan and Third World countries are more significant than many historians and social scientists are prepared to admit.[109]

Appendix 1 Women in the Birmingham trades[110]

Adams, Mrs (1777)	Iron works
Aston, Alice (1772)	Plumber and glazier
Bailey, Barbara (1776)	Jackmaker and whitesmith
Baker, Mary (1767)	Plateworker
Baldwin, Mrs (1778)	Watchmaker
Barnes, Ann (1791)	Ironmonger
Beddow, Elizabeth (1793)	Locksmith
Bell, Elizabeth (1767)	Glass pincher and buttonmaker
Bentley, Hannah (1774)	Blacksmith
Bradnock, Mary (1797)	Gilder, silverer and stamper
Bransby, Mary (1775)	Plumber and glazier
Chandler, Sarah (1774)	Buttonmaker
Dawson, Mary (1783)	Plumber and glazier
Deakin, Jane (1773)	Whitesmith and ironmonger
Fletcher, Sarah (1786)	Steel watch, toy and chainmaker
Garrison, Elizabeth (1784)	Brazier, pewterer and fine plate worker (father's business)
Gill, Anne (1756)	File cutter
Grove, Ann (1791)	Plumber and glazier
Hill, Sandra (1796)	Manufacturer of anvils, bisk irons, vices, hammers, all kinds of tinman and braziers' tools, press screws, mill pillers
Hoffmeyer, Elizabeth (1779)	Clockmaking
Hopkins, Mary (1763)	Ironmonger
Hughes, Mary (1793)	Nailor
Lane, Elizabeth (1767)	Licensed to sell plate
Lane, Sarah (1783)	Edge Tool maker and hammermaker
Lard, Lydia (1795)	Toymaker
Mercer, Elizabeth (1772)	Brazier and tin plate worker
Moore, Felicia (1795)	Sadler's ironmonger
Osbourne, Ann (1779)	Japanned clock dial manufacturer
Pagett, Mary (1767)	Wire drawer
Parker, Mary (1788)	Plater
Parkes, Sarah (1777)	Clock and watchmaker
Parratt, Ann (1765)	Ironmonger
Richardson, Mary (1773)	Tinman and coffin platemaker
Sly, Susannah (1786)	Plate
Russell, Mary (1767)	Bucklemaker
Whittaker, Martha (1797)	Wire worker and flour machine maker
Tuft, Margaret (1789)	Toy and watchchain maker

TRADESWOMEN MENTIONED IN CONNECTION WITH MISCELLANEOUS
PROBLEMS OF BUSINESS

Allen, Ann (1796)	Gilt toymaker
Baker, Mary (1767)	Licensed to sell plate
Baldwin, Mrs (1778)	Watchmaker
Barber, Elizabeth (1791)	Bucklemaker
Barnseley, Mary (1789)	Hammermaker
Bennitt, Eleanor (1794)	Nail trade
Bodington, Hannah (1765)	Milliner and bucklemaker
Bramwell, Ann	Nailer
Browne, Jane (1763)	Coal works
Clare, Sarah (1791)	Brass founder and silverer
Cooke, Mrs (1756)	Buckle rings and chapemaker
Cross, Mrs (1778)	Gun polisher
Darby, Rebecca (1797)	Ironworks
Davies, Mrs (1794)	Journeyman plumber, glazier and painter
Dudley, Mrs (1765)	Coalworks
Dumold, Mrs (1790)	Plumber and glazier
Evans, Ann (1767)	Owner of china warehouse
Fowke, Ann (1749)	Enginemaker
Godfree, Hannah (1775)	Buttonmaker
Goodchild, Mrs (1752)	Ironmonger
Greaves, Hannah (1790)	Plumbers and glaziers
Green, Mrs (1784)	Plumber and glazier
Hadley, Sarah (1745)	Anvil maker
Hartwell, Mrs (1793)	Watch manufacturer
Hopkins, Mary (1763)	Ironmonger
Latham, Jane (1762)	Bucklemaker
Orton, Elizabeth (1769)	Ironmonger
Parkes, Elizabeth (1789)	Ironmongers and cutlers
Piddock, Ann (1784)	Platers and bucklemakers
Reece, Mary (1769)	Ironmonger
Reynolds, Martha (1754)	Brazier
Rooker, Mary (1763)	Brass founder
Saul, Mary (1789)	Buttonmakers
Seagen, Ann (1784)	Plumber and glazier
Room, Mary (1792)	Japanner
Rowley, Mrs (1789)	Spoon maker
Salt, Ann (1797)	Hardware dealer
Stevens, Mary (1777)	Toymaker

WOMEN IN THE BUTTON TRADE

Wanted advertisements for women and girls:
    Button piercing (1773 and 1775)
    Filling and dipping buttons and annealing shells (1772)
    Carding plain, plated and gilt buttons (1788)
    Grinding steels at foot lathe or mill (1788)

4

The property of skill in the period of manufacture

JOHN RULE

I

Marx described a 'period of manufacture' coming between the period of the guilds with their regulated independent handicraft production and the mechanised production of the modern factory system (machinofacture). He noted that because the technical basis of manufacture remained handicraft skills, skilled workers retained a considerable power to safeguard their interests.[1]

The period of manufacture was not a static phase. It was characterised by an increasing division of labour and differentiation of skills:

Manufacture begets in every handicraft that it seizes upon, a class of so called unskilled labourers, a class which handicraft industry strictly excluded... Alongside of the hierarchic gradation there steps the simple separation of the labourers into skilled and unskilled.

The expansion of the latter group was however constrained. Capitalists would have liked to have exploited reserves of cheap unskilled labour more fully, especially that of women and children, but so long as hand skills remained crucial to the manufacturing process they were 'on the whole checked by the customs and by the active resistance of the male workers' who retained a preponderant influence: 'In as much as the integral mechanism which was at work in manufacture had no objective skeleton existing apart from the workers themselves, capital had continually to wrestle with the insubordination of the workers.'[2]

If strikes are taken to be an evident manifestation of worker 'insubordination' and of 'active resistance' then recent historical investigations have amply confirmed how frequent worker action was in eighteenth-century England and how right Adam Smith was to describe industrial disputes as endemic in manufacturing: 'The workmen desire to get as much, the masters to give as little as possible. The former are disposed to combine in order to raise, the latter in order to lower, the wages of labour.'[3] Strikes are only one aspect of insubordination and probably Marx had in mind

99

the difficulties experienced by employers in overcoming the notorious 'St Monday' and in imposing regular working habits upon their employees when he argued that the 'ample fact' that from the sixteenth century to the rise of large-scale industry, capital 'failed to become master of the whole available labour time of the manufacturing workers' best testified to their very considerable powers of resistance.[4]

Skilled workers were able through combinations, which in many cases had developed often effective tactics of industrial action, to exert a degree of control over the labour process and to face the employer in the labour market as a free bargainer: 'as independent owners of commodities, one an owner of money and the means of production, and the other of labour power'.[5]

Restriction of entry to the trade was crucial. Its cornerstone was the confinement of knowledge of skills and work practices to those who had served apprenticeships. In some trades these were seven years of formal indentured service. In others there were accepted equivalents, for example serving seven years with one's father could mean acceptance as a 'legal workman'. Levels of formality varied from trade to trade with rural crafts tending to be less rigid than urban ones.[6] It may be as useful to think of 'regular' as of legal workmen. This was the designation used by the weavers and shearmen of the west country when they gave evidence to an enquiry in 1802/3. By then formal apprenticeship had become rare among the weavers, but the labour force none the less recognised 'regular' weavers, embracing those who had learned under their fathers or other relatives without indenture but who had worked for seven years: 'a man who has a family brings them up without the expense of apprenticeship: serving seven years with him they are considered as lawful weavers'. To the suggestion that it had become the norm in Somerset to take boys 'in the nature of apprentices' but not to bind them, one weaver replied, 'It has been so through poverty.'[7]

Before the advent of the de-skilling shearing frame, the shearmen had become noted as a closely-knit craft group keeping a tight restriction on entry. Journeymen refused to work with those whom they did not regard as 'regular'. Yet even here there had been a substantial departure from insistence on formal binding: 'It is neither the one nor the other, it is not general.' The evidence of Thomas Lambeth who had been forty years a shearman is revealing. At first he asserted that he had been an indentured apprentice but as questioning proceeded some confusion became evident. 'Do you mean they are generally indentured?'; 'No, never, no writing at all, but they go to it as boys.' In fact, in Gloucestershire, the practice had become one of serving until twenty-one years old, usually meaning for five or six years. This still constituted a barrier through which young men had to pass to become 'regular' journeymen. By the end of the exchange Lambeth had come to realise that he had not in fact ever been an indentured apprentice: 'Did you understand the question when you were asked?'; 'No'. Such evidence suggests that enumeration from indenture records would very seriously underestimate the proportion of the manufacturing labour force thinking of themselves as 'regular' and to that degree as skilled.[8]

The level of skill required and a seven-year learning period needed for their effective practice, were real barriers to entry for some crafts. But in many (according to Adam Smith in most) apprenticeship was insisted upon primarily as a means of restricting entry to occupations capable of being learned in less than seven years. The object was to prevent 'overstocking'. In noting that in England the laws of apprenticeship had remained in force 'down to the end of the manufacturing period' Marx conceded that in part the distinction between skilled and unskilled labour had come to rest on barriers 'that survive only by virtue of a traditional convention' and by the fact that the 'helpless' condition of other groups of the working class prevented them from exacting equally with the skilled workers the value of their labour power.[9] In effect unions of skilled workers struggled to preserve and control apprenticeship as a functional equivalent of the modern 'closed shop': collective action increasingly replaced regulation by state or corporation as the means of restricting entry.

The period of manufacture was crucially one of transition. Had it been otherwise then resistance in defence of traditional or customary expectations would hardly have been as evident. The specialisation of labour increased and the separation of the worker both from the ownership of the materials upon which he worked and from the sale of the product of his labour became widespread. Nor was the period one of static technology. Historians have only just begun to appreciate the significance of technical changes in the period. These stopped short of mechanising production, but enabled very considerable productivity increases to take place in some manufacturing processes which remained still dependent on manual pace. Sometimes product changes in the direction of cheaper, less 'fully-fashioned' goods were significant in their impact on workers. General Ludd was not opposing the introduction of new machinery, but the employment of less-skilled labour on the knitting frames to turn out inferior stockings at lower wages:

> Till full fashioned work at the old fashioned price
> Is established by custom and law.
> Then the Trade when this ardorous contest is o'er
> Shall raise in full splendour its head

And colting and cutting and squaring no more
Shall deprive honest workmen of bread.[10]

Marx drew special attention to the workshop as a new form of social production: 'a product of the manufacturing division of labour' which in time, through its application of detailed labour, was to produce the machines which 'made an end of handiwork as the regulative principle of social production'.[11]

II

English skilled workers from the beginning of the eighteenth century down to about 1820 are the subject of this study. By others and by themselves they were commonly referred to as 'artisans'. It is a label fraught with difficulty and ambiguity. In some usages it suggests independent master craftsmen trading in a product made up from materials which they themselves owned: perhaps being themselves the employers of one or two journeymen. Contemporary usage was wider. In England especially, such independent masters were by the middle years of the eighteenth century a small part of those designated artisans. Skilled workers in general were so considered. The term generally described those who through apprenticeship or its equivalent had come to possess a skill in a particular craft and the right to exercise it. This restriction on entry was crucial. In some crafts the required level of skill was a genuine barrier, but in many others apprenticeship was rather an institutional limit on entry.[12]

Adam Smith wrote of twenty men working for wages for every one who was his own master and throughout the *Wealth of Nations* wages are understood to be 'what they usually are' that is, the contract of a worker who was one person with the owner of the stock which employed him who was another.[13] Twenty to one as a generalisation for Europe may be thought a ratio as notional as the Biblical forty years, but it certainly gives the correct impression for England, the economy with the most proletarianised labour force. Even so there were significant manufacturing towns and regions, notably the metal trades of Birmingham and Sheffield where specialised small-workshop production allowed a rather smaller ratio of master to men to persist. It has been calculated that by the end of the eighteenth century only five or six per cent of the working-class population of London, by far England's largest centre of artisanal production, were self-employed.[14] In England the class of permanent journeymen in urban trades was very large. Some occupations with low capital costs still allowed the traditional mobility from apprentice through journeyman to master. In the building trades men could move then, as they do today, from taking on contracts to working for wages as opportunities or need dictated. In some trades the movement away from self-employment was in progress. The larger shoemakers tried in 1738 to freeze out the small independent shoemakers and make them available for wage hire by seeking a governmental prohibition on the sale of leather in pieces smaller than the whole hide.[15] Even the pinmakers celebrated by Adam Smith as the classic illustration of the advantages of the division of labour, had at the beginning of the eighteenth century worked at home on small parcels of wire bought from second- or even third-hand dealers and sold their output weekly.[16]

Such independent production on purchased materials was not the usual case. Indeed it was not necessarily a desirable one. Skilled workers could be reduced to this kind of independence through inability to secure regular paid journeywork and could be among the poorest of their craft. Such 'garret' or 'chamber' masters were often looked down on by regular journeymen, whose powerful unions constrained their activities, as among the hatters for example.[17] When the London compositors complained in 1809 that high capital costs condemned them to permanent wage slavery whereas in other trades there was 'a moral certainty' of diligent and thrifty workers setting up as independent masters, they were greatly overstating the case.[18] Printers, with wages of £1 a week, according to Dr Johnson, for not particularly hard or especially skilled labour, belonged to that class of well-organised, regularly employed artisans like shearmen, masons, cabinetmakers, hatters and others, who earned more and were more regularly employed than most struggling 'garret masters'. Only fifty of London's hatters still worked on their own in 1777, a year in which their powerful 'congress' was giving their employers much cause for concern by preventing them from taking on the number of apprentices they would have wished and securing an effective 'closed shop'.[19] Until deskilled by machinery at the beginning of the nineteenth century, calico printers controlled recruitment and secured wages and conditions which lead one employer to dub them 'gentlemen journeymen'. It was the ability to preserve status and well-being which was the chief concern of most artisans rather than an ideal of self-employment.[20]

The small working clothiers of the West Riding buying their own wool and selling their cloth produced with the aid of one or two journeymen were much commented on as an exception to the organisation of labour in cloth manufacture generally. In the other main areas of production, in the west country and in East Anglia, master weavers were effectively a wage-earning labour force making cloth from yarn 'put out' by master clothiers, merchant capitalists who then marketed the finished cloth. The framework knitters of the east midlands were similarly paid by the piece for making stockings from yarn put out by master hosiers. Cutlers and other metal workers were also dependent upon the piece-rates paid by merchant capitalists.[21] Wage-earning craft workers of varying degrees of skill in town and country made up a large fraction of those engaged in English manufacture before 1820: if they were an 'elite' they were hardly a small one.[22]

From time to time such artisans sufficiently shared the perspectives of their employers to justify historians talking of a vertical consciousness of the trade, rather than of horizontal cleavage between masters and men. Common cause might be made, for example in seeking protection from 'ruinous' foreign competition. At times smaller masters might make common cause with journeymen against more capitalistically inclined employers seeking to use methods which threatened the well-being of both. However, it is to fly in the face of the evidence of endemic disputes to deny a form of labour consciousness to skilled workers before the industrial revolution.[23]

III

Of the values and assumptions which underlay the consciousness of skilled workers the most significant, because the most fundamental, was their sense of possessing a 'property of skill'. Until the late eighteenth century this was assumed rather than articulated. The right was implicit in the solidarity of the trade. Special forms of clothing such as the mason's leather apron and the ownership of the proper tools indicated its possession. Participation in ceremonies reinforced it, while attitudes towards outsiders, 'strangers', defined it. Statute or corporative law was presumed to guarantee it, while mythologies conferred upon it the legitimation of 'time immemorial'. Dr Linebaugh has contrasted the 'artisanal anonymity' of authorship of the wooden ship, the embodiment of the collective labour of the shipwrights and other yard craftsmen with the Great Western, an iron ship, 'a capitalist creation', named for Brunel, the great engineer.[24] The point is well made, but there is another dimension. The whole work, the ship, may have had 'anonymity of authorship', but its separate parts could reveal to those in the trade the handiwork of small groups or individuals. A skilled man could often recognise his own work and describe it still as 'his' work even when it had been alienated from him by sale. This hidden form of property, an element of continuing 'creative possession' is missed by a concept of property limited to a nation of alienated material rights, yet it describes the property that skill invents.[25]

The sense of a property of skill was then deeply embedded in the culture and consciousness of the artisan, as was the assumption of the respect of others for it. This respect seemed to be about to be withdrawn in the late eighteenth century and the beginning of the nineteenth century when the position of artisans was under threat of degradation. Then they articulated what they had always assumed, a specific rhetoric of property. In 1818 the *Gorgon*, commenting on disputes in the London printing trade, recognised that compositors acted from 'principle of self preservation' and from the 'very praiseworthy motive of preserving themselves from degradation'. This was based on the right earned by every workman who had served a proper apprenticeship. Not receiving a full remuneration for his labour during that time, he acquired in fact 'a property in his trade, for which he has paid the full price'. To expect submission to the lessening of the 'value of this property' was to expect an unreal degree of disinterestedness.[26] An address of 1818 to 'Brother Mechanics' – a term not used to describe the unskilled – warned that the despotism of the Combination Laws was removing their freedom in the disposition of 'the only species of property' they possessed, 'labour and talent'.[27] The watchmakers declared in 1817

...the apprenticed artisans have collectively and individually, an unquestionable right to expect the most extended protection from the Legislature, in the quiet and exclusive use and enjoyment of their several and respective arts and trades, which the law has already conferred upon them as a property, as much as it has secured the property of the stock-holder in the public funds; and it is as clearly unjust to take away the whole of the ancient and established property and rights of any one class of the community unless at the same time, the rights and property of the whole commonwealth should be dissolved, and parcelled out for the public good.[28]

IV

This was in bitter reaction to the repeal in 1814 of those clauses of the Statute of Artificers of 1564 which had required the serving of an apprenticeship to the skilled trades. The act was part of the collective memory of artisans, a legitimating basis for their actions in restraint of entry. The time of 'Good Queen Bess' was remembered in a verse of the saddlers:

> Her memory still is dear to journeymen,
> For sheltered by her laws, now they resist
> Infringements, which would else persist:
> Tyrannic masters, innovating fools
> Are check'd, and bounded by her glorious rules.
> Of workmen's rights she's still a guarantee
> The rights of artisans, to fence and guard.[29]

Even before the repeal of V Elizabeth was in question, some apprenticeship abuses were causing skilled journeymen to protest at threats to their 'property'. Facing the growth of disguised cheap labour in the form of 'outdoor' apprenticeship, whereby large numbers of boys were taken on not to live with and learn from their masters but to be paid low wages and cheaply lodged, the compositors of London saw a threat to the 'just and honourable means of subsistence' which had been obtained by the 'care and purchase of their parents and friends and by a legal servitude of seven years'.[30] Some authorities would deny to the handloom weavers of the early nineteenth century any pretensions to skilled status, but those in cotton were still insisting in 1823:

The weaver's qualifications may be considered as his property and support. It is as real property to him as buildings and lands are to others. Like them his qualifications cost time, application and money.[31]

Twelve years later after further increasing and intensifying competition from the factory, the *Weavers' Journal* was no longer claiming to speak for an occupation still within the ranks of the 'aristocracy of labour', but expressed the firm belief that 'property rights' still existed for other crafts and were properly supported by 'internal regulations'. No censure was due to those who, in seeking the due reward for their skilled labour, would 'bar the door against every intruder': should they do otherwise, they would be 'blind, mean, overawed or infatuated' in not acting in protection of their labour, which was 'their lawful property'.[32]

V

On the matter of 'lawful' property, the common law jurists had severe misgivings. Blackstone recognised that V Elizabeth had the authority of statute law, but thought it bad law nevertheless:

At common law everyman might use what trade he pleased but this restrains that liberty to such as have served apprenticeships ... the resolutions of the courts have in general rather confined than extended the restriction.[33]

Here the great lawyer was commenting upon a number of cases over two centuries in which judges' rulings had considerably worn away the firm edges of formal indentured servitude insisted upon in the statute. Most notable of these had been the decision that only those trades which had been in existence at the time of its passing were covered by the act. Recruitment of labour to industries like cotton was therefore not governed by it, and in a famous judgement Lord Mansfield refused to extend it to Lancashire weavers when in 1756 they sought to be placed under its protection when faced with an influx of cheap labour.[34] He argued both from the principles of common law and from the interests of trade, as did Richard Burn in the eighteenth century's most-used justice's handbook:

Indiscriminately to arraign the wisdom of our ancestors in requiring a long apprenticeship in all trades, might be deemed rash and presumptuous. It does not, however, therefore follow that regulations adopted in the infancy of trade and commerce, or even in their progress to a comparative state of perfection ... are never to be altered in conformity to existing circumstances.[35]

Behind the condemnation of apprenticeship lay the considerable weight of Adam Smith. No name was more often quoted in the contest between the organised trades and the employer interest which preceded the repeal of statutory apprenticeship in 1814. Smith had declared the institution to offend against 'the most sacred and inviolable property' which every man had in his own labour to exercise in whatever manner he thought fit which did no harm to his neighbour.[36]

The property of skill was not just a line to be defended against employers, but a frontier to be held against the unskilled they might seek to employ. It was an exclusive property and among those excluded were most women. Girls were more completely excluded from the skilled crafts in the period of manufacture than they had been in the guild era. Apprenticeships in the sense of genuine training for a trade were hardly open to them. Even where revenue and indenture sources indicate a sizeable number of girls being apprenticed to craftsmen there can be no presumption that learning a trade was the basis of the agreement: a girl would as likely be bound to a weaving household as a general servant. The effect of the rise of the journeymen's unions in reinforcing a gender exclusion already inherent in the operation of apprenticeship was noted seventy years ago by Alice Clark and has been recently re-emphasised. Sally Alexander has remarked that the successive steps in the breakdown of the handicraft system: exclusion from the guilds; the separation of home from workplace and the formation of trade unions further undermined the position of women in the labour market, while having the rebound effect of making them a source of cheap labour ready for the next stage when with machinery and the factory system the skilled men could be dislodged. Maxine Berg has argued that over the eighteenth century a striking difference emerged between the cultural and community basis of rural or family based manufacture and that of the workshop trades. In the latter, exclusion of women entailed the rise of 'moral communities of artisans' jealously defending 'independence' and 'rights' and involved in association outside as well as inside the workplace in ritual, custom and the male world of the public house. The point is an important one and the division in principle a real one. However, the two worlds are not wholly separable into workshop and cottage manufacture. Weaving was an occupation very largely carried on in the home, depending upon a family input of labour and one in which women increasingly took their place at the loom as well as the wheel. The dilution of the labour force clearly evident by the beginning of the nineteenth century has led some historians to suggest that handloom weavers should not be thought of as skilled labour. Yet the trade illustrates how very gradually a craft underwent the value changes associated with dilution and deskilling. Values not incongruent with those of the urban craftsmen emerged in the weavers' struggle of 1800–02 in the west country against the growth of weaving shops. The weavers petitioned for a proper enforcement of statutory apprenticeship and employed a lawyer to prosecute 'illegal' weavers. This resort to an old defence came in a region where women quite commonly wove and where many of the male weavers had themselves not served apprenticeships by formal indenture.[37]

It has been noted by Sally Alexander that although whole communities of weavers and knitters participated in the defence of customary rights, whenever community resistance was formally organised with democratically elected committees with powers to negotiate with employers, justices of the peace, and government representatives the men were in the forefront and were the spokesmen, women having been excluded from 'these forms of public speech'.[38] The vocabulary of grievance which underlay that public speech was that of skilled men and it responded to their sense of disinheritance of the right to practise their trades. In mind too was their status as fathers and heads of families as well as their independence through 'honourable' labour and their property in skill. Indeed, as Joyce has suggested, patriarchal values could supply a shared perspective of capital and labour, since the masculinity of skilled work could be a basis for various understandings with employers.[39] In fact definitions of skilled and unskilled work were as much rooted in social and gender distinctions as in technical aptitude. The product of nimble female fingers was often less valued than that produced by men with less dexterity. Josiah Wedgwood in the 1770s paid women flower painters only two-thirds of the usual rate for skilled men. In the growing cotton manufacture new occupations such as mule-spinning and weaving on Dutch looms were taken on by males and accordingly defined as skilled and as having a justified restriction over entry.[40]

Skill was then clearly a male 'property' and in that it was the distinguishing mark separating the artisan from the common labourer, it also represented a symbolic capital, an 'honour', the possession of which entitled its holder to dignity and respect as well as imposing the obligation of the proper performance of his craft. A language stressing value to the commonwealth, worth, pride and status characterises the early nineteenth-century manifestos of artisans.[41] The words 'honourable' and 'dishonourable' have themselves an eighteenth-century usage in distinguishing the better from the less-esteemed trades. Where artisans worked alongside labourers, as they commonly did in building, relations between the two clearly reflected the distance insisted upon by the former. Alexander Somerville worked as a labourer in a Scottish quarry in 1830 and found the masons to be 'intolerable tyrants' to 'the labourers'. Objecting to a presumed right of physical chastisement, he was offered the choice of having the work cease by a masons' strike or submitting to ritual punishment. This was to be held down over a stone while the masons' apprentices struck hard in turn with their knotted leather aprons. Leather aprons were the traditional wear of the skilled masons and the symbolism of the proposed humiliation is evident.[42]

Respect was also expected from employers. I know of no English incident as telling as that of the French journeyman who quit in anger when his employer dared to sit down at table without awaiting him. But Holyoake, after noting the harsh face which Birmingham's engineering employers commonly displayed towards their workers, noted that they behaved in a very different manner towards a handful of highly skilled men.[43] A poem composed, significantly, after journeymen had been defending their interests in a strike, displays as much a concern for mutual respect as it does for industrial harmony. It is from the London silk weavers in 1773:

> And may no treacherous, base, designing men
> E'er make encroachments on our rights again;
> May upright masters still augment their treasure,
> And journeymen pursue their work with pleasure.[44]

Similar sentiments were expressed by London's journeymen cabinet-makers at the beginning of a book of prices which they published in 1788. They denied that they were seeking to impose upon their employers, rather they were seeking to 'conciliate mutual regard – to be treated as men possessing an ingenious art'.[45]

Proper treatment of skilled men by their masters included no interference in the way in which they did their work, so long as properly made goods were produced to the quantum regarded as normal by the trade – 'full fashioned work at the old fashioned price' – as the Luddites put it.[46] There were several ways through which work control at the operational level was in the hands of the artisans. Hatters were expected to produce a given output, but although they worked on their employers' premises, they kept no fixed hours, coming and going at those of their own choosing. Skilled tailors' societies themselves fixed the measure of the output

which was 'a fair day's labour for a fair day's pay'. They would not allow
any workman who could not achieve it membership of the society, thus effectively excluding the inferior craftsmen from the better shops.[47] Under
the apprenticeship system, it was the skilled journeymen, rather than the
capitalist employers who had the training of the craft apprentices. Thus
the learner acquired his knowledge of the work practices of the trade as he
learned its skills. An apprentice in a silk-weaving mill in the early nineteenth century has recorded how he was always willing to do errands for
the journeymen, who in return showed him 'how to manage things that I
might have asked the foreman in vain to instruct me in'.[48]

Composition and ordering of the work-gang was frequently determined by the journeymen. Leaders, known as 'clickers' headed 'com-
panionships' of compositors evenly dividing the work among them
according to its difficulty. Naval shipwrights insisted that work-teams
were 'shoalled', that it made up of a mix of young and old, good and less
good workmen.[49]

There are several remaining questions about the nature of skill as a
property. We have noted the nature of its restrictiveness and we should
also note that its seeming contradiction of individual 'rights' earned the
dislike of jurists and economists. Radicals proclaiming the 'rights of man'
found difficulties as well. Thomas Paine recognised that laws which were
in existence for 'regulating and limiting workmen's wages' denied them
the freedom to make bargains over the 'personal labour' which was 'all
the property they have'. In proclaiming the virtues of the French Constitution in 1791 he seems to praise its insistence that 'all trades shall be free,
and everyman free to follow any occupation by which he can procure an
honest livelihood'.[50] Professor Dickinson has commented that very few
English radicals of the 1790s seriously considered using the economic
power of the working classes to bring pressure on their opponents: 'While
the workers themselves were beginning to combine to improve their
wages and conditions of work the radical theorists failed to perceive that
strikes and the protests of organised labour might be the most effective
means of bringing pressure to bear on the propertied classes.' The governing classes were terrified of the threat of 'combinations' yet the radicals
were for the most part too limited by middle-class conceptions of society
to recognise their potential.[51] A deeper reason may be the contradiction
between 'rights' of individuals and the rights of associations. Discussion
of the right to associate, denied of course to French journeymen under the
Le Chapelier law of 1791 was fraught with ambiguity.[52] There is an irony
in the petitioning of the prime minister, Lord Liverpool – often held to
have headed a 'counterrevolutionary' government – by a group of skilled
workers, the watchmakers, in 1817. They told him that in allowing the

repeal of statutory apprenticeship, he had bowed to the 'pretensions to the allowance of universal uncontrolled freedom of action to every individual' which had fostered the French Revolution and which, if allowed to prevail would 'hasten the destruction of the social system' so happily established by the British Constitution.[53] The irony however is for the historian to remark. It was probably not conscious on the part of the journeymen. Linda Colley has described the growth in loyalty over the reign of George III and its relationship to an 'anti-democratic' brand of patriotism which emerged in the French wars, 'a trend towards greater national consciousness' and the public's 'considerable acquiescence in the existing order'. It is hardly surprising that a group of artisans imbued with traditional and patriarchal values and whose rhetoric had come to insist on the value to the nation of their skilled labour should express such a sentiment.[54]

It is fundamental that the property of skill was not viewed as an individual property right, but as a collective one. Even though it was in part an inheritable property which fathers could pass on to sons, what was inherited was rather the use right to be exercised within the regulations and constraints imposed by the trade. This has already been discussed in the case of weaving, but it was widespread among the crafts. Dr Vincent is correct to stress that the arrangement and successful supervision of an apprenticeship was in the nineteenth century still the most important contribution that a father could make to his son's future prosperity, but entry to a father's trade often did not require formal binding. The Webbs wrote of 'patrimony' as a privilege of skilled workers from 'time immemorial' exempting from legal binding. A basketmaker from Bristol remarked in 1813 that many in that city who 'claim a right to work at the business' were sons of masters and journeymen and had served no formal apprenticeship. In some trades the right extended to all sons. In tobacco-pipe making for example, it was 'the custom to allow the children to follow the business', but in other cases the need to maintain strength in the labour market restricted the right: 'I was brought up under my father; it is a rule in our trade for the eldest son to claim to work at that trade' explained a fellmonger.[55]

The most evident obligation was for the craftsman not to accept work below the agreed rates or 'prices'. Within local labour markets these might sometimes be defined as 'customary' and prevail for long periods. A west-country weaver spoke in 1802 of a rate which had not changed through the twenty-six years of his working life: 'Nor yet in my father's memory'. In Gloucestershire in 1756–7 weavers were seeking to defend a rate which had been previously fixed at Quarter Sessions. Well-organised journeymen like printers and cabinetmakers had detailed printed price books which, even before the end of the eighteenth century, could be lengthy. The limits of the local labour market could be extended to some extent by the tramping system which brought intelligence of rates prevailing elsewhere. Journeymen who accepted lower rates might receive sanctioning visits from bodies of workers or be declared 'unfair' or 'foul' so that honourable artisans would not work alongside them or for their employers.[56]

There was concern for more than just the rate; the form of the wage was important. Skilled tailors allowed union members to accept work only at time wages and on the employers' premises. This was their defence against the advance of the sweating system with its piece-rate paid home work. The shipwrights of Liverpool refused to accept a system of piece-rates which, while it was rewarding to the younger and fitter men, was leading to the laying off of older men. The cabinetmakers, on the other hand, were by 1788 already specifying piece-rates in very great detail as a defence against the production of poor quality ready-made furniture. In the naval dockyards the introduction of 'task' work was resisted not only because it was thought that the intensification of labour would be a threat to health, but also because a change in the form of the wage might have threatened the basis on which overtime had been customarily calculated.[57]

Self-seeking individuals who declined to observe the customs of the trade met with the sanctioning disapproval of their comrades. Offending compositors found their type had been mixed by the 'chapel ghost'. Deviant cabinetmakers found the loss of their tools attributed to 'Mother Shorney', while in Sheffield similar sanctions were known as 'rattening'. In a number of trades workshop 'courts' inflicted fines or other punishment, for example in hatting, printing and in cabinetmaking.[58]

A critical area of control lay in ensuring that ambitious men did not engross more than their fair share of available work. When a newcomer to a London printing shop worked eighty-two hours in his first week, he was disconcerted to receive pay for fewer hours. The compositors had agreed a sixty-hour maximum week and he was told that his extra hours would be carried over to the next week for part of which he would have to 'mike' (idle). Liverpool shipwrights who took more than their share of work were 'drilled': that is, their fellows refused to work with them for a period of time thereby preventing them from working. By the beginning of the nineteenth century the union in the Thames yards had ensured that work was fairly distributed.[59]

It was crucial that the practices of the trade were followed by its practitioners if artisans were to retain control over the labour process and to resist the imposing by innovating employers of work routines which would intensify labour in the presumed interest of productivity or wage-saving. To this end, as Dr Behagg has shown, the workshop was partly a secret world, whose detailed practices are difficult for the historian to uncover precisely because they were protected from full knowledge by other than those who had been properly admitted to the 'mystery' of the craft.[60] Indeed that old word carried important meanings and indicated a sense of brotherhood, belonging, and rightful possession which more prosaic terms hardly impart. Ceremony and legend reaching back to a presumed antiquity are not as evident a feature of English journeymen's organisations as they are of French *compagnonnages*. They were nevertheless important inputs into the sense of solidarity crucial to the trade.

Processions marked the days dedicated to the various patron saints as it did the funerals of craft brothers. Ceremony was also evident in elaborate rituals marking initiation of apprentices. Conviviality was reinforced in the customary 'treatings' to beer expected from new entrants to shops or upon promotion. As Benjamin Franklin was to find in his days as a London printer, failure to meet traditional expectations in this area could bring as immediate a retribution as the breach of any other of the customs of the trade. The fines extracted by workshop courts were commonly spent on drink for the shop.[61]

Behagg has shown that workplace solidarity extended into after work hours. Particular public houses were patronised and used for other purposes than simply social drinking. Tailors used certain pubs as 'houses of call' where masters seeking labour could make contact with journeymen seeking work. Pubs served as headquarters for what might be termed 'union business' and for benefit clubs and friendly societies. Taking care of the needs of fellows and their dependents at times of distress was a major manifestation of the mutuality and pride of the artisan. Independence in this respect was highly valued. In hard times the common labourer had to fall upon the parish, but, boasted the watchmakers in 1817, 'it was scarcely known that any person in this trade ever applied for parochial relief'.[62]

VI

It has become a commonplace for historians of the labour movements of the early nineteenth century to stress their domination by artisans rather than by the newly emerging factory proletariat. Tailors, carpenters, shoemakers, building craftsmen, print workers and the like were the vanguard of a labour struggle which was 'born in the craft workshops, not in the dark satanic mill'.[63] This verdict has been delivered for France and for Germany as well as for England. Edward Thompson's classic study of *The*

Making of the English Working Class between 1790 and 1832 has been
said to describe not the rise of a working class in a form which has ever
since persisted, but artisans becoming politically active.[64] In the *Communist Manifesto*, Marx and Engels placed artisans as among those who
fought the bourgeoisie defensively. They had a reactionary rather than a
revolutionary consciousness in that they tried to 'roll back the wheel of
history'. They could develop a revolutionary consciousness only if,
through perception of their impending transfer into it, they deserted their
own standpoint for that of the proletariat.[65] Possibly Marx and Engels
had self-employed artisans chiefly in mind, although their ambivalent attitude to events in Germany in 1848 suggests that their insistence on the
factory proletariat as the destined bearer of revolutionary class consciousness blinkered them from a full understanding of the significance of
skilled workers in the development of labour organisation and consciousness and of socialist ideology.

If we accept that artisans were central in early nineteenth-century
labour protest, then, inevitably, many of the artisan values which we have
been describing for the 'period of manufacture' must be considered inputs
into the formative years of working-class consciousness, which in
England may be considered those stretching from the French Wars to
Owenism and Chartism. In an outstanding study of London during this
period, Dr Prothero understands artisans to have been members of the
'old specialised unrevolutionised handworking trades with a certain
amount of skill, but within wide limits a definite status connotation'. The
values which he ascribes to them have clear continuity with the eighteenth
century: concern for status and respectability, aversion to charity, emphasis on traditional privileges, conception of proper remuneration in traditional rather than in market terms, guild or guild-like ideas of
regulation of the labour supply, welfare concerns, labour funds, tramping
systems.[66] Indeed in many instances skilled workers reacting to pressures
upon their customary expectations and ways, explicitly looked back to a
past when their rights had been respected.

Historians have tended to pour scorn on notions of a 'golden age'.
Rightly so when it has been indiscriminately applied to a generalised pre-
industrial past. However when early-nineteenth-century artisans looked
back it was usually to more recent memories of better days. Cotton
weavers looked back to 1788 to 1803; framework knitters to 1755 to
1785 or possibly to 1809. The point is that as well as a folk memory of the
distant days of 'Good Queen Bess' or whatever, there was a much more
immediately relevant one for many groups who could date very closely
when decline set in for them. Sometimes, as with calico printers and wool
combers and shearmen, it had been caused by the introduction of machin-

ery, but more often it had been brought about by falling piece-rates as capitalist employers reorganised and restructured hand production in the direction of supplying ready-made goods from less skilled, sweated labour. Mayhew found many handworkers who spoke of recent better times: a shoemaker who began work in 1815 and who up to the 1820s could afford to play his '£1 a corner at whist' although he thought he had not been born soon enough to have seen the really good times and a sawyer remembered the times before machines had become capable of cutting the thin veneers, up to 1826 it had been 'as good a time for sawyers as ever it was'.[67]

Artisan attitudes persisted even into new work contexts. The first adult male factory workers of significance were the mule spinners. They defended their essential skill, restricted and controlled recruitment to their ranks and controlled the pace and intensity of labour. It has been suggested that despite the seeming incongruity they should be regarded as 'factory artisans'.[68] Some of what might be considered artisan values were emphasised more in the nineteenth century than they had been in the eighteenth. Readers of Frances Place's autobiography discover that status had always been important, but that marking that status by 'respectable' rather than 'rough' behaviour was in the closing decades of the eighteenth and early years of the nineteenth centuries a developing rather than a continuing characteristic. Place and others wrote of a discernible movement towards more ordered habits, sobriety and 'respectability' among London's artisans and their view was endorsed by Dorothy George. She claimed an improved status for the poorer classes as the 'average' working man became more educated, self-respecting and respected. There was an increase in parental ambitions for children, a new respect between masters and men, a 'growing spirit of providence and independence' witnessed in the increase of friendly societies and the decrease in drunkenness. This improvement for the 'average' man is misleading. Linebaugh is closer to the process at work when he writes of a division in the London working class between a predominantly artisan section already by the early nineteenth century operating within a wage-hierarchy and increasingly capable of organising itself politically, and the mass of the labouring poor 'distrusted by democrat and trade unionist alike for its fatalism' and largely antipathetic to wage discipline, being rough and ready to live by its wits.[69] It was from this more robust culture that artisans of Place's kind were drawing apart, if only to hold it at arm's length.

While it is true that artisans as a class had opportunities for education and leisure usages which were hardly available to the working people in general, Professor Hobsbawm's suggestion that irregular employment and fluctuating material standards provided conditions of too little permanence for the development of an 'aristocracy of labour' in the nineteenth-century sense of a distinctive cultural grouping seems well founded.[70] Fluctuating fortunes meant that for particular groups of artisans displaying cultural superiority was conditional and temporary. Ways of life characteristic of good times could, in worsening ones, be pushed to oblivion. Periods of secure employment and good earnings brought not only money but time. Then there could be leisure activities and the children could be spared from labour for schooling and wives from the need to toil the whole day alongside their husbands. For some there was time for the ale-house and robust sport, but for others for music or recreation. Sanderson has emphasised the decline in literacy among Lancashire's cotton weavers which accompanied their falling fortunes.[71] Samuel Bamford described his weaver father as a 'superior man' for his station in life in his liking for books and music, 'all in all he stood far above his rustic acquaintance in the village'. But Bamford senior in himself bridged the rough and respectable cultures of late eighteenth-century Lancashire. He was a good wrestler and at times still associated with the 'wild rough fellows' at the ale-house and danced, drank or, at times, fought with 'the moodiest or merriest of them'.[72] Where the material basis was secure enough, as in the Birmingham described by William Hutton, an artisan culture of independence, with a leisure dimension, a good level of literacy and a mutuality expressed through clubs and societies was discernible.[73]

To some historians studying the second half of the nineteenth century the formation and consolidation of an 'aristocracy of labour' was crucial in the accommodation of the working-class vanguard into the values of the capitalist economy.[74] The consciousness which spread among skilled workers in the early nineteenth century was neither of that kind, nor was it of the revolutionary form which Marx envisaged would be displayed by the factory proletariat as industrial capitalism developed. As we have seen, in the sense that they sold labour power rather than the product of their labour and were accordingly wage dependent whatever the form of the wage, large numbers of skilled workers in eighteenth-century England constituted a proletariat. Although within a 'craft consciousness' which certainly had a vertical dimension, they had in many trades developed a labour consciousness and enacted it in forms of collective pressure which suggest 'trade union consciousness'.

Just as Edward Thompson has characterised the labouring poor of the eighteenth century as 'rebellious' in the sense that a traditional culture was resisting in the name of custom and law those economic innovations which employers and, increasingly, rulers sought to impose, so labour movements of the early nineteenth century became radical in the defence of 'rights', standards, and traditional work practices.[75] As Stedman Jones has pointed out, they faced a developing capitalism at a time when its triumph did not seem inevitable. From this perspective Chartism was more than a tactical failure, 'it was the end of an epoch in which industrial capitalism itself had hung in the balance'.[76] To many in the England of the time the triumph of the machine seemed neither inevitable nor desirable, to others, notably Robert Owen, the benefits of the factory system were realisable without the evil consequences of 'competition' for the working people.

But for most groups of artisans who experienced decline and degradation in the early nineteenth century, the factory was not the direct cause. The anti-capitalist ideas which emerged were those appropriate to artisans facing 'merchant capitalism' in the form of monopolistic middlemen reorganising production in garment making, shoemaking or cabinet-making for the ready-made trade, or in building displacing the autonomy of the craftsman through 'general contracting'.[77] In so far as proletarianisation results from the appropriation of the product leaving the worker with no ownership stake in the productive process in which he is engaged then, as we have seen, it was a process well under way before the beginning of the eighteenth century and continuing with greater momentum through it. But there is another sense of appropriation beside that of the product and that is the appropriation of nature: what Marx understood as the subjection of the craft worker to the control and discipline of capital. While the factory system with its supervised labour and its machine-dictated rhythm of work is seen as the ultimate stage in this process, indeed it could be argued that full control over the labour process only becomes a possibility with the advent of industrialisation, it is clear that in a period when the factory system was in its infancy, larger numbers of workers faced intensification of labour and declining incomes through organisational changes which were only sometimes linked to technological developments.[78] They saw themselves as being exploited not by the factory master but by the merchant organiser of domestic production. That he performed no manufacturing function helped to identify this form of capitalist as 'parasitic' and 'non-productive'. By seeing themselves, therefore, as the true producers many depressed artisans came to identify themselves as 'labour' opposed to 'capital'. As Dr Prothero has amply shown this was not a false consciousness, for most who held it, it was an accurate analysis of their situation, just as the remedies to be found in Owenism and in Chartism aimed at restoring to skilled labour its proper dignity and well-being.[79]

In the early nineteenth century capitalist restructuring of production and of work advanced on a broad front and it was the shared experiences of workers in different trades which enabled that labour consciousness confined in the eighteenth century to the craft to become something wider. Many historians are sceptical of the extent to which consciousness broadened and insist that most skilled workers continued to protect their own craft interests aloof from wider concerns.[80] Yet there can be no doubt that however much the impact of general trade unionism in the early nineteenth century is played down, it remains a manifestation of a wider labour consciousness which is hardly thinkable in the eighteenth-century context. Dr Behagg has shown for Birmingham how a wider consciousness emerged among the metal-working artisans in the 1820s.[81] Political repression, in particular the attempts at proscription of trade unions added to the growing sense of oppression and of embattlement, as did the increasing disillusionment with the regulative intervention of government.[82] The exclusiveness of a craft-bound trade union consciousness broke down only gradually and far from completely and even when and where it did so it was capable of reassertion.[83] In general, because it attempted to retain a frontier between the skilled and the unskilled it could never develop naturally into a broad-based working class consciousness – even if at times an awareness of this strayed uncomfortably into the discourse of Owenism – but it was an historically specific labour consciousness which identified 'capitalism' as the enemy, labour as the source of wealth, and which reflected the real experiences of artisans and seemed congruent with their traditional values.[84]

5

'L'ouvrière! Mot impie, sordide...': women workers in the discourse of French political economy, 1840–1860

JOAN W. SCOTT

L'ouvrière! Pour tous ceux qui, comme Jules Simon, ont lu dans le grand livre de la vie réelle, ce mot sonne aux oreilles comme le synonyme, comme le résumé des choses cruelles: douleurs, privations, misères, prostitution.

Hippolyte Dussard, *Le Journal des économistes*, 1861

At the Paris Salon of 1861 Auguste-Barthélemy Glaize exhibited a painting called 'Misery the Procuress'. The picture is dominated by an old hag, shredded rags exposing an ugly drooping breast and bare leg. She drags a walking stick (her stance recalls figures of Death) and points or beckons with crooked fingers to the lights of a distant city. Behind her, working assembled around a candle, are some earnest young women in rural clothing. One holds a spindle; beside her is a spinning wheel. In front of the hag are a group of voluptuous, naked women, spilling out of or on to a horse-drawn chariot that is moving rapidly towards the city. The painting depicts not so much a static contrast as a narrative of transition: from country to city, from traditional to modern society, from order to disorder, from appropriately female attire and behaviour to sensual degradation and corruption. The transformation of wise into foolish virgins is effected by the old woman, whose hideousness warns us, but somehow not her victims, of the fate that awaits them. For the artist, it was also important that his subjects were workers. 'How many young women,' he wrote in the catalogue, 'giving up work, throw themselves into all the vices brought on by debauchery in order to escape this spectre that seems always to pursue them?'[1] The spectre was, of course, Misery, defined in the words of one critic of the time, as 'the mother of despair and infamy, of prostitution of all kinds'. But Glaize's words were as ambiguous about causality as was his painting. For the abandon of the young women seems to emanate from themselves; rather than being driven to a horrible fate, they rush off with a certain pleasurable eagerness to embrace it. Misery is as much a warning about the consequences of unleashing women's (natural? inevitable?) tendencies as she is the cause of their fall.

This ambiguity about women and misery characterised much of the debate about women workers during the nineteenth century, a debate that captured public attention in 1858–60 (the very years Glaize was painting his canvas) with the publication of a number of studies including Julie-Victoire Daubié's, 'La Femme pauvre au XIXe siècle' which won the Academy of Lyon's competition in 1859, and Jules Simon's *L'Ouvrière* (1860). Indeed, the acclaim Glaize's painting received probably stemmed from the fact that he captured so well the terms of his contemporaries' discussion. Maxime du Camp said as much in his comment; he found the painting 'absolutely fantastic and nevertheless fantastically real, comprehensible to all'.[2]

The publication of these studies placed the issue of *l'ouvrière* at the forefront of debates on morality, economic organisation, and the situation of the working classes. It also linked the concerns of political economy with the general debate on women that raged in this period – what one historian has called 'La Querelle des femmes of the Second Empire'. Indeed, the years 1858–60 saw an outpouring of books specifically on Woman: Proudhon's *De la justice dans la Révolution et dans l'église* (1858) foreshadowed his more virulent diatribe, *La Pornocratie ou les femmes dans les temps modernes* (published posthumously in 1871); Michelet's *L'Amour* (1858) and *La Femme* (1860); and the feminist responses to these works by Juliette Lamber Adam, *Idées anti-proudhoniennes sur l'amour, la femme et le mariage* (1858), and Jenny d'Hericourt, *La Femme affranchie* (1860).[3] The question of working women served to focus some concerns about independence, legal status and appropriate female social roles, although it was not central to all aspects of the debate on the woman question.

For economists the theme of *l'ouvrière* was not new in 1858–60, although the subject itself was central as never before. References to women had long figured in the discourse of political economy in nineteenth-century France, if only implicitly or as part of a general discussion of the working classes. That discourse included the voices of theorists propounding a new economic 'science', and critics of all kinds – protectionists who attacked the notion of a free market, moralists who feared that economic development undermined social order, socialists who railed against individualism and competition, and feminists who questioned the effects of new divisions of labour. In fact, it is inaccurate to place these voices in clear opposition to one another as in a formal debate for they overlapped in important ways, forming what Denise Riley has dubbed a 'web of cross references', intersecting at some points, diverging sharply at others.[4] One of the important points of intersection was the representation of working women; a shared conception about femininity, sexuality and social order that permitted the exchange of opinions and ideas about the effects of industrial development on French society.

In this chapter I want to approach the discourse from one perspective, that contained in or directly referred to by political economists. These were the men (and a few women) who took it upon themselves to define the terms of a new science of economics (the workings of the market and of the organisation of the production and distribution of wealth), to codify its laws and discipline its practitioners. They addressed themselves to 'public opinion' and to legislators as they aggressively sought to translate their views into policy. Through public addresses, a journal (*Le Journal des économistes*, founded in 1842), and an organisation (*La Sociétée d'Economie Politique*) they announced their views to the world. They had an eminent representative in the academy – the holder of the chair of Political Economy at the Collège de France – as well as members in the Académie des Sciences Morales et Politiques, chambers of commerce, and local and national government offices. However beleaguered political economists felt as they urged unwilling governments to institute free trade in the 1840s and 50s, they had a crucial impact on the articulation of the new economic order. For, having established the intellectual and institutional power of their science through control of knowledge and access to government, political economists were able to provide the conceptual framework within (and against) which those addressing economic questions had to work.

I

References to working women in the writings of nineteenth-century French political economists were direct and indirect. The figure of the working woman served both as an explicit topic in discussions of poverty, wages, occupations, and the family and as a metaphor for disorder. It is often impossible to separate these usages for, as we shall see, they refer to one another, as is the case in Glaize's painting. Most of the discussions of working women also involved considerations of cities; indeed two kinds of cities and two kinds of problems were constantly evoked. The first was the situation of young women on their own in urban centres such as Paris (*femmes* or *filles isolées*), working for a pittance and so swelling the ranks of the urban poor. The second were the denizens of new manufacturing centres, women who worked long hours tending machines, and who lived in households as members of units that only barely resembled normal families.

Femmes isolées

The term used to refer to independent women workers was ambiguous. In the regime of the policing of prostitution, *femmes isolées* referred to clandestine prostitutes who were not registered in one of the houses where the trade was permitted.[5] In surveys of workers, such as the *Statistique de l'industrie* prepared by the Paris Chamber of Commerce in 1848, *femmes isolées* denoted women wage earners (usually seamstresses or dressmakers), living alone in furnished rooms where they sewed garments at piecerates for the ready-made clothing trades.[6] The fact that the term was the same was not coincidental. Ever since Parent-Duchâtelet's massive study of prostitution in 1836 it was generally recognised that casual prostitutes came from the ranks of working girls.

> Of all the causes of prostitution, particularly in Paris and probably in other large cities, there is none more active than the lack of work and misery, the inevitable result of insufficient wages. What are the earnings of our dressmakers, our seamstresses, our menders, and in general all those who occupy themselves with the needle? ... let one compare ... the price of their labor with that of their dishonor and one will cease to be surprised to see such a great number fall into a disorder that is, so to speak, inevitable.[7]

Parent's analysis also included explanations that were not strictly related to wages or working conditions. He thought that, in addition to misery, 'vanity and the desire to glitter in sumptuous clothing, along with laziness, is one of the most influential causes of prostitution, especially in Paris'.[8] Such desires could run rampant when young women lived and worked outside the surveillance of employers or parents. As the authors of the *Statistique* of 1848 noted, 'dissipation' and 'disorderly conduct' were associated with 'women working in their rooms and ... those who are free to do what they wish at the end of the day'.[9] In fact, the occupational status of such women was, in the eyes of the *Statistique*'s authors, 'doubtful'. It was never clear whether their wages came from respectable work or from prostitution: 'One notices sometimes the traces of a well-being that their avowed occupation cannot justify.'[10] The condition of independence whether it unleashed insatiable desires or brought misery and unemployment led to prostitution.

The luxury and wastefulness associated with prostitution provided a striking contrast both to forms of necessary (and self-regulating) consumption that kept economies functioning and to appropriate (and self-limiting) forms of sexuality. An article in *Le Journal des économistes* in 1842 made the connection between consumption and sexuality explicitly. Its author located criminality not in poverty, but in passion, in 'moral misery' brought on by 'immoderate desires'. He warned against too rapid

an increase in the standard of living of 'the lower orders' which might
overstimulate desire:

We must take care, in seeking to accelerate their progress, not to set in motion a
disordering of their passions.[11]

The interchangeable usages of *femmes isolées* suggested that all such
working women were potential prostitutes, inhabiting a marginal and
unregulated world in which good order – social, economic, moral, political – was subverted. Rhetorically, then, the use of the term *femmes
isolées*, with its ambivalent references, had a double effect: it conflated
certain types of working women with prostitutes and it also identified
sexual licence with misery. The ambivalent causality (misery or bad
morals?) was less important than the association itself because there was
only one cure for sexual licence and that was control.

Commentaries on women workers acknowledged various categories
and forms of female employment, but the situation of *femmes isolées* preoccupied those writing about women workers. Political economists
lauded workshops in which skilled mistresses supervised and instructed
apprentices (the analogy was to mothers and daughters) and they granted
the necessity and the utility for married women to earn wages by combin-
ing home work with domestic chores. But inevitably, their writings passed
over these instances to the question of misery and thus to the dilemma of
the *femmes isolées*.[12] This was because *femmes isolées* revealed the stark
reality of women's economic status; in their pathological condition one
understood the 'natural laws' of women's wages.

What were these laws? As articulated by Jean-Baptiste Say, one of the
early theorists of French political economy, and repeated by his followers,
there was a fundamental difference between the calculations of men's and
women's wages. A man's wages had to maintain the worker and provide
for the reproduction of the labour force; his wages included subsistence
costs for his children and wife, 'natural dependents' who could never be
entirely self-supporting.[13] Women's, like men's, wages were set by the laws
of supply and demand, but an additional factor operated in the competition for women's jobs. Those women who for some reason had to be
self-sufficient always faced competition from women in the 'natural
state', that is those who needed only to supplement a family's income and
who therefore were willing to work for less than a subsistence rate. Say
recognised that the inverse might be logically true in the male labour
market – that unmarried men with no dependents might seem less costly
to employ than those married and could therefore drive wages down
below family subsistence rates. But he reminded his readers of the long-

run consequences of this system: workers would not reproduce, future supplies of labour would diminish and wages would have to go up.[14] ('Wages go up when two employers run after one worker; wages go down when two workers run after one employer' was the maxim cited in treatise after treatise on theories of wages and profits.) The solution was to set male wages – for those single or married – to include the costs of reproduction. For, according to political economy, reproduction was an economic concept not a biological function. It had to do with the provision of supports for life, the accumulation of human capital, not the production of life itself. For, as Say pointed out, 'The difficult thing is not to be born, it is to subsist.'[15] Subsistence prepared a child for manhood, built up the strength and skill eventually required for work:

This capacity ... can be considered a capital that is formed only by the annual and successive accumulation of sums [by the parents] assigned to develop [the worker].[16]

What is now referred to as 'human capital' was acquired and measured solely in monetary terms, as the 'sums' allocated to rearing a child or the 'wages' paid to an adult man. For this reason the worker's wage had to be set higher than that required for his individual maintenance; the additional amount represented an employer's investment in the next generation of workers. A woman's labour in childbirth and her activities caring for children did not figure in these calculations. Childbirth and childrearing were rather the raw materials on which economic forces acted, the elements of nature with which human societies were built. Say defined production as the activity that gave value to things, that transformed them from simple matter into exchangeable items of recognised value.[17] In his lexicon reproduction was a synonym for production:

Sometimes production is called reproduction because it is, in effect, nothing more than the reproduction of materials in another form which gives them a value ... The word production is more precise because the wealth in question does not come from the material itself, but from the value given to the material.[18]

Reproduction in our more exclusively demographic use of the term was included in this concept of production. Whether the capital was human or not was beside the point, the emphasis was on how value was created and by whom. By a kind of mathematical (and circular) logic, fathers were deemed the agents of transformation of babies into adults since their wages included subsistence costs. These wages, which in theory recognised and reimbursed workers for their part in the creation of value, became in relation to the household a means of conferring on the father the status of value-creator. By attaching a monetary value to human development (and imputing it all to the father's wages) women's contribution, both as domestic workers and wage earners, was rendered irrelevant.[19]

In part this had to do with a certain level of abstraction – the man's wage included (subsumed) all social labour costs including his particular expenditure of labour power. But the representation of production–reproduction as a male activity came also from a conception of the economy that depended on seeing nature as both its analogue and its antithesis. The economy was said to be a natural phenomenon with laws akin to those in the physical world; the status of political economists as scientists rested, after all, on their claim to observe in human activity the autonomous laws of the economic order. If the economy was a natural phenomenon, its activities involved the transformation of matter, of nature's bounty, by humans into things of value. The distinction between natural matter and the creation of value was defined in the oppositions: birth/subsistence, raw material/products of value, nature/worker, mother/father. In this scheme women's contributions to the social value acquired by children were both acknowledged and obscured because men's wages were seen as covering or reimbursing these costs. At the same time women's wage work was denied the kind of value-creating status attributed to men's. Women were by definition not workers and thus incapable of creating the same kind of value. The workers' newspaper *L'Atelier* put it precisely in a preface to a discussion of the problems of women wage earners:

Although women's work is less productive for society than that of men...[20]

The asymmetry of the wage calculation was striking: men's wages included subsistence and reproductive costs, women's wages required family supplements even for individual subsistence. In both cases, membership in a family was assumed (and encouraged), but the results were quite different. Men could live on their wages whether single or married; women could not. Men could realise the liberty of individual choice; women were enmeshed in a net of dependencies that always carried with them obligations and duties to others. Men came, in a sense, to embody the possibilities of individual liberty advanced by theorists of political economy, women became the dependent social beings the theory assumed them to be. Although critics of political economy argued that all wages should minimally guarantee male and female workers' subsistence, the theorists replied that this was impossible since women's wages were 'incomplete' without some contribution from a man. Or, as Eugène Buret put it in his 1840 study *The Misery of the Working Classes*:

Woman is, industrially speaking, an imperfect worker. If a man doesn't add his earnings to the insufficient wage of his partner, sex alone constitutes for her the cause of misery (le sexe seul constituera pour elle une cause de misère).[21]

Buret used sex in a double sense: as a reference to women's socially acceptable activities – what we now call gender – and to denote the physical act that beyond certain boundaries led to depravity and corruption. *Femmes isolées* demonstrated that outside the context of the family neither work nor sex could bring women acceptable returns.

But women could work within family structures. The issue in these discussions of *femmes isolées* was not that women were unfit for work or that work unfitted them for maternity. Indeed, some studies of wages and the distribution of wealth assumed the importance of women's contributions to household budgets. And studies of women workers pointed out how well-behaved were employees doing work appropriate to their strength and sex, and subjected to careful supervision in family-like settings. Good behaviour, moreover, led to financial well-being, for those who practised thrift and moderation somehow managed quite well despite low wages. The corrective to women's low wages was, in fact, not only financial support from men, but the decorum associated with the repression of desire – the desire to live beyond one's means and the desire for sexual indulgence both associated, of course, with prostitution. Here political economists implicitly took on their socialist critics, some of whom had used the figure of the prostitute to symbolise the plight of all workers under capitalist exploitation. They did not argue the question directly, but simply asserted a contrary definition grounded in the authority of their science. If socialists had pointed out that the sale of labour power was no different from the sale of women's bodies, that economic and sexual exploitation were of a piece, political economists established a careful distinction between the productive and disciplined use of 'muscular force' and the wasteful, self-indulgent aspects of sexual activity.[22] By locating sexuality in women's bodies, furthermore, they established a gendered contrast: between work and sex, productivity and wastefulness, discipline and indulgence, male and female. If economic productivity and moral order were to be maintained, the male principle must prevail. This meant that the patriarchal family – a hierarchical, interdependent entity – had to be the school for and embodiment of order. The ambivalent figure of the *femme isolée*, by linking misery and sexuality, demonstrated the consequences of all lives lived outside regulated contexts.[23]

The implications of the discussion went well beyond references to the reality of women's lives. *Femmes isolées* represented the domain of misery, a world of turbulent sexuality, subversive independence and dangerous insubordination.[24] They embodied the city itself.[25] For some writers they exemplified urbanisation's worst effects ('the blasts of unspeakable exhalations, the pell-mell of fumes, of evil emanations and bad dreams that hover above our darkened cities');[26] for others they were the source of the working-class demoralisation so evident in large urban centres. In fact cause and effect were usually not clearly sorted out in the political economists' writings. The figure of the *femme isolée* instead functioned evocatively. In their association with prostitution, these women carried the 'moral leprosy' that made large cities 'permanent centres of infection'; they permitted expression of or simply expressed those 'tumultuous passions' which, in time of political upheaval – as in the Revolution of 1848 – threatened to overturn the entire social order.[27] *Femmes isolées* were at once a concrete example of and a metaphor for economic and social deviance. The political threat posed by their situation underlined the need for government intervention.

In the presentation of the problem of the *femmes isolées* we see political economy's incorporation of moral science into its discourse on the production of wealth. This process has been well described by Giovanna Procacci, who notes that the 'grafting of morality onto economics' in the first half of the nineteenth century made 'possible the elaboration of a whole set of technical instruments of intervention'.[28] What those were and how they operated are not our concern here, but it is important to note that intervention was addressed to the family and not the economy.[29] The family was seen as the natural regulator of morals, whereas the economy was self-regulating in a realm outside human control. Yet the laws of each were interconnected and – in the language of political economy – discoverable by scientific observation as were 'the laws of (magnetic) attraction or gravity'.[30] It is impossible to separate moral from economic considerations in the writings of these political economists.[31] Analyses of wages, for example, linked gender and economics: the 'natural dependency' of women on men within families explained the differential between male and female wages; the 'natural laws' of supply and demand explained why women would always have to depend on men. One set of 'natural' laws articulated and constructed the other. And any discussion of the plight of *femmes isolées* assumed and reasserted the 'fact' of women's inferior or, in Buret's formulation, 'imperfect' standing as wage earners and the consequent necessity of keeping them within a family structure.

In the discussions of *femmes isolées*, indeed of women workers generally, we see a complicated interplay of concrete and metaphoric usages. It is impossible to separate these either in their import or in their effect. Indeed we must take account of both concrete and metaphoric usages, whether we are talking about the reality of women's lives, about political policy, or about economic theory and its practical applications.

Women workers in manufacturing cities

Two themes, integrally related, are evident in political economy's discussions of women workers in manufacturing cities. One had to do with
the impact of machinery on work itself. The new division of labour
brought a regime of interchangeability – of product parts and workers.
When mechanical power could be substituted for human strength, at least
one of the marks of difference between men's and women's work could be
erased. The other had to do with the physical space of factories, city
streets, and workers' homes where the 'promiscuous intermingling' of the
sexes took place. This implicitly referred to the levelling of differences at
work, but was presented as a separate concern. The issue of women's
employment in factories, then, involved not only a consideration of wages
and working conditions, but also of the relationship between industrialisation, urbanisation, and the sexual division of labour.

With the inroduction of machinery, jobs had acquired a certain homogeneity. In fact, in the 1840s and 50s, machines were used only in a limited
number of places in France, mostly in textile production. And even in the
textile industry, the labour market remained sexually segregated. Yet political economists recognised that the potential of machinery was to dissolve all differences among workers. Critics of the new division of labour
objected to the worker's loss of individuality – 'he can be replaced by
whoever comes along'[32] – and of skill, the mark that distinguished between 'les bons et les mauvais ouvriers'.[33] Proponents claimed that
machines had so simplified work that those who could not be employed
before because of weakness or lack of training – women and children –
now had opportunities to earn wages.

[machines] create jobs simple enough to trust to those who until now have not
been able to work, to children and women, and, in general, to the weakest part of
the population.[34]

This resulted in a more productive use of socially available labour power.
In addition, since differences of 'muscular strength' were no longer
required, and since such strength had been a factor in male and female
wage differentials, a certain equality between the sexes might be achieved.
The labour market might as a result be more open, demonstrating the
virtue of 'liberté du travail'.

Direct discussions by political economists of the economic effects of the
substitution of female for male labour or of the creation of jobs that had
no requirements of skill, strength, age or sex, were often aimed at critics of

the new regime, especially workers. Male workers' charges that the new organisation of labour was the source of poverty and misery were dismissed as contrary to fact and to the principles of the free market. Thus in 1862, *Le Journal des économistes* editorialised in favour of admitting women into print shops and condemned the protests of printers as an unjust interference with women's rights: 'sexual difference (la différence du sexe) is a consideration of no value; it disappears before the unity of human nature'.[35] Yet it would be a mistake to take assertions like this out of their specific discursive context (as part of an argument with workers about employer policies). For the discourse of political economists was, in fact, obsessed with sexual difference as a measure of the moral impact of mechanisation. Commentators noted, for example, that machines had wreaked havoc in all-female trades, such as spinning, by dissociating them from feminine skill and household locations.[36] But the question of the impact of machinery on job distinctions was taken up most often in discussions of morality framed in terms of the consequences of the spatial mixing of the sexes. This, and not the nature of work itself, was the preoccupation of the major accounts of factory life published in the 1840s and 50s.

There were many accounts of factory life written in this period by investigators affiliated with the Académie des Sciences Morales et Politiques, among them Louis Villermé, Louis Reybaud, and Armand Audiganne. Like travellers in foreign lands, these men journeyed from city to city, recording in minute detail the new and strange sights they had seen.[37] Their reports were reprinted in *Le Journal des économistes* or *La Revue des deux mondes*, and then in book form. They attained wide circulation and acquired tremendous authority, and their views were cited as scientific evidence for various analyses and programmes put forth in the period. Indeed, these accounts, providing as they did the moral dimension for economic science, fed into debates on the future of French industrial development that raged in the 1840s and 50s and they were used by both sides – those who urged unfettered economic growth, mechanisation and free trade and their opponents who advocated restricted growth, small-scale production and protective tariffs. What is striking is how important sexual difference was in the construction of the terms of the debate.

Dr Louis Villermé's sensational accounts are typical of the genre and his preoccupation with sex has been noted by historians.[38] Villermé compared the poverty and disorder of the various cities he visited in terms of their relative levels of sexual disorder. In the worst cases, certain neighbourhoods of Lille for example, promiscuity, incest, obscenity and prostitution were rampant and they were evident both at work and at home.

What! you mix the sexes in your workshops when ... you could so easily separate them? Are you then not ignorant of the licentious discourses which this mixture provokes, of the lessons of bad morals which result ... and of the driving passions which you encourage as soon as their voice begins to make itself heard?[39]

Even in factories where men and women worked at different tasks, the fact that everyone arrived and left at the same time led to promiscuity and fostered the practice of young girls working a 'fifth quarter' of their day as prostitutes.[40] The mingling in the streets continued in households:

I would rather add nothing to this description of hideous things which reveal, at a glance, the profound misery of these unhappy inhabitants; but I must say that in several of the beds of which I have just spoken I have seen individuals of both sexes and of very different ages lying together, most of them without nightshirts and repulsively dirty. Father, mother, the aged, children, adults, all pressed, stacked together. I stop. The reader will complete the picture, but I warn him that if he wishes it to be accurate, his imagination must not recoil before any of the disgusting mysteries performed on these impure beds, in the midst of obscurity and drunkenness.[41]

The publicist Theodore Fix, writing on the condition of the working classes in *Le Journal des économistes* several years after Villermé's study had appeared, cited the 'grave disorders' (which indicated political disturbances as well as moral offences) that followed from the situations the doctor had described. In opposition to those who argued that manufacturing itself was responsible for the disorder apparent in factory towns, Fix insisted that moral corruption caused poverty. Thus he called for a 'police des manufactures' as a way of raising living standards in factory towns. Fix offered examples of employers who had taken measures to regulate their workers' conduct, even at some financial cost. They rigorously separated the sexes, regulated hours so that men and women did not mix in factory corridors or on the streets, and expelled anyone who engaged in obscene conduct. 'These sacrifices ... are always largely compensated and their factories are among those that prosper most.'[42] Whether others shared Fix's solution or not, they shared his description of the symptoms.[43] 'Pell-mell' was the recurrent phrase used to designate the irregularities that existed, a random scattering that defied natural hierarchies and separations, that made home and workplace indistinguishable, that dissolved the meanings of the differences between women and men.

Women workers were emblematic of the problem. Their fate in factory towns was regularly contrasted with the situation of women in all-female workshops or of those working for wages at home. Although it was often acknowledged that women workers earned good wages in factories – better than in any other female work – the moral effects outweighed these economic gains. Factory women were said to be exposed to vulgar company, seduced, torn from the cares of household and children, or, alternatively, allowed to discover in the company of others the pleasures of sensuality, the taste for luxury, the possibility of fulfilling sexual and material desire. In contrast, women employed in all-female workshops (usually of relatively small scale) or at home were depicted as chaste, orderly and well-prepared for the responsibilities that marriage and motherhood entailed.

What is striking about these purported descriptions of factory towns is how exaggerated and inaccurate they were. For one, men and women were not usually indiscriminately mixed in factories; jobs and workrooms tended to be segregated by sex. Moreover, men and women shared space on the streets of small towns, on farms and in households, in much the way they did in manufacturing centres. Indeed, a characteristic feature of any family or household was the mixing of age and sex in the same physical space. How can we explain the contradictions? – by attending to the rhetorical as well as the literal functions of these writings; by examining the contrasts used to constitute meaning. These accounts try to render as physical detail what were in fact abstract qualities. Thus in Villermé's descriptions the effect is achieved by lining up obscene conversation, incest, darkness, and filth in implied opposition to decorous language, private marital intercourse, light, and cleanliness. The graphic portrayal of promiscuous mingling stood for the absence in industrial cities of the defining characteristics of good order: hierarchy, control, stability, all expressed as a matter of the customary relationship between women and men. 'Public morals are profoundly relaxed in the big cities,' wrote the authors of a book on abandoned children, '...they are especially so in the industrial cities where a very great number of workers of both sexes live together in one place.'[44] Somehow the equivalency – workers of both sexes, not men and women united in families – illustrated and explained the problem. The disorder of unregulated sexuality flourished where the social lines of sexual difference had become blurred.

If the absence of distinctions between the sexes indicated 'grave disorder', then the moralisation of the working classes required that sexual difference be articulated and enforced. It was in these terms that political economists examined the impact of wage work on women's domestic responsibilities and began to describe maternity as woman's primary 'natural' labour. The metaphoric use of female sexuality to talk about working-class misery or disorder implied for them a literal solution – attention to the lives and activities of working-class women.

II

The long discussion of the condition of the working classes in terms of women's disordered sexuality culminated and changed (but did not end) in 1858–60, in the context of negotiations for and then passage of the free trade treaty with England. Concluded in January 1860, this document doomed all attempts to stop the progress of urban industrial growth. Critics and proponents agreed that France could meet the English challenge only with further mechanisation and by intensifying the pace of economic change. What would the moral effects of this kind of development be? That question called forth responses that spoke at once to the 'querelle des femmes' and to economic issues, explicitly spelling out the terms of sexual difference, particularly as they applied to women's 'natural' roles.

Political economists explored questions of morality through detailed investigations into women's work and wages. Jules Simon (professor, publicist, member of the Société d'Economie Politique) published his articles on 'Le Travail et le salaire des femmes', first in *La Revue des deux mondes* and then combined in a book called *L'Ouvrière*, which appeared in 1860. Julie-Victoire Daubié, a young governess and virtually unknown until she submitted her winning entry to the Academy of Lyon's competition in 1859, published parts of her essay first as 'Quels moyens de subsistance ont les femmes' in *Le Journal des économistes* in 1862–3 and then as a book, *La Femme pauvre au XIXe siècle*, in 1866. Both Simon's and Daubié's studies were about the facts of women's manual work (there was no talk of professions or jobs requiring high levels of education) and some reviewers read them only as that.[45] But they were also moral statements less preoccupied with economic matters than with general questions of order and justice. These two studies were addressed to popular audiences, to that informed readership known as 'public opinion', but they also belonged to what I have referred to as the discourse of political economy. They drew on and spoke to the knowledge and ideas propounded by political economists; Simon accepted their precepts, Daubié occupied a critical position within the discourse.

Although their subject was more narrowly construed as working women, these studies were situated in the tradition of earlier scientific reports on the condition of the working classes. Simon explicitly evoked the method of first-hand observation used by his predecessors (Audiganne, Reybaud, Villermé):

I have not seen everything and I have not told everything I have seen; but there is not a single misery recounted that I haven't witnessed and that still doesn't oppress my heart.[46]

Daubié took a somewhat different tack, for she had neither reputation nor standing nor membership in a learned scientific society. She achieved the authority of her text by muting her own voice and instead citing historical documents, informed sources, and government reports. Yet at crucial moments she introduced dramatic anecdotes which, though she did not claim first-hand experience of them, made her appear a witness to the stories she told.[47]

Like their predecessors these were self-consciously moral works which assumed that economic laws had been accurately described and instead concentrated on moral (and what we would call social) science. Simon's first line announced his intention: 'The book you are about to read is a book about morality.'[48] Daubié insisted there ought to be 'treatises of moral justice as prologues to treaties of commerce' and clearly saw her own work in those terms.[49] Simon and Daubié established the need for moral considerations in an overly materialistic age by citing (sexual) pathology. Both books evoked the same images of prostitution, incest, and disorder apparent in earlier studies; it is clear that they assumed readers were already familiar with those studies. Yet the tone and emphasis of Simon's and Daubié's books contrasted sharply with the earlier works in their concentration on positive solutions. While prostitution and incest had been Villermé's focus (and titillation), Simon worshipped at the altar of an idealised motherhood and Daubié, more practically, sought ways to improve the position of working mothers. If the older investigations understood working-class disorder in terms of women's unregulated sexuality, these studies focussed on mothers as the key to orderly family and social life. If the older studies detailed the breakdown of order in terms of a loss of sexual difference, these studies imposed a grid of sexual difference as a means of achieving or maintaining order in social and economic organisation. If before, women's sexuality posed the entire problem of a disruptive working class, now maternity (depicted as an asexual female physical function) seemed to indicate a potentially more manageable working class; calls for the protection of maternity, moreover, implied a new vision of the relationship between labouring classes and middle classes, workers and the state.

In effect, Simon and Daubié simply reversed the emphasis of earlier constructions, making explicit what had before been implicit (that modest women and good mothers were the antitheses of prostitutes, that discipline and domestic order were the opposite of misery). The effect on representations of women workers was striking: they were now portrayed more often as victims torn by economic necessity (misery) from their 'natural' labour as mothers and wives, or from the work and workplaces appropriate to their sex. The real danger to be avoided was not so much uncontrolled sexual passion, but lost maternal sustenance – the key not only for the proper education of children, but for the support and strength of family life. If the explicit focus had moved, however, from negative to positive representations, sexual difference was, as earlier, established not as a systematic comparison between women and men, but solely in terms of the 'natural' purposes and physical characteristics of women's bodies.

Simon and Daubié had different agendas in their reports. He was a prominent commentator on social affairs who would later become one of the Third Republic's important legislators. She was a self-defined feminist, who would earn the first baccalauréat awarded to a woman (in 1862) and who would lead campaigns against government regulation of prostitution and for women's suffrage in the early years of the Third Republic. Simon wrote his book in the name of society, citing and endorsing Michelet's views on the female character; Daubié wrote in the name of women, making a claim for the importance of women's (economic) independence. The differences of argument and intention between them were crucial, but the similarities were also revealing. In both cases discussions of women workers converged on the question of motherhood, viewed as the defining quality or characteristic of femininity.

Jules Simon's L'Ouvrière

L'Ouvrière began with a dramatic contrast between advances in technology and science and the degradation of family life. Mechanisation had substituted women for men in industry because 'according to the law of wages' women were cheaper to employ. This employment in itself actually improved women's material situation because the wages they earned in factories were higher than those paid elsewhere. What then was the problem? Simon cited Michelet's anguished cry:

L'ouvrière! impious, sordid word that no language has ever known, that no age ever understood before this age of iron, and that holds in balance all our supposed progress![50]

And then added his own explication: 'The woman who becomes a worker is no longer a woman.'[51]

The contradiction woman/worker had several manifestations. Women did what was formerly men's work; they left the 'hidden, sheltered, modest life, surrounded by warm affection, that is so necessary to their happiness and to ours...'[52] for the factory where they mingled all day with women of 'doubtful morality' and men, some of whom 'dominated' them (the sexual innuendo seems intended) as supervisors; they exerted more physical force at work than was appropriate for their bodies;[53] and they earned wages that might lead them to question their husband's authority at home.[54] Distinctions within the family were levelled: there was no longer a mother and father, but two workers; there was no longer a family to return to at the end of the day, only a dirty lodging where children were abandoned and deprived of a mother's love. Factory shifts even ignored the differences between day and night – all that was natural and once taken for granted had been disrupted.

According to Simon there were still models of normality and these, interestingly, involved women earning wages, but in domestic settings or very small workshops where natural differences could be respected (silk spinning and weaving in the region around Lyons were exemplary). For Simon, the ideal was a family enterprise in the countryside, where women worked at delicate tasks suited to their weaker condition, interrupting production to care for children and husband, to infuse the household with loving spirit, to embody and 'personify' the family.

It is necessary that women be able to marry and that married women be able to remain at home all day, there to be the providence and the personification of the family.[55]

Women at home guaranteed the kind of behaviour that conserved resources and prevented the misery that followed from (men's) tendency to wastefulness and dissipation. For men's wages were designed to support families if managed carefully and used in the kind of 'moral' atmosphere only women could maintain. Those who argued that raising men's wages would restore women to their rightful place at home misunderstood the causality, according to Simon. It was necessary first to implement morality, then men's wages would be adequate for family support.[56] The economy, this argument assumed, was not susceptible to intervention, nor was the family. But while political economy had provided the insights according to which institutions might be moulded to economic 'laws', moral science had not sufficiently detailed the importance of the natural roles of men and women for the organisation of family life.

Simon rarely referred to men, though when he did he assumed they did hard labour, outside, away from the household. The evocation of men – as productive wage-earners – came through implicit contrasts with women. Simon's most eloquent (and memorable) descriptions elaborated his idealisations of woman;

Woman grows only with love, and love develops and strengthens only in the sanctuary of The Family.[57]

If there is one thing that nature teaches us with evidence it is that woman is made to be protected, to live as a young girl close to her mother, as a wife, under the protection and authority of her husband.[58]

We can write books and invent theories on duty and sacrifice, but the true teachers of morality are women. It is they who softly counsel the right, who reward devotion with a caress ... All material improvements will be welcome; but if you want to improve the condition of women workers and at the same time guarantee order, revive good sentiments, make the country and justice understood and loved, do not separate children from their mothers![59]

What was at stake was the essence of femininity and that had to do with love, morality and maternity. Wage-earning as an activity undertaken by women was not harmful as long as it did not distract them from their 'natural vocations', indeed it kept them from boredom and periods of useless inactivity. But it was not by wage-earning that women created social value, it was by exemplifying and enforcing family morality.

I have used the term 'social value', but Simon did not. References to the creation of social value, indeed of any value by women, were absent from Simon's conceptual vocabulary. He seems to have relegated the language of value to matters of technical economics which was not appropriate for discussing what women were or did. Rather, Simon's entire text was constructed in opposition to material, monetary concepts: women were associated with a secularised spirituality, with love and feeling; they lived in a domain outside the economy and their behaviour was detached from it; their qualities were inherent in their physical make-up, linked, above all, with the functions of motherhood. Women effected the transformation of others: under their tutelage children became moral, loving beings; men became responsible, disciplined husbands and fathers; even wages achieved their true value when 'morale' prevailed in a household. But this was not value-creating activity precisely because it could not be recognised in monetary terms. To do so, in fact, would be to undermine women's effectiveness, to reduce to cash terms, activity of literally unmeasurable importance. What women created, after all, had no quantifiable exchange value in the market for it was not the physical force or the capacity for labour of children that mothers produced. Those qualities still depended on subsistence as provided by the father's wage. Rather, women inspired those behavioural characteristics on which depended not so much a society's productive capacity or its wealth, but its stability and the bases of its social organisation. All of this left in place, indeed it took as axiomatic, political economy's earlier definition of production, and of men as value-creating (and therefore wage-earning) producers. While Simon brought to light and to social relevance the domestic and childrearing activities of women, he did so without challenging the calculus of political economy. Instead, he constructed the meaning of his text with a new set of oppositions: economic/non-economic, workplace/household, factory/family, material/spiritual, physical growth/moral education, wage-earning/moralising, economy/society, worker/mother, male/female.

To recognise in these contrasts the 'ideology of domesticity' or 'the doctrine of separate spheres' is at once to get and miss the point. There is, of course, in Simon's work a theme now familiar to historians of nineteenth-century Europe and North America, thanks largely to the research into the history of women. But to label the theme and assume we therefore know what it means is to miss the chance to see when and in what contexts these kinds of ideas were articulated as well as how, specifically, they worked. In Simon's case it seems fair to conclude that he drew on the views of earlier critics of capitalism (those of romantic/Catholic socialists, for example) who argued from the Bible that woman's destiny was the labour of childbirth and the responsibility of maternity and that wage labour was therefore an unnatural activity.[60] But the timing of the publication of his work is also crucial and it helps explain his equivocation on the question of whether or not industrial growth could be stopped. Clearly Simon thought not, and at every point he threw up his hands about the impossibility of saving less efficient small workshops instead of building new factories. Indeed his book offers no economic solution, no way of turning back the clock. One critic was so annoyed at Simon's refusal to suggest policy that he deemed the book, 'a long moan uttered by a man of sensitivity and talent' and wondered what the impact of such a study could be.[61] The impact seems to me to have been ideological, not immediately programmatic. For it provided a kind of compromise with opponents of free trade who had warned that rapid industrial and urban growth would sap the (moral and physical) vitality of France and who, in 1860, hysterically denounced the treaty with England as the fruition of their worst fears. In his discussion of women workers, Simon accepted some of the critique offered by protectionists, but he also pointed out (reluctantly, his tone suggests) that history could not be reversed. Simon's discussion of the true nature and mission of women set forth an alternative way to understand the future. He developed and endorsed a vision of moral order and social organisation detached from, unaffected by, and yet perfectly compatible with an economy of unlimited industrial growth.

Simon's book was offered as a study of the facts of working women's lives but it was really an exercise in prescription and idealisation. His most urgent and exhortative statements were about femininity, not about work, and he eschewed all discussion of practical solutions to the problems he described. Simon insisted that neither legislation nor coercion could change the direction of social organisation, but he did suggest that a process of 'education and institutions' might eventually have some effect.[62] In no small way his book constituted part of that process of education by offering a normative statement about womanhood as a goal to be attained. The idealised family with woman at its centre was the model according to which people might increasingly choose to live. The remedy to be hoped for was 'the return of the mother to the family ... to family life ... to the virtues of the family'.[63] Indeed once the natural bases and the salutary social impact of the family were explained, it would achieve in reality its theoretical promise: 'It is always to be wished,' Simon wrote, 'that facts be made to accord with institutions.'[64] The title of Simon's book, then, represented dismal facts that were contrary to the institutional necessities of the family: 'L'ouvrière' was the antithesis of 'la mère'.

Julie Daubié's 'La Femme Pauvre'

Julie Daubié approached the study of women workers differently from Simon, but she began with many of the same assumptions. Like him, she equated immorality and disorganisation with the loss of clear lines of sexual difference. One of the destructive impacts of industrial wage labour, she argued, had been to erase certain institutionalised sexual distinctions, thereby depriving women of legitimate economic activity and moral protection. Men or machines (or both) had usurped women's traditional trades – spinning, embroidery, lacemaking – leaving them with only unskilled menial occupations. The loss of exclusive rights to practise these trades meant for women the loss of customary skill, of work appropriate to their 'natural aptitudes', of legal and moral protection, of jobs, and of wages that contributed significantly to subsistence.[65] The regime of industry erased the lines of difference:

Today the mother is forcibly torn from her family, the wife from her husband, her household, the work of her sex; childhood has become the prey of the most avid speculation; the young girl..., the weak, and the strong, all riveted to the same chain as slaves of industry, have to perform equal labor.[66]

This system produced irresponsible men who monopolised all advantages, and exploited women who bore without compensation the burdens of 'civilisation'.[67]

These burdens took their toll on the physical constitution of women – the bodies of young girls were martyred to debauchery and seduction, the bodies of mothers were unable to suckle infants so worn out were they with fatigue. Daubié graphically painted the losing struggle of women against steam-driven machines in terms of physical violation:

The woman who competes with machines, struggling for speed against wheels and gear, has squandered her life to industry without receiving in exchange the certainty of her daily bread. But it is not enough that industry has slain her body, industry also has killed her soul.[68]

She underscored this image by citing doctors who concluded that, 'from the point of view of health, the condition of working women is much more deplorable than that of prostitutes'.[69]

Prostitution represented the physical and moral abuse of women, the perversion of their proper vocation, which was motherhood. Wrote Daubié, 'in all well-constituted societies, the woman ought to be above all wife and mother and her most beautiful work will be to bring a man into the world'.[70] As bearer of children and director of the household, woman personified the family; when men agreed to support their wives and children, they acknowledged their social duty to protect the family (and, by extension, the country).[71] In effect, they enacted towards the institution of the family the same maternal solicitude mothers naturally expressed for their children. Daubié's vision of an ideal moral order, then, echoed Simon's: morality rested on a sense of responsibility to others developed in families at whose centre was a woman.

Like Simon, Daubié did not refer to maternity, to the example women set, the moral instruction they gave, as having 'value'. She accepted political economy's equation of value with wage-earning and so assigned domestic functions to a separate sphere. At the same time, however, she thought it possible for women to create value in the labour market and to use their wages, if necessary, for the sole support of their children. In a clear disagreement with political economy, she saw nothing inherently different about women's and men's productivity, and for that reason she insisted on equal wages for both sexes. In fact, she argued that women's social status would be enhanced if they had access to decent paid labour. But she also thought that work, though it might be necessary, was not a desirable solution for married women.

Daubié addressed as separate issues what for Simon and others were inherently contradictory concepts – wage labour and motherhood – in an effort to provide practical solutions to the pressing problem of women's poverty. In her view, this problem had two related causes: the monopoly by men of previously all-female trades or of trades perfectly suitable for women, and the selfishness of men, embodied in the Le Chapelier Law of 1791, who pursued individual rights (seducing and abandoning young women, drinking away family resources, refusing to contribute to household expenses) instead of fulfilling their social duties.

I have searched in vain for man's duty in social organisation; I have found only his right to the unlimited liberty to oppress. That, if I am not mistaken, is the node of all questions of work and political economy.[72]

If the poverty of women was caused by men, then women must be given the power to seek redress of their grievances. Simon's solution of simply returning women to the home would be futile in the absence of laws that could limit oppression or force men to recognise their duty. Daubié agreed that the long-term remedy was a 'moralisation' of men (both workers and employers), but she maintained that this would only be achieved by strengthening the position of women. And that would come neither from a return to the past nor from idealised pronouncements, but from the implementation of equality – equality before the law, equal participation in making laws, equal access to training and apprenticeship in all jobs, and equal hourly pay.

Equality, in Daubié's view, would not eradicate sexual difference; it would put women in a position to protect themselves. First, equal access to jobs would enable women to break unjustified male monopolies of trades perfectly suited to women (such as printing) and to enter those trades 'that bring out naturally the attributes fitting' to their sex.[73] Second, equal pay would remove the pressure for women to work to excess in violation of their natural inclinations and it would permit single women to support themselves without having to depend on (and thus become sexually vulnerable to) men. Here Daubié implicitly rejected the asymmetrical wage calculus of political economy, assuming instead that women were, like men, 'naturally' independent and that wages ought to provide any individual worker's subsistence. Women's natural physical limits ought not to disqualify them from wage-earning because the wage conferred the status of producer, it did not reflect inherent capacities. Third, legal rights would enable women to force seducers to acknowledge paternity and recalcitrant husbands to recognise their financial obligations to their families. Equality before the law would give women the power to enforce normative rules of family organisation in very much the structural terms that moralists and political economists envisioned them.

In effect Daubié addressed two problems and offered two apparently different solutions to them. The first problem was economic in origin and had to do with the pressing fact that women needed to work and that existing jobs and wage scales made subsistence impossible. The effects of this situation were both material and moral. For single women the result was 'misery or shame' – both of which led to debauchery and death – for married women the result was not only individual poverty but the sacrifice of their children. The second problem was moral in origin and had to do with the fact that men had abandoned their families, pursuing liberty instead of fulfilling their duties. This had an economic effect especially on married women and made it necessary for them to supply the subsistence their husbands should have provided; it also had a moral effect, disrupting family organisation and social order. Despite the fact that she pointed out that material and moral causes and effects were related, Daubié offered two separate solutions for the two problems she had described: the first – for single women – equality in the job market; the second – for married women – the legal power to enforce paternal responsibility.

In a sense, the second solution cancelled the radical import of the first, for it suggested that equality was a compensatory measure for women who had not yet married, or who could not marry, or whose husbands were delinquent providers. And by endorsing political economy's view of men as the major source of subsistence (economically responsible for the reproduction of the labour force), Daubié left in place the theoretical formulation that defined women (as a category, whether single or married) as 'imperfect' wage-earners. Though her practical solutions were a far cry from Simon's and though gender power relationships were the cornerstone of her analysis, Daubié remained within the conceptual boundaries earlier set by political economy, accepting the notion that work and family (economics and morality) were separate spheres when in fact it was precisely the relationship between them that lay at the heart of the wage calculation.

III

In the discourse of political economy women workers were a prominent topic. They served at once as an object of study and a means of representing ideas about social order and social organisation. Political economists focussed attention on women workers because they seemed to reveal something of the problematic of urban/industrial development, especially its moral dimension. Through that act of observation, women workers became an essential part of the conceptual vocabulary of moral science, the means by which normative rules were articulated and applied. Even Daubié, who made the plight of women themselves the central issue and who eschewed idealised metaphoric representations (insisting instead on the complexity of concrete details), participated in the same process. That process involved a double move that at once set women workers apart from the larger world of work as a distinctly deviant case and made their situation central to the resolution of the problem posed by the urban working classes.

The marginalisation of women workers rested on and reinforced political economy's presentation of its economic and moral science in terms of the 'natural' qualities of women and men; the invocation of nature legitimised certain percepts and put them beyond the bounds of dispute. This was the case for the discussion of women's lower wages as a result of their 'natural' dependency (a function of motherhood) and the projection of a desirable moral/social order in terms of sharp lines of sexual difference, spatially divided between home and work, physically divided between men's 'muscular force'/productivity and women's maternity/domesticity.

The discourse of political economy with which I have worked here was clearly idealised and surely ideological and it tells us little about what work meant to the women who performed it. None the less it did not take place in a realm apart from the economy or politics or 'real life'. Rather it set the definitional terms according to which policy was debated and programmes enacted and even fundamental critiques – such as those of socialists – were developed.[74] The marginalisation of women workers was, then, an historically produced effect which must itself be critically examined. Historians who treat women workers as marginal to processes of urbanisation and industrialisation mistake historically constructed meanings for objective facts and thus miss at least half the story. For it is precisely by studying the terms of women workers' marginality that we can discover some of the central issues of public policy and political debate in mid-nineteenth-century France. Through such an approach, we not only see a new dimension of history, but we put ourselves in a position to interpret – and perhaps to change – one of the ways in which the meaning of work has been constructed.

6

The languages of factory reform in Britain, *c.* 1830–1860

ROBERT GRAY

It is now widely recognised that nineteenth-century industrialisation was a complex and uneven process. Recent work has emphasised the expansion and transformation of domestic and craft forms of production, alongside or as an alternative to the growth of the factory; within the factory itself, historians have noted the persistence and adaptation of old skills, and the emergence of new ones, rather than any unilinear process of de-skilling.[1] Attention has also been drawn to the artisan base of much popular protest and labour organisation; there can be no simple equating of 'working class' with 'factory proletariat'.[2] This more complex account of early industrial capitalism is welcome. But if simple notations of the 'industrial revolution' have now to be abandoned, we still need to retain some sense of overall transformation. Different industries and regions followed different paths, but there may nevertheless be a common 'logic of process' at work;[3] there was certainly a widespread contemporary perception, for example in popular radical and Chartist literature, that diverse struggles were shaped by similar forces.

Industrialisation can thus be seen as a process of cultural change, and historians have begun to explore the different ways in which work patterns, conceptions of work and their relation to family and community were changing. Workers, employers and concerned observers were attempting to formulate languages in which to negotiate their relationships to each other and to a changing environment. What came to be named the 'factory question' was, during the second quarter of the nineteenth century, a site for contending ways of seeing these issues. The factory was a concentrated metaphor for hopes and fears about the direction and pace of industrial change. Its significance for British industrialisation thus extends beyond the direct impact of factory labour, or the numerical weight of those engaged in it. On the one hand, the uncontrolled growth of the factory system, with its concomitant concentration of capital in the hands of monopolising 'factory lords', could be linked to a range of issues

relevant in textile manufacturing communities and more widely: the
weavers' distress, the poor law, rural depopulation. On the other hand,
the factory, in the context of educational reform and enhanced moral
discipline, could be presented as the symbol of economic and social progress. In this perspective the factory was not the problem but, given some
collateral changes, the solution. While emphasis on the factory system
and its workers must be heavily qualified in any balanced account of industrialisation, the debate around factory labour was nevertheless central
to changing conceptions of work, within and beyond the factory itself.

In this chapter I attempt to explore some of the wider ideological and cultural dimensions of factory reform. The story of the ten hours' movement,
and the major sources for its study are fairly familiar ground, and it is not
the intention of this chapter to tell that story again.[4] I want rather to offer a
reinterpretation, in the light of wider concerns with industrial labour,
class, gender, the state, and the languages through which these were represented. Such themes have received increasing attention in recent work,
and factory reform has proved a rewarding topic for bringing them
together. The factory acts have been variously interpreted, from Marxist,
functionalist and administrative perspectives, and all this work has added
to our understanding. But all these perspectives tend, in effect, to construct the process of reform as a single prolonged battle, involving the
same protagonists and the same issues. Often this leads to an implicit tele-
ology; factory reform is the unfolding of some inherent logic of capital,
industrialism or bureaucratic state regulation, with more or less aid from
operative class interests and a rather vague entity called 'humanitarian
sentiment'. As with all teleologies, this schematises complex historical
processes, and reduces their open-ended possibilities at any given moment
to a single destiny. It is frequently assumed, for example, that the model of
inspection and enforcement that developed after 1833 constituted the
only rational and effective form of regulation, with a consequent dis-
missal of alternative popular understandings of law and its enforcement.
Factory reform had different meanings to different protagonists, and
these meanings changed over time. Some meanings became preferred over
others in the languages of public debate. Insofar as there was a redefinition of this kind, it may have some bearing on the stabilisation of industrial society, and the construction of a broader social and political
consensus.

This re-examination of the debate on factory labour takes its inspiration from recent work in a number of cognate fields. Studies of the early
Victorian 'revolution in government' have attempted to place the internal
workings of the state in a wider social and ideological framework, paying
special attention to the figure of the official 'expert' and his claims to auth-

oritative social knowledge.[5] Socio-legal studies of the judicial and administrative construction of issues are of particular relevance here, and have already provided important insights into factory regulation.[6] Recent work on industrial change and the labour process has already been mentioned; this draws attention to the diversity of patterns of development, and has begun to examine the interrelations of work, culture and community. Feminist historians have insisted that social change and state regulation have to be seen in terms of patriarchy as well as class; the labour process itself is shaped by gender.[7] Finally, attention has been drawn to the constitutive role of language in forming social identities and movements.[8] My work arose from a concern to bring these perspectives together in a study of the factory question.

Language and the construction of public debate is a central concern. Power in society is exercised partly through the privileging of particular modes of discourse, and the disqualifying of others; when subordinate groups speak it is in a 'borrowed language'.[9] But – and this has perhaps been the historian's characteristic intervention in 'post-structuralist' cultural theory – there is a danger of seeing this in an over-deterministic, static, and ultimately functionalist way.[10] Discursive hierarchies are more settled in some periods than others. Different discourses address different areas of life, and, even in relatively settled periods, the boundaries can be ill-defined, squabbled over and renegotiated. It is arguable that a period of crisis is definable in the 1830s – not only in terms of the familiar 'political' and 'social' history of the decade, but in a deeper cultural dislocation, defined precisely by the presence of alternative languages whose boundaries were unsettled. For example, as I shall argue below, moral languages drawn from evangelical religion or the romantic imagination claimed to address the workings of labour markets. The 'condition of England' debate of the 1840s may perhaps best be seen as part of a process of settlement, though one that never effected any definitive closure. The changing terms of debate on factory labour would seem to give some support to this way of seeing the cultural politics of the period.

I want to argue, then, that the emergence of factory agitation in the early 1830s was marked by a rich and diverse range of modes of discourse, with distinct radical implications. This range was effectively narrowed in the further development of the struggle. To recover such shifts it is essential to guard against teleological and schematic readings. Thus the factory movement is often seen in terms of a particular reading of opinions and alignments in the 1840s, with emphasis variously placed on 'enlightened' big employers, factory inspection and bureaucratic feedback, evangelical or Benthamite public opinion, protectionist gentry looking for a stick to beat the Anti-Corn Law League, and the operatives' own organisations. This is arguably a simplified version of the 1840s, and it certainly cannot be read back into the emerging debate of the 1830s. The 'enormous condescension of posterity' has edited out much of the diversity, and some of the radical edge of the earlier debate. Discursive boundaries, which in the early 1830s were undefined, came to be more firmly drawn, and the continuing struggle for a ten hours' bill was conducted in this changing context. The present chapter is an attempt, first, to establish the diversity and the radical implications of the debate of 1830–33; second, to suggest more tentatively some of the ways in which this range was narrowed, and factory reform could be reconstructed as part of a symbolic social settlement in the late 1840s and through the 1850s and 60s.

I

The early ten hours' movement had a number of strands, loosely held together by a rhetoric variously composed of evangelical religion, conceptions of a due social balance threatened by unregulated economic change, popular radical ideas of fair employment and labour as property, and patriarchal values. Such rhetorics embodied notions of a 'moral economy' counterposed to the aggressive economic liberalism of the manufacturers' lobby, but also alternative conceptions of political economy itself, based on a more measured pace of growth, development of home rather than export markets, and the protection of labour as the key productive resource.[11] This clustering of views might often represent itself in terms of appeals to tradition and a 'paternalist' mutuality of interests, with the values of a 'rural' society taken as a touchstone to judge the excesses of industrialism. But labels like 'paternalistic traditionalism', so often employed to explain some of the support for factory reform, require further examination.[12] The honest yeoman or squire as moral touchstone is a rhetorical device; it positions the speaker within his discourse and enables him to articulate a moral voice resonating through a range of potential publics. Richard Oastler, who played a pivotal (if self-dramatised) role in organising a ten hours campaign around such feelings, liked to represent himself in that way.[13] Oastler's own affiliations were in fact to commercial circles in the West Riding towns, as well as to agriculture; and industry and agriculture, town and country were anyway scarcely on separate planets, least of all in the West Riding.

Oastler is of interest, partly because he brings together, in a unique stylistic mixture, the elements of the early factory movement, to produce a kind of populist traditionalism or 'Tory Radicalism'. Evangelical religion and gothic romanticism – a sensibility about childhood suffering in terms

of the 'monstrous' – are particularly important resources here. The much
quoted account of Oastler's discovery of the cause of factory children, by
a chance conversation with his friend John Wood, a Tory worsted spinner, has all the motifs of evangelical conversion.[14] The conversation may
have been as much to do with the appropriateness of a public campaign,
as with the discovery of the problem. Michael Sadler was certainly talking
of 'infant slavery in these accursed manufactures' and denouncing political economy and the 'earthly selfish and devilish' policies of Huskisson
and Peel in January 1829, a year and nine months before Oastler's famous
Leeds Mercury letters.[15] Oastler uses language in explosive ways that set
him apart from other propertied 'friends of the poor'. Overworking
employers and their apologists could be denounced in disturbingly direct
terms, often through the gothic motif of unmasking:

Now, Sir, with the most abhorrent disgust, I turn from your letter to yourself. I
know not who you are, – what you are; I only know you as the author of *that*
letter; – whether you are descended from patrician or plebeian blood, I care not
... I *suppose* you to be a Christian 'so called;' – but I *know* you are the writer of
that letter, which stamps – for ever stamps – infamy on your name! – Hereafter,
every thing cruel, disgusting, and abominable will be expressed thereby.[16]

The terrors of child labour are uncovered in the interstices of 'normal',
avowedly Christian and philanthropic everyday life; 'the tears of innocent
victims' wet 'the very streets which receive the droppings of an "Anti-
Slavery Society"'.[17] References to 'factory slavery' could be more than a
rhetorical flourish: they might lead in to an analysis of the economic dependence of adult, as well as child labour. Moving his Ten Hours Bill,
Sadler asserted that 'the employer and the employed do not meet on equal
terms in the market of labour', regardless of the age of the labourer.[18] The
factory system could be seen as concentrating capital at the expense of artisans and small masters; 'the common people here say "The Factory
System has *robbed* us of *our* capital, *our* trade, and *our* labour"'.[19]

Such statements relate to the context of the West Riding, where the
uneven development of mechanisation had concentrated some of the
worst problems of child labour, especially in the worsted mills; while a
resilient artisanal and out-working economy was under pressure from the
growth of factory production in the woollen trades.[20] Substantial sectors
of the propertied classes – merchants, gentry, professional men – saw
their interests and values as identified with the artisanal and domestic
economy, and feared the threat of unchecked factory concentration to
community cohesion and social balance.[21] It is possible to overplay the
specifically Tory components of this kind of paternalist feeling: such attitudes cut across the political spectrum, from 'traditionalist' Tories to

Whigs, to a patrician radicalism. Such gentry and merchant philanthropy embraced the ten hours' movement with sentiments ranging from crusading fervour to a rather condescending platform presence at public meetings.[22] Among political leaders, at both central and local level, there could be an element of opportunistic calculation, a search for the line of least resistance by the otherwise non-committal – a feeling perhaps hitched to the ten hours' bandwaggon in 1831–2, then unhitched by the manufacturing lobbies and the authoritative tones of the Factory Commission. Public figures adopted a more measured language than Oastler, with resonances of eighteenth-century natural theology: 'it has been ordained by the Almighty Creator of the Universe that the rays of the sun shall not always shine upon us, but that ... winter shall succeed summer'.[23] Arguments from design were often expressed by medical men; children would have stronger bones had 'the Divine Author of our being' intended them to work long hours in factories.[24] And the appeal to 'common sense', defined in ways that overlapped both its eighteenth-century philosophical and everyday uses, was one unifying theme in the ten hours coalition; the Factory Commission was attacked on the grounds that 'it implies the want of Common Sense or Honesty' to dispute that twelve hours was too long for children.[25]

The radicalism of artisans and operatives shared many of these intellectual and stylistic resources. A remarkable pamphlet by George Crabtree, 'an operative', *A Brief Description of a Tour through Calder Dale*, makes ironic use of the genre of romantic topography:

We entered a beautiful valley and passed a mill belonging to Mr Hinchcliffe, it is filled with power-looms and propelled by steam.... We jogged up the valley, admiring its beauties, which indeed were exquisite in some parts of it; its rocks and precipices made us almost imagine we were contemplating the wildness of Alpine scenery.... But on a sudden, as though by magic, a Factory burst in our view.[26]

There are certain particular emphases in the operative voices. The political language of radicalism, itself saturated in romantic imagery, helped define ways of seeing industrial labour, in terms of 'freedom', 'tyranny' and 'slavery'. John Doherty's *Poor Man's Advocate* repudiated the term master as 'unworthy of being used by, and degrading to, all but such as are anxious to be tyrants, or willing to be slaves'.[27] The polemical use of the term slavery by Oastler or Sadler had a peculiar resonance among operatives, and could slide, as we have seen, from a reference to children to a generalised view of factory owners as monopolising 'tyrants' and a critique of the dependent and unequal position of the adult male worker. The Huddersfield Political Union argued in Painite terms:

no individual, or any number of individuals, has a *right* (nor ever had, nor ever will) to exercise a power over another, or any number of individuals, which if exercised over themselves, they would consider, and call unjust ... social right either does or ought to emanate from the natural one.[28]

In the evocation of 'slavery' and 'tyranny' this rationalist Jacobin language could connect with the language of common law constitutionalism, and thus with Oastler's brand of populist Toryism, as well as the radicalism of figures like Cobbett. The stock platform rhetoric of popular radicalism was an amalgam of these languages.

Operatives tended, as we might expect, to give more concrete accounts of particular abuses. Witnesses at Sadler's Select Committee – by no means all of whom were simply recalling conditions in their own childhood – went into considerable detail about recent changes in the labour process, especially the intensification of labour associated with piecemeal mechanisation in the cloth-dressing trades where 'the work is very laborious at the gig, and it is very necessary to be uncommonly careful'.[29] Popular radicals emphasised the link between overwork and low pay. While individuals might raise their earnings by working longer, 'you must for the *whole*, reason collectively ... over-production invariably sinks, not indeed the *intrinsic*, but the *exchangeable* value of every article or commodity'.[30] The operative voice may also be distinguished by a greater readiness to name names. This is certainly a feature of Oastler's rhetoric, and one which probably did much to create his reputation as a dangerous man given to inflammatory language; but his polemics seem most often to be directed at those who, like Holland Hoole or Vernon Royle, entered the lists as champions of the employers. Crabtree's *Tour through Calder Dale* sought out detailed information about the treatment of children and other practices, as well as canvassing the clergy for their opinions and publishing the results. Of the seven firms he mentioned, the four that can be traced in the factory commissioners' questionnaire of 1833 appear to be on a fairly small scale, employing less than 50 hp and less than 100 workers; some of these rural mills may indeed fit Elizabeth Gaskell's picture of the down-at-heel yeoman or small squire realising that 'the "beck" running down the mountain-side ... can be turned into a new source of wealth'.[31] Doherty proclaimed 'the justice of exposing tyrannical employers' and regularly listed employers engaging in night-work and other abuses in *The Poor Man's Advocate*. In Manchester, however, it was the biggest firms that were attacked; five out of seven employers listed were among the twenty-two leading firms in the city.[32]

Operatives' views of the factory question appear to place some emphasis on the protection of adult workers. This should not, however, be taken to mean that the concern with children was merely tactical – or even hypocritical – as the Factory Commission and many subsequent commentators have implied. It could reflect a perception that the need to send children to the factory was a function of the bargaining position of adult workers: 'our adult Operatives have generally no more choice than their children'.[33] Any improvement would thus be seen in terms of the position of labour in general, and adult men's labour in particular. In the West Riding this may have been related to ideals of a family economy, threatened by the diminished earning-power of men and the employment of children away from the home; apart from the impact on family life and the health of the children, this could deprive out-working households of crucial additional labour, and disrupt the succession of generations within the local economy.[34] One preoccupation of Sadler's Committee was the age at which boys bargained for themselves with an employer. Eighteen was cited as the age when 'you were your own master' by a witness from Gomersal, while in Leeds 'I always bargained for wages ever since I began to work for wages'.[35] Such statements certainly have to be read in the context of Sadler's proposed restriction of all under eighteen; but the implied normative ideal is nevertheless significant, and may itself underlie the demand to restrict teenage hours. In Lancashire cotton the emphasis was on the individual earning-power and job security of the adult male spinner, and the maintenance of his position as an artisan within the factory. It is noteworthy that John Doherty, denouncing the abuses of an industry employing a large and increasing proportion of women and juveniles, adopted the radical rhetoric of the 'freeborn Englishman' and addressed himself predominantly to the 'working man': 'Is the personal liberty, or the actual imprisonment, of a very large portion of the king's subjects, *a mere matter of private business*? Is the act of stripping men of large portions of their property by violence, *a mere matter of private business*?'[36] Women and juveniles are present as victims to be protected by the manly exertions of husbands and fathers, rather than addressed as protagonists in their own cause.[37]

Patriarchal values thus pervade the debate on factory labour, but, as Joan Scott has argued with reference to Parisian artisans, values are differently appropriated and defined in different contexts; this process of appropriation leads to varied and contestable specific solutions to problems of work, family life and their interrelations.[38] In the factory debate of the early 1830s, the main emphasis seems to be on the deleterious effect on 'health and morals' of long hours of child labour, and the deficiency of formal schooling and/or moral education within the parental household (possibly visualised as a domestic manufacturing household). Within this general argument about children, however, girls and their fitness for future marriage and motherhood were the focus of particular anxieties.

Such concerns are expressed across the spectrum of support for the Ten Hours Bill and beyond.[39] The regulation of child labour – or, in the perspective of radical operatives the effective protection of adult male labour – would enable girls to grow up into 'domesticated' wives and mothers. Thus the concern about child labour connoted concerns about gender. In a characteristic rhetorical slide the figure of the helpless factory child could suddenly become gendered as a girl, just as the figure of the ideal independent free labourer became gendered as a man. In Oastler's powerful image of Holland Hoole's own children driven to the factory, it is the girl's fate that is foregrounded: '"Emma is of sufficient age, – she must go to the factory;" – and for this, he deducts – three shillings a-week; – *her wages* from *your* parish pay!!'[40] And sexual innuendo could be employed in knockabout attacks on factory commissioners or employers: 'There are no crooked legs under the Petticoats – none at all – no ulcers under the stockings.'[41] Anxieties about childhood, seen in terms of innocence, danger and dependence, focussed particularly on the female child, and implicitly on adult femininity as well.

Patriarchy, in its diverse interpretations, could provide some common ground on which issues of industrial labour might ultimately be negotiated. But such values could refer to differing versions of an 'ideal family'. For operatives this was linked to views of fair exchange and the fair employer, analogous to those of the 'artisan ideal'.[42] Notions of the property of men in their skilled labour, entitling them to regular work under fair conditions and to a degree of moral independence and respect, seem to have extended beyond the ranks of artisans narrowly considered, to include mule-spinners, weavers, wool-combers, cloth-dressers and others. Ideas of fairness could have different meanings. The property in labour and access to livelihood could be located at the level of the individual (skilled?) 'working man' – as was perhaps to become the dominant meaning from the mid nineteenth century – the household considered as a producing unit, or a whole community network of interdependence and exchange, composed of non-monetary as well as monetary transactions.[43] In *The Poor Man's Advocate* reciprocity and equal exchange are constructed in terms of the wage bargain, 'for if a working man perform his contract to his employer, if he gives value for all that he receives, there can be no obligation, much less any inferiority on his part'.[44] In the woollen trades fair employment could be seen in terms of the maintenance of an out-working family economy and artisanal control over parts of the labour process threatened with disruption by the growth of factories. Such views might be shared by the proprietors of 'domestic mills', who regarded their mills as 'no factory', but a facility servicing the domestic clothiers. As Abraham Wilkinson, employing twenty-three boys and men

in a mill at Dalton near Huddersfield, argued, 'the more you shorten the
... hours in the factories (I mean where power is applied) the more you
enable the industrious and highly valuable domestic clothier to come
nearer in competition with the opulent factory master'.[45] There were important areas of artisanal control in the diverse processes of woollen
manufacture, 'greatly more numerous than those required by any other
textile manufacture',[46] even where these processes were becoming more
concentrated and subject to the piecemeal extension of machinery. In the
production of worsted, weavers and wool-combers were concerned to
restore a deteriorating bargaining position in face of the big spinners and
the threat that de-skilling would 'DRIVE the Weaver from his Loom, and
the Comber from his Shop'.[47] The employment of a predominantly female
and child labour force in the spinning mills also meant that artisans' conceptions of fair employment could endorse paternalistic control of the
'health and morals' of these dependent categories. There appears to be a
gender difference in the apprehended dangers: knee deformities associated with piecing could undermine boys' later earning capacity as weavers
or combers, while dangers to the moral welfare of girls undermined their
fitness for domestic duties.[48]

Popular Methodist preachers often articulated these concerns: 'he was
always preaching against the Factory System, Describing them as "*Little
Hells*", their steam looms "*Rattling Devils*", and he frequently tells the
Masters they will *all be Damned!*'[49] Such criticisms could go along with
praise for the 'good master' and the invocation of reciprocal duties.

I should be the last man in the world to relax the three-fold chord of *affection*, and
dependence, and *obligation*, which should bind the employer and the persons
employed together – no, Sir, I would rather twist it a *little* tighter. I would have
every factory-master to consider himself as a *father* to his numerous family, and
command and *forbid*, and *smile*, and *frown*, and *correct* and *reward* as a
father... Then reciprocal duty and affection would be delightfully profitable.[50]

Appeals to moralise employment relations through a sense of mutual obligation were a frequent theme of ten hours' propaganda, which might,
indeed, be seen as one of the sources of the language of industrial paternalism. The meanings of such appeals for operative audiences are distinctly
ambiguous, especially given the observed behaviour of most actual
employers. Insofar as notions of mutual obligation in employment were
endorsed, this might be interpreted, either as evidence of a residual
deference and traditionalism, or as a purely calculative use of a dominant
rhetoric. Both these interpretations may be too simple. The appropriation
of a shared language has to be decoded in relation to its specific referents.
It was a language of negotiation, a moral vocabulary which could have a

critical edge, based on the perception that 'there is a difference in factories'.[51] The extent to which radicalism developed a structural critique of
industrial capital during the 1830s is a matter of continuing debate,[52]
although that debate has proceeded with remarkably little reference to the
factory question. It is certainly true that the attack on 'factory tyrants'
was tempered by perceived distinctions between the practices of different
employers – in themselves a universal feature of workers' views of the
employment relation – together with the public stance of exceptional
employers like Fielden and Wood. Even at the tensest moments, spaces
were kept open for a more accommodative language. Some of the contradictions of this are registered in Crabtree's account of the Fielden works at
Todmorden; noting the noise in the weaving-shed ('well might Mr. Farrer
call them *"Rattling Devils"*') and the exhaustion of the girls employed
there, Crabtree abruptly changes tone:

Father went to her and told her to be *good girl*, and mind her work; Well thought
I, if *Parents* manifest such cold indifference towards their offspring, there is no
wonder that avaricious masters act in the manner they do! Leaving the works I felt
inward pleasure of thus having had the opportunity of viewing the extensive
works of a Philanthropic individual, that has risen by his industry, to a princely el-
evation.[53]

Fielden and Wood were of course exceptional, and employers' attitudes
constitute a spectrum from Fielden's outspoken support for a ten hours'
bill to hard-line opposition to all regulation. Employers' practice also
varied, to some extent independently of public political stances, and contained its own ambiguities – for example, the difficult relation between
working-class independence, itself a figure of liberal, as well as popular
radical rhetoric, and the paternalist claims of the 'good master'. The latter
might anyway be a rare and endangered species in the conditions of the
1830s, and claims to this status could be vigorously contested. Reporting
workers' resentment at the financing of a chapel from the profits of their
exploitation – 'a corner of that chapel of mine, and it all belongs to his
work people' – Crabtree 'began to reflect on what Mr Rogers had said
about several Benevolent, Humane and charitably disposed masters'.[54]

Appeals to the mutuality of interests formed part of a moral vocabulary, which expressed workers' ideas of fair employment, and was critically deployed in attempts to mobilise a community consensus.
Operatives' voices are to be heard in particular inflections of these shared
languages. Community opinion, expressed in a series of local polemics
against 'tyrannical' employers and later against the factory commissioners, was an important site for the construction of these values. Crabtree
and Oastler's tour of Calderdale was followed by a protracted battle of

placards, in which the employers were attacked as 'tyrants and cowards', and counterattacked by accusing Oastler of 'receiving Corn law Rents and a Corn law Salary'.[55] As the reference to the Corn Laws – and Oastler's frequent allusions to the hypocrisy of entrepreneurial dissent – suggest, there is often a hint of sectarian and party-political special pleading in such polemics; this was to be projected into national political alignments in the 1840s, though its importance for factory reform can be exaggerated. But imputations of ulterior motives should not be allowed to obscure the wider confrontation of values within the local community, in which Oastler found himself allied to popular radical secularists and dissenters. The demand for a public hearing is a characteristic theme: '*Come out ye Tyrants; I accept your "Challenge"*, and I want to know your names.'[56] In what appear to be headings for a speech, Oastler moves from 'Ashley's Bill' and 'Althorpe's Bill – Preamble' (a reference to the 'over-critical' preamble of the Bill, deleted under pressure from the manufacturers' lobby)[57] to 'Free agents', 'Caning', 'Bad Fathers', and 'Mr Fielden'; then to more detailed points about overwork and truck, concluding: 'Dick – tea 3/-6d ... wholesale warehouses at Rochdale say "Oh put it sideways it will do for Crag [sic] Dale masters to sell among their work-people"!'[58] These attacks were clearly disturbing to employers – all the more so, perhaps, for being posited on a moral judgement of individual conduct. Complaints about the 'undeserved imputation of cruelty and avarice', and the 'sentiments of ... placards posted on the walls of our town' recur in employers' submissions to the Factory Commission.[59] One of the employers mentioned by Crabtree, W. H. Rawson of Sowerby (woollen manufacturing, 30–40 hp water), asserted that statements at public meetings and in Sadler's evidence 'are totally inapplicable to this mill, or any mill in this neighbourhood'.[60] The Factory Commission was thus an intervention in a series of ongoing community polemics.

This context helps to explain popular hostility to the Factory Commission. Halifax operatives protested in turn at the 'attempt made by the Millocrats through their despicable tools the Commissioners, to misrepresent the motives and to vilify the character of the whole operative body'.[61] Anger at a parliamentary delaying tactic and suspicion of a whitewash operation staffed by Whig jobbery contributed to such sentiments. But there was also a wider confrontation of two modes of discourse, alternative models of social knowledge, the legislative process, law and its enforcement. Sadler's adult male operative witnesses were clearly presented as representatives of their trades and communities, the bearers of a corporate social experience of relevance to the legislature; they were repeatedly asked about the 'opinion of the people' in their neighbourhoods, and emphasised the general support for a ten hours' bill.[62] The manufacturers' lobby, the factory commissioners, and historians of the 'optimistic' school have all made much of the pre-selection and rehearsal of Sadler's witnesses. But it is clear from reading the minutes of evidence that these men were the chosen, and probably in some way elected representatives of structured constituencies. The presentation of prepared cases through the select committee procedure was a well established practice, long adopted by lobbies of all kinds, whereas royal commissions aroused considerable opposition, across a spectrum from Tories to popular radicals, as unconstitutional innovations, smacking of Star Chamber despotism.[63] For the commissioners, with their Benthamite cast of mind, facts and opinions had an atomistic existence, and could only be aggregated by expert investigators. As J. P. Kay, a key figure in the definition of state expertise, argued, select committee reports 'are never so minutely accurate as those results obtained from statistical investigations; ... they frequently utterly fail in ... convincing the public'.[64] Leading manufacturers of course had weightier facts and opinions to offer, while any structured representation of working-class opinion, such as that organised through short-time committees, was seen as illegitimate agitation by 'that class of men who entitle themselves, unfortunately with some truth, the delegates of the workpeople'.[65] This does not, however, mean that the commissioners gave a simple endorsement of the manufacturers' views: allegations of Whig jobbery and whitewash, although both elements are certainly to be seen in the Factory Commission, underestimated the new resources and practices of the emerging liberal state. The ten hours' movement seems to have been caught off balance by the commissioners' recommendations and the 1833 Factory Act.

Opponents of the Commission emphasised the voice of the community against such claims to expert knowledge. On his home ground at Huddersfield Oastler demanded 'an open Court' and denounced the commissioners as 'a set of *Briefless* barristers and of *Feeless* doctors'; Dr Thomas Chalmers, of all people, happened to be in Huddersfield that evening, and the burning in effigy of the commissioners, an unpopular MP, and 'another unpopular master-manufacturer' clearly induced a certain *frisson*: 'The spectacle I am sure is a depraving one, and fitted to prepare the actors for burning the originals.'[66] Opposition to the enquiry, and subsequently to Althorp's Bill also implied a view of legislative intervention and law enforcement distinct from that of the commissioners and the general direction of factory legislation thereafter. W. G. Carson has drawn attention to 'symbolic' aspects of factory legislation and to the ways in which administrative and judicial practice provided a space for the negotiation of more accommodative definitions.[67] For popular radicals and populist Tories like Oastler, legislation was seen in terms of the

endorsement and sanctioning of communal norms, rather than the intervention of bureaucratic state agencies. This vision underlay the weavers'
petitions and resistance to the new poor law, as well as the way a ten
hours' bill was seen. The unmasking of 'tyrannical' employers belongs in
this context. Such feelings were to be briefly focussed in the debate on
'personal punishment' at the Wibsey Moor meeting in July 1833. This
issue divided Oastler, with by all accounts the overwhelming support of
the operatives, from Ashley and most other propertied supporters of the
ten hours' movement, as well as from the approach of the 1833 Factory
Act. Oastler at one point advocated the pillory – significantly a form of
punishment with elements of community exposure – as well as prison for
offending employers.[68] Some of his bitterest language, in the period of
'disunion and deflation' following the 1833 Act, was devoted to attacks
on offending manufacturers and conniving magistrates. In *The Unjust
Judge, or the Sign of the Judge's Skin* (1836) he uses an image taken from
a sermon of Latimer about a corrupt judge who was flayed alive, to attack
George Goodman, mayor of Leeds, for dismissing a case under the Factory Act; and in the famous 'law or the needle' speech at Blackburn he asserted that without respect for the law there could be no respect for the
employers' property.[69] Law is seen as the moral voice of the community,
for the protection of the weak against the powerful, and the people owe
obedience insofar as this duty is fulfilled.

These populist conceptions of law perhaps marked a growing distance
between the language of Oastler, operative radicalism and Chartism and
the more measured tones of Lord Ashley and other patrician 'friends of
the poor', as well as of Benthamite social reform. Ashley wrote privately
to Althorp, when agitation was at its height in the summer of 1833, warning him that 'the people are desperate'; he was writing privately, he
explained, 'because arguments drawn from intimidation are both unfit
for the ears of a legislature, and improper excitements to the parties
whose cause is urged'.[70] With the developing debate on the 'condition of
England' the more radical critiques of the factory system and the state
came to be marginalised, in the context of continuing and determined
struggle for a ten hours' bill. Factory reform was thus a matter of how the
'problem' was to be authoritatively defined, as much as of contentions
over the actual length of the legal working day. The factory question continued to carry a diversity of meanings, but some of these meanings came
to be more centrally represented than others in the construction of a selectively interventionist liberal state. The nature of that intervention was
partly shaped by the employers' responses to factory agitation.

II

The textile employers did not constitute a homogeneous group, and recent work has begun to explore divisions among them.[71] Apart from variations in industrial structure and market conditions, with corresponding differences in work relations and employer practices, there were marked political and cultural divisions; the claims of 'Manchester Liberalism' to speak for the manufacturing interest as a whole, or even for Manchester itself, are open to question. There was a significant Anglican and Tory presence, and, within the liberal community, differences between the narrow economism and philistinism caricatured by Dickens and the broader vision of more established manufacturing dynasties. Particular attention has been drawn to the unitarian intellectual networks of liberal reform in Manchester;[72] this emphasis, which figures in the following discussion, rests on the group's strategic role in public debate, rather than on their typicality of employers as a class. The significance of Manchester as a regional centre should be borne in mind here; leading manufacturers throughout the region, drawn together by the Exchange, were participants in Manchester society. Despite its extensive service economy and consequent occupational diversity, which must qualify any picture of Manchester as a town polarised by the factory,[73] its cultural institutions could refract the experience of the whole cotton region. Although Leeds and Bradford provided a certain focus for the woollen and worsted industries, there was no single equivalent to the role of Manchester in cotton.

Attitudes to factory reform arose from readings of the legitimate economic interests of employers and of the 'manufacturing interest' to which they felt themselves to belong, but also from wider considerations of their status, cultural aspirations and claims to authority. While employers, especially in cotton, generally constructed their interests in terms of the market (as defined in some version of Ricardian economics), they might feel uneasy about an apparently uncontrollable competitive process, an unease sometimes expressed in complaints about the irresponsibility and short-sightedness of speculative investment and marginal producers.[74] Economic interests were rarely understood in the narrow cash nexus sense caricatured in the 'Manchester man'. The aspiration of the 'average' business owner was perhaps less to maximise profits and growth than to reproduce his position and that of his family (although the Hobbesian logic of an unstable and fiercely competitive industry might make continued growth the only alternative to falling behind).[75] It is becoming apparent from recent studies that the practices associated with industrial paternalism were not confined to a few evangelical zealots – though such

individuals may have undertaken initiatives with particular enthusiasm
and adopted particular styles – but were quite widespread pragmatic
responses to problems of labour recruitment and control, as well as expressions of the civic duty of men of property.[76] Here again, the functioning of capital cannot be understood without reference to patriarchy and
the middle-class family. The part played by women in the construction of
industrial paternalism, and thus in the consolidation of an industrial
bourgeoisie needs fuller investigation; women could be actively engaged
in schooling, the management of housing, charity and moral surveillance,
while the moralisation of employment relations could be linked to the
redeeming influence, in all classes, of the feminine virtues (for example in
the novels of Elizabeth Gaskell).[77] The family was a much-used metaphor
for the proper relationship between classes. Religious discourse was often
the site for constructing such values, and anxieties about an anarchic
market, cut-throat competition and social dislocation could induce sensitivity to the language of evangelical critics of the factory – a sensitivity
sometimes displaced onto an extreme defensiveness.

Such feelings seem to have cut across the political and religious spectrum. There is no necessary association of paternalism – which might or
might not be accompanied by an openness to critics of the factory – with
Tory critiques of industrialism, or with orientations towards the gentry.
Tory manufacturers, like Oastler's antagonist, Holland Hoole, could be
aggressive exponents of liberal economics; indeed Oastler's polemics may
have been inspired partly by a sense of betrayal.[78] It is thus hard to find
systematic associations between political and religious alignments and
views about factory reform. Such associations were dependent on specific
industrial and community contexts, and would need to be traced out in
those contexts. The most obvious clusterings of opinion appear to be
centred on the Manchester elite in cotton; and the Bradford worsted
manufacturers in the West Riding. A group of leading cotton manufacturers combined a defence of the factory system with support for the
characteristic liberal project of education and moral improvement; this
group opposed the Ten Hours Bill, and orchestrated the characteristic
themes of the commissioners' investigation in response to it, but were
divided over the desirability of more limited measures. Bradford seems to
have had a particularly high level of employer support for factory legislation, though not necessarily for the Ten Hour Bill (see below, Table 2),
linked to a group of Tory-Anglican worsted spinners.[79] This apparently
reflected a sense of moral responsibility as employers of child labour –
John Wood insisted on the need for small children as piecers, and justified
a ten hour day on this ground[80] – and the desire to control undercutting
competition and stabilise the labour-force. According to his overlooker,

Wood offered greater stability of employment, provided sick pay, kept a higher ratio of children per machine, with some apparently on stand-by, as well as offering generally better conditions and humane treatment (though corporal punishment was used).[81] One can discern here the outlines of a strategy of higher productivity from a stabilised labour-force, underpinning the evangelical language of the humane master. Other manufacturers may have been more or less uneasy about the implications of unregulated competition, but felt constrained by that very competition.

The relationship between industrial paternalism and factory reform was a shifting and ambivalent one. Paternalistic controls over the labour-force were justified in a language of mutual obligation, reciprocity, and the mission of the enlightened manufacturer as improver of the poor (in the last analysis, by virtue of offering them employment); and this language may well have been felt as an ethical imperative by some manu-facturers, who were then obliged to live the contradictions of subordi-nation based on mutual obligation co-existing with market calculation. Conversely, competitive effectiveness and the further accumulation of capital were the conditions which enabled employers to fulfil their moral mission. The languages of liberal economics and social organicism were not locked in some metaphysical conflict, but could complement each other – as they necessarily did in the construction of a hegemonic liberal ideology.[82] But the balance between them was a problematical one, and the drawing of boundaries was a contentious matter. Industrial paternal-ists could be fiercely defensive about state intervention in what they saw as their domain, and evinced a marked sensitivity to public criticism of their practices, a sensitivity reflected in some of their responses to factory agitation. Any perceived advantages of legislation in controlling compe-tition had to be balanced against concerns with autonomy and the auth-ority of the employer.[83] The spectrum of attitudes to factory reform reflected changing perceptions of how such contradictions were to be re-solved at any given moment.

When the factory issue exploded in the early 1830s the textile manufac-turers found themselves in a rather isolated and vulnerable position. Sub-stantial sectors of the propertied political nation, especially members of what remained, after the Reform Bill, a gentry parliament, might be responsive to the ten-hours' lobby. Manufacturers themselves were div-ided. Initial responses were often at a defensive 'economic-corporate' level, composed of arguments about the importance of the industry, the investment and employment dependent on it, the threat of foreign compe-tition and apologetic special pleading. For example, Holland Hoole described the Manchester Whit processions of factory children 'well clad and often even elegantly dressed, in full health and beauty, a sight to gladden a monarch – not to be paralleled perhaps in the whole of the civilized world'.[84] In woollen and worsted manufacturing initial responses to the *Leeds Mercury* letters were confused,[85] one effect of the prolonged struggle over factory reform may, indeed, have been the creation of a more coherent 'manufacturing interest'.

Of more strategic significance in reshaping the terrain of debate were the initiatives of certain leading cotton manufacturers and intellectual groupings allied to them – the circles of liberal rational dissent and the Manchester Statistical Society. Such arguments could acknowledge the need for more effective regulation – but also for voluntary effort based on enlightened self-interest and civic duty – while displacing the factory as the decisive site of social anxieties.

The evils here unreservedly exposed, so far from being the necessary consequences of the manufacturing system, have a remote or accidental origin, and might, *by judicious management* be entirely removed.[86]

The recognition that an effective regulation of child labour was the pre-condition for the favoured liberal solution of education was qualified by a concern with market conditions, and the characteristic move of linking amelioration to the repeal of the Corn Laws. This perspective of liberal reform may be related to the position of big, often second-generation capital in cotton, and the requirements of a more 'educated' and efficient labour-force. Effective regulation might also be a way of stabilising the industry and restricting undercutting competition. The characteristic language is that of Benthamism and political economy, infused with a quasi-evangelistic sense of moral purpose. Concluding his *Enquiry into the State of the Manufacturing Population* (1831) on an almost apocalyptic note, W. R. Greg called for:

some cordial, faithful, vigorous, and united effort . . . on the part of the influential classes, to stem that torrent of suffering and corruption, which is fast sweeping away the comfort and the morals of so large a portion of our poorer countrymen; and which, if not checked, will soon send them forth into the world, desperate, reckless, ruined men.[87]

The resources of political economy were central to this position, but they were framed by a moralising discourse of social reform.

Greg's pamphlet, and his friend J. P. Kay's *Moral and Physical Condition of the Working Classes* (1832), were in some respects keynote statements for the project of liberal reform. 'Evils' are recognised, but in terms far removed from the language of factory slavery. Greg is nevertheless unusually outspoken in this liberal context, and some of his ambiguities are indicative of wider confusions of opinion. Greg emphasises very strongly – possibly too strongly, even for most 'reforming' manufacturers – the necessity of a restriction of hours to make education a serious possibility. And he appears to favour a ten hour day, and to justify this by arguing that improved efficiency would make shorter hours economical. But this is qualified by reference to the economic situation of the industry, and 'the shackles and drawbacks to which the Cotton Manufacture is subjected'.[88] Whatever Greg's intentions, his pamphlet was to be cited by ten-hour-day publicists.[89] Oastler evidently read it with attention, and annotated it in his inimitable manner. The reference to ten hours, already italicised, is underlined with a red marginal mark; while opposite the qualification about free trade Oastler wrote 'here Mr. Greg permits his philosophy to eclipse his reason'. And Oastler sometimes takes particular exception to Greg's choice of words: 'what a singular word is this "sloth" to be applied to a man who is [avowedly?] in a perpetual state of *over* exertion'; Oastler paid similar attention to Kay, underlining references to the enervating character of factory work, demoralisation, poverty and disease.[90] Oastler again alluded to Greg in 1836, quoting his more apocalyptic phrases in *The Unjust Judge*. A decade later Fielden referred to Greg as a man 'who wrote a pamphlet in favour of a Ten Hours' Bill, and then altered his opinion (a laugh)'.[91]

In the context of hardening alignments on the factory question Greg's pamphlet may have been something of an embarrassment. The launching of the demand for restriction to ten hours of all under eighteen by Oastler, apparently in an attempt to cut across the qualifications and prevarication over Hobhouse's Bill and probably also to counter the electoral appeal of Whig reform,[92] made Greg's reference to ten hours less acceptable. It is noteworthy that Kay, arguing on similar lines to Greg, referred in general terms to the desirability of reduced hours, but saw this as impossible 'in the present state of trade ... without occasioning the most serious commercial embarrassment'.[93] The early output of the Manchester Statistical Society, in which Greg and Kay both played prominent parts, reflected similar concerns.[94] The proliferation of social concern, organised around issues of education, moral discipline and the urban environment can be seen as a kind of displacement of the factory question. Greg himself would seem to have retreated from the more outspoken aspects of his position in 1831. In evidence to the Factory Commission he made no allusion to his earlier arguments, but reported on his continental tour and the dangers of foreign competition; answering the commissioners' questionnaire as proprietor of one of the family mills, he argued that the cotton trade was in 'too precarious a state to make any further restrictions advisable or safe'.[95] Greg was later commissioned by the Statistical Society to prepare a summary of the Commission's findings: his conclusions are as reassuring as those of 1831 had been disconcerting; 'the principal charges alleged

against the factory system, are here most triumphantly refuted'.[96] The selective appropriation of Greg's arguments by more radical critics of the
factory system, and his own apparent volte-face suggest a hardening of
alignments and closing of the manufacturers' ranks in the struggle to
defeat Sadler and Ashley.

The figure of the enlightened large employer and the association of the
worst practices with backward and marginal producers was a thrust of
the Factory Commission Report, the subsequent debate and much more
recent commentary. This image could be adopted, either to argue that further restrictions were unnecessary and dangerous interferences with the
capital accumulation which underpinned better conditions, or to argue
the necessity of legislation to strengthen the hand of the 'good' employer
and generalise such practices. Employer witnesses at the Commission
were drawn almost entirely from the biggest cotton firms. Whatever conclusion should be drawn about structural change and plant size, in terms
of public representation it was the biggest firms that led: 'Horse power
counted, not heads'.[97] Opinion among these leading manufacturers was
by no means homogeneous, though it seems to have been more coherent
in cotton than in wool or worsted. One group, led by Henry Houldsworth, expressed support for a judicious extension of restrictions, while
implacably opposing ten hours (eight of the sixteen signatories of this
memorial were among the twenty-two leading firms in Manchester).
Others, including such noted industrial paternalists as the Gregs, Ashtons
and Ashworths, opposed further restrictions, while Holland Hoole alluded to the aggressively hardline pamphlet which had aroused Oastler's in-
dignation.[98]

Both groups of employers included figures associated with the Manchester Statistical Society, and there were thus differences in emphasis
among advocates of liberal reform. There were shared emphases as well,
on the economic situation of the industry, enlightened self-interest, education and a moralised and improved labour-force, however the relationship among these might be interpreted.

It is difficult to generalise about the opinion of more 'average' employers. The questionnaire circulated by the factory commissioners does, however, afford some picture of a broader spectrum of employers. There are
many difficulties with these returns, and, quite apart from the serious
problems of omissions and under-enumerations (such important centres
as Oldham, Ashton and the Wakefield and Dewsbury woollen districts
are either severely under-represented or entirely omitted), any classification of the opinions expressed in the returns is bound to be in some
degree arbitrary and impressionistic.[99] In the analysis which follows I
have tried to classify as 'favouring legislation' only those responses that

Table 1 *Factory questionnaire 1833, Cheshire, Lancashire, Yorkshire: employer support for further legislation, by sector and power*

	Employers supporting legislation, reported horse-power:						Total in	% supporting
	0–49	50–69	70–99	100+	Not stated	Total	returns	legislation
Cotton	15	8	3	4	9	39	260	15
Wool	15	–	3	1	1	20	147	14
Worsted	21	4	1	1	–	27	88	31
Of whom supported ten hours, reported horse-power:								
Cotton	1	–	–	–	1	2		0.8
Wool	2	–	–	1	–	3		2
Worsted	1	3	–	1	–	5		6

Source: Factory Commission, Supplementary Report, PP 1834, XX, 1.

appear to see legislation as positively desirable, and not those which are prefaced by such remarks as 'if we must have a bill, then . . .'; the very frequent expressions of support for restriction on the moving power by Lancashire respondents have not been counted, as they were in response to a semi-hypothetical question as to how *any* law might be enforced.[100] The calculations based on these returns are not offered as a complete survey, still less a representative sample, but as a rough indication of distributions among those firms enumerated by the commissioners.

These figures do suggest that support for legislation was not confined to the largest manufacturers, though they may of course have been the opinion-makers in this respect (see Table 1). Differences between areas (Table 2) may be some indirect indication of such influences. The highest proportions supporting legislation appear to be in Manchester – the cotton metropolis, where employer opinion was probably most developed – Bolton, Blackburn and Wigan (though too much weight should not be attached to this in view of the small numbers enumerated). The low proportions in smaller centres ('other') and the intermediate position in the Stockport and Hyde district would seem to lend some support to the picture of less enthusiasm for legislation among the 'country spinners'.

Woollen and worsted masters were less prominent in the public debate – or rather, their participation in local debates was less strongly projected outside the locality. Polemics were conducted in the press, in petitioning and counter-petitioning and in broadsheets, rather than in the pamphlet

Table 2 *Factory questionnaire 1833, Cheshire, Lancashire, Yorkshire: employer support for further legislation, by district*

	Supporting legislation	Total in returns	% supporting legislation
Manchester, Salford	18	92	20
Stockport, Hyde etc.[a]	7	55	13
Bolton	4	11	36
Wigan	3	11	27
Blackburn	2	10	20
Other	2	37	5
Lancs./Cheshire total	36	216	17
Leeds	8	53	15
Huddersfield	8	50	16
Bradford	16	34	47
Halifax, Calderdale	4	45	9
Keighley	5	18	28
Other	10	121	8
Yorks. total	51	321	16

Source: See Table 1; discrepancies in totals from Table 1 are the result of inclusion here of flax and silk.
[a] Including Mottram, Dukinfield

literature which some Lancashire masters were so quick to produce. Overall, the proportion favouring legislation – which in this case meant the application of any legislation at all beyond the cotton industry – was comparable in wool to that favouring further restriction in cotton, and notably higher in worsted. Comparing the main worsted centres, however, there is markedly more support for legislation in Bradford than in Halifax and Calderdale. As in Cheshire and Lancashire, there is less support for legislation outside the main centres, but the difference is not so marked. This may reflect the greater diffusion of the woollen industry, and the persistence of alternative values based on domestic manufacture which might favour legislation.

The language used by employers, whether they favoured or opposed legislation, also provides interesting contrasts between sectors and regions. Replies from the cotton districts seem more standardised, generally arguing, whatever the conclusions reached, from the competitive position of the industry and the problem of cyclical fluctuation. Opponents of further restriction, like Henry Ashworth, anticipated 'the extension of rival manufactories abroad' resulting from 'a considerably

diminished rate of profit, a material increase in the cost of the article produced'; the inevitable consequence would be 'diminished wages and want
of employment'.[101] Most supporters of legislation, on the other hand, saw
it as of paramount importance to frame legislation judiciously so as to
avoid 'any reduction of the profits of the master beyond what will encourage the outlay of capital fast enough to give employment to the work-
people'.[102] Most Lancashire responses tended to be variations on these
themes, often in a simplified form. John Fielden, of course, had an alternative version of the economic problems of the cotton industry, and his
support for a ten hours' bill certainly has to be seen in terms of his interpretation of the interests of manufacturers, and not just his popular
radical political base in Oldham. Fielden had been involved in attempts to
fix weavers' wages on a voluntary basis since the 1820s, and was constantly attempting to get other manufacturers to agree to work short time
as a counter-cyclical measure.[103] Fielden himself is not included in the factory returns, whether because of deliberate boycott or non-enumeration,
but one Manchester spinner, Thomas Flintoff, argued in Fieldenesque
terms that twelve hour working led to 'over-production, and consequent
low prices'.[104]

Woollen and worsted manufacturers' responses seem less standardised
than most of those in cotton, suggesting a more inchoate state of opinion.
Among opponents of legislation there is less emphasis on foreign competition – although this is generally mentioned, it is not much elaborated –
and more on the absolute rights of property 'in this country where freedom is tolerated'.[105] Opponents of legislation also talked in terms of
the necessity for 'man' to labour 'wherever Providence has cast his lot';
moreover 'PROVIDENCE' [sic] required children to work for their keep.
(Oastler annotated that particular remark 'miserable stuff!!'.)[106] There is
a good deal of special pleading: the labour is alleged to be light, the atmosphere more healthy than in cotton or flax.[107] Supporters of legislation
argued simply that 'restrictive hours would be beneficial', 'legislative
enactment [is] the only way to protect children'.[108] This could, however,
be placed in the context of wider conceptions of economic 'interest', divergent from those that were becoming dominant in the 1830s. One small
worsted spinner in Calderdale (10 hp steam, fifty-one workers) saw
restriction as 'what every reasonable man will agree to, except the large
mill-owner' enabling the small producer to survive the competition of
overworking steam-powered mills; while the proprietors of 'domestic
mills' servicing the small woollen clothiers could articulate a vision of a
balanced domestic economy: 'let the steam engine (which cannot feel) do
the chief part of the labour that is required to be done; and let human
beings, especially children, be spared, *but not starved* in this land of

plenty'.[109] The Yorkshire woollen and worsted districts were thus marked by relationships of factory, mill and domestic production, town and country, large and small manufacturers different from those in cotton; these relationships were formulated in a diversity of economic discourses. But it was the voices of cotton employers that set the terms of further debate.

The variation in employer attitudes and opinions cannot adequately be described in terms of differences between big, technically progressive and small, technically-backward concerns. Legislation had different implications in cotton with its history of existing, albeit ineffectual, restrictions, higher proportion of steam power and greater urban concentration, from wool or worsted (which in turn differed from each other). The question of stopping the moving power is only the best-known aspect of such differences. Even employers with a broadly similar 'reformist' outlook, like those associated with the Manchester liberal elite, could differ on the proper balance between state and voluntary initiative, the advisability of given proposals, tactics and timing. The Factory Commission Report certainly projected the views of such 'enlightened' manufacturers, and it is not surprising that the Manchester Statistical Society should see the findings as a vindication – they were, after all, relaying back the essential points of an argument the Manchester intelligentsia had been busily constructing. However, it may be too sweeping to conclude that the 1833 Act 'marked a great victory for at least a segment of the manufacturing interest'.[110] Certainly the Act marked a defeat for the ten hours' movement, and one which caught it off balance. But it left no one happy, and matters remained unsettled. The relay system, for example, was never widely adopted, even by the large urban-based manufacturers whom it is often supposed to have suited.[111] And the battle over enforcement took place in the context of problems of labour supply, followed by deep recession in the later 1830s. Even employers generally favourable to shorter hours and compulsory schooling might oppose the implementation of such a measure at that time. Whatever the congruence between particular measures and the interests of sections of employers, and whatever benefits they might, *ex post facto*, have perceived, most extensions of factory legislation were vigorously resisted.[112]

This employer resistance related particularly to the implications of state enforcement for the authority and autonomy of the employer, and to fears that continuing public debate would legitimise the ten hours' delegates. John Marshall, while giving general support to Althorp's Bill, nevertheless complained (in notes for a speech that was not delivered) that some of the commissioners' suggestions were 'objectionable', reflecting 'the same rancorous spirit which has guided the conduct of persons out of doors'.[113]

The commitment of some employers to schooling and the regulation of the age of employment had to be balanced against a marked sensitivity about any kind of 'outside interference'. This was dramatised, almost certainly with the desire on both sides to make a test case, in the famous conflict between Henry Ashworth and Leonard Horner.[114] As Ashworth noted, it was paradoxical that Horner should cite his school 'with expressions of approbation' then prosecute him for a technical offence.[115] But the paradox captures the essential ambivalence of the enlightened manufacturer. Accommodation to factory legislation was to become part of an image of the rational factory system and the benevolent employer that helped form the industrial paternalism of the third quarter of the nineteenth century.[116] Many of the practices associated with paternalism, and many of the languages used to justify it can be seen earlier. But their articulation together was an *ex post facto* rationalisation, and depended on further transformations in the meanings attached to the factory question.

III

The redefining of the factory question belongs in a wider context of the shaping of the Victorian state and the accommodation of interests within it, and the construction of 'social reform'. The legislative and administrative process opened spaces for negotiation among divergent positions; the language of official expertise and social knowledge functioned as a language of negotiation, but carried with it deeply embedded assumptions and ways of seeing. Evangelical Tories like Ashley could enter a dialogue with Benthamite liberals within this framework.[117] State intervention in a number of spheres was shaped by a series of compromises among contending forces. If the 1830s saw the elaboration of projects of Benthamite rationalisation, and vigorous resistances to them, at both popular and ruling-class levels, the 1840s saw modifications of this project through its incorporation into a broader governing consensus, which shaped the agenda of the 'condition of England'.[118]

Attention has been drawn to the role of claims to expert knowledge in this writing of public agendas, and some of the factory inspectors would seem to fit this picture.[119] However, their role was in many respects reactive rather than initiatory.[120] Insofar as they were zealots, it was for the wider liberal project of education and moral discipline linked to class conciliation, as much as for any specific regulation of factory labour. Indeed, the debate about state servants as 'zealots' should not be allowed to obscure the fact that even routine and pragmatic responses were conditioned by ideological frameworks; speaking or writing requires language, and language is not the neutral medium that some historians, themselves perhaps too much inside the common sense of the state functionary, suppose it to be. The constitutive role of state expertise is thus to be seen in the reordering of agendas, as much as in agenda-setting initiatives. The factory inspectors had initially been inclined to defer to the expertise of leading employers; they were, Saunders later claimed, 'led to believe that a serious injury was about to be inflicted on all classes engaged in manufacture' by the age stipulations of the Act.[121] The pressure of popular agitation, and the parliamentary defeat of Poulett Thomson's amendments to the Act pushed the inspectors to take a more independent line. John Lawton, a former Manchester operative and member of the short-time committee, claimed at Ashley's Select Committee of 1840 that the appointment of 'shadow inspectors' by the short-time committees had led to a marked improvement in the efficacy of inspection.[122] Popular outcry and the desire to contain unrest pushed the inspectors, parliament and elite public opinion to take a firmer line on enforcement. But if Leonard Horner was responding to outside pressures and grappling pragmatically with the difficulties of his job as he saw it in strife-torn industrial communities – an experience which may well have produced moments of exasperation with both employers and operatives – he was nevertheless an active interpreter to a wider public of the meaning of his functions. In a pamphlet of 1840 he presented the benefits of factory regulation in terms of the growth of more rational attitudes among both employers and workers; the law was now accepted by many employers and 'the most considerate and best disposed among the work-people themselves'.[123] In a characteristic liberal refrain, 'acts of violence and lawless outrage' by 'these deluded people who followed the Chartist leaders' were attributed to 'their deplorable ignorance'.[124] The enlightened manufacturer, who realised that 'it will cost a great deal less to maintain, in food, clothes, and lodging, two strong healthy men employed to perform a piece of work, than would be required if we had to employ three men to do the same work, because of their inferior muscular power',[125] was complemented by the figure of the 'considerate and well disposed' working man. Horner thus outlined a perspective of moral order and economic efficiency, appealing to the longer-term rational interests of employers and workers, and projecting the role of state servants in monitoring this diffusion of rationality.

State expertise in this area should not necessarily be seen in terms of the advocacy of any specific measure (it was limited in its capacity to address the labour process, for example; the factory commissioners' attempt to do so in their suggestion of relays had met with mixed success); but the intervention of the official experts produced an atmosphere where the desirability of regulation, linked to education, moral improvement and efficiency, could be established. The terms of legislation emerged from wider processes of struggle and bargaining, in which parliamentary politics and official administration played an important role. With the involvement of the short-time committees in pressure to enforce the existing law (albeit with a view to exposing its inadequacy), operatives' organisations were drawn onto this terrain of bargaining and negotiation, while still insisting on the necessity for a uniform ten hour day. The 1840 Select Committee, chaired by Ashley and including Fielden, Brotherton and Hindley, with, at the other end of the spectrum, R. H. Greg, marked an important moment in this respect. As its report noted, the committee's terms of reference were 'limited to an ascertainment of the operation of the Act, of its defects, and of the probable remedies.... It was not a new law that was required by The House, but the fulfilment of the intention of the existing law.'[126] The 1833 Act could then be placed in a consensual perspective of progress, while leaving open the extent of further progress or the nature of further legislation:

Your Committee must congratulate the House and the Country on the partial success of their efforts for the removal of many evils, which, down to the year 1833, had accompanied the employment of children and young persons in factories; much, unquestionably, yet remains to be done; the actual condition, nevertheless, of these young workers, contrasted with the state in which the first enquiry found them, is such as to give Your Committee considerable satisfaction for the past, and good hope for the future.

Action to remedy defects in the Act, while remaining within its broad intentions, would remove 'the several causes of heartburning and mutual distrust between the employer and the employed ... by the revival of a good understanding on all sides'.[127] As its terms of reference indicate, the committee was largely taken up with problems of enforcement, especially the vexed questions of age certification and the rights of entry; and much of the evidence is from the inspectors and their subordinates, the superintendents.[128] But while the recommendations were confined to these issues, the proceedings provided a platform for ulterior positions. Fielden questioned witnesses on the intensity of labour, pursuing the controversy about the distances covered by piecers in a day's work; while Ashley challenged employers on their moral responsibility for the children they employed, which, he implied, went beyond mere legal obligations.[129]

The factory question in the 1840s, like other aspects of the 'condition of England', was characterised by the construction of a debate in and around the state, to which a range of interests and opinions felt they had some access, although by no means an equality of access. Some voices were privileged over others, but this did not produce a uniformity of discourse – still less of opinion, and opinion might always vary, sometimes on 'technical' grounds, within a shared language. A variety of positions could then be organised into a debate, around a language of negotiation, a common reference to 'the prosperity of the trade, and the welfare of the nation'.[130] This contrasts with, for example, the polarisation between Sadler's Committee and the Factory Commission (Ashley's Committee significantly, but inaccurately alluded to the latter as 'the first enquiry').[131] Factory reform is a particularly interesting aspect of the construction of such debates, in that an organised and articulate body of working-class opinion was present on its own behalf. The 1840 Committee sat at a time of deep depression and threatening Chartist agitation: there was indeed much 'heartburning' in the industrial North, and the insistence on a rhetoric of improvement and mutuality may reflect anxiety rather than confidence.

Anxieties about distress, moral degeneration and Chartist insurgency – often seen as linked in ruling-class opinion – created a public for the social knowledge produced in the debate on factory labour. Official enquiries and public debate on such issues as factory reform, the weavers, poor relief, education and children's employment were summarised and paraphrased in journalism and fiction, ranging from the weighty analyses of the quarterlies to more popularised presentations. Industrial tourism, in which pamphleteers like Crabtree and factory commissioners and inspectors had engaged for reasons of social commitment or official career, seems to have been a growing phenomenon in the 1840s, attracting the idly curious as well as the socially earnest.[132] Much of this literature in fact recirculated a limited stock of impressions and anecdotes, such as the story of how Ashworth's fruit was left intact by starving operatives in 1842.[133]

Two particular emphases of this proliferating literature worked to incorporate social criticism into the liberal vision of a rationalised factory system. First, by its very nature the development of state regulation and the associated public debate tended to project a series of distinctions between 'good' and 'bad' factories and masters, just as, among the operatives, concerns with fair wages and employment produced analogous distinctions. Critiques of the factory system could be recuperated in terms of such judgements, especially as it was argued that the best conditions were to be found in the biggest and most technically advanced factories, so that improvement would result from the further growth of the factory system. As Horner argued in a celebrated exchange with Nassau Senior:

The law was not passed for such mills as those of Messrs. Greg and Co ... Messrs. Ashworth ... and Mr. Thomas Ashton .... But there are very many mill-owners whose standard of morality is low, whose feelings are very obtuse, whose governing principle is to make money.[134]

One motif is what might be termed the 'industrial pastoral'. If the 'country spinner' could sometimes be presented as an undercutting competitor, the well-regulated mill village with the manufacturer as industrial squire could be presented as a contrast to the poverty and demoralisation of the town centre. Cooke Taylor describes Ashworth's Turton in these terms, and the *Ten Hours Advocate* reprinted a rather similar account of Fielden's mills, though with a different political message: 'the air is most salutary, and the natural advantages of the place so great, that, in spite of the excessive labour to which the operatives are subjected, they in general appear cheerful and healthy'; there is no mention of 'rattling devils' or exhausted children.[135]

Second, as the agenda of the 'condition of England' extended into mines, child and female labour generally, the weavers, out-work and sweating, and urban conditions, the factory lost its centrality as a focus of social concern. Indeed the very possibility of regulation in concentrated sites of production was held out as a token of the superiority of the factory over other forms of labour. Oastler and the radical operatives had projected a vision in which the regulation of the factory, and the protection of labour generally was the key to remedying social distress; and this emphasis persisted, for example, in the anti-machinery rhetoric sometimes present within Chartism. The authoritative public opinion elaborated in the debate on the 'condition of England' saw social problems as separate, and the evils of the factory as by no means the worst – though possibly the most readily remediable – form of social distress. Education and a morally improved labour-force became the key. In part this enumeration of discrete social evils arose from a series of polemical assertions and counter-assertions by contending interests (lending some credence to the view of the 1847 Factory Act as the protectionist gentry's revenge for the repeal of the Corn Laws). Factory masters often pointed to the existence of worse problems elsewhere; and in the case of the weavers quite near at hand. Ashworth made a point of showing Lord John Manners the severe poverty in Bolton,[136] and Cooke Taylor argued that it was necessary to find a situation, like Turton, where 'the influence of factories could be seen undisturbed'.[137] Representations of the well-regulated factory in 'undisturbed' conditions – which might well include lower wages as well as cleaner air and company welfarism – proposed the factory as the solution rather than the problem. And reformers often argued that further legislation would enable the factory to fulfil its ideal function.

The eventual introduction of a fairly effective Ten Hours Act could be seen as a logical development within this ideological framework. However, that development was at every stage bitterly contested, and can be explained only by popular pressure. There appears to be a certain shift in

the language of the ten hours movement, as it became drawn into the parliamentary and administrative debate. This is perhaps registered in the
histories of the movement produced by participants like 'Alfred' and
Philip Grant. The shift from militant opposition to the Commission and
all its works – which is documented more fully than by many subsequent
historians – to the battles over enforcement and a Whiggish view of the
1833 Act as an inadequate and faltering first step in the right direction is
indicated but not explored and explained.[138] The ten hours' movement
itself seems to have taken some distance from the more explosive
moments of the 1830s. Welcoming Oastler's return to public activity in
1846 the *Ten Hours Advocate* introduced the familiar theme of his over-
coloured language, expressing pleasure that 'he is resolved to use moderation and argument in all his speeches'.[139] The general tone of the
Advocate (published in 1846–7 in the lead-up to the 1847 Act) is one of
quiet determination, reasoned optimism and appeals for class conciliation. 'The time ... is fast approaching when the force of public opinion
will accomplish an object which avarice alone can retard.'[140] More radical
interpretations of the factory question certainly persisted, for instance
within Chartism, whose personnel probably overlapped the short-time
committees. Noting this overlap, Grant nevertheless claims that 'in no
instance in any of the agitated districts was there recorded, within our rec-
ollection, one seditious speech by any member of a Short Time Committee'.[141] Visiting the textile towns in the depth of depression in 1841
Ashley was duly gratified by the restraint of the operatives: 'What a sin it
is to be ignorant of the sterling value and merit of these poor men! A few
words of kindness are as effectual with them as a force of fifty thousand
soldiers on a French population.'[142]

The ten hours movement, then, deployed a rhetoric of class conciliation, and composed its arguments increasingly from a repertoire of evangelical moralism – of Ashley's rather than Oastler's brand – and
Benthamite enlightened self-interest. Factory reform became part of the
construction of the Victorian liberal state. But the engagement in this process was never an uncritical one, and the liberal state itself has to be seen
as a space for struggle and negotiation, rather than an incorporative
machine. The parliamentary consensus around more effective enforcement did not mean the abandoning of ulterior positions. As Lawton told
the Select Committee, 'speaking for myself, and for a very large majority
of the operative spinners, I should recommend ... 10 hours a day, and a
uniform working day for the whole'.[143] He also suggested a divergent
view of enforcement; with a uniform day for all, the common informer
could observe when the mill started, in contrast to the 'inquisitorial' proceedings of the superintendents (the summary fining of operatives, the

burden of obtaining new certificates on shifting mills, and the removal of the inspector's office from Manchester were particular grievances).[144]

The debate on factory reform thus continued to embody distinctive operative perspectives, though these were perhaps less centrally articulated, and less challenging than in the 1830s. Ten hours' propaganda insisted on the minimal protection of labour, including in the last analysis adult men's labour. This was constructed as a moral imperative, and a necessary limit to the sphere of political economy. Men had a right to work and a decent livelihood, regardless of the state of the markets: 'property itself was the creature of society, and could only exist rightfully and permanently on conditions consistent with the welfare of the whole community'.[145] Linked to this emphasis on minimal protection as an absolute right was the firm insistence that only an effective ten hours' bill could settle the issue: the Whigs 'had miscalculated the stern stuff of which the friends of the Ten Hours were made' in imagining that Althorp's Bill could be a satisfactory settlement.[146] The demand for ten hours had the virtue of simplicity (despite the complications of water and steam power and restrictions on the mill engine) and could hold together operatives in diverse situations and with diverse understandings of what such a measure might achieve. If, as Marx sometimes suggests, factory legislation is in some sense in the logic of capitalism, there is nothing in that logic to fix the standard working day at ten hours. The 1833 and 1844 Acts and the problems of enforcing them owed much to the continuing pressure from without for a ten hours' bill; and these battles helped convince some employers that *any* measure that would settle the issue might be better than continued uncertainty. The Ten Hours Bill, Grant wrote later, was a 'Charter of ... liberties' and he exhorted operatives to be 'firm in its maintenance'.[147]

IV

The Ten Hours Act, together with the repeal of the Corn Laws, came to form part of a symbolic 'social settlement', underpinning the apparent social harmony of the mid-Victorian period. Contrasts between the prosperity and harmony of the third quarter of the century and the distress and unrest of the second quarter seem to originate in the retrospective constructs of contemporaries, and historians should certainly subject such notions to critical scrutiny. In mid-Victorian conventional wisdom the absence of factory acts became part of a collective memory of the 'bad old days', an unacceptable face of capitalism that no doubt worked to make its current face seem more benign. Thomas Wood, an engineer and son of a handloom weaver in Bingley, remembered his days as a piecer: 'Going to the mill in those days was vastly different to what it is now. There were no inspectors, no public opinion to put down flagrant cases of oppression, or of cruel usage.'[148] W. R. Croft dedicated his *History of the Factory Movement, or Oastler and His Times* (Huddersfield, 1888) to a William Armitage of South Crossland, 'recognising your unwavering and persistent adherence to the principles of human liberty and social freedom throughout the world, at a time when it was hazardous to speak one's mind and espouse the cause of the people'.[149] Croft's work, which claims to be based on the recollections of local people, would thus seem to be part of the liberal recuperation of radical and Chartist memory that characterised the 1870s and 80s, notably in Frank Peel's *Risings of the Luddites*.[150] One of Croft's informants recollected seeing Oastler display a handful of bloody hair, allegedly from a girl assaulted by a violent overlooker – 'Behold! another bloody trophy of tyranny!' – and Croft comments 'I hope for the honour of Huddersfield that this story is not true ... now, at all events, there are no factories in England better regulated than those of Huddersfield.'[151]

From the 1860s the factory agitation could be recalled, within a rather bland liberal consensus, as part of the general progress of society. Reference to Oastler's 'emotive language', combined with some recognition that he had a valid point, is a frequent element in this placing. Oastler seems, however, to have been warmly remembered by the operatives, and been admitted to the civic pantheon on that account. In a celebratory volume of 1868 produced in aid of the new Leeds Infirmary Oastler is duly commemorated, the next entry being devoted to none other than Sir George Goodman, the 'unjust judge' of 1836; both presumably qualified as *Eminent Men of Leeds*, striving to do good according to their lights, and the antagonisms of the 1830s are not mentioned.[152] In Liberal Bradford a statue of Oastler was inaugurated in 1869 before a crowd of a hundred thousand, 'the final mammoth rally'.[153] Visiting the sculptor's studio, W. E. Forster wrote to Matthew Balme:

...the possession of the monument will I cannot but think be precious to Bradford both on account of its merit as a work of art & as a memorial of a good man & a great cause.... If I could find any fault it was with the children that they were too healthy looking – rather like what Oastler & his fellow-workers have made Bradford mill-children than what they were when he struggled for them – but it is too much to expect of a sculptor that he would not make his figures as good looking as in him lies.[154]

For employers, the improvement associated with the Factory Acts became part of the image of the well-regulated factory as the site of that economic, social and moral progress that the Victorian bourgeoisie liked to represent as its mission in life. And the public debate on factory labour in the 1830s and 40s was, as we have seen, one source for the language of reciprocal rights and duties in industry. The evangelical strand in factory reform, against a background of economic adversity and popular agitation, seems to have encouraged a reappraisal by some employers, or at any rate provided a language in which they could construct their motives and values.

The fierce animosity displayed against mill-owners during this agitation, and the unmeasured abuse heaped upon masters by their own workpeople, led me, and doubtless other employers, seriously to review our position, and to ask ourselves if we had done our duty to those over whom Providence had placed us?[155]

This public enthusiasm for factory legislation was, however, uneasy and ambivalent. Part of the thrust of Edward Akroyd's argument (just quoted) was to defend the factory system by the familiar tactic of scoring points at the expense of those large sectors of employment which remained unregulated, and to exhort other employers (like those of Birmingham where Akroyd was speaking) to follow the example of social responsibility provided by the big textile manufacturers. In advocating factory act extension Akroyd emphasised the element of education and moral discipline; extension would in effect mean compulsory schooling, while 'minute and vexatious regulations' in the workplace were to be avoided.[156] The factory inspectors clearly saw themselves as agents of moral improvement among the operatives, as much as their protectors from unscrupulous employers.[157]

The impact of this within workplaces, and the degree to which such rhetoric corresponded to norms which were internalised and reproduced in work relations is of some relevance to the making of industrial paternalism, and demands fuller treatment than can be undertaken here. It would seem that the formal requirements of the Factory Acts, as well as the rhetoric of public debate may have worked to augment employers' authority – an authority that some employers seem to have had thrust upon them – while limiting their freedom in other directions. According to Robert Baker's much-used handbook on the Acts (1851) 'a person is considered to be employed in a factory when doing any kind of work whatsoever within the entrance walls of any factory, whether for or without wages', and the employer or his agent ('any manager, overlooker, slubber ... or other person employing persons under him, whom he himself sets on is an agent') are responsible for the conditions of protected categories thus employed.[158] One Keighley firm asked the inspector to endorse their managerial appointments; he refused as 'we have no authority to confirm or disallow any arrangements you may make with your own men for the observance of the Factory Acts'.[159] Statutory regulation may thus have helped to formalise and standardise managerial practices, perhaps through the space it created for the diffusion of social knowledge about factory practices as much as through its formal requirements. Employer responsibility for events within the juridically defined space of the factory involved some tightening of control, as well as the amelioration of conditions; the overworking employers of the past were allegedly 'as much sinned against as sinning' through embezzlement, 'mill robbery' and other depredations.[160] As important as the actual requirements of the law, was the construction of the moral responsibility of employers, extending beyond minimal compliance. Employers at the 1840 Select Committee were challenged on this by Ashley, for instance in an exchange with Richard Birley:

I speak to you as an honest man ... whether you do or do not consider it to be a duty on your part to make yourself sure that the certificate [of age] speaks the truth? – ... I consider that we are bound to take every ordinary precaution, but I do not consider it is my duty to pay more special attention to that point than I do to other parts of my business.[161]

Some of the pressure for an enlarged view of employers' responsibilities seems also to have come from operatives' resentments about employers' evasion of responsibility by summonsing parents or adult employees.[162] In this respect the debate surrounding factory legislation may have been one site for redefined conceptions of work, the wage bargain and the respective spheres of responsibility of employers and workers.

Factory reform thus had some bearing on the making of mid-Victorian industrial paternalism. To decode more fully the rhetoric of the responsible employer would demand a more detailed investigation of the actual workings of legislation, including the important issue of the efficacy of enforcement and the exercise of administrative and judicial discretion.[163] The extent to which the factory acts meshed in with changes in the labour process and a stabilisation of the reciprocal expectations of employers and groups of workers is an important issue here. It is difficult to disentangle the effects of specific legislative measures from wider changes, which were themselves variable as between industrial sectors and localities. If the symbolic meanings of factory legislation helped stabilise textile communities around the figure of the responsible manufacturer, this has to be placed in the context of a generally expansive economic climate. In the worsted industry, for example, the transition to machinecombing seems to have been eased by this favourable context; Akroyd and other paternalist employers were praised for the way they had minimised distress and the displacement of adult male labour.[164] The provision of relatively stable employment underlay the social leadership of employers; even those without other claims to distinction had the merit of 'circulating a vast amount of money in wages'.[165] In this economic context the factory acts might function as an important symbol of 'industrial legality' and reciprocity between employers and workers.

The growth of any such sense of reciprocity was necessarily rooted in changing workplace relations. Changes in the labour process were not as such dictated by the terms of the factory acts, but by conflict, negotiation and shared understandings within the framework set by the acts (insofar as they were observed). Thus the restriction of women by the 1844 Act may have helped consolidate the male spinner-piecer system in cotton, but this outcome was the effect of workplace bargaining in which the terms of calculation had been altered for law-abiding employers and operatives by removing one advantage of adult women over teenage men as piecers, since adult women were now restricted on the same terms as 'young persons'. The general effect of legislation was not to exclude women, but to define terms for their participation in waged factory labour, balancing off the domestic role against waged work – a balancing act performed at some cost to the women involved. However, the rhetoric of public debate, and informal workplace bargaining may have encouraged a redivision of labour on gender and age lines. Job segregation within the workplace probably became more defined and organised, with moral concerns about mixing on the factory floor and dangers to unmarried girls; while some large employers banned the employment of married women, thus possibly helping to produce a dual labour market in the localities concerned.[166] Equally, the stress on education may have produced a stratification of the labour-force, between half-time factory children and their families and those able to afford full-time schooling; it was the latter group, Akroyd asserted, who had the best prospects as adult operatives.[167]

The consensual rhetoric of factory reform could have differing meanings in specific industrial and local contexts, requiring more detailed examination by local case-studies. In particular, it will be necessary to investigate how far 'public' languages of state reform coexisted with more 'popular' languages in workplaces and communities. For operatives, the factory acts may have been important as a symbol of 'industrial legality' (Philip Grant's 'charter of liberties'), especially where trade unions were relatively weak. And the construction of women and juveniles as protected categories reinforced notions of the adult male 'breadwinner' as an independent free labourer. The long struggle for a ten hours' bill could be seen in retrospect as an important victory for working-class pressure, evidence both of the moral integrity and determination of working people and of the ultimate receptivity of the legislature. This class dimension is not always immediately apparent. In the various near-contemporary histories of the movement the operatives are certainly present, but it is not *their* role that is celebrated, so much as that of propertied sympathisers like Oastler, Ashley and Fielden, and, by extension, all men of goodwill, regardless of creed or class.[168] At a deeper level, however, the constant operative support for such enlightened and humane men, and their acknowledgment, in turn, of the workers as moral agents was an assertion of working-class identity. There is a substratum of collective pride in the operatives' affection for a figure like Oastler:

The sacrifices you so nobly made, regardless of reproach, calumny, and persecution – while battling for the weak against the strong, for truth against error – for principle against expediency.... We know you feel, that you have not lived in vain. Of that fact we are the evidence ... one of the results of the factory legislation in this part of Yorkshire, is, as you always said it would be, the best of good feeling between masters and workmen...[169]

Thus declared the Huddersfield operatives in 1856, presenting Oastler (then living in retirement, in reduced circumstances in Guildford) with a suit of broadcloth 'knowing you will not like it the worse, because it is given to you by the factory workers'.[170] The history of factory reform could certainly be viewed as a vindication of the operative short-time committees' fundamental assertion that only a uniform day would be effective and that a ten hour day was necessary and desirable. This had moreover prevailed against much 'expert' and authoritative testimony from employers and others to the contrary.

Factory reform was in this sense an important site for renegotiating some of the inherent contradictions of liberal ideology. The market of liberal economics – as the economists themselves realised – existed in a legal and moral framework. But the setting of that framework, and the drawing of boundaries around it was a matter of continuing contention. As Fielden described the dilemma of the government and their commissioners in 1833:

But they are 'political economists'; and though, *as men*, they could no longer screw up their minds and hearts so far as to sacrifice any more limbs and lives of infants, the science would not suffer them to invade the 'freedom of industry', by involving the adult in that protection which they were obliged to give to the child.[171]

Much debate was concerned with the drawing of such boundaries – between morality and the market, dependent and free agents, the state and the rights of property, the household, the factory and the school. This contention was open in the 1830s, when varied kinds of discourse – popularised romanticism, evangelical religion – claimed to have something to say about the operation of labour markets and the experience of industrial work. From the 1840s the boundaries appear more settled, with an authoritative discourse of reform and moral improvement framing economic and Benthamite languages with a moralising social commitment. This seems to have worked effectively as a language of negotiation, incorporating more radical critiques into a liberal vision of a moralised and rationalised factory system, which could then be held out as a model to other sectors of economic activity. But, as a language of negotiation, liberal reform could only resolve contradictions by reproducing them. Divergent meanings and emphases were never far below the surface, and the boundaries of discourse were jealously guarded. Whatever social harmony prevailed in the mid-Victorian decade has to be seen as a fragile construct rather than an achieved and stable state. A fuller history of factory reform will have to investigate the subterranean currents below the smooth flow of consensual rhetoric.

7

Time to work, time to live:
some aspects of work and the re-formation of
class in Britain, 1850–1880

KEITH McCLELLAND

I

As we trudge through the 1980s it is now widely accepted that not just capitalism but also the socialist alternative is in a crisis of both definition and practice. One central element of that crisis concerns the core conception of *who* is to make socialism. Raymond Williams has pinpointed one aspect of the problem. Writing of that powerful and dominant tradition of thinking which fixed the wage-labourer as the decisive agent, he comments that many theories of socialism, and more specifically the form of trade-unionism, came to be centred 'not only on the working man but on the man *at work*', which 'often amounted in practice to the *isolation* of this one powerful form'.[1]

This essay explores the foundations of this focus upon the 'man at work' within the emergent practices of some trades and trade unions in Britain between 1850 and 1880. And while I think that these practices had important implications for the subsequent development of British socialism – in all its forms – this essay does not explicitly address those consequences. Rather, it is limited to an examination of the working class prior to the creation of modern socialist ideas about work and its meanings. Moreover, the focus here is upon parts of a working class which contained a considerable diversity of forms and contexts of labour, female and male, paid and unpaid, within an unevenly developed capitalism.[2]

Those with whom I am mainly concerned here are only one, distinctive, section of this working class: adult male skilled workers in engineering and shipbuilding and related metal-working trades, and even more specifically those on Tyneside. The essay is, as a consequence, quite concentrated in the material used. However, there are a number of reasons for this delimitation. In the first place, such workers have been central to debates on the re-formation of the working class in the period, especially in discussions about the emergence of a supposed 'labour aristocracy'.[3]

Secondly, the forms of trade-union organisation which these men built and the conceptions which they held about the nature and place of their labour in the society as a whole exemplify some of the changes in the historical meanings of work which were occurring. Thirdly, they were working in industries and an area in which one can see a quite major development: the consolidation of industrial capitalism as a whole system of economic and social relationships.

Tyneside had a number of specific features.[4] Its economy and geography were dominated by the emergence of a relatively small number of large-scale companies which had a stability and solidity which came to be visibly implanted on the landscape. In moments of economic boom like the early 1870s they were joined by more ephemeral, speculative ventures. But the core companies were ones that lasted, at least until the catastrophes of the twentieth century. There were about ten such engineering companies, some of which employed upwards of 1,000 men, while the biggest, Armstrong's engineering and ordnance works, employed 3,800 in 1863. Similarly, in shipbuilding about a dozen companies dominated, with the leading ones tending to even larger size: by 1880 Swan Hunter's was employing 6,000–7,000 while Palmer's of Jarrow employed 8,000 by the end of the 1880s.[5] Of course, there were smaller companies than these, but this was a world not of the small workshops of Birmingham or London but of the pervasive influence of a relatively new kind of capitalism that structured the physical and social communities in which it was lodged. Moreover, this was not a world in which both men and women were employed in paid industrial labour, as in the Lancashire cotton districts, but one overwhelmingly of men's work. So far as one can tell from inadequate census figures and other sources, relatively few women worked in formal, paid occupations.[6]

The labour force that built these companies was not only large and concentrated; it also contained a substantial core of *skilled* men. While there are considerable difficulties in defining skills, for the moment I mean those who would generally have served a formal apprenticeship or who had worked for (usually) five years at the trade, and were recognised as 'tradesmen' by themselves and others.[7] In engineering, the skilled trades of fitters, turners, patternmakers, blacksmiths and others formed perhaps 40–50% of the whole work-force; in shipbuilding the platers, riveters, angle-iron smiths and others formed a slightly higher proportion, at around 50–55%.[8]

Such men were generally thought of by contemporaries as 'artisans' or 'mechanics' and were also frequently thought to be sharply divided from the rest of the working class.[9] However, such rigid classification was inattentive to some of the more ambiguous and loosely defined classifications

of others. In the first place, there were differences of status at the workplace which could be observed, as when 'A Son of Toil' referred to the
'blacksmiths, turners, fitters &c.' as 'second-class tradesmen'.[10] Second,
the 'artisans' were often seen as part of a wider group which itself might
be vaguely defined, as when, for example, shipwrights in Liverpool were
referred to as simply part of the 'labouring' or 'humbler classes'.[11]

The difficulties of accepting too readily social classifications which
were quite frequently ambivalent or imprecise are compounded by the use
of the terms 'artisan' or 'mechanic' to refer to workers such as those with
whom I am concerned. Iorwerth Prothero has convincingly argued that
the artisans of the early nineteenth century are best thought of as those
men of varying degrees of skill who were members of 'the old, specialist,
unrevolutionised handworking trades' while the more restrictive term
'mechanic' should be used to refer to the 'skilled artisans', 'the better-off
journeymen who belonged to trade societies'.[12] But to refer to the skilled
men of the second half of the century who were working in industries like
engineering and shipbuilding as 'artisans' or 'mechanics' in these senses
detracts from some of the *differences* between the 'old' and the 'new'. Certainly there were distinct similarities in the attachment of the skilled man
to his trade; certainly these were men who invested their work with their
own considerable knowledge and skills, not least because of the continuing heavy reliance on them of large sectors of even the most 'advanced'
sectors of British capitalism.[13]

Levels of skill in the engineering and shipbuilding industries varied,
both between trades and sectors, and it would be a mistake to suppose
that skills were purely the property of those who were recognised as being
'skilled'. For example, platers' helpers in the shipyards certainly had skills
which were developed in highly specific tasks.[14] But to take simply one or
two trades generally recognised as skilled, the persistent importance of
'handicraft' abilities, of varying kinds, is undoubted. In locomotive engineering, fitters did virtually all of their work by hand, using scrapers, files
and chisels to adapt 'each part of an engine to its place with the most
minute exactness'. The blacksmith's trade required 'much above the
average in intelligence and education' and to excel in their craft needed
'powers of manual dexterity [and] habits of observation and of adaptation'. Or in shipbuilding, it was said of the plater, one of the boilermaking trades, that he did his job by 'beating down the projecting parts of the
edge with his hammer till he considers it sufficiently straight, and when
well done a sound joint is made; but ... the *degree* of accuracy thus
attained is very much at the discretion of the workman'.[15]

Yet at the same time there was a vital difference of context in which
such labours were performed. The difference was essentially one of con-

trol over the forms and relations of production. The technological and
economic transformations of engineering in the 1830s and 1840s and
after, and of shipbuilding from the 1850s with the rise of iron shipbuilding, were built on the destruction of older forms of production and the
reconstitution of a new division of labour with new skills and tasks. But
the range of skills was both different from and less all-encompassing than
hitherto. While a degree of immediate on-the-job control and autonomy
persisted, which in some trades like boilermaking was pretty considerable, this has to be seen in relation to the major result. The economic and
technical compulsions to labour for capital and the more fragmented
division of labour within both these industries meant that no *single* trade
could exercise control within the whole labour process to the extent that
the millwrights had been able to do in engineering or the shipwrights in
shipbuilding.[16]

One dimension of the more systematic control of capital over labour lay
in the attempt at least to impose a more rigorous regulation over time and
conduct. If a general diminution of the 'normal' hours of labour in British
industry was occurring between 1850 and 1880 there was also an attempt
to impose a more regular working day, although this was always subject
to workers seeking to reduce by formal or informal means the actual time
they put into work (a point to which I shall return).[17] At Stephenson's
locomotive factory in Newcastle, to take only one example of quite widespread practices, the workman's time was regulated by a time-board upon
which was written the time, the articles he was working on, and the engine
or other machinery they were for. Reinforcing this was regulation of conduct. The company's rules included the imposition of fines for damaging
equipment, making excessive noise, smoking, leaving work without
giving notice to one of the foremen, and many others, including even one
for coming in or leaving by 'any Door other than that adjoining the
Office'.[18]

It seems likely too that workers were under continual pressure to work
harder. How far this was so is virtually impossible to judge. Certainly the
incomplete estimates of productivity in these industries or for the economy as a whole all suggest a general upwards movement in the period; but
the extent to which this was due to a greater intensification of labour, how
far to changes in capital equipment or the reorganisation of labour processes cannot be statistically established.[19] But many workers clearly
thought that they were having to work harder as the period went on. For
example, John Allen of the Boilermakers' Society told the Royal Commissioners of 1867 that while there had been a 10% increase in the wages
of shipyard riveters, there had been a 50% advance in the amount of work
done. Indeed it was said of riveting in the 1890s that it 'is a difficult trade

to learn, a hard and exhausting one to follow, wearing a man out in his youth, for no one ever saw an old riveter'.[20] And of course when men struck for reductions in their hours, as the engineers did in their great strike of 1871, they did so in part because of the 'present excessive hours of labour'.[21]

There was assuredly a widespread expectation that people should work hard. The necessity of 'work', of various kinds, was one of the most compelling, saturating, values of the culture. Condensed in the discourses upon the nature, purposes and meanings of work which emanated from commentators ranging from Carlyle to Samuel Smiles, Ruskin to the political economists, were not only arguments about the nature and possibilities of economic relationships but also those about individuality, morality and religion. The complexity and diversity of these views cannot be explored here: evidently, they drew upon many sources, including Protestantism, Romantic critiques of industrialism, and hard-faced utilitarian notions of what it was to be human or, more particularly, a man.[22] However, what I would emphasise here are just two aspects of the discourses of work. Firstly, manual labour was seen by many as a necessary, burdening, compulsion. For instance, the economist J. R. McCulloch gave voice to the persistent belief that 'the eternal law of Providence has decreed that wealth can only be secured by industry – that man must earn his bread by the sweat of his brow'.[23] Yet, secondly, work of this kind was also seen as an activity to be celebrated, not only in the writings of Carlyle[24] but also by those who found the virtues of work in the ordinary materials of everyday life. A journalist wrote of Hawks, Crawshay's Gateshead ironworks in 1854: 'The stern duty of WORK – hard, sweating, energetic work – presides over the whole.'[25] More than this, labour was celebrated as part of a single project in the creation of a national culture grounded on work and its productions. Addressing workers at an anniversary meeting of the Mechanics' Institute in Elswick, Newcastle, the Rev. Rowland East proclaimed, 'what a glorious thing labour is!' (which might, he added as a good protestant, be succeeded, not preceded, by pleasure). His sentiments were complemented by those of G. W. Rendel, a partner in Armstrong's, who saw labour as one of the essential foundations of the nation and Tyneside's contribution to this as particularly distinctive:

Happily, the spirit and industry of the people have proved equal to the call made upon them during the last 30 years, and have earned for our country the honour of leading the way in mechanical science, as well as the more solid advantages of wealth and plenty. Newcastle, more perhaps, than any other town, has contributed to this result; and amongst the men of Newcastle, those who have worked in the Elswick Engine Works have taken a prominent place.[26]

II

But if there were continual exhortations from employers and others to work, and work hard, how did workers themselves feel about their labour? While a commanding fact of the period from the 1840s was the continuing, if uneven, expansion of the economy, what was also of great importance was the sense of the permanence of the system. The apparent fixity of economic relations and institutions came to be a quite central assumption of the thinking and practice of the kinds of workers discussed here.[27] 'By commerce we live' declared the miners of St Hilda's colliery in South Shields in a demonstration of 1873,[28] and many like them came to believe that their futures, as workers, were bounded by and dependent upon the future of the economy as a whole. At its most global, this was frequently articulated in terms which were consonant with liberal ideas of free trade and the growth of the economy on a world scale. Liberals like Richard Cobden believed that the world was composed of competing individual nations. If, like individual persons, they were able to pursue their self-interests then the greatest happiness of the greatest number would be ensured. Sharing much of this vision, the Boilermakers' Society thought that world economic progress, the extension of commerce and manufacture, was opposed by trade restrictions and war. But what would guarantee peace was free trade, as it guaranteed the general economic welfare:

What we want is free trade pure and simple, that we may have the markets of the world open to us, and then we can hold our own against all comers.

Between them, free trade and peace would entail the 'advancement of liberty, justice and equal laws all over the world'.[29]

Yet if workers existed in a world felt to be both permanent and one which held out the possibilities of progress, it was also one in which scarcity and insecurity were governing facts and fundamental structures of their lives. There was chronic insecurity not only for the abysmally-paid seamstress or the labourer, but even for the better-paid engineering fitter or boilermaker. As a basic fact of life it underlay the attitudes of workers and unions to how they should effectively operate and it established an exceptionally important boundary of what was thought to be possible. Moreover, this was not seen as something which simply concerned the worker as an individual. When trade-unionists and others contemplated the potential terrors of scarcity of jobs they were well aware that they spoke not just as individuals, nor even as part of a collectivity of workers within particular trades and industries, but, usually, as men who had dependents. These men knew that they lived with the constantly gnawing possibility that any gains in wages or conditions of work might

be short-lived and melt away as quickly as snow in summer. As Robert
Knight of the Boilermaker's Society said, workers must:

make the best of the sunshine we now enjoy, for as certain as night will return, so
surely will the clouds of depression again surround us with gloom, loss of work,
and consequent suffering to ourselves and families.[30]

What produced insecurity was the nature of an economy in which men
and women were picked up, tossed about and thrown down by its uncontrolled booms and slumps. Knight, whose views were shaped by shipbuilding, an industry subject to more intense fluctuations than almost any
other, commented:

These unhealthy, feverish spurts, followed by years of idleness, are not conducive
to the best interests of the workman and those dependent upon his earnings. What
we desire is a steady, progressive development of trade that will be a guarantee of
constant, permanent employment for those bread winners who have to supply
food for more mouths than their own.[31]

How workers understood their relation to this economy was not however a simple reflection of the brute facts of its apparent permanence or of
insecurity. It was refracted through the available discourses which
attempted to make sense of what that world was like. One important
dimension of this was the decline of an alternative to the prevailing orthodoxies.

In the first half of the nineteenth century a popular political economy
had been formed which posed a very considerable challenge to the developing, dominant, precepts of 'classical' political economy. Noel Thompson has summarised that challenge:

Classical writers were accused of elaborating theories which bore little relation to
the objectively observed facts of exploitation, poverty and general depression; of
formulating, instead, theories designed to defend the interests of capitalists and
landowners; of obfuscating the true causes of general impoverishment and
material distress suffered by the labouring classes; of constructing a political economy purged of any ethical dimension; of concerning themselves exclusively with
how to maximise the rate of capital accumulation rather than how to optimise the
distribution of wealth and, therefore, viewing Man as a means of increasing production rather than regarding his welfare as the sole goal of economic activity.[32]

But by the 1840s, as Thompson also argues, popular political economy
had entered a period of crisis and degradation as an effective practical and
theoretical critique of capitalism and classical political economy. Indeed,
the crisis bit so deep that few were to envisage the possibility of any radical alteration in the nature of economic relations until a new socialist
vision began to be available and take hold in the 1880s. There was not,

however, an utter abandonment of the preoccupations of earlier generations in the intervening period: as I shall argue, one of the most important elements that was sustained was the *moral* dimension of the popular critique. But the 'internal' weaknesses of the theories propounded were exposed by their inability to cope with changing 'external' circumstances. Above all the problem was that while a plausible explanation of distress and crisis was offered, what could not be done was to explain continuing economic growth and relative prosperity.[33]

There was, in the subsequent period, a general narrowing of the range of discussion of the nature of economy and economic relations. There is little which had the vibrancy and quality of exploration of the 1820s and 1830s. Nor was there any popular theoriser to emerge of the stature of William Thompson, Hodgkin or Bray. Rather, those who dominated the discussion of economy were the political economists and those who translated their relatively abstract theories into 'practical ideology'. As Philip Harwood told his audience at the London Mechanics' Institution in 1843:

The mysteries of economical science are mysteries no longer; the recondite wisdom of the Smiths, Says, and Ricardos has become the diffused convictions, the common sense of society.[34]

This 'common sense', whose doctrines 'remain unimpeached' and are 'unattackable' for 'they are true now and will be true to all time',[35] not only defined this or that economic 'law' but the whole field of activity of what was thought to be 'the economy'. Although as a practical ideology it was certainly not free of moral and cultural assumptions and maxims[36] – how could it be? – as a theory it abstracted 'the economy' from other kinds of human relationships and activities and declared that men and women were subject to its 'laws'. Political economy, thought John Stuart Mill, does not concern itself with the whole of man's nature or with his human passions or motives 'except those which may be regarded as perpetually antagonizing principles to the desire for wealth, namely aversion to labour, and desire of the present enjoyment of costly indulgences'.[37]

In one sense, workers saw labour and capital as bound together in a single project, unified by the economy. But at the base of this was a continuing adherence to the view that labour was the foundation of wealth and society, that simple idea which, in different forms, has been of the utmost importance to so much radical and revolutionary social and political thinking over the last 200 years. It was regarded as axiomatic, as part of the common sense of working men, that they were 'the producers of wealth by labour' and that the workman was the 'founder of society, the substratum of social prosperity'.[38] As a sailcloth weaver and former

Chartist of North Shields, Thomas Thompson, put it, it was 'the artizans, the mechanics and the seafaring population who produced the country's wealth'. Or as Ralph Currie, an engineering worker at Stephenson's, said: it was the working classes who had built the steam engines and had been the great colonisers and had 'cleared the wild bush and made the desert blossom'.[39]

However, labour was defined as *one*, distinct element in the productive process. Capital was seen as another. If labour was the 'arch of society, capital is the keystone'. While capital was derived from labour it had assumed a difference from it in that it was possessed and concentrated in the hands of those who were not labourers. The Chainmakers' Society thought, like John Stuart Mill, that capital was 'accumulated labour, useful inventions and acquired skill which had been handed down from the past'.[40]

The acceptance of capital as having both a distinctive and legitimate place rested, in this period, on the effective practical abandonment of any claim in terms of 'the right to the whole produce of labour'. When John Burnett of the engineers defined the nature of labour he said:

Political economy defines labour as the voluntary exertion of mental or bodily faculties for the purposes of production, or as the action of the human frame directed to the manufacture of useful articles.[41]

What is of interest about such a view is not only the appeal to political economy as the defining set of ideas about the nature of labour but also that it implies no theory of natural rights. For when earlier radicals and workers had claimed that they had a 'property' in their labour they espoused the belief that to have such possessions was to have a natural right, as producers, to the products of their labour.[42] At the same time Burnett's view of the purposes of production retained something of the belief that the goal of production was the welfare of the whole, the achievement of the general good.[43] But it was a view largely sundered from both the 'right to the whole produce' and its corollary, a theory of exploitation.

In this period after mid century what became much more pronounced was the belief that capital, as well as labour, had a rightful claim to a share of the product. Labour's position as the founder of wealth was seen to be the structure upon which capital rested: between them the two elements were the most important constituents of the whole economic machine. The *Chainmakers' Journal* offered one view of this. Originally labour had been recompensed by their own products: the gold-digger who found gold was remunerated for the labour he had expended. But there then emerged – it was not explained how – the landlords and capitalists who each wanted their shares which were 'natural deductions from the original wages of labour'. The result was that now any increase in wages could only be derived from an increase in capital because capital was accumulated past labours.[44] This was to accept a good part of the doctrine that the level of wages was determined by the amount of capital available to pay wages. Indeed the Nine Hours League claimed in 1871 that the fact that they accepted this showed:

that we really know what we are doing [for] we all remember our own interest in the extension of the capital which is destined for the payment of our wages better than to stop its flow recklessly and for a mere whim. We know that whatever we do which diminishes or stops the flow of that capital must react with heavy effect upon ourselves.[45]

What was increasingly seen as determining the share of labour and capital in the product were the governing 'laws' of political economy and of supply and demand in particular. It has now become part of the historiography that, by and large, trade-unionists by the 1860s were rejecting political economy 'by word and deed' and that in so far as they accepted any part of it they did so on 'practical' and pragmatic grounds, taking from it only what appeared to suit their particular interests.[46] Certainly there was a range of opinion of the validity of its doctrines and there is a good deal in the notion that trade-union practice did not accord wholly with its precepts. However I think such a view underestimates the extent to which these workers took those 'laws' as the first premiss of their actions and felt constrained by them. As the Iron Founders' Society put it, they disliked the laws of political economy but 'as practical men, we must accept the situation, it being out of our power to alter the position at present'.[47]

In other words, the relations between capital and labour were accepted as being structured, at bottom, by the market. Given this and the legitimate place of capital, it was fully accepted that the *ultimate* determination of the market relation, and particularly the wage, was supply and demand for labour. Thus capital or the employers 'have a perfect right to get their work done as cheaply as they possibly can'.[48] On the other hand it was both proper and necessary that labour also operate according to market demands. Charles Blake, secretary of the Tyne and Wear Chain Makers' Union, told the annual meeting in 1861:

since the commencement of the present Union they had directed their attention to obtain the best wages the state of the market would allow, and to prevent employers obtaining an exorbitant profit out of their labour. Masters always had a right for a fair profit upon their capital invested, and remuneration also for their business capacity, but when trade was prosperous it was the business of workmen to see they enjoyed their share of that prosperity.[49]

But Blake, and men like him, also insisted that collective organisation and action – *union* – could mitigate the consequences of those 'great natural laws' for 'our experience leads us to believe that these great laws are quickened in their operation by a little artificial aid, and trades unions supply that assistance'. In short, the 'artificial' modified rather than fundamentally altered the 'natural' and set limits upon what employers could do to the men. Practically speaking this meant that it would be 'unrealistic' to imagine that trade unions could raise wages in a depression or prevent reductions: that would be to transgress the ultimate limits of the 'natural'; but what they could do was to 'accelerate an advance of wages, or ... retard reductions'. It also meant that in practice there was no 'natural value' or 'nominal price' for labour in the sense that employers imagined, that is, the lowest price or wage they could get away with. Rather, the wage was 'whatever the workman is able to obtain from the employer' and the collective strength of union would amplify his capacity to do so.[50] I shall return to the questions of the wage and the union a little later, for while the building of the union was seen as the central instrument by which men might regulate the relations between capital and labour, its foundations lay in the *trade*, whose boundaries were not yet formally fixed in the institution in many industries.[51] So it is to the trade that it is necessary to turn.

III

For skilled men it was the cardinal importance given to the trade which was what distinguished them from the unskilled or those 'without trade'. The primary purpose of collective organisation, formal or informal, was to protect and regulate the trade in which men believed they had a 'vested interest'. The printers said that the object of their society was to 'protect the rights, privileges, and usages of the letterpress printing profession' and such sentiments were widely shared.[52] Bound up with these notions too was the idea that men had a 'property' in the trade which was acquired through apprenticeship. The Birmingham Wire Weavers' rules of 1869 summarise this:

Considering that the trade by which we live is our property, bought by certain years of servitude, which gives to us a vested right, and that we have a sole and exclusive claim on it, as all will have who purchase it by the same means.[53]

The importance of these notions was emphasised long ago by the Webbs and their central place in the eighteenth- and nineteenth-century artisanal culture has been recently stressed by John Rule and others.[54] By the second half of the nineteenth century they were being weakened in some degree, at least to the extent that the decline of the 'right to the whole produce of labour' and the emphasis upon the market relation tended to nullify their potentially anti-capitalist concomitants. However, they persisted in the importance which tradesmen attached to apprenticeship and the transmission of skills. After all, if such men had nothing else then they did have this property or, as some put it, 'our only capital, namely skill and labour'.[55]

Skilled workers had a tremendous sense of pride in their work and skills, symbolically represented in both the ownership of personal tools, as Hobsbawm has emphasised, and in the fact that when unions like the Boilermakers' Society held public demonstrations, as they did on Tyneside from 1865, they carried models of ships as well as the tools of their trade.[56] There was not only the sense that their skills were indispensable to production but, more than this, that those who possessed them were the repositories of knowledge about it. Moreover, knowledge may be embodied in the individual workman, but it was necessarily a collective knowledge, passed through time by collective experience and learning. The Boilermakers' Society expressed this when, contemplating the threat of an influx of unapprenticed labour in the early 1870s, they asked:

who trains, instructs, and qualifies ... lads to become thorough workers in the trade – does the master? No; the instruction these lads receive comes from the men; and when a man has spent years in acquiring a perfect knowledge of his trade, such acquisition becomes his own personal capital as much as the gold or silver he carries in his pocket.[57]

Of course, the actual ability of the men to protect apprenticeship and their collective knowledge was coming under considerable pressure. By the end of the century the numbers able to practise full apprenticeship regulation were smaller than either those having formal regulations but who were unable to enforce them or those who had no such controls. Yet if formal indenture could not necessarily be hung on to, at least a union like the Amalgamated Society of Engineers could insist, as they did from the beginning, that for a man to belong to the union and to be a recognised member of his trade he must have served at least five years at it.[58]

What also threatened the men was the structural division of 'mental' and 'manual' labour. In both engineering and shipbuilding there was a growing separation of the two and a developing fragmentation of knowledge about the *whole* production process. This was embodied, in part, in the rise of the professional engineer or naval architect and the creation of distinctive design departments in the companies.[59] This and the division of labour on the shop floor put into question what the tradesman's knowledge was knowledge *of*. There is apparent a certain loss of knowledge of the whole, reflected in the Shipwrights' Society telling the Royal Commission on Labour in the 1890s that they were considering offering inducements to get properly trained men, perhaps by sending them to naval architectural classes, so that they may have 'a theoretical as well as a practical knowledge of the trade, and so that they may more thoroughly understand the construction of the vessels they are building'.[60]

Yet if knowledge was preeminently of *the trade*, the importance of this should not be underestimated. On-the-job learning remained by far the most important way of transmitting skills, in the relative absence of the means of acquiring technical knowledge elsewhere. Certainly no engineering company could have done without the intelligence and adaptability of the patternmaker who 'today ... may be employed on a pattern, the like of which he has never seen before, and to-morrow on something quite different, and many of these patterns are of supreme difficulty and need deep and careful thought'.[61]

The learning of technical skills was imbricated with the construction of social identities. As Thomas Wright wrote, 'the social phase of life in a workshop – the phase embodied in the customs and the traditions of "the trade" – is generally the first into which the beginner is initiated'.[62] It was here that some of the definitions of the work-group were established and sustained, including not only the collectivity but also, as integral to it, the integrity of the self of the worker and his 'manhood'.

Apprenticeship continued to be defined by many as a period of 'probationary servitude' in the manner of the Birmingham Wire Weavers. It was a state, that is, of a kind of necessary 'unfreedom' through which it was essential to pass if a lad was to emerge as both a competent workman and an independent, free man. This is evident in the terms used, not least in the notion of being 'bound' or of 'serving' one's 'term'. Charles Manby Smith wrote that when he had finished his apprenticeship he was 'free from all bonds and indentures'. Towards the end of the century, Paul Evett, also a printer, found that having learned the 'art and mysteries of the trade', 'my term of servitude had expired'.[63]

Evett also indicates the other dimension of this in that he had not only acquired the right to the trade but also that he had grown to 'man's stature', that he had made the transition from being one of the 'boys' or 'lads' to being one of 'the men'. Such transitions were ritually celebrated by drinking and eating as were other rites of passage like marriage or becoming a father. In 1843 for example, Thomas Wood, an engineer, 'was called upon by the custom of the shop to provide a supper for the men'. Among shipwrights at about the same time, those who became apprentices or got to the end of their time had to pay large sums – between one and five pounds – for drink, often leading to two or three days of 'idleness' and 'drunkenness'. Men paid too for getting married: among Scottish cotton spinners they also paid if they had been spinning a pair of wheels in the same shop for a year and had *failed* to get married. There were also payments made, by employers as well as men, when the products of labour were completed.[64]

Such customs did not go uncontested. There were rules imposed by employers like Stephenson's mentioned above. Some shipbuilding employers successfully put a stop to the 'allowance' system in the yards in 1858 although at the cost of a strike by the shipwrights who, to the exasperation and incomprehension of the local paper, clung to their pint of beer with 'tenacity'. Still, the employers were not wholly successful in the short run: three years later, Emanuel Young, a shipbuilder and magistrate of North Shields, declared his intention of putting an end to footings in the yards (fees in drink demanded of new apprentices), a move welcomed by the South Shields Total Abstinence Society who resolved to write to all the Tyne shipbuilders commending the action.[65] But in the long run, these pressures, and those coming from unions like the Boilermakers' Society, who were, as I indicate below, consistent opponents of drink, probably had the effect of removing drink from the work-place but only by keeping it to the pub.

Where the customs of the trade persisted they were enforced by strict and sometimes brutal 'rules', although it is possible that these were on the decline in the period. The shipwright who came to work on a Monday morning with dirty shirt or shoes or unshaved might simply be fined; but the new apprentice who had failed to pay his footing suffered 'flogging with a handsaw from time to time' and 'other mal-treatment' until he paid up. Enforcement had the power and rituals of law as well. Among Scottish blacksmiths there were 'courts of justice' in which 'he who presides wears a quantity of tow (in many cases) around his head, in imitation of a wig, and is styled the "Lord Justice Clerk". The decisions of these judges are final; and such as do not comply with them, are compelled by persecution to leave the shop.'[66]

What was also learned in the workshop was the distinctively masculine. The defining of sexuality in the workshop is clearly an extremely difficult subject to get at but it is hinted at by, for example, Thomson's *Autobiography of an Artisan* written in the 1840s. He recalled that as an apprentice he had felt himself to be an outsider, for he could not join in the 'mad roysterings' of the other lads: as a result he was the butt of their 'coarse jokes and taunts'.[67] It is made more explicit by T. R. Dennis, a cabinetmaker writing about practices of the 1920s but which could hardly have been new. As an apprentice he was subjected to sexual humiliation by the others. Cast on to a bench by them, his trousers were pulled down and his genitals were 'painted' with glue and saw-dust. 'God knows how a girl must feel when molested', he wrote, but 'I felt awful.' Yet he could not tell his mother (although she guessed that something had happened) and he could not expect his father to complain for 'all apprentices got tricks played on them' and if fathers protested 'then boys would be called "cissies"'.[68] As this also indicates, such grotesque 'games' were probably licensed by the men but in ways which, like all 'licence', required that the limits be known. Apprentices could taunt each other but not the men, even those who were labourers. As 'A Working Man' wrote:

If a journeyman detects an apprentice 'coming it strong' in the way of ordering about a labourer, he will immediately come it strong in putting down the offender; sometimes in a literal sense by a well-directed 'clip under the ear', if he be a young boy, while if he be too old for that eminently practical form of remonstrance, a severe 'tongue-dressing' will be administered.[69]

The preservation of this route to being an independent tradesman necessitated defending its transmission from one generation to the next, preferably through a patrimonial system of apprenticeship inheritance. E. P. Thompson has observed that for workers 'the critical point of familial transmission has [been] ... at the point of giving the children "a start in life"'.[70] One might add that so far as the skilled workers were concerned this had a distinctly agnatic bias. Evidently the extent to which sons were able to inherit their fathers' trades is a matter of dispute and uncertainty. But there cannot be much question that it was at least an important part of the aspirations of the tradesmen. Among iron founders, it was said in the 1890s, it was generally the sons who got into the trade; among boilermakers in the depression of the 1880s the Society was having to impress upon its members that the pressure of fathers to get their sons into apprenticeship was leading to the market being overstocked, to the consequent detriment of the trade; and among shipwrights, again by the 1890s, it was being accepted that patrimony was on the way out and that their union ought to take eligible lads, regardless of whether their fathers were in the trade.[71]

A challenge to the patrimonial could be accommodated; but any serious assault on apprenticeship itself would lead, it was thought, to a general degradation of the men, a crushing of the spirit which would extinguish a good part of being human. Leave the question alone, said the Boilermakers' Society, and the conditions of 'men' – by a 'slip' they assimilated women and children to the category – would suffer:

First of all wages fall, then a large number out of employment; wages fall again; then men are in work, and then they are out, and still matters grow worse, until we become like the nail makers, and other trades we could mention, where father, mother, and children are all employed to earn such a miserable subsistence as makes life itself weary and desolate, and which has eaten all manhood and independence out of them, wages being so low that for shame they can go no lower.[72]

IV

Degradation was thought to be quite likely for it was widely believed that while there were employers who were particularly bad, perhaps *all* of them had the potential to treat the men with contempt. Some reserved special opprobrium for those engaged in speculation and reckless competition. At times this was expressed in terms which would have been readily understood earlier in the century as when the Iron Founders' Society complained of the corrupting role of 'middlemen and speculators who gamble with the products of millions of toilers' while 'the lot of the worker is a bare subsistence while in the prime of manhood, and often (but for Trade Unions) a pauper's fate in old age'. But it was primarily the direct employer of labour who was the chief enemy, partly because he too was ultimately bounded by that 'law' of economy, 'a law that is ever at work, as steadily and silently as time, which is ... that as commerce is now carried on, there is a constant tendency to bring down wages to the lowest level'. Obedience to this law might result in the capitalist keeping the worker in a 'state of bondage' (or 'slavery') but behaviour of this kind by employers was largely seen as a contingent matter and correctable if only they attended to their moral responsibilities. Surveying the recent history of capital–labour relations in 1873 Robert Knight wrote:

were the history of strikes faithfully written, a great number might be traced to bad manners on the part of supercilious employers, who, by good luck, have acquired wealth without the feelings of gentlemen, and who were not morally fit for the important post of captains of industry.

But against this were the 'good' employers, those many 'excellent gentlemen' who were anxious and wishful to deal as fairly with their workmen as they possibly can, and believe in paying operatives an equitable remuneration for their skill and industry'.[73]

The sense of the moral was of vital importance. For if the economic was seen as the first premiss, the primary determination, of action, there was a profound belief that the system could be subject to human intervention and that such intervention should be closely attentive to needs. With the practical shrinking into the background in this period of the two great alternative methods of regulation of economic affairs which had been looked to earlier in the century – state intervention and co-operative production – it was labour acting in union which would play a decisive role in this, because employers would be held in check and be compelled to be mindful of their duties towards workers. For their part, the men expected that they should behave in such a way too: if they had rights they also had obligations towards the employers. In other words, union was seen not only as the pursuit of particular claims concerning wages, hours and conditions of work, but also as a kind of morally purifying agency which would dissolve the bad and the corrupt. In this sense it was thought to be possible to construct a world of 'reciprocity' pivoted on a morally regulated exchange of labour against capital.[74]

Some were optimistic about the realisation of this possibility. The *Chainmakers' Journal* in the 1850s felt that the relations between employers and employed already rested on consent. 'Great industrial enterprises are conducted ... not by force, but by willing labour' and the consequences of this were that the world was progressing to

the improvement of the physical condition of the masses of mankind; to the free intellectual development of all; to the abolition of the remnants of feudal tyranny; and to the recognition of the independence of the worker, of his dignity and importance, in this conquering of the material world, which is the distinguishing characteristic of the civilization that now exists.[75]

It was a view belied not only by the actual conditions of insecurity in which chainmakers and other workers actually lived but also by the continuing struggles which workers had to put up in order to build and sustain trade unions in the face of persistent economic and politico-legal obstacles. The Boilermakers' Society achieved virtually 100% unionism in the shipyards of Tyneside by the 1870s but, for most, the situation was inimical to trade-unionism. Only gradually was opinion among employers shifting towards an acceptance, willingly or otherwise, of its existence; until the reforms of the 1870s, the unions' legal position remained uncertain, while the use of the Master and Servant laws had been widespread in the 1850s and 1860s; and, above all, economic conditions made it virtually impossible for any but those able to exercise fairly tight control over the labour market to sustain organisation. Even for skilled engineers the building of a viable ASE in the north-east was a protracted business. The trade-union movement certainly had established a permanent place in society by the 1880s, but only by continuously attending to its organisational roots.[76] So, in important ways, the kind of optimism displayed by the chainmakers was not realistic. But the *aspiration* that underlay it was central to the moral cosmology of trade-unionists and to their desire to bring order to the always potentially unstable and disordered world that threatened them. The nature of that threat and the remedies for it were summed up by the Iron Founders' Society in 1880:

We are desirous to be at peace with capital; the two interests, capital and labour, should work harmoniously together, for they cannot otherwise succeed in the full acceptance of the word. If we are to hold our own against all comers, the sooner this principle is recognised by each side the better it will be for both. Quarrels only recoil on those who create them; both suffer immeasurably by continued warring; each interest has duties to perform as well as rights to expect. This law must be acted up to before peace can be restored; selfishness, treachery, want of union and united action among the ranks of labour, and often a dissatisfied spirit, when things are going on tolerably smooth, create disastrous results. On the other side we have overbearing greed, a desire to become rich in an unusually short time, a needless competition to take work at a figure at which it is impossible to pay, and for which first-class work to be turned out is out of the question altogether. All these combinations of evil work out the inevitable injury of both interests.[77]

The countering of 'selfishness' among the ranks of labour and the regulation of the employers necessitated the imposition of order and discipline on the men for unions knew that 'prior' to the formalised union, and co-existing with it, was a system of 'informal' bargaining and attempted control of the workplace. The story of this is complex and cannot be gone into at any length here,[78] but some of the dimensions of it may be suggested by reference to time and wages.

To what extent workers' abilities to regulate time in informal ways were diminishing in this period is an open question. In general it is evident that practices such as St Monday were under attack but how successfully is uncertain.[79] However, stealing back time from work unquestionably persisted (as of course it still does). Thomas Wright said that 'keeping nix' was probably the first thing an apprentice in engineering learned. This 'really important job'

consists in keeping a bright look-out for the approach of managers or foremen, so as to be able to give prompt and timely notice to men who may be skulking, or having a sly read or smoke, or who are engaged on 'corporation work' – that is, work of their own.[80]

Harry Pollitt recalled that at the turn of the century in Lancashire, when the men returned from a holiday the boilermakers would congregate in the yard. The eldest would pick up a brick and announce:

'Now lads. If t'brick stops i' th'air, we start; if t'brick comes down, we go whoam.' I do not remember any occasion on which we did not 'go whoam'.[81]

Such practices appear to have been widespread and were particularly prevalent when economic conditions were favourable, especially for those on piece-work. There were persistent complaints by the Boilermakers' Society of men staying away from work to drink, as in 1881 when it said that 'stopping off drinking is the greatest evil that our trade and society has to contend against'.[82]

Stealing time was complemented by the practical regulation of working
time by the work-group itself, who maintained either a 'customary' standard or one that had been recently won through action. This entailed both
the regulation of how the work was done and the time spent doing it. The
puddler, it was alleged, could do more than he did but practice had established six heats as the proper quantity 'and as soon as he finishes this he
goes home, leaving his furnace for an hour or more doing nothing'.
Among the chainmakers, 'in the North an approximation is made
towards a fair and reasonable day's work, by mutual agreement among
the chainmakers themselves' although, it was added, in 'the south'
(by which was meant the Midlands) an 'extravagant' amount of work
was performed. Custom could also sometimes be concerned with the
maintenance of an acceptable minimum. J. P. Grieve of the Thames shipwrights in the 1840s said that 'we cannot work harder; if a man does
not do his proper quantity of work, his master and his mates look blue
upon him'.[83]

The importance of the customary in the determination of the wage level
has long been stressed by Eric Hobsbawm.[84] Informal regulation of it was
dependent upon, among other things, the time that was put in. For those
on piece-work, a system that was spreading in the period,[85] and who had
some degree of effective bargaining power and autonomy in the workplace, there was at least the chance of keeping their earnings relatively
high. Yet this might also be dependent on the absence of a formal system
of collective bargaining, because of the absence of agreed standard rates
for the job. In 1882 the Boilermakers' Society complained that the prosperous state of trade appeared to some members as a justification for
pushing up the rates. In these circumstances 'a sort of "inner circle" is constituted by a few workmen, who meet in the yard and decree what shall be
the price paid on certain jobs'.[86]

However, the unions thought, and generally correctly, that the overall
wage level did not go up unless there was regular trade-unionism. This entailed the suppression of some of the practices of 'informal regulation'. I
do not wish to suggest that what *this* meant was the wholesale suppression of a pristine, morally unsullied rank-and-file, untainted by the
evils of bureaucratisation. It did mean, however, the unions giving shape
to and leading the men in ways which were, by their own lights, unselfish.
The claims of the collective were placed above those of individuals and the
responsibilities of the men to each other were insisted upon. Yet at the
same time both of these concerns were drawn into a sense of 'responsibilities' to capital. One may see this in respect of the wage. Daniel Guile
told the Royal Commission on Trade Unions:

One good effect of a union is that every employer shall pay the same price for his labour... Now if all men were society men, and asked a fair day's wage for a fair day's work, and all masters were willing to abide by that rule, then all masters could go into the market on the same footing.[87]

The notion of a 'fair day's wage for a fair day's work' which many espoused 'had, and has, little in common with the ideal of buying in the cheapest and selling in the dearest market' and, as Hobsbawm also notes, the criteria for a 'fair wage' depended on physiological, technical, social and moral considerations, including, one might add, the consideration that the wage should be sufficient to maintain both a man and his dependents.[88]

Workers could be tenacious in hanging on to the moral determinations of the wage level. The market might shape what wage it was possible to get but there was a limit commensurate with a particular job below which no self-respecting man would go. Shipwrights, it was noted in 1860, would rather become wagon builders, house carpenters or even labourers at 2s. 6d. a day rather than work as shipwrights at 4s. 'The Shipwrights' Society urges each of its members to withstand strictly any infringement of their rights.' In the 1880s the Boilermakers' Society asked if men should receive *any* wage rather than remain idle, to which their emphatic answer was no. The market was not, as yet, offering a decent wage so 'wait until you can sell your mechanical skill for something like a fair remuneration'; and what was fair was that which did not offend against a man's sense of his own dignity: 'the breast which burns with manly independence would rather work as a common labourer than sell his mechanical skill for a mere pittance'.[89]

This sense of dignity and justice was especially evident when it came to the question of piece-work, to which most unions in metals, engineering and shipbuilding were formally opposed, even if they were often unsuccessful in preventing its spread and had to recognise it in the end.[90] Their objections tended to have four strands. Firstly, it impoverished the workman and benefited the employers because the latter were continually seeking to reduce the rates. It also led to unhealthy competition and unemployment among the men: 'it often gives to one man what ought to be enjoyed by three or four'. Secondly, it made the men work harder: 'its tendencies are to ultimately compel men to work at the utmost limit that nature will allow'. Thirdly, it produces *bad* work and demoralised the worker. This was particularly so where sub-contracting was involved. In iron and engineering works, for example, the moulder who was a contractor 'is made a kind of middleman – a sort of whipper-in, and he has to drive, it may be, a better man than ever stood in his shoes, and he gets cent. per cent. out of him'. And this 'slave-driving' was antipathetic for 'inferior work is produced by the cheapest and least skilful labour that can be procured'. Finally, it injured the union, not least because of the insecurity it produced. Where wages were arranged on time-rates 'the workman feels somewhat settled, which is one of the things a respectable man wants' and

it is a fact that the workmen who oppose the system are the best, the most intelligent, the soberest, and the most religious of the working class. Piecework, and work performed by very imperfect boys and pretenders, at half wages, do more harm to the trade of this country than anything else we know.[91]

These notions of justice did not just concern the men's duties to each other; they also embraced felt obligations to employers in terms of the moral contract. The Boilermakers' Society were very keen on advocating a sense of obligation. The members, they said, must remember that 'the duty of everyone is ... to faithfully render the work each is paid for', and that while the central function of the union was to get a fair wage

it is equally incumbent upon them to insist that employers are treated by its members with equity and justice. It is by enforcing these principles that stability to trade is secured, the material prosperity of our members advanced, and the well-being and usefulness of our association guaranteed to future generations.[92]

Equity and justice required that the employers treat them decently as well, although they were thought to be quite likely to be derelict in their duties, as I have mentioned, and it also came to require the establishment of the legal and political conditions necessary for the existence of this market equality, a central concern of the campaigns for the vote and the reform of the labour laws in the 1860s and 1870s.

V

Those campaigns, especially for the vote, were able to bring together in some measure considerable sections of the working class, at least in the north-east. They certainly spoke for more than just the skilled unions.[93] However, the building of the trade unions also entailed drawing certain distinctions within the class. In the first place, there was that internal to any union, between the good unionist and the bad. The good was the kind who turned up to meetings and played an active part; the bad included both those who were loathe to see the union weakened but would not do anything much to sustain it and those who failed to pay their subscriptions and eventually got expelled. In sum, as the Boilermakers' Society said, 'first, intelligence; second, selfishness; third, Dead to Duty'.[94]

The more important distinctions were those concerning the unions and their relations to the rest of the working class, and these were generally of three kinds. There were those lines drawn against those who were members of a trade but were not members of the union. For the printers 'non-members are not recognised "in times of peace or war"' while the Iron Founders thought that all non-unionists were, by definition, morally corrupt, tending to be 'drunkards, idlers, and very improvident men, that do not care for their wives, or children, or themselves, and I lament to say [are] very often ... defrauders'.[95] Such an attitude could produce odd results, with any sense of solidarity with other skilled men being determined by whether or not they were organised. Thus, for example, the Boilermakers' Society would not support platers, riveters and holders-up in a strike at Hawthorn's on the Tyne in 1863 because there were non-union men involved.[96]

Second were those distinctions drawn against competing unionists. The vested interest of the trade was often jealously guarded although this did not always preclude wider solidarities, evident in political demonstrations or around such issues as the use of the 'document' against the building workers in 1859, for here was at stake the existence of trade-unionism itself and 'labour's right and cause'.[97] But the right to the trade in work was a different matter. In shipbuilding sectionalism was rife, although not as severe as it became at the end of the century. Most notably in this period of the establishment of iron shipbuilding there was great mutual antagonism between the boilermakers and the wooden shipwrights, the latter regarding the former as an 'inferior class of men', as Mayhew observed. In the 1850s and 1860s this lack of cordiality persisted as each group attempted to map out its territory within the division of labour. The shipwrights remained contemptuous of the 'iron men', eventually at some cost to their own trade, while the boilermakers fined those who worked with the shipwrights on iron work.[98]

In engineering too there was sectionalism. In the Tyneside shops there were at least twelve unions of the 'craft' kind, that is either recruiting from a single trade like the patternmakers or from closely related ones like the ASE, although the ASE was clearly predominant. As in shipbuilding one of the problems that all unions faced was marking out their own, distinctive, areas of eligibility and function. The evidence of disputes in the industry suggests that in matters of bargaining in the 1850s and 1860s the unions operated as individual groups but fighting each other appears to have been less pronounced than in shipbuilding. One central reason for this was that formal unions were much less well-established. Moreover, the greatest dispute, the long, arduous and eventually successful strike for

nine hours in 1871, demonstrated that sectionalism might not be a fixed
and insuperable part of the landscape. It is significant that the issue was
fought over hours, for here was an issue that could potentially unify all
grades of workers, at least where men's time was more closely regulated
by employers than in shipbuilding. The hours' issue was the only one in
the 1850s and 1860s which could unite workers across industries; in 1871
it united about 10,000 men across trades within an industry and stimu-
lated an explosion of demands for a shorter working day, both throughout Tyneside and elsewhere in the country. But its permanent effects in
transcending the boundaries between the organised trades were relatively
short-lived. While it engendered an expansion of trade-unionism and
altered the pattern of bargaining with employers, the major beneficiary of
this on the workers' side was the ASE. And as the informal collectivity
who had fought and been fused by the strike broke up in the depression of
the later 1870s, those who remained in the individual trade unions tended
to become fixed into the relatively inert structures of an increasingly sec-
tionalised engineering unionism.[99]

A third distinction drawn within the working class was against the unskilled and those thought to be dependent within forms of paid work. One
may see this, first, in the attitude to domestic service, largely of course a
woman's occupation. One commentator observed in the 1860s that 'there
are few of the employed class who would not prefer a herring and
potatoes in a room of their own to the choicest meals in the servants' hall'
for 'public opinion among the class at the present time is in favour of the
independence of factory and other day work'. The contrast was, in sum,
'*independence* against *dependence*', or, as one male servant put it: the life
of a servant was 'something like that of a bird shut up in a cage. The bird is
well housed and well fed but is deprived of liberty.'[100]

That a person was not wholly free as a domestic servant was also felt to
be the case with some kinds of labourers. There were, wrote 'A Working
Man', two types of labourers – the 'attached' and the 'unattached'. Both
were distinguished not only by being without handicraft and union but
also by being 'servants unto servants'. However, the attached labourer
was the 'servant of many masters, of every artisan in the shop, as well as of
foremen' and although he might be acknowledged as 'a man' he will not
be regarded as either a 'brother' or as an 'equal'. On the other hand, the
unattached labourer, engaged in work like dock-labouring, at least had
one advantage over the attached: he was 'more free'.[101] Moreover, where
the unskilled formed a *union* they might attract the support of the skilled.
For example, the printers gave money in the 1870s to agricultural workers
and shipyard labourers among others because they were unionists but
refused it to striking lead workers because they were not.[102]

If the gulf between the skilled man and the labourer was sometimes wide, and sometimes fixed, it was not always so.[103] Where uncertainty could arise was at the margins. One example of this was the position of the caulkers in boilermaking. In the mid 1860s the issue arose of whether or not the union should admit them and it turned on two matters: the nature of the work and whether or not they were 'independent'. The north-eastern members of the union argued that their proficiency as workmen entitled them to membership. Where shipwrights were being employed to do the job they were simply incompetent: 'if it were not for the assistance of two Caulkers ships would never float'. But it was also argued that, unlike platers' helpers who were 'dependent on the beck and call of Platers', the caulkers 'as a body are independent of all others', symbolised in that they 'will not in the majority of shops let anyone touch their tools'. In the event, the arguments failed to convince, for the executive and other members stuck to their position that the trade was not a distinct one.[104]

These lines of distinction that unions drew belied the universalism of their claims to be treated as equal to the employers in the market and deserving of respect and justice. For if collective organisation was essential so that 'we working men as a class ... [may] ... better our conditions as every man has an indispensable right to do', and action such as on hours would benefit 'the whole working population',[105] then should not *all* workers be able to advance their claims? Evidently, the universalism of the aspirations was limited by the effective particularism of much of the practice, a conflict which may be seen in the case of the shipyard platers' helpers.

While the relations between the skilled tradesmen and their labourers varied, those between the platers and helpers is a notorious instance of domination and subordination in which the subordinate was, in any reasonable sense, exploited. Throughout the 1870s and 1880s the relationship was fraught with antagonism, breaking out into open conflict from time to time. The conflict came to focus on the system of wage payment, the platers being paid by the piece, the helpers by time, either directly by the plater or by the employer. The helpers' challenge to this was to demand that they too should be paid by the piece, a challenge fiercely contested by the platers on the grounds that the helpers had 'no responsibility in the actual work'.[106]

This manifestly unjust and unequal relationship was vigorously attacked by J. Lynch, one of the helpers' leaders, in a paper to the Industrial Remuneration Conference in 1885. The platers, he said, worked at a high pace in order to give themselves time off from work, which forced the helpers to work both extremely hard and to lose money. The

Boilermakers' Society had of course also complained of men taking time off from work; but they saw it in terms of the mens' duties to the employers, not other workers. The consequences of the system for the helpers was to yoke them to the insecurities of the future:

the platers and other workmen had ample means to provide for the future, but the helpers had no chance to make any provision for prospective hard times.

But like the boilermakers against whom they complained, the helpers both accepted the economic situation as determinant yet apprehended it through moral categories. The relationship with the platers was not one of the bonding of equals but of bondage. And just as any form of oppression degrades both oppressor and oppressed, in this instance the relationship was 'demoralising to both plater and helper'. Formal equality might be thought to obtain – 'they are nominally fellow-workmen' – but in fact it was grossly unequal, resulting in a kind of 'unfreedom' for the helper: the plater was a 'taskmaster', the helper a 'serf'. The effects of this were specified by Lynch in terms which were similar to those used by the Boilermakers' Society about capitalists. The system:

lowers his self-respect, it cripples his energies, it makes him slavishly subservient to the plater, and, I regret to say, in many cases, disloyal to his own class, and the general effect of it is to degrade him immeasurably in all respects, besides making his work very much more unpleasant than it need be.[107]

VI

While unions constructed a vision of, and certain lines of division around, forms of paid labour they also saw themselves as having wider social functions which derived, in good part, from the values associated with work. 'We have only one object in view,' said the Iron Founders' Society, 'to make the man a better mechanic and the mechanic a better man.'[108] Yet if the relations of work were the starting point of what a man and a collective could be, some felt that work bounded existence too much. John Stuart Mill thought that 'Anglo-Americans' were distinguished by seeing the whole of their life in their work,[109] a view also taken by the Lancashire socialist Allen Clarke when he wrote of the cotton workers:

The factory folks are, in the main, conservative, slow to change. They have no true idea of life. They believe that they are born to work; they do not see that work is but a means to live.[110]

Work might even provide some of the lexicon of 'dreams'. 'When a man is not happy in his work he seeks to escape in dreams', wrote Taine. For some skilled workers whose work was ultimately bounded by capital, which determined what their pride and knowledge was to make, their 'dreams' might embody both fantasies of creation and the impossibility of their realisation, as Thomas Wright indicates:

Those who when in their cups talk 'shop' – and many do, since work is the only subject on which many of them *can* talk – will begin to display their knowledge now. With no other tools or material than the stem of a pipe, beer sloppings, and a public-house table, they will in a few minutes erect stupendous palaces, construct locomotives and steamers capable of unheard-of speed, design ordnance of hitherto undreamt of destructive powers, and otherwise demonstrate that they could, if they were so minded, revolutionise the mechanical world by merely making known a few of their original ideas.[111]

But if work was seen as bounding existence it was also to be escaped from. Clarke was very conscious of this. Although taking a rather ascetic view of what factory operatives ought to be doing, what underpinned his description was a belief that capitalism and the machine exhausted the abilities and capacities of men and women. The 'mental strength' of factory folk was not, he thought, very great:

They cannot bear any long strain of thought or study; they prefer light and sensational reading. For poetry and good literature they have no inclination. Their minds, like their bodies, are weakened, and crave spiced and seasoned rubbish, even as at every mouth-meal their sickly appetites must be coaxed with pickles, vinegar, or some other saliva stimulant.

What shaped those appetites was a refusal of the domination of work over non-work time.

Some few seek recreation in Sunday-school work and prayer meetings, but these are the minority; the majority want stirring amusements, lively and intoxicating – something to make them forget.[112]

Thirty years earlier, W. A. Abram had made similar observations about Lancashire factory workers: 'the omnipresent and probably the strongest sentiment of this people is an inveterate repugnance to factory work, and a constant desire to get away from it'.[113]

Among the skilled workers of the north-east, the utter repugnance of work was less than this: they were not subject to the machine in the way of Lancashire. Yet, still, there was an apparent desire to refuse the wholesale domination of work. 'We aspire to bring about the day when all who live shall work; and all who work shall live' said a speaker at a 'nine hours' meeting in 1866.[114] And to 'live' was not just to refuse work in some degree but also to affirm that the social relations 'within' the workplace ought not to dictate one's life outside it. The *Chainmakers' Journal* offered one statement of this position. Inside the workplace a moral and social contract was struck with the employers, but outside one was, or ought to be, free of their constraints:

the swarthy artizan ... claims, and justly, that when he has performed his con-tract, he is at liberty to follow the best of his inclinations. If the employer wishes to control his actions out of the workshop, and to determine whether he shall unite with his fellow-labourers to raise his wages, what church he shall belong to, what thoughts he shall think, the worker turns round and answers rightly, ''tis not in the bond'.[115]

Practically, the refusal of the utter compulsion of work was realised through those formal and informal methods of stealing back time which I have already mentioned and the most important instance of it was the 1871 strike, a self-conscious rejection of the sway of work in the economy over what was *not*-economy. Men might be shaped by and identify with what they did at work but they must also be able to re-create themselves outside it. 'A Unionist' of Jarrow wrote:

If man is to be a progressive animal, he must have some time to improve his mind. Surely God did not give man the knowledge to invent machines, simply to increase the capital of the wealthy, but for the benefit of man, by reducing his hours of toil, so that he may cultivate his intellectual faculties as a reasonable being, and rise in the scale of creation. If the masters would but concede the small 'boon' of one hour to the working bee that makes the honey, they would reap a rich harvest of gratitude ... Learning is much talked about at present, but, if the labourer cannot get to the 'Institutes' where it is to be had ... it is like starving a man outside a cook shop – there are good things inside but they are beyond his reach.[116]

Yet what were men to do outside work? Those like this unionist persist-ently presented an ideal of non-work activities which was preeminently that of the respectable and independent worker. At the centre of this was the belief that those who were independent and in possession of their 'manhood' were those able to maintain *dependents*. The conditions necessary to realise this lay in work and collective activity for when they had caught the 'golden moments as they fly ... using them rightly, we shall soon find that we are happier men, better husbands, fathers, and brothers, and worthier members of society'.[117] But where men could be like this was in the home. Their representation of this was consonant, in some respects, with that 'domestic ideology' which Catherine Hall has described.[118] The dependent wife would soften the potentially brutalising facts of everyday working life, and nurture her husband's happiness. As Robert Knight wrote:

What is wanted for every working man is a *well regulated home, that* should be his greatest attention. The principal source of human happiness lies in the exercise of domestic affection.
  This involves in it the regulation of our labour in such a way that we may have

the opportunity of sufficient intercourse with our families. A life of work, and nothing but work, is no life for a man, we should have

'Leisure to live, leisure to love, leisure to taste our freedom.'

To work with the hands is the necessary, and under right conditions not the unhappy destiny of our race, but as Adam Smith says 'the man who works so moderately as to be able to work constantly, not only preserves his health the longest, but in the course of the year executes the greatest quantity of work'. Let us remember this truth for the sake of those who are dependent upon us, also that our family life ought to be the source of our purest happiness, where all the hardness and selfishness of our natures may be tempered and subdued by the atmosphere of our homes.[119]

Yet the vision of the respectable moral and social order was constantly threatened by the disruptive intrusions of 'the rough'. The question of drink was central to this. There were certainly significant numbers of working-class men and women who supported temperance; but it would be mistaken to suppose that those who did were solely skilled workers or their wives, or that, in turn, skilled workers and their wives did not go on the booze. One temperance advocate in Newcastle regretfully admitted that 'habitual drunkards' included 'some of the best mechanics and tradesmen' and that 'the boiler-makers drink more than the others [while] the miners are very good at it too'. And it was not just that men drank: drinking occurred not only at work or in the pub as an alternative to work but was also the focus of those liminal states marking the transition from the spatially separated places of home and work. Some (who were on piece-work) drank before going into work in the morning, but above all they drank on Saturdays. Leaving work at dinner time, many went straight to the pub or beerhouse 'and drank a very large amount of their wages away before [going] home, and that is continued on to the closing hour'.[120]

Drinking habits or involvement with the drink trade were not confined to men. The Boilermakers' Society complained that some of their members kept beershops, which were presumably largely run by their wives, and in Jarrow, a town completely dominated by Palmer's shipyard, 'rough' behaviour among women – some of whom were, one would guess, the wives of skilled workers – was thought to be widespread in the 1870s: 'Women drank as much as men. Women fought in the streets as only women fight, with fists and nails, using the latter until they drew blood.'[121]

Drink was imbricated too with a threat to the sexual ordering of society. While pubs were preeminently places to drink and talk, and perhaps even to dream like Wright's men, they were also places for young men and women to meet, to dance, to sing and to do so in ways which led, so some thought, to the inevitable 'demoralisation' of young women.[122]

Obviously, this is not the place to survey the full range of 'recreational' activity among skilled workers.[123] I merely wish to emphasise that trade-unionists might present themselves, particularly when addressing 'outside' observers like Royal Commissioners, as helping to create a respectable working class, but that that ordering encountered limits within the constituency of skilled workers themselves.[124] It did so not only in the pub but in the heart of the respectable vision itself – the home. The model might affirm a picture of men and women sharing home and familial life, and there was, no doubt, much in this.[125] However, it must be doubted if this was wholly typical, partly because of the appalling housing and social conditions on Tyneside, so that the sheer amount of time that was spent in the home or in family-centred activities was probably quite limited. In Jarrow, the absence of gardens and healthy places of recreation might help to foster drinking and fighting among some women; among the men, the same commentator noted, 'the artisans were silent and sullen'.[126]

Even among respectable artisans there was an evident degree of separation of many of the activities of men and women. The sober trade-unionist might go to his building society or trade-union meeting, his chapel or working man's club; but his wife's world was centred on the home and the street.[127] Moreover, while the respectable working-class home was ultimately dependent on a decent wage coming in, the actual construction and sustenance of respectability was, as Ellen Ross has shown, often heavily dependent on the work of women – in how money was spent, in the maintenance of cleanliness, in establishing and keeping up good relations or, at least, appearances with the neighbours, in educating children and, not least, in providing a counterweight to the sometimes lax behaviour of unrespectable or wavering husbands.[128] Harry Pollitt's parents were one example of this. His father, a striker in a boilermaking shop, was given to drinking a bit too much, betting, and, one senses, keeping a distance from an altogether too serious world of the respectable. But his mother was a religious woman, a passionate cleaner of the house, antagonistic to drink, and it was from her that Harry learned not only much of his early education but also his socialism. Or to take one more, earlier, example of this tension which might exist within the home, G. J. Holyoake noted that 'many married women become members [of co-ops] because their husbands will not take the trouble, and others join the store in self-defence, to prevent the husbands from spending their money in drink'.[129]

This world of 'women's work' scarcely came into the purview of trade-unionists in their representations of work and its social relations. For them the lines between work and non-work time were formed around a particular definition of what was and was not work and 'economy'. The institutions they built were a great achievement: by 1880, while still facing considerable obstacles, the core of a better organised, more disciplined and more powerful trade-union movement than in any other country had been established. Yet at the same time the movement was premissed upon not only the drawing of distinctions around forms of labour but also on a moral and social vision that took as its central agent and antagonist to immoral capitalism (if not capitalism itself) a particular construction of 'the working man' – limits which were not to be seriously questioned until late in the century and which, in important respects, still remain unsurpassed.

8

'A time to every purpose': an essay on time and work

RICHARD WHIPP

St Augustine asked where time came from. He said it came out of the future which didn't exist yet, into the present that had no duration, and went into the past which had ceased to exist. I don't know that we can understand time any better than a child.

Graham Greene, *The End of the Affair* (London, 1951), p. 179

INTRODUCTION

This essay deals with one of the essential yet curiously neglected aspects of the historical meanings of work, the relationship between time and work. The main aim is to set the labour process in its appropriate technical and social contexts. Work here is seen as a process and a social activity. The essay focusses therefore on time as a key element of both the formal organisation of work and the experience of labour. There are three main sections dealing with: concepts of time; the problem of time/work discipline in British industry; and an examination of the relationship between time and work in two contrasting industries, ceramics and automobiles.

The first section offers a synthesis of the literature on time which is useful to historians of work. Time as a separate object of study has, ironically, been rather neglected by historians. However, a growing awareness of the way writers from different disciplinary backgrounds have tackled the problems associated with conveying the nature of change and the dynamic aspects of structures, events and experience, has suggested alternative ways in which historians may treat time. Geographers, anthropologists and sociologists and, in particular, some French historians have explored the distinctive temporal framework associated with different social processes. These scholars all undermine the notion, often implicit in historical writing, that western society has become increasingly regulated by a single means of time reckoning: clock time. The broad conclusion drawn from recent research is that time is not an object existing independent of people and objectively dividing their life into precise units. Instead, time is more diverse and necessarily social and subjective.[1]

The second part of this chapter uses this understanding of time in order to reveal the importance of time as a central feature of the organisation and experience of work. A critical examination of the influential statement on time/work discipline by E. P. Thompson in 1967 is long overdue. The thesis of Thompson, and others, indicates the relevance of the subjective definition of time for the early phase of industrialisation in Britain. However, it maintains that in temporal terms working life has, in the nineteenth and twentieth centuries, become increasingly standardised and lar. This essay will argue that time is not so easily, nor uniformly, converted into a commodity under capitalism. The linear progression identified by Thompson from 'task-based time' to clock time is not well founded. Moreover, he ignores the varieties of perception and use of time and consequently underestimates the continuing diversity of people's experience of time in relation to work. An alternative picture will be offered based on an awareness of the social construction of time by management and workers. Time in relation to work is for management and employees a potential commodity which has to be created and its control and disposal negotiated. Above all, a single mode of time/work discipline was not established once and for all. Rather time in relation to work has been continuously shaped, defined and contested by workers and employers in the context of changing structural pressures contained within the spheres of production and social reproduction.

The third main section of this chapter uses primary material drawn from research into the history of work organisation in the ceramics and automobile industries. These sectors represent two extremes of industrial work. One notoriously craft-based and 'traditional' while the other is often taken to be the form which best symbolises modern mass production. The two examples are used to draw out the multiple and changing sources of time reckoning and control in work. The essay closes with two pleas. The first is for a more open approach to the way time in industrial societies is structured by an array of possible forces. The second is for a greater sensitivity by historians to the plurality of time-reckoning modes which exist in and around work and their interrelations.

CONCEPTIONS OF TIME

Although time is central to the historian's craft few have made it the subject of formal study. Britain has no school which corresponds to the French Annalists or individual scholars directly comparable with Braudel or Ladurie. Indeed the reception given in this country to these French historians whose work is founded on a novel understanding of time has been decidedly mixed.[2] British historians' discussions of time have generally been related to the relationship of past, present and sometimes the future. Much historical writing often contains assumptions concerning the progressive dominance of the calendar or clock as part of the process of modernisation. However there is an increasing number of studies which, although they deal with time only implicitly, can be used to question the prevailing approach to time in history. Research on time within adjacent disciplines not only strengthens the challenge but can lead to an alternative appreciation of direct use to the study of time and work.

The subject of time is usually dealt with by historians either when they reflect on their discipline in general or when they seek to defend it against the assaults of others. Simmel's 'The problem of historical time' is one of the few attempts to tackle the problem directly. He concludes that the question of the relationship between time and other components of history has not been answered 'with the clarity that is desirable, nor even with the clarity that is possible'.[3] His examination of time is confined to essentially philosophical considerations.[4] None the less, he highlights a central problem for all historians. Historical writing is 'suspended in a perpetual compromise' as it must embrace two extremes. One is the continuous process of history which has 'no lapses or gaps'; the other relates to the unique, unrepeatable nature of events. However, little practical assistance is given by Simmel in solving this dilemma[5] and as we shall see, it has been left to others to link the two extremes.

In recent years the need to justify history's existence as a subject of study had prompted historians, of whatever persuasion, to return to the theme of past and present. Eric Hobsbawm in the Glass memorial lecture argued that:

All prediction about the real world rests to a great extent on some sort of inference about the future from what has happened in the past... All human beings and societies are rooted in the past – that of families, communities, nations or other reference groups or even of personal memory – all define their position in relation to it.[6]

In a more combative vein, Tilly not only agrees that 'we live in history and cannot escape it by assuming it away; when something happens, what has happened before shapes how it happens'. He also castigates sociologists for their timeless, unhistorical models.[7] Indeed the dialogue between historians and sociologists has revealed that the major difference between the two is not so much to do with the conventional division between generalising and particularity but the extent to which place and time enter into explanations of events and actions.[8] However, in spite of historians' general sensitivity to the problems of change, the arbitrary nature of periodisation and an awareness of long-term continuities coexisting with major break points and crises, few have attempted systematic studies of time.[9] Apart from work on pre-industrial societies (influenced by anthropology) historians have allowed the picture of the rational progression of abstract, clock time with industrialisation to persist. Mumford's assertion that the clock not the steam engine was the key to the machine age has remained unqualified. In fact, the linear progression of time-ordering of life according to the clock has been perpetuated in a recent work subtitled 'clocks and the making of the modern world'.[10] The line runs, apparently, from the Chinese invention of astronomical clocks, to the religious structuring of the day by canonical hours, through Renaissance timing devices to the watches of the late eighteenth century, and thereafter a range of chronometers of ever-increasing sophistication. Newtonian, mathematically-based, objective concepts of time are said to have spread throughout the western world. The increasing obsession with speed and time is noted from a number of significant turning points. These include the standardisation of national time-structures in response to the spread of the railway (and later the wireless). The key event was the Prime Meridian Conference of 1884 which established Greenwich as the zero meridian, set the length of the day and divided the earth into twenty-four time zones. Some point to the First World War and the resulting establishment of the wristwatch as an accepted coordinating device.[11] Western public institutions are seen as having been governed increasingly by officially-sanctioned clock and sidereal notions of time during the nineteenth- and early twentieth-century period of industrialisation.[12]

The most notable departure from this view has undoubtedly been the Annales school and the work of Bloch, Febvre and later their doyen, Fernand Braudel. Braudel's prodigious output has resulted in a series of major works which include: a study of the Mediterranean world in the age of Phillip II, a multi-volume work entitled *Civilisation and Capitalism*, and a host of writings on the nature of history.[13] His work rests on an approach to time quite at variance with the orthodox view, while his methods constitute one of the most sustained attempts to transcend the compromise which most historians are forced to make when representing both the continuity of history and discrete events.[14]

Braudel's work pioneered a form of history which operates on three time-levels, namely, geographical, social and individual time.[15] At the base of the model is history that is 'almost changeless'; that is the history of people in relation to their surroundings. Next comes the history of social groups and groupings and finally the history of individuals which embraces the events and rhythms of their life courses. Each level has its own temporal character. The base is associated with the long duration of natural (including seasonal) growth and movement which unfolds very slowly. Social time relates to the 'gentle rhythms' of social activity and their deep-running currents. Lastly, at the level of the individual, history has to be ultra-sensitive to the short 'nervous vibrations' of human rhythms.[16] Braudel, in common with Ladurie has tried to create a language of time which encompasses the 'multifarious, contradictory times of man' as well as the long duration of climate or demography for example. Both draw attention to the structures of thought which are associated with the various units of time and movement. They note how cycles, events or crises tend to mask the regularities and permanence of particular economic and social formations.

In his desire to draw attention to the 'longue durée' Braudel's vision has become increasingly deterministic. He remarked in a recent interview that, 'for me it is not man who makes history it is history which makes man'. Yet it is unnecessary to accept this aspect of his vision since Braudel's work is open to less pessimistic interpretation. Braudel himself notes the 'infinitely repeated opposition between the instant of time and that time which flows more slowly'. Above all it is the identification of a plurality of times associated with human activity by Braudel which has prompted many social scientists to re-examine both their understanding of time and its application to specific aspects of social change.[17] Indeed, it is this renewed appreciation of the importance of time which necessitates a re-evaluation of our understanding of time and work.

Early in this century, Durkheim had drawn attention to the way 'fundamental categories of human thought' such as number, time and space are modelled upon features of social organisation. Similarly, Bergson had earlier argued against straightforward mathematical conceptions of time since this inevitably excluded the experience and perceptions of the individual.[18] These writers clearly influenced the work of anthropologists such as Mauss, Evans-Pritchard and Lévi-Strauss.[19] Many anthropological studies concentrated on comparisons between industrial and non-industrial societies and indicated their differing methods of ordering time, studies which influenced the early work of Thompson and other historians. However those anthropologists who have made time their main area of research do not accept this simple differentiation.

Sorokin for example, warned against those accounts which concentrated only on sidereal time. He argued that each social process has its own temporal framework and that the calendar is often of limited use in understanding social rhythms. Moreover he contended that time changes unevenly within groups and may be experienced and understood differently between societies. Above all Sorokin maintains that the way time is perceived within a social context (he uses the term socio-cultural time) means that the passage of time becomes a 'creative, modifying and transforming agency'.[20] Similarly, Mauss, in his approach to time was anxious to highlight reciprocal relationships and the way social groups and the members modify categories of time and space through experience. He based these conclusions on detailed study of the Eskimo social organisation of time in relation to season, soil, morality and religion. Furthermore, he maintained that these variations in the experience and ordering of time were by no means unique for they were present, albeit deeply embedded, within modern industrial societies.[21]

Somewhat belatedly, these themes have been taken up by sociologists. William Grossin observes how far from time-ordering becoming more regular, quite the opposite is true. He sees that each academic discipline appears to construct its own appropriate 'time standards'. In general, as he puts it, 'we forget that every activity generates its own time'.

Despite the apparent 'transcendance' of the clock and its authority to offer time as an 'exterior product' for everyone to choose how to use it, 'man's activities will find their place in the many cells of time, be it unique, standard, external or impersonal time'.[22] Peter Laslett has moved the subject of time and society on even further. He agrees at the outset with the central value of understanding time in relation to social characteristics, since, 'each form of social change has its own time scale, and therefore its own pace'. The object of research for him has now become their investigation with a view to establishing a rank order of paces of changes.[23]

Clearly Newton's definition of time in 1687 as abstract, absolute and mathematically based ('flowing without relation to anything external') was especially attractive to the progressive spirit of nineteenth-century administration and public life. The hope of erecting a single superior, objective means of time-ordering of society is seen in government legislation and the continued search for increasing accuracy of measurement. The most sophisticated atomic clock measures a second as 9,192,631,770 cycles of the frequency associated with the transition between the two levels of energy of the isotope caesium 133. The idea that time is somehow objective has apparently been increasingly accepted with the spread of the clock, together with the notion that time has become a commodity to be spent, lost, wasted or saved.[24]

Yet a combination of the Annalists with specialist writers from anthropology and sociology presents a formidable challenge to the received idea that industrial societies have become dominated so completely by clock time. They have questioned the supposed ascendancy of abstract, objective time over all others. Mead observed that we are subject to a 'psychological illusion if we assume that the rhythm of counting and the order which arises out of counting answer to a structure of passage itself'. On this basis, 'to set up time as a quantity having an essential nature that allows of its being divided into equal portions of itself is an unwarranted use of abstraction'. Burgess uses literature to show the depictions of 'subjective, internal time' citing the examples of Sterne, Wilde, Kafka, Joyce and Proust. Similarly, students of leisure have confirmed that time is more than astronomical and quantitative: it is social and qualitative. The result is that 'uses of time acquire quality and meaning from the beliefs and values, and the routines of life'.[25]

A consideration of both specialist and non-specialist writers concerned with the issue of time leads to the following proposition. The assumed dominance of abstract, objective sidereal and clock time is mistaken. Rather, these officially sanctioned public means of time reckoning have only been one possible means of time-ordering. Given the diverse, subjective perception of time within differing social settings they have not embraced all aspects of life (even in industrial societies). It is now clear that clock and calendar time exist within the plurality of time-reckoning modes associated with the rich combination of time perceptions. Western societies may have become increasingly conscious of clock time but, as Clark shows, within them even single organisations require a multiplicity of time-reckoning modes for their joint continuity. Attempts to synthesise these understandings of the multiple time-ordering modes has barely begun.[26] Yet an awareness of both the objective and subjective, public and private, structural and social conceptions of time allows a more profound understanding of time and work in history. It can do this by alerting the historian to the diverse means of interpreting time or duration in work, the range of sources and hence the uncertain outcomes over the issues which the time–work relationship raises.

TIME/WORK DISCIPLINE

The way in which historians have approached the specific relationship between time and work has, until recently, largely followed the orthodox understanding of time in industrial societies. One of the most influential statements was made by Edward Thompson in his *Past and Present* article of 1967 on time/work discipline. Thompson, and those who have adopted his analysis, argued within the conventional view that work became increasingly time-ordered during the last two centuries; an ordering based on clock rather than natural or task-based time.[27] In the light of broader understandings of the nature of time, as well as subsequent insightful research into work, the Thompson thesis requires an overhaul.

Thompson's article was informed by early anthropological studies of non-industrial societies and their time patterns. He used work by Evans–Pritchard, Bourdieu[28] and others to argue that the transition to a mature industrial society entailed 'a severe restructuring of working habits – new disciplines, new incentives, and a new human nature': all were directly related to 'changes in the inward notation of time'.[29] The natural rhythms of pre-industrial rural and urban life based on task time were replaced by stricter codes related to production governed by the clock. In the latter, this measurement comes to embody a 'simple relationship.... Those who are employed experience a distinction between their employer's time and their "own" time. And the employer must *use* the time of his labour.... Time is not currency: it is not passed but spent.'[30]

The thesis is backed up by a detailed and vivid account of aspects of the transformation process in this country during the eighteenth and early nineteenth centuries. Thompson admits that the transition to work based on clock time was sometimes difficult. He cites the way people 'clung tenaciously' to pre-industrial habits in general and how in England in the eighteenth century the transition was protracted and fraught with conflict.[31] However, his central thrust is that the establishment of the 'familiar landscape of disciplined industrial capitalism, with the time-sheet and the time-keeper' occurred via activity both internal and external to the workplace. Inside, these included the division and supervision of labour, bells and clocks and money incentives. Outside, the preachings of moralists, school authorities and the suppression of traditional fairs and sports amounted to a considerable 'propaganda of time thrift' by which new labour habits were formed.[32] Thompson concludes with a clear statement: in mature capitalist society 'all time must be consumed, marketed, put to *use*' and that 'all varieties [of capitalist society] are marked by time-thrift and by a clear demarcation between "work" and "life"'.[33]

Thompson's view is buttressed by studies from within history and elsewhere. The very title of Douglas Reid's piece 'The decline of Saint Monday 1766–1876' directly supports the idea of the relentless suppression by employers of unofficial Monday holiday practices by workers.[34] Similarly Bienefeld, in a study of working hours in British industry, reinforced the demarcation of work and non-work activities as well as accepting the notion of 'normal hours in the major trades and industries of Britain'.[35] This of course has been the conventional approach to work–time outside history, in government publications and many economic and sociological accounts.[36] Even those employers who have been seen as either 'welfarist' and 'progressive' in the twentieth century apparently continued to rely on quite elaborate means of clock-based labour discipline as in the case of Rowntree's in the 1950s. Apart from reflections on the nature of time by Shackle and others, economists lend further credibility to Thompson's assertion that in capitalist societies all time must be used or spent, in their theories of rational time-allocation as a scarce resource in work and non-work activities. Graphic accounts of certain extreme occupations with regard to time such as Cottrell's account of time and the railroader in America are clear examples of the strength of 'inward notions of time' induced by modern employment.[37]

Thompson's thesis was both path-breaking and persuasive. Yet although the general direction of his argument holds broadly true, that direction is overemphasised at the expense of alternative understandings. In the light of the discussion in the first section his view can now be seen as too partial and in need of qualification and extension in a number of respects. There are four features of Thompson's interpretation which require adjustment. The modified perspective which results is then well placed to intersect with a host of new research into work. This intersection may then offer an alternative model for understanding time and work.

The four main criticisms are as follows. Firstly, Thompson gives far too much weight to the ability of employers to develop 'a greater sense of time thrift' and hence increasingly commodify time at work. Whilst the economic forces unleashed by the process of industrialisation were unquestionably powerful, in this country it was the limited growth of direct managerial control of production and the varieties of devolved work-organisation which stand out. In telling international comparisons Bendix and later Merkle point to the pragmatism of British management in the nineteenth and twentieth centuries. They show how industry advanced by 'a series of practical organisational inventions devised to meet immediate needs'. Industry relied therefore on a mixture of close, personal, managerial control of work, together with degrees of craft and workgroup self-regulation. It was this experience which led to the way 'Taylorism as a philosophy of organization was rejected most strenuously by the British'.[38]

Secondly, the almost linear progression from task-based time to clock time on which his thesis rests is overdrawn. As is now known, in both the previous centuries not only were there forms of industry which failed to make this transition in any clear way but also sections of supposedly mature industry did not experience the move so simply. In product markets where flexibility was at a premium, task-based arrangements persisted. Raphael Samuel demonstrates how 'capitalism did not grow up all of a piece, and its nineteenth-century development, though swift, was also highly uneven'. Mining is a good example: the 'disparities were nowhere more extreme'; handcraft work continued alongside large-scale industry.

Management, as distinct from our images of coal owners, was 'comparatively underdeveloped'. Brutal managerial regimes notwithstanding, brickmakers successfully resisted new machinery, while in the Cornish tin mines, work was put up for auction each month and let out to 'tributers'. Here, as under the Scottish 'darg' system or 'the family berth' of the Cheshire saltworkers the immediate organisation and timing of work was largely the responsibility of the workers concerned.[39]

Thirdly, control of time in relation to work was not established once and for all as phrases such as 'the familiar landscape of disciplined industrial capitalism' imply. 'Time-sense in its technological conditioning' and 'time-measurement as a means of labour exploitation' were not imposed unilaterally. As Marx noted for the nineteenth and Montgomery for the present century, it has been the 'irregular habits of the workpeople' which continued to obstruct 'the regulation of the hours of labour'. Herbert Gutman showed how in America British workers were noted for how they 'worked hard but in distinctly pre-industrial styles'. This included discretionary movement in and out of the workplace, and highly irregular working weeks made up of 'bursts of great activity' followed by periods of unofficial holidays.[40] Definitions of appropriateness with regard to time have been subject to negotiation and contest with each generation and according to changing market and social contexts. Uncertainty has been the keynote of such contests.[41]

This leads to the fourth criticism. Thompson seriously underestimates the continued range and diversity of how time is experienced by people as both workers and actors in other social settings and the interrelations of these experiences of time. Although citing a 1967 example of the way 'the rhythms of women's work in the home are not wholly attuned to the measurement of the clock' he fails to appreciate the way paid labour and domestic work, and their attendant definitions of time, continued to interact throughout the uneven maturation of industrial societies. Perhaps Gregory's critique of Thompson on a broader scale is applicable here. In accepting a picture of the wholesale restructuring of time and work under capitalism he makes an over-direct correspondence between the dynamics of economic growth and the dynamics of social or cultural life.[42]

The integration of all the possible sources of time reckoning and their impact on work which recent developments in time studies suggest is a much larger future project. However, it is possible to sketch the possible outline of a simple taxonomy. If it is accepted that multiple time-reckoning systems have continued to operate in advanced economies and that they must be understood in relation to both their social construction and more abstract forms, then a good deal of current historical research can help to build an alternative model. This model of time and work must embrace at least three main levels: the sector, the community, and the enterprise.

A number of writers have found that the sectors of the modern economy are far more than just artificial creations of the Standard Industrial Classification. A sector refers to a segment of the economy in which a given activity occurs. Strictly speaking it is not the same as an industry. An industry is concerned with a single classification of products whereas a sector logically groups together related classifications of products. A good example is the automobile sector which includes passenger cars, commercial vehicles and component makers; another would be the wool, cotton and jute industries within the textile sector. Clearly, sectors have varied in their homogeneity and they differ in key respects such as their degree of integration, geographical dispersal or the extent to which they are drawn into foreign markets or penetrated by overseas producers. Yet it appears that there may be important common factors within a sector which may effect the rhythms of development within firms and their temporal character. Some have contended[43] that the conditions in which a given sector emerges (for example, electricals and chemicals in the late nineteenth century) may critically affect the subsequent character of market relations, connections with the state and what become accepted as best-practice methods. In practice, sectors acquire distinctive languages, bodies of thought and assumptions. They also develop general rules (often entirely uncodified) which help to account for the way firms evolve in general but also for their particular approaches to time and control. Similarly sectors vary markedly in the pace of technological and market change thereby imparting very different experiences of time between individual workplaces. Analogies have been drawn with biological cycles to distinguish sectors in their infant, maturing and senile phases.[44]

Rather than seeing the development of modern industries in terms of a unified process even with different phases historians now recognise its essentially uneven character between sectors. In particular, any one sector may contain, at the same time, specialist and mass-market producers; firms therefore using craft techniques adjacent to those employing batch or more tightly synchronised mechanised production methods. More especially it is now realised that there is no necessary linear progression from craft to factory, to mass production. Sabel and Zeitlin show not only that there have been alternative paths but that in periods of market upheaval and rapid technological change it is quite possible for firms to revert to modified versions of earlier methods.[45] Similarly, the notion of an ineluctable line of progression in technology or work-organisation has been further eroded by renewed interest in the long-term cyclical activity of the economy and individual sectors. Freeman's reworking of Schumpeter on innovation or Ramsay's analysis of workplace bargaining both rely on the nature of the business cycle and periodic crisis of productivity. Both underline the essentially volatile, long-term pattern of activity between sectors.[46] Taken together the diverse characteristics of sectors in the past two centuries weaken the notion of a common time-pattern across them. Rather, activities within them were structured by a range of quite different time-frames which are vital to an understanding of the temporal character of work.

A similarly important level of analysis for explaining both the organisation and experience of work-time is the community. Although there has been considerable debate over the precise meaning of the term community, research by social historians over the past decade rebuts Thompson's assertion that work and life became so totally separated. Put more positively, it is now realised that the workplace continued to bear the imprint of the world outside. Moreover, the two spheres of work and non-work can be regarded as not separate but reciprocal in their relationship.[47] In the broadest sense community may be understood not only in terms of shared economic experience reinforced by common attachment and association but also in terms of moral obligations. These codes of behaviour have not been all-embracing nor universally accepted by people in a given location; they have often led to competition and division.[48]

These notions of obligation and mutuality have been connected to work in a number of ways. Some geographers have discovered these mechanisms working across regions in the nineteenth century: this comes as no surprise to historians long aware of the concentrated and localised development of industry in Britain. Gregory's study of the Yorkshire woollen industry in the eighteenth and nineteenth centuries does not reveal a simple downward imposition of clock-time discipline. Instead there existed throughout the district 'a grille of intersecting responsibilities and deferences' which defined what was required of owner and employed both inside and outside the workplace. These were in turn subject to the working of the business cycle and the vagaries of fashion. Production was punctuated therefore by season and market but together with 'considerations of moral economy'.[49] As I have argued elsewhere these features of industrial life did not disappear as factory production spread but continued to inform the relationship between work and non-work activities.

Perhaps the strongest expression of the continuum between the two spheres, with regard to time, comes in the home or family. Maxine Berg shows how in domestic manufacture, time-ordering in work was a product of both household and technical pressures: a picture reproduced by Benson's study of so-called 'penny capitalism' in the nineteenth century.[50] Hareven's study of work in the New England mills between 1880 and

1930 elaborates this theme. She distinguishes between the time-frames of industry, family and individual but does not accept any straightforward dominance of 'industrial time'. Instead, her examination of family and work-time is both contextual and dynamic, taking into account workers' motivations and wider economic forces. As she puts it: 'industrial organisations are not constant over time just as the internal organisation of the family changes over the life of its members'. The emphasis is on uncertain outcomes. Timing becomes crucial in the experience of work. In other words, the relationship between individual, family or industrial time-frames is important. The points of intersection between an individual's or family's life-cycle with wider economic movements become vital in understanding how people experience work in a total sense. In Hareven's study it is the point at which a family's life-cycle encountered the great depression of the US textile industry in the 1920s which helped explain the subsequent actions and indeed capacity of a family to survive.[51]

It is at the level of the enterprise where Thompson's projection of time/work discipline has been especially superseded by subsequent scholarship. Whilst market considerations increasingly conditioned the organisation of work these forms of organisation were by no means uniform and unchanging. Simmel showed how the London tailors in the eighteenth and nineteenth centuries changed their mode of work-organisation. In times of peace the tailors operated a decentralised format: during periods of anticipated warfare their work was rigidly and hierarchically organised via the inns, the centres for government contracts. Similar alternations underlay the work-organisation of the Birmingham arms industry.[52] Others have indicated how industrial production remained tied to the rhythms of the natural seasons together with the dictates of selling 'seasons' and fashion in the consumer goods areas.[53]

Whether from the perspective of managers or workers, the processes of industrialisation in Britain do not seem to have yielded a single, commonly accepted mode of time/work discipline. Owners and managers did not acquire a readily agreed managerial science. Quite the reverse: accountancy and specialist managerial hierarchies along with a clearly defined clock-based time-saving and costing methods emerged erratically. Even in the early twentieth century in manufacturing industry, tied as it was to the slow growth of mass markets, management continued to rely on indirect, delegated means of controlling production. These did not contain the ability to monitor and control all features of work-time in precise or systematic ways. It was said after the First World War that:

The failure of British management to gain complete control of the production process, even during a war crisis, was critical in leading post-war management to reject direct control as a viable strategy.[54]

On the shop floor, recent overview accounts of the literature on work and industrial change cite the repeated discovery that technological change has tended to produce a 'decomposition of skills rather than a unlinear process of downgrading'. Besides a rich literature on shop-floor work culture which confirms the ability of workers to refashion successive management time-cost systems (for example, Taylorism and Bedaux schemes), there are also accounts of work in the past which reveal the variety of pace, rhythm and time-ordering. The irregular patterns of work-activity of Gregory's textile workers are mirrored in Alfred Williams' breakdown of the working week in a railway factory, or Hassard's investigation of firemen's struggle for a so-called 'normal working day' between 1833 and the 1970s. Contrary to Bienefeld it was not until 1974 that the notion of continuous duty was replaced by a nationally operative 48-hour week.[55] Research into hospitals with their pervasive service ethic, reveals that nurses are 'able to arrange time-tables so as to thwart consultant's intentions' via the nurses responsibility for scheduling.[56] Returning to the overlap of work and home, as Keith McClelland shows for the north-east engineering industry in the 1850–1900 period, or Joyce more generally for work in the nineteenth century, the traditional practices of St Monday, for example, have persisted. Such practices, however informal, eroded the simple notion of the working day and the rational division of work from life outside.[57]

CERAMICS AND AUTOMOBILES

The necessarily brief and allusive outline in the second section by no means covers all the possible sources of time/work ordering. Instead it has given an indication of their range from the structural to the processual levels. The following section uses two examples to illustrate the plurality of time-reckoning systems involved in industry and the uneven unfolding of time/work discipline. Although Thompson notes the slowness with which a version of time/work discipline was established in the pottery industry it is more important to realise why that was so. In pursuing that question via our three-tier model it becomes clear that the sources and perceptions of time-ordering at work remained diverse and often in competition.

Apart from being one of the most distinctive industries to emerge from Britain's industrialisation, by 1900 the Staffordshire potteries region was by any standards 'the world's greatest pottery industry'. It accounted for almost a third of the world's ceramic export market, employed 46,000 workers in 1911 and was, according to *The Times* in 1917, 'a great industry, valued at £7 million a year'.[58] At the sectoral level the unity implied by the inclusive term pottery is rather superficial. During the nineteenth century the industry diversified into its modern form of a group of related sub-industries. Down to 1850 earthenware remained the foundation together with stoneware based on cheaper clays. China or porcelain manufacture expanded. A variant of porcelain known as parian was added to the range after mid century to satisfy the demand for statuary ware. Brick and tile production increased parallel to the growth of industry and towns. Two sub-industries which were spawned in the later part of the century were the sanitary and the electrical trades. Sanitary ware with its superior finish grew to replace the enamelled goods of Wolverhampton while new electrical porcelain served the needs of the early electricity industry.[59] Each of the seven sub-industries presented quite different market, technology and company profiles. Work-time therefore assumed a rich mosaic of forms derived within the various settings of the sub-industries.

Besides being dispersed unequally among the six towns of the region the seven sub-industries exhibited large differences both between and within them. Varying permutations of materials and making techniques made an enormous product range possible thereby ensuring a wide spread of work-forms. Even a single product type would be produced in different ways. The work required to make a nine-inch plate could differ between two firms in the same Longton street due to the way a clay body's plasticity varied when mixed in a different firm's recipes.[60] The whole character of work varied between sub-industries. Earthenware and china, for example, were in sharp contrast. In 1917 it was noted how 'the production of earthenware is a business; the making of porcelain an art and craft'. Electrical porcelain production was differentiated from the other sub-industries by the greater impact of scientific requirements and the higher standards of pyrometry which necessitated closer technical control of production by management.[61]

The sub-industries were also divided by the characteristics of the product market. Some produced for domestic, personal demand, others sold mainly to industry. Similarly, the differing degree of participation in home or foreign markets added further distinctive time pressures on each sub-industry's pattern of work. In 1902 home demand was said to be notable for its 'steady and substantial' quality 'not being subject to violent fluctuations either as regards quantity or style'. Rhythms of work in companies which produced for imperial markets (51% of pottery exports in 1900) were still regarded as stable but those exporting elsewhere (e.g., the US) faced severe competition and potentially fearsome disruption.

The exporters to the empire could leave production techniques largely unchanged while the second category were forced to take up any new methods which would lower costs and add to competitiveness.[62] Moreover, no two product markets were alike during the 1880–1930 period, or beyond. Although generally the pottery industry resembles the experience of the older British staples, each sub-industry performed very differently. Even in the same year or month different sub-industries enjoyed entirely opposite trading circumstances and hence rhythms of work.[63]

Stratification of the pottery industry according to firm type also stands out. As Samuel points out for the nineteenth century in general, production took on a range of forms which were not uniformly equated with the factory system. Similarly for pottery the 1857 census shows that in earthenware over 60% of pottery masters employed less than twenty men. What emerged by the mid nineteenth century was a three-layered structure of productive unit type, each with very different work styles. At the base were the smallest, often self-employed and with little capital. These produced mainly cheap ware, often on contract to larger firms. At the top were the leading companies: highly capitalised, engaged in world markets and using ceramic consultants to control production processes involving over 1,000 workers. But there is an intermediate layer made up of specialist firms with often high-quality output for specific markets. While the larger firms were generally the most sophisticated in work-control techniques, the smallest 'penny jack shops' were noticeably more direct and crude. The medium-sized firms did not have the same imperatives as the other two categories given their specialist markets and the need for quality and exclusiveness above cost and volume.[64] Finally, the natural and selling seasons overlay the pottery industry to add to the variegated patterning of work-time. Given the susceptibility of clay to the weather the rhythm of pottery production had to pay attention to the climatic seasons. Yet the selling seasons of each sub-industry also diverged between consumer, 'useful' or decorative ware (e.g. Christmas or commemorations) and the way sanitary and brick production was linked to the building cycle. Moreover, this range of time-structures in the pottery industry was not transformed or simplified by any aggregate economic shifts (e.g. 1880s or the 1914–20 period): if anything they appear to have added to the complex rhythms of both pottery production and employment relations.[65]

The pottery firm shows how the notion of a dominant general mode of time/work discipline sits uneasily with local evidence. Although they were anxious to increase control of materials, costs and labour, management's capacity to do so was extremely variable. Managerial control of production remained relatively primitive in the pottery industry. In 1921, many potbanks were apparently 'characterised by an absence of anything like an office'. The sector clearly lacked a precise ceramic science and so pottery manufacture was guided by essentially empirical knowledge.[66] In spite of the public debate on 'scientific methods' during the 1900–20 period only a few of the larger companies possessed a sound costing system. W. G. Fox told the English Ceramic Society in 1916 that 'there is abundant evidence that cost taking is a minus quantity with many firms'. As late as 1940, only a third of pottery firms kept cost accounts which distinguished labour and material costs for each part of the production process. Outsiders chided pottery manufacturers for their 'want of system' as they continued to rely on more direct, implicit forms of control. These centred on sub-contracting and piece-work with its crude method of ensuring high output by workers. Internal sub-contracting had the advantage of saving managerial time spent in supervision by removing the need to control all workers directly: it also dispersed the risks which production entailed from owner to sub-contractor. Overall managerial control was sustained by limiting craft or workgroup regulation and discretion to separate parts of the production process.[67]

Above all, the absence of a demonstrable managerial time-ordering of work in the industry was best expressed by the lack of clocks on most potbanks. In spite of the generally recognised impact of the First World War on the spread of personal timepieces, an accountants' report on the pottery industry in 1924 found that few establishments had official time clocks. In the same way an international report on the world pottery industry found that Britain had no easily recognised office which could be called 'time keeper'. Indeed hours of work varied so widely that there was no standard working day. As R. Stirrat, a moulder wrote in 1920: 'We have no set time for stopping and starting here, that is in regards to moulded work, should any job be given out, a piece-work rate is at once fixed on. So the Boss troubles no more about one's coming and going.'[68]

The pottery production process itself was 'infinitely sub-divided' due to the low levels of mechanisation and the reliance on craft skills to produce such a varied product range. The largest potbanks contained over 100 departments or shops. Even the smallest had thirty separate workshops based on the central production sequence of mixing, potting/making, firing, dipping, decorating and packing. There were few machines which simplified tasks and integrated them into a flowline even within the six main phases. The Ministry of Reconstruction found in 1918 therefore that the pottery industry did not require large supplies of electrical power because it was 'very largely split up into small shops which do not need a great deal of machinery'. Neither product standardisation nor increased mechanisation synchronised production into a unified time-sequence. On the contrary there were notable delays between departments. The hold-ups between mixing and potting, making and firing were notorious, often resulting in conflict over work-time between workers which rivalled in intensity the disputes between management and workforce.[69]

The idea of standard working methods and times breaks down even more when different parts of production are compared. Slip-making, which took two or three hours, contrasted with the intensity of flatware production, this differed again from the firing department's oven work which was spread over two days.[70] The equally intricate division of labour in so labour-intensive an industry meant that the potbank work-force was made up of a collection of very small occupational groupings often working in workgroups of around four to eight people confined to the tiny workshops. No uniform perception of working emerged among them. Craft skills and attitudes and the rich customs of the workshop were indulgent of clock-based time. Colin Sedgly's description of his ver-satile 'fitting' trade in the potting department defied regulation and stop-watch ordering in March 1919:

I am not a polisher but a china or potters fitter which requires a lot of training and takes years to learn to become efficient in the business as figures, ewers, vases, bowls, &cetera [sic] are made in sections: and I have to grind and fit them perpen-dicular and horizontally true then stick them together with a body composition and send them through the kiln and make them one whole piece, work that requires great care and skill besides mental capacity. There are about 5,000 shapes to remember how they have to be fixed.

Such people could not be mechanised: they and others, such as the makers, dippers or firemen, provided a flexibility which accommodated the infinite variations in materials, temperature and clay plasticity which no machine could approach. The tiny workshops therefore became satu-rated with their own codes which arose spontaneously among workers in order to regulate such an unsynchronised production process. Worker or-dering of time became a necessity if the competitive pressures between or within workgroups were not to overwhelm them. Work-sharing is a good example. When the work sequence was interrupted a workgroup met and decided how the available work would be divided. Each worker was then given a stint or stent of articles to produce in his or her time. Even when demand was high it was noted how 'the equalisation of work between one team and another is arranged by the men'. Factory inspectors concluded therefore that potbanks were 'places by themselves, with hardly any supervision'.[71]

The depiction of a plurality of time-reckoning modes connected with the pottery industry is completed by examining the overlapping worlds of work and community. The interdependence of the potters' orientations to

time with the organisation of the industry stands out. Without doubt the
staple industry dominated life in the region. The 400 potbanks individually and collectively threw a shadow over the potters' homes. Most potters lived within walking distance of their workplace.[72] Yet this physical
dominance was not translated into a straightforward superiority of
work-time over all other activities. In practice, work and domestic
routines remained bound in a number of ways. These can be seen in
the influence of family and kin relations and also in the way wider
collective perceptions of time were formed and sustained across the
six towns.

A potter's family life was directly structured by the demands of the irregular working patterns in the industry. The most frequent breaches of
the Factory Acts in the area during the 1900s arose from the uneven but,
overall, lengthy work-cycles of pottery manufacture. On the other hand,
within a tradition of self-determined work routines, potters not only
accommodated such variations they also learned to convert that irregu-
larity to their own use. Workers therefore exploited the many breaks in
production to stop, attend to children or other dependents. Indeed, pottery workers and employers legitimated the activity by labelling these
periods 'play'. The word signified that a person was temporarily not actively engaged in pottery work but it had no pejorative connotation of
work avoidance; a meaning which differentiates the Staffordshire word
from its use elsewhere. It was this intermittent quality of pottery work and
the way it was interwoven with outside activities which led Clapham to
remark in 1938 that the potters were able to retain control of time in a
way usually associated with the pre-factory age.[73]

In part this interweaving of home- and work-time was facilitated by the
extent of family employment. By 1900 50% of the workforce was female.
Contrary to popular images of the working-class family in the past, in the
potter's household each member had duties which were designed to
ensure the continuation of joint work and domestic routines. Workgroups
(often family- or kin-based) allocated work in a way which recognised
domestic requirements and family needs: this was especially necessary
given the high incidence of industrial disease. Women of course were central to such accommodation and developed their own time-ordering
devices which united paid and unpaid labour; without this capacity the
pottery industry could not have operated. Families also understood the
work-home relationship via longer time perceptions. Potteries' families
helped determine the timing of key events in their children's projected
employment careers. Older members negotiated points of entry to work
and once inside they informed the progression of younger kin among the
skill and status hierarchies.[74] This picture is confirmed by the high levels

(up to 60%) of kin-based job succession. It is made more intelligible by the long-term connections of potters and their families with specific firms or areas.[75]

On a wider scale the potters also constructed their own collective versions of the passage of time within the industry. Inside each sub-industry potters generated marker points for negotiations of their employment contract related to points in the selling year (especially March) as well as more customary points, such as Michaelmas. Potters' union leaders and labour representatives on the local councils led a campaign across the six towns against the refusal of Anglican priests to hold Sunday funerals and weddings: a practice which pottery workers wished to continue since it fitted in with their unpredictable work-cycles which often embraced Saturday working.

In the same way, the collective consciousness of the potters contained some especial perceptions of time. This was seen in the highly selective memory and reconstruction of time past. The best example of this phenomenon was the way in which the exceptional, industry-wide disputes of 1879, 1892–3 and 1899 were selectively reproduced as almost immediate precedents during the more usual localised conflict of the 1900–1930 period, the lapse of up to forty calendar years notwithstanding. A significant outcome of the multiplicity of time-ordering in the pottery industry appeared in the continuous problem of creating either a single industrial union, one inclusive manufacturer's association, or a unified bargaining system: problems which still persist today.

The selectivity of the potters' reconstruction of time becomes a key means of understanding the course of industrial relations within the ceramic sector. The high incidence of strikes in the 1900s were clearly related to current issues (especially new technology) and market conditions but the prime motivation on the potters' side was derived from memories of events in the 1880s and 1890s. Noah Parkes, a union organiser, during the 1908 sanitary disputes based his actions on his perception of how 'the great improvements in the pottery industry in the last twenty years had gone vastly in favour of the masters and now the potters wished to take their share'. The way in which the actions of Lord Hatherton (an arbitrator) in 1879 were continually cited by negotiators in the early twentieth century draws attention to the way highly subjective constructions of the past inform actions in the present.[76] Indeed, interesting comparisons with car workers emerge. As will become clear, the impact on labour of the changes in markets, management and work in the early 1970s was intensified by those workers' attachment to relations and work practices which had evolved over decades. Although in a mass production sector said to be the antithesis of ceramics, car workers, like potters, used such constructions of time past to legitimate their position on the new patterns of work of the 1970s.

The descriptions of work in the car industry have been amongst the most vivid accounts by social scientists of modern industry. At first sight the car industry would seem not only worlds removed from pottery manufacture but also an example which fits Thompson's thesis rather better. However, in the British car industry, while the development of mechanised production appears to equate with the received image of a highly-synchronised and tightly-controlled time/work discipline, the reality within given companies was less straightforward. Once more, it is the late emergence of a clearly-defined managerial time/work discipline and the coexistence of multiple time-structures which stand out.

The abiding impression of car work has been derived from a series of famous portrayals.[77] Walker and Guest's investigations of American car plants in the 1940s and 50s concluded that a time/work discipline clearly based on production technology was pervasive. Hence:

the nature of work itself, the fractionated repetitive conveyor pacing, profoundly affected all aspects of the quality of their working lives ... there was virtually no participation of the workers themselves in decisions affecting their work lives.[78]

A substantial body of writing supports these conclusions. A review of the British car industry of the early 1970s took up the line of technological dominance and stated how 'one of the major characteristics of the industry is its domination by the mass production process'.[79] Yet research on the British case points to the inability of this approach to cover all aspects of car work, its over-reliance on American experience and the high degree of technological determinism involved. A brief examination of time and work in a British car firm (the Rover Company) informed by our three-tier perspective of sector, enterprise and community contexts reveals a different picture.

At the sector level a number of features of the UK car industry distinguish it from the American-based images of time and work. First, as Turner et al. stress the 'way work is done' is the result of a number of interrelated variables, each operating within different time dimensions. These have included, the length of track, number of work stations, a production line's model-handling capacity and the number of operators per task. The variations in the time cycles of different operations can be considerable. Their research in the 1960s also uncovered how working time in a car factory could be punctuated by both technical and informal breaks in production. Although they agree that the 'moving tracks enforce their own supervision' it was also apparent how 'men are their own managers, there being considerable scope for personal discretion to be used in doing even the simplest and most menial of jobs'.[80]

Detailed accounts of car work reinforce this differentiated experience of work, the variable impact of technological change and the ability of workers to regulate important aspects of their work routines.[81] They show how the slowness of British companies to adopt capital-intensive production techniques and the reliance on payment systems to maintain output made for weak managerial control of production.[82] Secondly, the British sector does not fit the US and European models of industrial relations built on unified, national bargaining institutions. In Britain a fragmented structure persisted with negotiation located predominantly at the shop-floor level. Set against a background of minimal formal management training in this country these did not lead to the highly developed union-'management' of workers, as suggested by Bardou for other European countries.[83]

Thirdly, general accounts of the car industry have featured a three-stage scheme of technological development: unique product production around 1900; rigid mass-production of a single model from 1913; and more flexible mass-production developed and diffused from the 1920s to the 1960s. While the scheme holds true for the US industry, Britain's car sector does not fit this course in either the pattern of change or its timing. Whereas the American experience relied on a set of clearly-defined corporate strategies laid down as early as the 1920s, the UK producers (larger in number) struggled to find such consistent policies within a more fragmented and unstable market. The early elimination of craft skills and craft organisation of production in America was not seen in Britain. The slow emergence of a mass market, the different selling-season rhythms compared to the US annual car-model change, and the high variability of demand did not lead to increasingly specialised plant or divisional corporate organisation in Britain. Here the 'best practice' examples of production technique and company form continued to enshrine flexibility as a necessity. Anglo-American comparisons carried out by UK car engineers in 1940 and a major review of Austin techniques in 1947 showed US methods to be inappropriate to their needs.[84]

Although located in the semi-luxury, medium-sized section of the car market the Rover Company is a good example of the distinctive pattern of company growth in Britain, the multiple time-frames in which work was carried out, and the slow growth of mass-production. The Rover Company began making cars in 1904 in Coventry and maintained an independent existence down to 1967 when it merged with the Leyland Motor Corporation (later BLMC).[85] The company's market position set the broad time-structure for the internal organisation of work. In 1912 the company offered one of the largest vehicle ranges. After 1920, Rover faced increasing price competition from Austin and Morris. Rover's weak capacity to reduce production costs led to a major crisis between 1928 and 1932 when the company almost went out of business. From 1933 under new leadership the company formed a new policy of limited production for the medium-sized, semi-luxury car market. After temporary aeroplane production in the Second World War the product range was extended to include the Land Rover and four-wheel-drive vehicles.[86] From 1946 to 1963 the company maintained its policy of quality and engineering sophistication via the 'P series' of cars: the P3 from 1948, P4 from 1950 and the P5 in 1958. In 1963 the P6 sparked off a further crisis as the company attempted to change its market position and expand production.[87]

Rover management developed a business strategy which rested on devolved forms of control which came to embody a diversity of time-ordering devices. Rover management's main expertise lay in product design. Throughout the 'P series' they were noted for 'imaginative and advanced design' in direct contrast to the low rates of innovation in the American corporations. This resulted in a very uneven long-term process of product change at Rover since new car projects did not appear in conventional four- or five-year cycles. The Range Rover took two attempts between 1961 and 1971 while the P5 went through six main reworkings in fourteen years. These unpredictable changes in product naturally led to comparable reorderings of production each time.[88]

In the area of production Rover, like other UK car firms, did not follow the Fordist principles of centrally-directed, highly-synchronised, machine-paced production. Rover managers' main principle was 'to minimise the complexities of management'. The integration of product, production and work-organisation was much less than in the US. According to Robson, down to the 1970s, 'product planning as we know it to-day simply did not exist'.[89] The company, for example, had 'little idea' of prospective demand for the Range Rover in 1971. Elaborate managerial hierarchies did not arise. Product and production engineers, far from working to rigid model policies prided themselves on their small, flexible, organic, design teams and their weekly, informal liaison with production staff.[90]

Production techniques were therefore less developed. Rover is a clear example of the generally low levels of investment in new plant in the UK car industry and the fitful introduction of new, machine-based technology. A reconstruction of the main assembly plants of the company also reveals the slow developments of an integrated fabrication cycle. The Coventry Meteor factory in the 1920s was where 'departments have to be added where space was available, regardless of whether the position were [sic] ideal from the viewpoint of internal works transportation or the progress of parts'.[91] In 1936 although the Helen Street works shows a main final assembly track, it was noted how 'few sections of the track are mechanised'. The new factory at Solihull in 1946 was termed 'continuous flow production' requiring time-and-motion study. Yet, sub-assembly was still by bench construction and track speeds were very slow since hand-work predominated. Even in the 1960s the full integration of the P6 operations was weakened by the delays involved in the dispersal of production and assembly over two main groups of factories.[92]

In the organisation of work the absence of a 'scientific' approach to management was compensated for by Rover management's use of direct, personal lines of authority. Outsiders found the 'team' approach of the company 'inbred' and based on 'continuity of personnel and their practices'.[93] Management relied on devolved forms of organising work but backed up by a range of cultural and ideological persuasion. At the centre of these means of securing worker co-operation and adherence to company policies was the inculcation of a 'life-time' perspective to work at Rover. In a technical sense this was fostered by apprenticeship schemes open only to relations of existing workers: but it was reinforced by the development of long-term work and community relationships which informed worker perceptions. These included reinforcement of a company time-narrative at each new model launch for instance, or the development from 1945 of share and pension schemes for employees.[94] The company decided in the 1950s therefore that 'the best road to success was to build a limited number of quality cars by employing and looking after a highly skilled and talented staff'. Skill levels remained high.[95]

Although it was one of the first companies to experiment with the Bedaux time-and-payment system in this country in the 1930s Rover leaned heavily thereafter on piece-work arrangements in common with the rest of the industry. The detailed organisation of production was therefore the effective responsibility of the workgroup which learned to accommodate the irregular rhythms of market and inter-plant supply lines. It was on the shop floor that the most intricate patterns of perceptions of time arose. As in the pottery industry the key characteristic of piece-work was the way management gave only general orders regarding tasks. Workers were expected to 'carry out the necessary detailed operations implied by these orders'. Workers concentrated on issues related to their work stations or group's task responsibilities and payment: a concentration which produced a strictly localised perception of task-pace and regulation, which could not be generalised over the whole workforce of a plant or the company. Track workers were preoccupied with the base-rate payment per minute while trim workers were more interested in the rate per hour they could negotiate. The variety of timing and hence uncertainty of payment was compounded by the generally unsynchronised

supply and production operations. As a long-serving track worker reflected 'you never knew what you were going to earn'.[96]

The community dimension to work and time in the case of the Rover
company has already been suggested by the development of 'life-time'
careers there. However, with over half the workforce living within the
borough of Solihull the relationship between work, community and time
was experienced in a number of ways. Two examples indicate how industrial pressures did not determine work-time patterns unilaterally. In
the 1970s management attempts to introduce double-shift working were
successfully resisted on two fronts. One was via conventional union bargaining which centred on the workers' rejection of the market need for the
volume of production which would require a second shift. But the second
front was opened up by the families of those workers who objected to the
proposed night shift because of its disruption of family routines and life. It
is significant that the combination of these two fronts during strikes in
1977 and 1978 meant that management abandoned its plans.[97]

A second example of the community aspect of work and time is more
difficult to convey to those outside the industry. The secrecy over new
models and car projects in general is notorious. New car launches and factory openings are closely-guarded secrets. Car workers would appear to
be at a severe disadvantage over such crucial timings and all that they
imply for changes in future work. Whilst Rover management undoubtedly decided on the course and timing of such projects (as in the P6 of
1963 or the SD1 of 1976) car workers at Rover had their own means of
monitoring such projects and using that information to structure their
actions in the future. Therefore, in the case of the SD1 car, skilled proto-
type and pre-production workers kept friends and colleagues informed of
key developments. The mixture of kin and social networks which operated both in the Solihull factory and within the borough spread the information. As a result, the stewards who entered the new SD1 factory in June
1976 had already planned their sectional and plant organisation in
advance. Their plans rested on detailed knowledge of task-times and line-
speeds derived not from official manuals but from the interaction of work
and community relationships.[98]

Moreover, it was this rich spread of localised time/work organisation
when confronted by increased sectoral instability of demand and general
inflationary pressures, which led to record levels of (unofficial) disputes in
the 1960s at Rover. At the heart of this conflict was the way sectoral
rhythms overwhelmed the workgroup's capacity to handle such uncertainty and hence gave rise to the much hated increase in 'waiting time' and
its lower rates of pay.[99] It is a measure of the radical changes initiated by
the crisis of the 1970s in the car industry that falling productivity and

increased competition have forced management to refashion the accepted relationships between sectoral and company time-ordering. Management now considers it vital to regain control over this range of time-frames and time-reckoning systems which had operated in the industry for so long.[100]

CONCLUSION

The purpose of this essay has been to suggest the ways in which the time/work relationship may be approached: it is by no means comprehensive. As Keith McClelland's and Maxine Berg's research indicates, industrialisation did not impose an all-embracing, single time/work discipline. In parallel with the range of social and economic forces it unleashed in terms of the time/work relationship industrialisation opened up a stream of possibilities. Above all, it is the heterogeneous forms of time and how they are differently perceived which emerges on closer inspection. As Pahl has argued,[101] social scientists should not uncritically accept the definition of time embodied in supposedly rational, modern, economic exchange. Historians, by the same token, will not understand the meanings of work in the past if they too rely on the received idea of the linear progression of a so-called objective, public, mathematical ordering of time.

An understanding of the time/work relationship informed by both the subjective constructions of time and the plurality of time-reckoning modes which have continued to operate in industrial societies is proposed. This approach sees work-time not created or determined by the needs of capital alone but rather as structured from multiple sources. These methods of time-ordering and synchronisation relate not only to the clock or machine but also the cyclical patterns of season, family and life-course, as well as the diverse perceptions derived from various social groupings inside and outside work. Moreover, the consistent feature of time/work discipline has been that in spite of formidable attempts to commodify and appropriate it by management, work-time has always been uncertain and quintessentially difficult to control; not the least because of the highly personal and subjective bases on which it often rests.

An analysis based on the social experience and construction of time offers possible ways forward for historical and contemporary research into work. The historian's task is to explore how the various time-ordering mechanisms intersect. In doing so there are a number of scholars from adjacent disciplines who can assist in this project. They range from geographers such as Thrift who use the notion of a time-structuring process; to sociologists of Moorhouse's kind, sensitive to the fluidity of work and non-work boundaries; and on to anthropologists such as Godelier who are keenly aware of the diverse ways in which language is used to represent the many facets of work.[102] And then there are those authors from literature who seem to have long appreciated the social basis of time and its implied order. A very recent and apt example might be the opening lines of Graham Greene's *The Tenth Man,* set in a French prison in the Second World War.

Most of them told the time very roughly by their meals, which were unpunctual and irregular: they amused themselves with the most childish games all through the day, and when it was dark they fell asleep by tacit consent – not waiting for a particular hour of darkness for they had no means of telling the time exactly: in fact there were as many times as there were prisoners.[103]

9

The 'work' ethic and 'leisure' activity: the hot rod in post-war America

H. F. MOORHOUSE

SOME ORTHODOXIES IN THE STUDY OF 'WORK'

In post-war America full employment and the changes associated with a general rise in real incomes caused a number of analysts to ponder the nature of work, its meanings, and its effects on the individual. Quite often the targets of this attention were workers in the automobile industry, and it was in this period that labour in automobile factories (this labour very narrowly conceived) was elevated to an iconic status, such that labour on the track or line became, somehow, the explicit or implicit model of what most modern work is like, or would soon be like, and in which major guidelines for investigation were provided such as repetition, boredom, degradation, de-skilling, and so on, all spun round a central thread of alienation.[1] Such studies helped establish an orthodox tradition in the social analysis of work which is still dominant today, given added weight, if not much more depth, by a renewed Marxist interest in the labour process in the last decade.[2]

One of the largest of these post-war studies was carried out by Kornhauser. His book, pregnantly titled *The Mental Health of the Industrial Worker*, emerged out of interviews with over four hundred male Detroit workers and their spouses carried out in 1953–4.[3] Kornhauser, like so many other students had no doubts that 'work' was synonymous with job, or of its significance for the individual:

clearly work not only serves to produce goods and services, it also performs essential psychologistical functions. It operates as a great stabilising, integrating, ego satisfying, central influence in the pattern of each person's life. If the job fails to fulfil these needs of the personality, it is problematic whether men can find adequate substitutes to provide a sense of significance and achievement, purpose and justification for their lives.[4]

Such confident proclamations underpin many other, much more recent, studies of work, its meanings, and effects, but Kornhauser departed somewhat from the orthodox tradition in that he at least tried to establish whether his workers found 'compensations' in other aspects of their lives for what he believed to be their routinised work. However, his search led him to conclude that only 10–15% of his sample were engaged in hobbies or pastimes which:

are of genuine current significance in their lives as sources of pride and enjoyment.[5]

The destructive effects of modern work were not, it seemed, checked by other activity. Kornhauser, despite his excursion, was able to swing back into the path of orthodox analysis by deploying more assumptions. He exemplifies an approach to the study of work which is both quick to assume the crucial existential significance of some conceptually unclear 'work', and also demands that, if *other* activities are to enter into consideration as possible sources of pride, fulfillment, identify formation, and affirmation, they must pass the most stringent scrutiny as to their *moral* worth. The dismissive use of terms like 'hobby', 'pastime', 'amusements' is indicative here, and Kornhauser's analysis abounds with phrases like '*serious* reading', '*shallow* routine pastimes', '*genuine* self-expression', '*challenging* quests for knowledge', and the like, where an undisclosed and undiscussed moral evaluation merges with what purports to be detached appraisal, and operates so as to exclude various categories of action as being unworthy sources of meanings, purpose, and self-definition. So Kornhauser excluded that considerable percentage of auto-workers who insisted that all their spare time was devoted to house, car or garden. He excluded those who referred to gambling or drinking, and the 20% who alluded to sports (including hunting). All these were joined by those who said visiting or TV-watching was their main leisure activity. Kornhauser's residue was composed only of the boat-builders, violin-makers, and short-story writers. Such value judgements, concealed in commonsense concepts and taken-for-granted connections, reek of the power of the 'work ethic' which may, or may not, have penetrated the minds of most workers but is certainly lodged, as a moral ideal, in much of what purports to be the analysis of work and its meanings.

This criticism of Kornhauser's book is intended to reveal a quite widespread set of assumptions which underpin most orthodox study in this field, and which serve to simplify the real puzzle of issues which lie around work, its meanings and effects. The most important of these assumptions are that:

(1) 'work' is paid labour;
(2) it is just this work that is the crucible in which social identity is forged;

(3) the dominant values of capitalist society did, and do, without much
equivocation, stress just this work as the critical area in which male
life is played out.

Feminist critiques, it is true, have shaken this set of assumptions somewhat, but still the weight of their objections have not forced most analysts
to really think what they mean by the concept 'work', and to assess the
variety of values surrounding that term. Recently, a critique has been
developing within, as it were, the sociology of work itself.[6] In their books
Rose and Pahl both point to the fallacy of treating 'work' as equivalent to
the regular paid labour of, usually, men and both point out that what are
all too often claimed to be 'new' attitudes or 'departures' from 'old' values
invariably rest on comparisons with an implied or idealised past based on
no or inadequate evidence as to exactly what such attitudes or values were
in earlier periods.

Rose concentrates on the issue of whether some 'work ethic' *ever* affected the behaviour of most workers. This scepticism is most refreshing, but
his analysis does tend to dwindle in force because his attention is directed
at paid labour and so other activities, other labour, does not attract the
careful scrutiny he applies to the meanings of 'work' as conventionally understood. Indeed, he is led to argue that a 'work ethic' cannot now represent truly bourgeois values since modern economic performance
depends on avid consumption. The activities of the modern sales effort:

reinforce a broader hedonistic frame of mind which is directly at odds with the
bourgeois doctrine of deferred gratification.[7]

and he refers to:

an immensely competent advertising and promotion industry whose creative elite
possess every skill needed to reassure people of their personal right to self-
indulgence, to frequent escape from social obligation, and work commitments, to
an undue concern with time, or from worries over budgeting.[8]

In such quotes Rose reveals that he has not entirely escaped the frameworks imposed by the assumptions of the dominant tradition. He certainly simplifies the accomplishments of the groups in modern capitalism
who work with and on culture and symbols, *and* assumes they produce an
undifferentiated, one-dimensional ideology of easy indulgence in leisure
time.

Pahl's text concentrates on discussing the various types of work that
were and are done in society, and makes a useful distinction between
employment (paid labour) and work, which is conceived of as a very
broad category encompassing all productive activities (paid and unpaid),
reproductive activity, and some consumption. Such a broadening of the

key term has great implications for orthodox study, for if 'work' is the place where 'man makes himself' and if, 'work' is an unclear concept, with many dimensions, then it is by no means clear which *work* is to be afforded centrality in identity creation, or perhaps all are important, or perhaps relative weights change through time or through a life. Each work may have its own ideologies and preferred meanings which can vary through time and space. Pahl catches part of what is at issue here in his concluding remarks that:

the work ethic is alive and well: people enjoy working and there is plenty to do. Often they may not particularly enjoy their employment.[9]

However, Pahl does concentrate on examining the work done and tends to neglect questions of meanings and associated ideologies, and occasionally suggests that the existential significance of various types of work can be illuminated by quantitative measures, whereas what is of the essence here is the varying quality of labour times. Moreover, Pahl's stress that work (in all its forms) is a strategy of households directed to a project of 'getting by' and 'cosiness' means that he both neglects independent, individual work strategies, as he recognises,[10] and tends to adopt too instrumental a view of what work is done for. So he has little to say about work in relation to expressive needs, self-presentation, and symbolic display. He does appreciate that such labour is done and is promoted in society:

the development of consumption as a form of work is, perhaps, the dominant new element that capitalism has imposed on household work strategies.[11]

but he does not investigate the qualitative significance of such work and relegates mention of it to footnotes or throwaway lines. And, as with Rose, Pahl tends to assume that advertising and marketing always link to 'new' needs and 'new' commodities.

So, even these important new critiques of the orthodox tradition do not really touch on all of the important issues involved in recasting the study of work. In particular, if there are many *types* of **work**, and the meanings of each can vary, then there is a great need to focus on the way people learn about work and are socialised to various meanings. For there is no intrinsic meaning to any piece of labour. Meanings have to be attached, sustained, promulgated and learned. Now most analyses, and, again, Kornhauser's is a typical example, rather vaguely assume that the dominant values of capitalist society do present some 'work ethic' which is both smooth and unequivocal in tone, and paramount in the messages emanating from the major institutions of society.

Neither of these assumptions is obviously correct and, at a bare minimum, students of the meanings of work need to be alive to a diversity of dominant sources presenting rather different messages about work. They need to be aware also that while dominant values will provide a good deal of input, albeit in a more complex and contradictory fashion than is often suggested, other sources exist with their own institutional supports which will mediate and mix with dominant views. Specifically, class, gender, and ethnic cultures will make complex inputs, as will quite precise occupational ideologies formed in varying workplaces which will have both formal and informal expressions: from union rule books to workgroup norms. Acceptance of even this point makes it clear that the meanings of work are not likely to be neat and simple, or form some uncomplicated 'ethic' but are rather likely to be jumbled and variegated, so that any individual has a whole range of types and levels of meanings on which to draw, and with which to understand or appreciate the labour they are doing at any particular moment. The notion of 'a work ethic' as central to the experience of work – even when this is understood as paid labour – simplifies this issue since it picks out only a few of the heterogenous meanings which circle around labour and promotes these as 'the most important'.

One of the fullest descriptions of the work ethic is provided by Rodgers when considering nineteenth-century America:

The central premise of the work ethic was that work was the core of moral life. Work made men useful in a world of economic scarcity. It staved off the doubts and temptations that preyed on idleness, it opened the way to deserved wealth and status, it allowed one to put the impress of mind and skill on the material world.[12]

This formulation is preferable to most, if only because Rodgers understands that worry about the dangers of sheer idleness form part of dominant ideologies about work. In all too many analyses the 'work ethic' has been slimmed down to equate to a craft ethic or professional ethic – work as a vocation – in which, it is argued, the job should yield a sense of mastery, control over materials and techniques, command of technology, an engagement of hand *and* brain in solving problems and so on. This then becomes linked to another aspect, as alluded to by Rodgers, that the job should allow the opportunity for development in personality, *and*, though the rather imprecise connections are usually quickly skated over here, an opportunity for advance and mobility in material terms.

The problem with this kind of formulation of the 'work ethic' is that it posits far too simple a relation between objective task and subjective perception: the most routinised and paced paid labour requires some worker's knowledge to be applied if the task is to be done in the optimum way, and thus virtually *all* jobs provide the raw material for workers to regard themselves as 'skilled', even if this is not institutionalised. Pride can be obtained from doing *any* job, even the most menial, well, in the eyes of bosses or other workers. The respect of significant others in the workplace can be what is sought and valued, and this does not depend on the abstract quality of the task to be done.[13] Or work can gain meanings by being defined as a sacrifice, through which the individual yields himself or herself to unpleasant tasks or routine in order to meet obligations to others – usually wife, husband or children, and so gain respect.[14]

However, and more crucially, the tendency to align 'a work ethic' with a craft job ethic has meant that there are numerous meanings around work which have received – from history, sociology, or Marxism – little attention. Even Rodgers' formulation misses a lot of these. The meanings of work which circulate around its role in marking passages in the life cycle – adulthood, retirement – is a good example. Others concern meanings which arise out of the job's location in quite particular contexts: thus purpose and identity can be summoned out of working for a well-known firm, or in a glamorous location, or from being linked with broad ideological notions of 'scientific progress', or from being associated with a desirable product.[15] Car workers call on all of these to locate their work and infuse it with meaning. Nor has work as an area for the experience and display of sheer strength, endurance and courage been much discussed, yet, for males at least, such values are of some importance and by no means nestle easily with the craft ideal. Much hard, routine, labour is infused with meaning because it allows a physical confrontation. Life in any industrial concern is fraught with danger. Many labour processes routinely produce potentially dangerous incidents. The radical response to this is to analyse why such processes have come to be in the service of profit maximisation, but much less analysed is the response of workers to such recurrent situations, and the way danger and bravery, drawing on notions of masculinity, become important in the meanings surrounding work.[16] Men can gain pride, respect, confirm identity, by pitting themselves against fear or furnace.

So, and while the others I have mentioned certainly do not exhaust the stock, there are many ideologies which lurk around work and which provide meanings, and only some of these are caught in orthodox appeals to the power of some 'work ethic'. Clearly then the actual position confronting the student of work is extremely complex, for there are many types of **work** in a capitalist society and many ethics or ideologies about work. The task has to be to trace the ethics that apply to different kinds of work, for only if some activities can be shown to be intrinsically trivial and devoid of ideological justifications, should they be written-off by social analysis as inadequate sources of pride, identity, and social understanding. In the rest of this paper I want to consider these matters by looking at the automobile *in use* (where it is usually ignored), at the automobile as an object in consumption. I have adopted this strategy to try to indicate what meanings are evoked there, what values, beliefs, and cultural injunctions surround the motor car in this area of life and what, if anything, this suggests to us about the definition of work, and the social location of the 'work ethic'. The aspect of the automobile in use I want to consider is its incarnation as 'hot rod', but I must stress this is only an example of a host of other automobile-related 'leisure' subcultures which could be scrutinised, all of which have their own institutions, literature, heroes, calendars, and their own ideologies which often seem to draw on what is called the 'work ethic' but which, in hobbies, enthusiasms, interests, and passions, are not related to paid labour. So the hot-rod subculture is far from unique or odd.

THE HOT-ROD SUBCULTURE

In 1947 *Fortune* magazine estimated that while real incomes had risen by 40% in the 1940–7 period, discretionary spending was up 160%.[17] In the next decade credit for the purchase of automobiles rose by 800%, and in the 1950s general consumer indebtedness rose three times as fast as personal incomes.[18] By 1955 around one-third of spending units in the *lowest* quintile of incomes owned a car,[19] and by 1958 5.9 million teenagers had a licence to drive and around one and a half million teenagers owned cars.[20] In short, the years after the war were that period of affluence when most Americans became comfortable and well-off compared to their parents or to pre-war standards. The automobile was the symbol of this change and came to a new peak as commodity *and* as a cultural symbol.

In just this period the 'hot rod' became significant in the lives of a large number of (mainly young) Americans. A culture was created around the term with definite values, interests, a special vocabulary, and a variety of informal and formal institutions: used car lots, races, clubs, events, speed-shops, magazines, local and national associations. The term was used for abuse and admiration in the news media of the time, while the cinema, radio, TV, and books drew on the culture for background and for symbolism, refining and spreading its messages.[21]

The main theme of the culture was the modification of 'Detroit iron', the 'lead barges' which were the American production car. There was both a technical and an aesthetic aspect to such modification. The aura which hung around the culture, and its presentation in the media certainly was that of a 'hot' car, a speedy vehicle engaged in racing, often illegally on public highways. But, in fact, engineering and ornamentation, the desire to go faster and the wish to look sharper, were combined or separated in all manner of ways to provide a variety of sub-cultures, styles, and specialisms. And, of course, like any other activity, there was a continuum of commitment: from simply bolting a few shop-bought accessories onto your car, to creating, through one's own labour over many months, a streamlined dry-lake special.[22] The horizontal and vertical dimensions of attachment to the hot-rod culture provided many niches for individual placement and many permitted the exercise of skilled manual labour and intense mental work of design, costing, and racing.

The ethos of this culture, expressed through the specialist magazines and books of post-war America, is not one of redolent passivity but rather of urgent prescriptions to labour, to strive, to plan, to exercise skill, to compete, to succeed, to risk: themes like those supposedly typical of some traditional 'work ethic' but now directed to unpaid time.

The main myth of the culture is of buying a junked Ford for a few dollars, of reclaiming various parts from it, and with these and some other standard and custom accessories reassembling, via a great deal of hard and skilled labour, a high performance vehicle.

Jaderquist's manual *The New How To Build Hot Rods*, first published in 1957 and through to its sixth printing by 1977 is, like other books, full of pictures revealing how to do it yourself. The emphasis is on study, problem solving, initiative, making do and saving money by 'knuckle scraping' and 'back breaking' in an overall tone that would have heartened Benjamin Franklin:

Tools, remember, are only extensions of your hands, arms and fingers. Unless the original will and muscle is there, the finest tools in the world are useless.[23]

In Horsley's *Hot Rod It: And Run For Fun* of 1957 the bias of the text and photography is on the never-ending business of understanding the machine, especially the engine, in theory and practice. This kind of theme coexists with messages which stress, not occupational success, but, say, that working on your hot rod after paid labour is a source of satisfaction whatever your occupation, or that all rodders form a special community of interest, or that there is a relation between your rod and personal style and identity. Mass-produced automobiles, it is held, are standardised as the result of an inevitable compromise: they are, therefore, nobody's 'dream machine', whereas:

Your rod expresses you in more than just looks. Its quality of workmanship and roadability, as well as its power advertise your status and power as a rodder. You want to be able to point to your car with pride and say, 'want to take a ride'.[24]

In this chapter I want to focus on *Hot Rod* magazine, the pivot of this sub-culture.[25] My material is drawn from reading each monthly issue of this magazine from January 1948 to December 1960. This periodical took a very active role in trying to control and shape the nature of 'hot rodding'. For, in post-war America, this term referred to two distinct activities. In its common and mass-media usage it pointed to a highly visible, relatively affluent, teenage lifestyle which seemed to turn on drive-ins, noise, jalopies held together with chewing gum, and 'dragging the strip'. The phrase *also* denoted a much less visible, less publicised, technical and achievement-oriented amateur sport of automobile racing against the clock which had developed on the dry lakes of California from the 1920s and which had its own organisations. This small group of often older men (especially as war veterans returned) felt threatened by the mass-media use of the term, and the moral panics that ensued. This group feared that threatened action by legislators and authorities against the street-racing teenagers might curtail their rather serious and all-American activity. They met with police, civic officials, and parent–teachers' associations to put their views, and *Hot Rod* was set up, in large measure, as a voice for respectable rodding. Its publishers and early writers were all lakes enthusiasts.

The magazine was first published in January 1948 with a print run of 5,000 copies, by 1950 200,000 copies were produced each month, and by 1956 it was promoted as the world's top-selling automobile magazine with half a million copies sold each month and a claimed readership of well over a million.[26] In short, this magazine was a great commercial success and soon outran its initial constituency. As sales spread across the USA, and as the lake-beds of California cracked under increasing use, it was in the van of creating a new participant and spectator sport – drag racing – which became what, it asserted, real hot rodders did and wanted to do. It had very close links with the National Hot Rod Association, founded in 1951, which was, and is, the major organisation in the big sport of drag racing which, in the mid 1970s, ran events catering for four and a half million spectators and half a million (mostly amateur) competitors.[27]

This kind of ephemeral literature which hangs around free-time pursuits is rarely examined *but* on the numbers of readers alone I think I can stake some claim as to the worth of looking at this magazine as an important vehicle of value transmission. If that is granted, and we might well think that such material may be read with much *closer* attention than a lot of other literary items which are given much greater prominence in social analysis, then I will add that *Hot Rod* is but one example of a host of other special interest magazines which did, and do, exist and in which 'leisure' is presented as a very serious matter indeed.[28] If, as I have argued, students of the meaning of work need to trace the actual type and diffusion of ideas about a variety of types of work, then it might be as well if analysts laid to one side the texts of Franklin, Alger and Weber, and picked up other examples of this type of the popular literature of contemporary capitalism.

To help in this process I want to review the messages, themes, values, and ideas that this magazine promoted and repeated. In fact there were a variety, but a large part of its message was taken up with the ideologies of activity, involvement, enthusiasm, craftmanship, learning by doing, experimental development, display, and creativity, all of these circulating around the motor car in unpaid time. I have traced this message as it related to mechanical labour, but it could as easily be illustrated in other aspects of hot-rod activity, about fuel for example:

on page sixteen is the first of twelve enlightening articles on fuel and carburation.[29]

Or driving, for many articles urged that, whether on the strips or streets, a true hot rodder should be a top class driver: knowledgeable, cool, able to marry mental awareness to manual dexterity to foresee and forestall danger. So what follows is but one facet of an ideology covering many other rod-related activities. *Hot Rod*'s conception of its younger readers was that they were a group of normal males who, being American, were attracted to mechanics, tinkering, competition, and the search for success. Because these combined speed and the automobile, readers were always on the brink of lawlessness. They could succumb to temptation. They must not be allowed to be idle. They must have the right path constantly set before them. They required leadership, organisation, and a sympathetic control. The magazine tried to accomplish this in part via the individuals and cars it featured as the measures of success in this 'leisure' pursuit and in part by its overall ideological tone.

This magazine does not present hot rodding as an activity for the idle or for the spectator; it is not about triviality or passiveness or easy hedonism. The bottom line is that nothing good comes easy:

Stuart has been developing the same engine, a 1934 Ford for the last eight years. He has constantly improved it and hopes to improve it even more in the future. At one lakes meet a rod went through the block, shattering a four by eight inch hole in the side of the engine. He salvaged the pieces, welded them together and welded that piece into the hole. Performance was not altered.[30]

Almost every month there is a story about someone who works several hours a day, 300 days a year, on their rod. Nor can it or should it be a matter of money. In 1949 when the editor asked for snapshots of readers' cars to be sent to the journal for publication he remarked:

By the term 'good car' we do not necessarily mean one that has thousands of dollars sunk into it. Most of us cannot afford that. We do mean a car that reflects good workmanship and ingenuity.[31]

The hot rodders' project is presented as a serious one. Indeed the magazine argued it was just this that distinguished the true hot rod ('the million of us') from the 'shot rod', i.e. those cars which have only the surface appearance of what an ignorant public think is a hot rod, owned by people who 'do not burn the midnight oil', whereas:

A real hot rod is a car that is lending itself to experimental development for the betterment of safety, operation and performance, not merely a stripped down or highly decorated car of any make, type or description or one driven by a teenager.[32]

These kind of messages spill out of the numerous technical articles about engines, components, fuels, etc.; through DIY pictorial strips; in the assessments of featured cars; in stories of individual achievement; in the technical question and answer section; on the readers' letters pages; and in the editorials. So in January 1951 when the magazine tries to get a hot rod (with a truck engine) into the Indianapolis 500 track race, it muses:

Whether it qualifies or not, the car will still long be remembered as a tribute to American ingenuity and the average man's desire to build something of his own design, with his own hands.[33]

The emphasis was not simply on working with metal but on theoretical understanding, scientific knowledge, and designing skill:

In many cases you can improvise, but when you can't, take it easy. Save your muscles for the gym and use your head in the garage.[34]

An outline of some typical articles may indicate what I mean. In November 1948 the magazine printed the first part in a series of 'Building a Hot Rod'. The titles of the successive monthly articles were:

(1) Glossary of terms
(2) Classification and selection
(3) Running gear part I
(4) Running gear part II
(5) Power plant part I
(6) Power plant part II
(7) Power plant part III
(8) Power plant part IV
(9) Roadster completion

If this does not give the flavour, then consider the subheadings of the Power Plant Part I article:[35]

(1) Disassembly of engine
(2) Inspecting and reboring block
(3) Increase in power output
(4) Reasons for porting and relieving
(5) Methods of porting
(6) Methods of relieving

And so it goes on through the years with articles on 'Crankshaft stroking: more engine torque and how to get it'[36] one month and 'Do a better valve job'[37] another. Such knowledge was not regarded as important in its own right. What mattered was its application. The magazine had a particular philosophy both on the reasons for American economic success and on the importance of applying and testing knowledge in a practical, down-to-earth way. It argued that the true American genius was to translate and improve on a basic invention and:

American youth is the most advanced among the nations of the world in mechanical know-how, the attribute which has kept this country foremost in progress. Building cars, studying engines and learning basic mechanics, the essence of hot rod activity, is one of the greatest contributing factors to such progress.[38]

This is a theme constantly stressed in the Korean War period. In 1951 an editorial reflected that hot rodders were doing the job in the motor pools at the war front and in the training camps:

We take pride in the fact that we possess great mechanical know-how. In a measure, the very essence of American armed might rests in our ability to maintain technological superiority over the rest of the world.[39]

The mass media was proud of this but was quick to condemn 'the schools of experience' in which this pre-eminence had its birth. It was not a natural trait nor could it be learned from textbooks, rather:

young Americans must learn to do by *doing*, there is no substitute or shortcut for actual experience.[40]

This stress on learning by practice and not via books, was a repeated theme in the magazine and was underlined as a characteristic, indeed crucial, American trait. In general, the magazine was sceptical about 'experts with slide-rules' who could impose restraints on invention and imagination. In 1952 it reported how two rodders were trying to create a car capable of 300 miles an hour. Many said this is impossible:

But it is an accepted fact that hot rodders don't always *know* what can't be done, so they go ahead and *do* the impossible anyway.[41]

The hot rodder was the practically-oriented underdog who could exasperate theorists and could match Detroit. The Motorama car show of 1954 provided an opportunity to show that:

backyard built cars and the people who build them are capable of matching or surpassing the world's finest.[42]

When individuals were featured it was as enthusiasts or mechanics, their paid occupations were either not mentioned or mentioned in passing – they were not significant. What mattered was their absorption in the activity, the technical details of their car, their sweat, and dedication to their task. The theme of this kind of article was on the unity of mental and manual labour. So when the magazine featured Fred Iges' roadster in February 1950, after plenty of technical data, the article ran:

Using a 1925 Model T body, Fred filled and smoothed all the contours and added many original ideas to the lines of the car. The turtle back was welded to the back of the body and leaded in smooth. The deck lid is made of sheet aluminium to save weight, and the joined edges have been filled with a special cold solder. A metal worker by profession, Fred has done all of the body in his backyard garage. Faced with the problem of getting short louvres punched in the curved edges of the hood and side panels, Fred manufactured his own jig and dies and stamped the louvres himself. Power behind the dies was provided by use of a heavy hammer.[43]

This is a fair example of featured individuals. A craft-like approach to the task, attention to the smallest, apparently insignificant detail, was often held up as the route to success in building or racing, and was sometimes contrasted with attitudes found in paid labour. In 1948 an industrial designer praised hot rodding as:

it encourages the development in our youngsters of the art of mechanical artisanship. This artisanship is seldom found in the auto-brotherhood. There is so much sloppy work performed in the great majority of garages that it becomes a rarity to see a mechanic who is proud of his work.[44]

Or in 1959:

Incompetency among mechanics in garages and new car agencies has become a major problem for today's motorists.[45]

Akton Millar, dry-lakes veteran and elected official in hot rodders' associations presented a concentrated statement of the magazine's ethos in his article, 'Hot rods, I love 'em' in 1951. He never mentions his paid occupation, except to joke about being an infantry private in the war, but talks about his first hot rod:

Working nights and Sundays, I spent approximately four months building my car and enjoying every minute of it while I learned many new angles to car construction which cannot be found in a book.

And goes on:

I have always felt that successful participation in hot rod activities, as in any other form of activity is based on the age-old law of compensation in that the amount of effort one puts forward on a project determines the degree of education, fellowship and satisfaction which he may expect to enjoy in return. I have seen boys come into the organisation, compete in one or two meets and drop out because they found the competition too tough or the financial demands too great. Others work hard, sacrifice time and money, and remain in year after year eagerly awaiting the next event and the challenge it has to offer. One can compare the sport to a ladder; some take one step, others ten or more. But one thing is certain in all cases: the boys learn that there is a relationship between man and machine which cannot be found in any other sport. Words cannot describe the rewarding satisfaction of doing things with one's own hands, then seeing, hearing and feeling the gratifying results of hard labour and sacrifice. Nor can mere words ever convey the sensation that the hot rodder experiences when he gets behind the wheel of 200 plus horsepower and begins a run against the clock with the knowledge that he is about to demonstrate the union of speed and acceleration as personified in a hot rod of his own making.

Moreover:

Progress within the Association makes it necessary for one to change ideas, methods and styles constantly if he wishes to keep pace with the top men.[46]

Generally *Hot Rod* was not averse to intellectual reflections or musings about what the activity 'signified' or 'meant', and such analysis often suggested to hot rodders that what they were involved in was a reworking of old values in new contexts. In 1951 it reprinted an article by Balsey (a postgraduate student of David Reisman's) from an academic journal (the only contemporary academic piece on this subculture),[47] and a year later it published a long article by Dr P. E. Siegle – once on the staff at the University of Illinois but then consultant psychologist to the Maremont Automotive Products Corporation. His article – 'Psychological components of the hot rodder'[48] – related the sub-culture to a wider American culture which stressed initiative, competition, and free enterprise. It was about the:

opportunity to make more and better things. The ideal dream is that of a man alone with his raw materials, using his ingenuity and know-how along with his industriousness to produce a better *thing*.

And Siegle goes on:

There is an almost mystic quality to the picture of the young American boy working from scratch in the shop hoping to build a better hot rod. It fits with the American shibboleth of recognition for the ability to pull oneself up by the boot-straps. Hard work and luck are key ideas in the American success story.

Hot rodding allowed this. Indeed it was perhaps *more* in tune with the older virtues than was the modern 'conspicuous consumption' society where status came from the acquisition of goods and which was, anyway, frustrating and anxiety-provoking since competition was not clear-cut. Siegle also explained to his readers that rodding allowed an outlet for aggressions, and the achievement of mastery over machines, in a society where the relevance of older standards of personal success were by no means clear-cut. In Siegle's portrayal the hot-rod movement involved a more vital working out of basic cultural values than a rather flabby 'normal' life now allowed. Everyone would benefit:

from the opportunities the hot rod provides for the expansion of mechanical expression (which is really the heartbeat of the American socio-economic system). It's good for today's youth to have a place, either at home or in the community at large, where he can learn to build and use the ingenuity so prized by Americans.

And, Siegle ended, activity surrounding the hot rod was:

creative, educative, competitive, constructive, and masculine all of which are desirable elements in furthering the best in the American way of life.

I could give many other examples of the inspirational message of this magazine, only one of a number centring around car knowledge, modification and maintenance. Indeed, as readership increased, those in control obviously realised that it was being purchased by large numbers of people who were not hot rodders in any pure sense (about 30,000 the journal estimated). In 1953 the magazine added the logo 'The automotive how-to-do-it-magazine' under its main title on the front page, and the magazine began to broaden the definition of what could be considered a 'hot rodder' so as to cover all 'the mechanically minded' or 'motor minded Joes' as the publication put it.[49] These were people, so it said, who wanted to know more about the automobile than was available in other publications and who wanted to get a better performance out of their stock models. The magazine was often scathing about the so-called technical details printed in the mass media or in the advertisements of the Detroit companies. It sneered at the ordinary motorist who believed that because his speedometer registered 120 miles per hour he was actually *doing* 120 miles an hour. The magazine proclaimed itself as being for the insider, the knowledgeable, and so while the technical articles, and question and answer pages changed somewhat in the mid 1950s, so that a lot more attention was given to technical details of new cars and new engines, still, the DIY ethos and urgings to learn and to strive, to improve, to work on your car and make it better looking and better performing, remained cen-

tral in this magazine, were paramount in this magazine as it spoke to its
million and more readers each month.

DISCUSSION

The hot-rod subculture of post-war America can be dismissed as a trivial
topic, one to be shunned by the serious minded, of little moment to the
analysis of work and its meanings. However, if it is granted that 'work' is
a multi-faceted activity, and that the meanings of work are not to be
encompassed by invoking the power of some immutable 'work ethic',
then there is a real necessity to consider exactly what social sources are
promulgating what ideas about what work at any particular period, and
so the literature that surrounds popular pursuits is significant. The, more
or less, unexamined activities and ideological material of gardening, ang-
ling, cooking, do-it-yourself, boating, motoring, home-computing, sport
and so on, all have plenty to say about labour and identity, skill and self,
craft and commitment.

Of course, there are powerful arguments which suggest that in the post-
war period a basic cultural shift occurred with a devaluation of paid
labour as a significant area of life, with people's prized images becoming
focussed on the weekend-self or holiday-self,[50] but regardless of such
hypotheses about the varying importance of pieces of life, true students of
work would still need to consider the social organisation of a lot of enthusiasms and interests, and the kinds of ideologies which surround them.

My review of the themes contained in the specialist literature of a particular subculture indicate that the weight of its messages stood very close
to the mélange known as 'the work ethic'. The desire of the lakes enthusiasts to safeguard their sport, or at least a sport, and the mutation of some
of them into a creative elite who also sought to protect a bundle of economic opportunities which grew up around the sport, meant that hot-rod
literature rang with a serious tone. Its fire was trained on idleness, time
was to be filled with skilled activity, and success seeking. The journal
addressed its readers through an idiom stressing excelling through effort,
progress by trial and error, advance via defeat, and learning from
mistakes. Benjamin Franklin's nostrums that 'there are no gains without
pains' or 'God helps those who help themselves' echoed again and again
in subcultural argot and were pursued in action by the magazine through
its influence over the local and national organisations.

Hot Rod did not seek to challenge commonsense categories of 'work' or
'leisure'. Its language was, in the main, quite conventional. It spoke of hot
rodding as 'a hobby', as 'tinkering', as an 'avocation'. However, as the
quote by Akton Millar cited earlier indicates, *Hot Rod* often tripped over

the definitional problems more sophisticated analysis has now come to. In August 1950 the magazine featured the 'Recuperated Coupe':

The entire process consumed many hours in time and considerable expense in parts, but like many other car builders he took great pride in his work and enjoyed the work he was doing.[51]

Or another featured car is:

a real tribute to the craftsmanship that makes car building a great hobby.[52]

This, unrecognised, conceptual confusion (mirroring orthodox social analysis) carried out into mass-media surveys of the subculture. *Hot Rod* was instrumental in presenting its version of the activity in a well-selling novel, a number of low-budget films, and in popular radio and TV shows of the 1950s.[53] A *Life* cover story in 1957 (heralded with suspicion by *Hot Rod*) did speak of illegal street races but also told its readers:

These cars are usually hand built with much ingenuity and affectionate care by avid teenagers.

Life featured the 'Dream Boat' of 24-year-old Norman Grabowski, much admired in the Los Angeles drive-ins:

By working for five years on a poultry farm and as an extra for the movies Grabowski has earned the money it cost to hand make his machine – $8,000[54]

So a wider audience was made aware of the craftsmanship and expertise ethos of the hot-rod world.

Of course, the levels of achievement reported and honoured in the magazine were symbolic, not representative of the average level of effort or achievement in the subculture as the slightly apologetic tone of readers' letters about *their* cars indicates.[55] The specialist literature and its echoes in the mass media presented a mythological version of the hot-rod endeavour: stating what should be done if you wanted to reach the pinnacle. It was an optimistic version too. Nothing is said about botched jobs, or cars that look aesthetically awful, or perform badly as a result of home tinkering. There is little about racing accidents (when that racing is legal) while disasters – engines blowing, cars turning over – are presented as challenges, as opportunities for progress, not as being physically or financially crippling. The ethos is positive and exuberant, with little time to dwell on failure except as a stepping stone. The route to success, status, and self-satisfaction, is still labour, and practical, manual labour at that, but the appeal here is to something much higher than working for wages. Often the magazine suggested that the purpose of conventional work can be merely to provide the wherewithal for this finer pursuit.

However, in general the magazine, and most other hot-rod literature, had very little to say about paid labour. Sometimes, but by no means always, the employment of featured rodders is mentioned, but such references carry about the same significance as their home town. Of the jobs that are mentioned in this random and peripheral fashion, a high proportion (though not *that* high, given the place of automobile work of *all* kinds in the American economy at the time) are in automobile-related employment, and the vast majority are in skilled manual or petit-bourgeois occupations.

Hot Rod's search for respectability for the enthusiasm did lead it to sometimes suggest that 'know-how' could lead onto employment. In 1952 it reprinted a NHRA pamphlet – *The Hot Rod Story* – whose author argued:

That hot-rodding provides an incomparable proving ground for amateur experimentation and research is not open to question. That out of such activity – be it classified as a sport, hobby, or avocation – may arise some of our foremost engineers or designers of tomorrow is a reasonable speculation.[56]

Or in 1953, in reply to a decision by the National Automobile Dealers Association not to sell to hot rodders, the editor proclaimed:

The thinking men of Detroit's industry are increasingly aware that from such enthusiasm and enterprise can come the skilled manpower pool necessary to keep American wheels rolling.[57]

This theme was reinforced, as the magazine's circulation expanded, by regular full-page advertisements which also suggested that the hobby could be turned into employment. From the mid 1950s the Army and the Air Force regularly sought 'men with mechanical skill', while correspondence courses counselled:

> If you eat, sleep and live cars
> TURN YOUR HOBBY INTO A CAREER
> Get America's big-time, big-future
> AUTO MECHANICS, DIESEL COURSES
> at *home*, in your spare time.[58]

Then too the development of a paid elite of racers (greeted none-too-enthusiastically by *Hot Rod*) suggested another way that personal interest and paid employment could be combined, in advance to professional ranks. And the hot-rod literature does sometimes suggest that any rodder's ideal would be to marry hobby and payment. Bill Kenz, a racer and speed shop owner, remarked in 1951:

When cars are a man's hobby as well as a livelihood, there is always something new and interesting coming up ... there's *never* a dull day.[59]

Don Garlits, who metamorphised from Florida street-racing to world champion professional drag racer, recalls that when he left school in 1950 he took up a book-keeping job:

it was just taken for granted – including by myself – that I'd get a job of that kind. It was awful. Working conditions were all right. It simply boiled down to my dislike of the day-in, day-out drudgery of working with invoices and receipts, bills of lading. It was an utter drag.[60]

Hot-rod expertise gave the chance of a career to:

the kid who wasn't very good at schoolwork, especially all that English, but who could speak to engines. He could rest his fingertips on the hood of any car and detect its illness.[61]

However, this is not painted as an easy, simple, or always desirable option. It requires total dedication, single-mindedness, perseverance, and luck. There is a stress on the costs of professional success – injury, loss of friends, broken marriages, loss of family life.[62] Moreover, it is not presented as necessarily that enjoyable as in Prudhommes weary description of drag racing:

Six seconds sometimes feels like a lifetime – especially when you look out the side and there's a car right next to you. There are so many things that can happen. Tyre vibrations. The car gets out of shape. While the car is out of shape and while the tyres are shaking, not only are you concerned about beating the guy next to you, especially in a big race like Indy., but you're thinking '*I've got to fix that before the next round*'. There must be a million thoughts that go through your mind driving the six second run. Then people look at me at the end of the day and say 'Boy you sure look tired'. Doggone right. I have thought about every thought in the world.[63]

The stars of any subculture are important in the production of meanings as they serve both as the embodiment of ideological principles and allow lower-level practitioners to relate their immediate experience to mediated experience through similarities of circumstance and event. Stars exist at a higher but essentially parallel plane. However, heroes are not necessarily portrayed as entirely successful. In the hot-rod literature there is more than a hint that the drive required to reach professional status could involve failure as a human being.[64] *Hot Rod*'s stress was on an *amateur* ethos. It was quick to point out that professionalism could bring a displacement of goals so that running for fun could shift down into earning a living. For example, in October 1950 replying to letters asking why the times achieved by rodders were not filed as world records the editor stressed that hot rodding was a strictly amateur activity:

As long as the boys are running for the fun of it, rather than for the almighty dollar, the sport will remain a hobby and recreation. Main objective in entering any sport is for relaxation and the attainment of self-satisfaction.[65]

The professional elite were regarded both as craftsmen with mysterious secrets,[66] but also as having sacrificed some spontaneity and enjoyment. Amateur endeavour was not only seen as more authentic experience, untainted by an instrumentalism which could lead to scandals and cheating, but could be combined with calls to high standards of morality, attention to unwritten rules, and, indeed, financial *sacrifice*, much more than could be expected from any mere job.

In all, the hot-rod literature tends to be silent about any paid labour which is not connected to automobiles, and while reference to the possibility of moves into rod-related jobs can be found, they are by no means a major element in the specialist literature. In this, and in its incorrigible stress on the importance of manual labour (albeit founded on contemplation and study) *Hot Rod* presented a highly romantic vision of work and what it was for. The rodder was enjoined to see himself (and herself – women did feature) in the roles of craftsman, inventor, the independent artisan, and as practical dreamer, whose garage improvements and drag-strip experiments were, the magazine constantly asserted, monitored by Detroit and which paid off in the form of improved cars for everyone. As well, the literature stressed the experience to be gained through racing. This gave to life a rare quality of excitement, found when you were out there, at the edge, wheel-to-wheel, in competition. The magazine enjoined that fine workmanship and controlled aggression could be fused, in a way which allowed masculinity to be tested, celebrated and displayed. And unlike the confusion of much of the rest of life, racing on the lakes or strips offered plain measure of success and failure. There were clear victories, intelligible defeats, comprehensive standards of personal achievement and progress, laid down by the exact second hand of a timing device or the finishing line. So complex cultural imperatives of all kinds surrounding 'work' could be easily understood, obeyed, and applied in the drag race.

My example of the hot-rod literature is designed to show that injunctions to strive, to create, to study, and achieve are around in plenty in 'leisure' activities, and most people are touched by them in some part of their life. What is revealed when we look at the hot-rod subculture of the 1940s and 1950s are directives in its literature, and the carrying out in practice, of personally-chosen projects, not connected to paid labour: 'work' as hobby, as relaxation, as fascination, as something *you really want to do* rather than being forced to do. About feeling *good* by working hard. This I am sure is true of the literature of many other activities, but, I would argue, is especially significant in automobile pursuits. The automobile is a machine, it is technology: and people confront it, handle, know, master, and enjoy it in a way which is often very satisfying; as it was for the hot rodders. And the automobile is important as a symbol as well as a product. Words which are 'naturally' associated with it – mobility, freedom, pace, progress, competition – have parallels in other, apparently more 'important' areas of culture, and metaphors, allusions, if not direct substitutions from one cultural sphere to the other, are plentiful.

The assumptions which underlie a lot of social analysis define many areas of life as unimportant. The orthodox tradition of the study of 'work' and its meanings has largely ignored 'leisure', and when it has noticed it there has been a depiction in broad-brush strokes like 'trivialisation', 'passive response', 'incorporation by the mass media', 'hedonism' and so on. Such categorisations flatten out the varied contours of non-paid activity, avoid issues of the relative quality of time, and ignore ambiguities inherent in the way life has developed in capitalist society.

Special interests and specialist literature with its 'insiders'' views, 'expert' opinion, assurance of 'community', and assertions of authenticity, abound in modern capitalism but have been neglected by social analysis. In *Hot Rod*, as in much other literature, social identities were offered, arcane language was explained, mysteries of craft were laid bare, tasks were invested with purpose, each reader was addressed as part of a wide movement, and everyone was held to be implicated in 'scientific progress' and 'technological advance'. Those who operate as the cultural entrepreneurs of unpaid time,[67] working through unexamined texts and disregarded organisations, do draw on grander and long-established cultural themes, in order to explain and promote their activities, and make them respectable, but, in so doing, they can alter accents, replace essences, and shuffle significances, so that older messages ring out in new areas of life. Part of what they seek to do is to really rework the 'work ethic', locate it to unpaid labours and so, quite possibly, make it *more* psychologically meaningful for the bulk of the population than in earlier periods of capitalist society. Until social analysis gives such moral entrepreneurs and the transformations they achieve a lot more attention, then, I suggest, we will not know very much about the various meanings of a variety of types of work, and their differing significance for the individual.

Notes

1 THE HISTORICAL MEANINGS OF WORK: AN INTRODUCTION

Acknowledgements: My thanks are due to all the contributors, especially to those who so kindly commented upon an earlier draft of this introduction – Maxine Berg, Robert Gray, Keith McClelland, Bert Moorhouse and Richard Whipp.

1 B. Roberts, R. Finnegan, D. Gallie, eds., *New Approaches to Economic Life* (Manchester University Press, 1985).
2 M. Godelier, 'Work and its representations: a research proposal', *History Workshop Journal*, 10 (Autumn 1980).
3 S. Wallman, ed., *Social Anthropology of Work* (London, Academic Press, 1979). There is extensive citation of the anthropological literature in this volume.
4 The recent work of the sociologist Pahl on strategies of livelihood in the present British economic recession draws valuably on anthropological and historical work; R. E. Pahl, *Divisions of Labour* (Oxford, Basil Blackwell, 1984).
5 B. Messenger, *Picking Up The Linen Threads* (Austin, University of Texas Press, 1975).
6 See, for example, T. Ferguson and J. Cunnison, *The Young Wage Earner* (Oxford University Press, 1951); W. F. Whyte, *Street Corner Society* (University Press of Chicago, 1943); R. Jenkins, *Lads, Citizens and Ordinary Kids* (London, Routledge, 1983); also P. Willis, *Learning To Labour* (Farnborough, Saxon House, 1978).
7 Roberts, Finnegan and Gallie, *New Approaches.*
8 See, for example, D. Cannadine, 'The past and the present in the English Industrial Revolution, 1880–1980', *Past and Present*, 103 (May 1984); P. Joyce, 'Work' in vol. II, *Cambridge Social History of Great Britain 1750–1950*, ed. F. M. L. Thompson (forthcoming); also C. Sabel and J. Zeitlin, 'Historical alternatives to mass production', *Past and Present*, 108 (August 1985).
9 C. Geertz, 'Suq: the bazaar economy in Sefrou', in C. Geertz, H. Geertz, L. Rosen, eds., *Meaning and Order in Moroccan Society* (Cambridge University Press, 1979), cited in the illuminating introduction of B. Roberts to the Roberts, Finnegan and Gallie collection.
10 As in R. Turner, A. M. Bostyn and D. Wright, 'The work ethic in a Scottish

town with declining employment', in Roberts, Finnegan and Gallie, *New Approaches*.

11 As is apparent in J. Davis, 'Roles not laws: outline of an ethnographic approach to economics', in Roberts, Finnegan and Gallie, *New Approaches*.

12 S. Gudeman, *Economics as Culture: Models and Metaphors of Livelihood* (London, Routledge and Kegan Paul, 1986).

13 P. D. Anthony, *The Ideology of Work* (London, Tavistock, 1977).

14 R. Samuel, 'The gospel of work' (forthcoming), should fill this gap. It was hoped to include this essay in this collection.

15 M. Rose, *Re-Working the Work Ethic* (London, Batsford, 1985).

16 *Ibid.* pp. 84–5. M. Wiener, *English Culture and the Decline of the Industrial Spirit 1850–1980* (Cambridge University Press, 1981), is the source of much of this fashionable interpretation of the British middle classes. For a good critique of Wiener and others of the revisionist school see S. Gunn, 'The "failure" of the Victorian middle class: a critique', in J. Seed and J. Wolff, eds., *Cultivating Capital* (Manchester University Press, forthcoming).

17 J. Robertson, *Future Work* (London, Gower, 1985).

18 H. Braverman, *Labour and Monopoly Capital* (New York, Monthly Review Press, 1974).

19 For a discussion of the literature see P. Thompson, *The Nature of Work* (London, Macmillan, 1983).

20 S. Wood, ed., *The Degradation of Work?* (London, Hutchinson, 1983).

21 G. Salaman and C. R. Littler, *Class At Work* (London, Batsford, 1984), chs. 3–6.

22 A. Friedman, *Industry and Labour: Class Struggle at Work and Monopoly Capitalism* (London, Macmillan, 1977); R. Edwards, *Contested Terrain: The Transformation of the Workplace in the Twentieth Century* (London, Heinemann, 1979).

23 In particular, D. M. Gordon, R. Edwards and M. Reich, *Segmented Work, Divided Workers* (Cambridge University Press, 1982).

24 M. Burawoy, *The Politics of Production* (London, Verso Books, 1985). See also M. Burawoy, *Manufacturing Consent* (University of Chicago Press, 1979).

25 Burawoy, *Politics of Production*, ch. 1.

26 Gordon, Edwards and Reich, *Segmented Work*, offers such a context for the US, ambitiously so. For a historical critique see J. Zeitlin, 'Social theory and the history of work', *Social History*, 8:3 (October 1983).

27 Burawoy, *Politics of Production*, pp. 27–8.

28 Burawoy cites a number of works important in tracing the workings of consent, e.g. M. Hales, *Living Thinkwork: Where do Labour Processes Come From?* (London, CSE Books, 1980); W. Baldamus, *Efficiency and Effort: An Analysis of Industrial Administration* (London, Tavistock, 1961).

29 Joyce, 'Work', *Cambridge Social History of Great Britain 1750–1950*, vol. II (forthcoming).

30 P. Joyce, *Work, Society and Politics* (London, Methuen, 1982).

31 P. Joyce, 'Labour, capital and compromise: a response to Richard Price', and 'Languages of reciprocity and conflict', in *Social History*, 9:1 (Jan. 1984) and 9:2 (May 1984).

32 R. Price, 'Conflict and co-operation: a reply to Patrick Joyce', *Social History*, 9:2 (May 1984), see R. Price, 'The labour process and labour history', *Social History*, 8:1 (Jan. 1983).

33 Joyce, *Work, Society and Politics*, ch. 4.

34 For a brief but useful discussion of some of these matters, see Salaman and Littler, *Class At Work*, pp. 67–71.

35 H. Newby, C. Vogler, D. Rose, G. Marshall, 'From class structure to class action: British working class politics in the 1980s', in Roberts, Finnegan and Gallie, *New Approaches*, especially the citations of the work of D. Lockwood and J. Goldthorpe.

36 E. O. Wright, *Class, Crisis and the State* (London, New Left Books, 1978); also *Classes* (London, Verso Books, 1985).

37 Burawoy, *Politics of Production*, p. 88.

38 E.g., G. Stedman Jones, *Languages of Class* (Cambridge University Press, 1983); J. Foster, 'The declassing of language', *New Left Review*, 150 (Mar.– Apr. 1985); R. Gray, 'The deconstruction of the English working class', *Social History*, 11:3 (Oct. 1986); P. Joyce, 'The people's English: language and class in England 1840–1920' (forthcoming); W. Reddy, *The Rise of Market Culture* (Cambridge University Press, 1984).

39 See for example A. R. H. Baker and D. Gregory, *Explorations in Historical Geography* (Cambridge University Press, 1984); D. Gregory and J. Urry, *Social Relations and Spatial Structures* (London, Macmillan, 1985), also the journal, *Society and Space*.

40 Roberts, Finnegan and Gallie, *New Approaches*.

41 B. Roberts, 'Introduction', in *ibid*.

42 For a research agenda linked to the initiative, see D. Gallie, 'Directions for the future', in *ibid*. This shows how sparse is sociological knowledge of workers' attitudes to work, especially in such crucial areas as perceptions of economies and attitudes to job mobility.

43 D. Gallie, *In Search of the New Working Class* (Cambridge University Press, 1978); C. Sabel, *Work and Politics* (Cambridge University Press, 1982).

44 R. Whipp, 'Labour markets and communities, an historical view', *Sociological Review*, 33:14 (Nov. 1985).

45 This account is indebted to a paper presented to the 'History of Work' group of the History Workshop Centre for Social History by R. Gray, 'Approaches to the social history of industrial work: notes towards an agenda'. The essays of R. Johnson in J. Clark, C. Critcher and R. Johnson, eds., *Working Class Culture* (London, Hutchinson, 1979), chs. 2 and 9 are also of use.

46 Stedman Jones, *Languages of Class*, 'Introduction'; see also P. Anderson, *Arguments Within English Marxism* (London, Verso Books, 1980); K. McClelland and J. H. Kaye, eds., *E. P. Thompson: Critical Debates* (Cambridge, Polity Press, forthcoming).

47 For accounts of the 'labour aristocracy' debate with full citations see R. Gray, *The Aristocracy of Labour in Nineteenth Century Britain* (London, Macmillan, 1981); H. F. Moorhouse, 'The Marxist theory of the labour aristocracy', *Social History*, 3:1 (January 1978). For the latter, labour process twist, Stedman Jones, 'Class struggle and the Industrial Revolution' in *Languages of Class*, and Joyce, *Work, Society and Politics*.

48 A. Reid, 'The division of labour in the British shipbuilding industry 1880–1920' (unpublished Ph.D. thesis, University of Cambridge, 1980); J. Melling, '"Non-commissioned officers": British employers and their supervisory workers, 1880–1920', *Social History*, 5:2 (May 1980); the essays of Reid and McClelland and Zeitlin in J. Zeitlin and R. Harrison, eds., *Divisions of*

Labour (Brighton, Harvester Press, 1985); J. Zeitlin and S. Tolliday, *Shop Floor Bargaining and the State* (Cambridge University Press, 1986); C. Sabel and J. Zeitlin, 'Historical alternatives to mass production', *Past and Present*, 108 (Aug. 1985).

49 H. Cunningham, *Leisure in the Industrial Revolution* (London, Croom Helm, 1980); P. Bailey, *Leisure and Class in Victorian England* (London, Routledge, 1978).

50 For example, T. Hareven, *Family Time and Industrial Time* (Cambridge University Press, 1982); P. Kriedte, H. Medick, J. Schlumbohm, eds., *Industrialization Before Industrialization* (Cambridge University Press, 1981).

51 M. Segalen, *Love and Power in the Peasant Family* (Oxford, Basil Blackwell, 1983).

52 A useful discussion of symbolic discourse may be found in B. Martin, *A Sociology of Contemporary Cultural Change* (Oxford, Basil Blackwell, 1981), chs. 3 and 4. This has the virtue of applying symbolic analysis to the conditions of working-class life. Whether the application is adequate or not it is illuminating. See also H. Medick and D. W. Sabean, eds., *Interest and Emotion: Essays on the Study of Family and Kinship* (Cambridge University Press 1984).

53 See N. Abercrombie, *Class, Structure and Knowledge* (Oxford, Basil Blackwell, 1980).

54 Gray, 'Deconstruction of the English working class'.

55 E. J. Hobsbawm and T. O. Ranger, eds., *The Invention of Tradition* (Cambridge University Press, 1983).

56 See the works cited in n.38 above.

57 As well as Joyce, 'The people's English', see D. Vincent, *Literacy and Popular Culture 1750–1914* (Cambridge University Press, forthcoming); P. Burke and R. Porter, *The Social History of Language* (Cambridge University Press, 1987); P. Dodd and R. Colls, *Englishness: Politics and Culture 1880–1920* (London, Croom Helm, 1986).

58 See the essays on this theme in Hobsbawm's *Festschrift*, P. Thane and G. Crossick, eds., *The Power of the Past* (Cambridge University Press, 1985).

59 W. H. Sewell, *Work and Revolution in France* (Cambridge University Press, 1980).

60 Reddy, *The Rise of Market Culture*.

61 M. Sonenscher, 'The *sans-culottes* of the year II: rethinking the language of labour in revolutionary France', *Social History*, 9:3 (Oct. 1984). See also the essay of Sonenscher in a new and valuable collection, S. L. Kaplan and C. J. Koepp, eds., *Work in France: Representations, Meaning, Organization and Practice* (Ithaca, NY, Cornell University Press, 1986).

62 Godelier, 'Work and its representations'; T. Kusamitsu, 'British Industrialisation and design: with special reference to printing and figure-weaving in the Lancashire and West Riding textile industries' (unpublished Ph.D., University of Sheffield, 1982).

63 For a brief, stimulating treatment W. J. Ong, *Orality and Literacy* (London, Methuen, 1982).

64 M. Douglas, *The World of Goods* (London, Allen Lane, 1979).

65 A. Ludtke, 'Images of industry, silences of work: visualization as contested terrain in German industry 1900–1940' (forthcoming). I am grateful to Ludtke for a sight of his typescript.

66 See for example the interplay of work and politics in I. Prothero, *Artisans and Politics in Early Nineteenth-Century London* (Folkestone, Dawson, 1979).

67 C. Behagg, 'Custom, class and change: the trade societies of Birmingham', *Social History*, 4:3 (Oct. 1979).

68 C. Behagg, 'Secrecy, ritual and folk violence: the opacity of the workplace in the first half of the nineteenth century' in R. Storch, ed., *Popular Culture and Custom in Nineteenth Century England* (London, Croom Helm, 1982). Behagg's forthcoming book also takes up these concerns. I am grateful to Behagg for sending me parts of the manuscript of this book.

69 M. Taylor, 'The myth of the small master?: dependence and the community of the trade in Sheffield 1832–1867' (typescript). I am grateful to Taylor for a sight of this.

70 P. Bailey, 'Will the real Bill Banks please stand up', *Journal of Social History*, 12 (1979); A. Reid, 'Intelligent artisans and aristocrats of labour: the essays of Thomas Wright', in J. Winter, ed., *The Working Class in Modern British History: Essays in Honour of Henry Pelling* (Cambridge University Press, 1983).

71 Gray, 'Deconstruction of the English working class'.

72 Gray's research work involves consideration of these appropriations in the 1850s and 1860s; for other appropriations see Joyce, *Work, Society and Politics*.

73 For an interesting account see J. Mendilow, *The Romantic Tradition in British Political Thought* (London, Croom Helm, 1986).

74 For the identification of the Smilesian ethic as the one true work ethic, and for its appropriation to right-wing ideology, see Sir Keith Joseph, 'Introduction', Samuel Smiles, *Self-Help* (London, Penguin, 1986).

75 Cunningham, *Leisure in the Industrial Revolution*, ch. 2.

76 R. Price, *Masters, Unions and Men: Work Control in Building and the Rise of Labour 1830–1914* (Cambridge University Press, 1980).

77 Though providing a valuable distinction between custom and invented tradition Hobsbawm tends to exaggerate the decline and the social conservatism of custom, see Hobsbawm and Ranger, *The Invention of Tradition*, 'Introduction'.

78 S. Tolliday, 'The language of shopfloor bargaining: semi-skilled car workers 1930–1960', paper circulated for 'Work' section of 1983 History Workshop, Manchester.

79 Reddy, *Rise of Market Culture*, ch. 9.

80 Joyce, 'The people's English'.

81 The subject is little studied and is best approached through literature and song; see e.g. A. L. Lloyd, *Folk Song in England* (London, Lawrence and Wishart, 1967) and the citations in Messenger, *Picking Up the Linen Threads*.

82 C. More, *Skill and the English Working Class* (London, Croom Helm, 1980).

83 See also S. Alexander, 'Women, class and sexual difference', *History Workshop Journal*, 17 (Spring 1984).

84 Others are apparent in Joyce, *Work, Society and Politics*; and C. Evans, 'Unemployment and the making of the feminine during the Lancashire Cotton Famine', in W. R. Lee and P. Hudson, eds., *Women's Work, Family Income and the Structure of the Family* (forthcoming).

85 There are clear links with Foucault, *Discipline and Punish* (London, Allen Lane, 1977).
86 See also the works of Cunningham and Bailey on leisure cited above.
87 P. Bailey, 'Ally Sloper's half-holiday: comic art in the 1880s', *History Workshop Journal*, 16 (Autumn 1983). See also *The Victorian Music Halls* (Milton Keynes, Open University Press, forthcoming), vol. I, ed. P. Bailey, *The Business of Pleasure*, vol. II, ed. J. Bratton, *Performance and Style*.
88 R. McKibbin, 'Work and hobbies in Britain 1880–1950', in Winter, ed., *The Working Class in Modern British History*.
89 The north-east example may be contrasted with the textile manufacturing districts (cf. Joyce, 'People's English'): regional differences are important, and the attractive and repulsive powers of work are always finely balanced. Work and non-work time were often closely integrated, cf. Joyce, *Work, Society and Politics*, passim.
90 E. P. Thompson, 'Time, work-discipline and industrial capitalism', *Past and Present*, 38 (Dec. 1967).
91 T. C. Smith, 'Peasant time and factory time in Japan', *Past and Present*, 111 (May 1986).
92 P. Joyce, 'Work', *Cambridge Social History of Great Britain*, vol. II.
93 See also Zeitlin and Sabel, 'Historical alternatives to mass production'.
94 See also M. Berg, *The Age of Manufactures* (London, Fontana, 1985).
95 D. E. Williams, 'Morals, markets and the English crowd in 1766', *Past and Present*, 104 (August 1984); A. Charlesworth and A. J. Randall, 'Comment: morals, markets and the English crowd', *Past and Present*, 114 (Feb. 1987). My thanks are due to Adrian Randall for an exchange of information on these matters.
96 K. Snell, *Annals of the Labouring Poor* (Cambridge University Press, 1985), p. 100.
97 Vincent's *Literacy and Popular Culture* (forthcoming) has important, new things to say on this.
98 Martin, *A Sociology of Contemporary Cultural Change*, is interesting on the internal, symbolic structure of communities. She utilises the work of the sociolinguist Basil Berstein, and like Berg, that of Mary Douglas.
99 Reddy, *Rise of Market Culture*, is adept at making the familiar strange.

2 MYTHICAL WORK: WORKSHOP PRODUCTION AND THE 'COMPAGNONNAGES' OF EIGHTEENTH-CENTURY FRANCE

Archival material cited in this chapter was collected with the financial assistance of the ESRC and the British Academy, to whom I am indebted for research grants at various times between 1979 and 1985. Thanks to Patrick Joyce and Maxine Berg for comments on an earlier draft of this paper. The following abbreviations have been used in the notes: *AC* = Archives communales; *AD* = Archives départementales; *AN* = Archives nationales. I have retained the original orthography in all archival citations.

1 The ruling is printed in Emile Coornaert, *Les Compagnonnages en France du moyen age à nos jours* (Paris, 1966), pp. 350–54.
2 The *compagnonnages* still exist. For an account of their recent history, see Christian Faure, 'Vichy et la "rénovation" de l'artisanat: la réorganisation du compagnonnage', *Bulletin du centre d'histoire économique et sociale de la région lyonnaise*, 3–4 (1984) 103–19.

3 See E. J. Hobsbawm, 'Ritual in social movements', in his *Primitive Rebels* (London, 1959).
4 Cynthia M. Truant, 'Solidarity and symbolism among journeymen artisans', *Comparative Studies in Society and History*, 21 (1979) 214–26; Jean Lecuir, 'Associations ouvrières de l'époque moderne: clandistinité et culture populaire', *Revue du Vivarais* (special issue on *Histoire et Clandestinité: du Moyen Age à la Première Guerre Mondiale*; Albi, 1979) pp. 273–90.
5 William Sewell, *Work and Revolution in France, The Language of Labor from the Old Regime to 1848* (Cambridge, 1980).
6 *Bibliothèque historique de la Ville de Paris* 4371, *Rapport de la société philanthropique de Paris*, an XIII.
7 'On nous avoit parlé des compagnons de devoir, qu'on disait exister dans la classe des menuisiers et autres ouvriers en bois. Les menuisiers eux-memes nous ont declaré n'en avoir qu'une connaissance très imparfaite. Nous nous sommes informés dans les autres professions, et personne, jusqu'à present, n'a pu ou n'a voulu nous donner des renseignements sur ce compagnonnage. Il est couvert d'un voile impénétrable. C'est probablement une espèce de france-maçonnerie qui échappera toujours à nos investigations.' *Ibid. Rapport de 1821.*
8 *Ibid.*, 'terme qui répond à celui d'apprenti'.
9 Agricol Perdiguier, *Le Livre du compagnonnage* (Paris, 1839).
10 There are several accounts of the *compagnonnages*. The fullest, and in many ways the least tendentious, remains E. Martin Saint-Léon, *Le Compagnonnage* (Paris, 1901); Coornaert, *Compagnonnages*, contains a valuable selection of documents, but its value is limited by its author's neglect of the usual apparatus of notes and bibliography. Coornaert, in particular, assumes that all forms of association created by journeymen were really *compagnonnages*. See too Henri Hauser, *Les Compagnonnages d'arts et métiers à Dijon aux XVIIè et XVIIè siècles* (Dijon, 1907); Germain Martin, *Les Associations ouvrières au XVIIIè siècle (1700–1792)* (Paris, 1900; Emile Levasseur, *Histoire des classes ouvrières et de l'industrie avant 1789*, 2 vols. (Paris, 1900). For one attempt to come to terms with their ritual, see Mary Ann Clawson, 'Early modern fraternalism and the patriarchal family', *Feminist Studies*, 6 (1980) 368–91.
11 The subject awaits fuller study. See J. M. Roberts, *The Mythology of the Secret Societies* (London, 1972).
12 See however the remarks in Steven L. Kaplan, 'Réflexions sur la police du monde de travail au XVIII siècle', *Revue historique*, 229 (1979) 17–77; and David Garrioch and Michael Sonenscher, '*Compagnonnages*, confraternities and journeymen's associations in eighteenth-century Paris', *European History Quarterly*, 16 (1986) 25–46.
13 There has been no comparative study of journeymen's associations. On England, see E. P. Thompson, *The Making of the English Working Class* (London 1963); E. J. Hobsbawm, 'The tramping artisan', in his *Labouring Men* (London, 1964); C. R. Dobson, *Masters and Journeymen* (London, 1980); John Rule, *The Experience of Labour in Eighteenth-Century Industry* (London, 1981); Iorwerth Prothero, *Artisans and Politics in Early Nineteenth-Century London* (Folkestone, 1979); Clive Behagg, 'Secrecy, ritual and folk violence: the opacity of the workplace in the first half of the nineteenth century', in Robert D. Storch, ed., *Popular Culture and Custom*

in Nineteenth-Century England (London, 1982); and, for examples of ceremonies of initiation in the English trades, the works cited by Behagg, p. 175
(note 24).

14 On Germany see Andreas Griessinger, *Das symbolisches Kapital der Ehre*
(Frankfurt, 1981) and, for an attempt at a comparative study (which does
not, however, deal with ritual) Ulrich-Christian Pallach, 'Fonctions de la
mobilité artisanale et ouvrière – compagnons, ouvriers et manufacturiers en
France et aux Allemands (17e–19è siècles)', *Francia*, 11 (1983) 365–406.

15 See Hobsbawm, 'Ritual in social movements'; there is equally no reference
to the *compagnonnages* in Maurice Agulhon, 'Working class and sociability
in France before 1848', in Pat Thane *et al.*, eds., *The Power of the Past,
Essays for Eric Hobsbawm* (Cambridge, 1984).

16 Truant, 'Solidarity and symbolism'; Lecuir, 'Associations ouvrières de
l'époque moderne: clandestinité et culture populaire'.

17 Natalie Z. Davis, *Society and Culture in Early Modern France* (London
1975).

18 On the limitations of the concept of popular culture, see Carlo Ginzburg,
The Cheese and the Worms (London, 1980) 'Introduction'; David Warren
Sabean, *Power in the Blood* (London 1984), pp. 1–36; Dominick LaCapra,
History and Criticism (Ithaca, NY, 1985), pp. 45–94.

19 For a fuller discussion see Stuart Clark, 'French historians and early modern
popular culture', *Past and Present*, 100 (1983) 62–99.

20 See below, p. 42 n. 39.

21 The best known of these accounts was J. F. Lebrun, *Histoire des pratiques
superstitieuses* (many editions; see the 1751 edition, vol. IV, pp. 60–68).

22 See below, pp. 40–41.

23 Jack Goody, ed., *Literacy in Traditional Societies* (London 1968), pp. 28–
34. See also E. J. Hobsbawm and T. O. Ranger, eds., *The Invention of Tradition* (Cambridge, 1983), pp. 1–14.

24 It was 'le plus approprié à nos moeurs et à notre indépendance', see Jean
Vial, *La Coutume chapelière: histoire du mouvement ouvrier dans la Cha-
pellerie* (Paris, 1941), p. 115.

25 See Michael Sonenscher, *The Hatters of Eighteenth-Century France* (Ber-
keley, California, 1987).

26 Accounts of the origins of the rites are printed in Coornaert, *Compagnonnages*, pp. 341–48.

27 AC Troyes. FF *supplément* (unclassified, 30–8–1782); unless otherwise indicated, all the following citations come from this dossier.

28 *Ibid.* 'La cérémonie consiste à se mettre à genoux et à être baptisé avec du vin
et à jurer par son sang qu'on ne révélera jamais rien de ce qui se passe dans les
assemblées des associés.'

29 *Ibid.* The initiation of the other journeymen followed the same pattern as the
first. According to one, the rituals

consistent à faire mettre le récipiendaire à genoux sur une serviette, à lui verser du vin
sur la tête en lui disant, 'Enfant, je te baptise au nom du Père, du Fils et du Saint Esprit,'
et à lui faire jurer au récipiendaire qu'il le tiendra toujours dans son compagnonnage et
de ne rien dire de ce qui se passe.

A second journeyman described how those already initiated 'le firent entrer
seul dans la chambre, le firent mettre à genoux, lui verserent sur la tête du vin

et de l'eau, disant qu'ils le baptisèrent. Ils le firent jurer de renoncer à tous les Gavots et Espontons, et en dressèrent un acte.' Again the *mère* of the *cabaret* was given a ribbon 'qui est le présent accoutumé pour la mère des compagnons, parce que ladite mère leur avance la bonne chère'.

30 *Ibid.* 'en prenant le partie des armes, Mr. le lieutenant général de police voudraient bien oublier sa contravention'.

31 *Ibid.* 'Tant mieux,' Vivarais exclaimed, 'il y a longtemps que nous attendions un troisième pour recevoir nos aspirants'.

32 *Ibid.* 'Ils n'avoient pas de Maître Jacques'.

33 *AD Seine-et-Marne* B (non-côté), Bailliage de Montereau, 11–9–1763. 'Je suis compagnon ainsi que mon camarade que voila,' he said, 'quoique nous soyons d'une autre vacation, si vous voulez nous vous ferons la conduitte.'

34 The journeyman glazier Jacques-Louis Ménétra described how he and his fellow *compagnons* had celebrated the feast of Saint Luc in Lyon in 1763: 'Le jour se fait avec pompe, l'on n'a jamais vu une fête pareille. Tout Lyon veut nous voir passer deux à deux au son de la musique moi en tête ayant deux rubans à la troisième boutonnière, le père des compagnons à ma droite. Le pain bénit porté est d'une grande grandeur démusurée par quatre apprentis. La fête se passe et le repas très triomphalement.' Daniel Roche, ed., *Journal de ma vie. Jacques-Louis Ménétra, compagnon vitrier au 18è siècle* (Paris, 1982), p. 128.

35 'Il a ésté reçu par maître Richon, maistre architechte, à l'auberge de la Providence ... en présence de plus d'une vingtaine de compagnons tant remerciés qu'autres, parmy lesquels il se rappelle le nommé Jolicoeur d'Agen qui est encore compagnon quoyque marié, cadet Berant de Bordeaux qui est aussi marié, le nommé Roussai qui a remercié.' *AD Gironde.* 13B 212 (25–11–1754).

36 'L'usage etant parmi eux d'éprouver le passant sur le devoir, il s'est éxercé à différents éxercises ... avec ledit compagnon,' *AC Troyes.* FF *supplément* (29–1–1771).

37 *Ibid.* 'avec lesquels ils ont fait le bossu et recommencé le devoir'.

38 *AD Gironde.* 12B 350 (10–8–1774). A number of master joiners were involved in an assembly of journeymen when the rules of one of the rites of the *compagnonnages* of Chalon-sur-Saône were drawn up in 1666, 'suyvant l'antient coustume que nos predecesseurs nous ont laissés, tant pour le proffit des maistres que celluy des compagnons'. Master joiners in Lyon were deeply divided over a police regulation prohibiting the ceremonies of the *compagnons du devoir* in 1735. A majority (67) called for the total suppression of the *devoir*. A minority (41) claimed that it was beneficial to the trade, 'en ce qu'elle attire en cette ville les compagnons du devoir, lesquels ayant travaillé dans plusieurs villes des differentes provinces ... sont bien plus experimentez que les autres compagnons qu'ils appellent gavots'. *AC Chalon-sur-Saône.* HH 20; *Bibliothèque de l'Arsénal.* 8° J 4684, Statuts des Menuisiers de Lyon, sentence de police (2–6–1735).

39 An anonymous description of the rites of the *bons-drilles blanchers-chamoiseurs* sent to the *procureur-général* of the Parlement of Paris from Chalons in 1767 contains an almost identical account of the ceremony of initiation. Paul Bondois, 'Un compagnonnage au XVIIIè siècle: le devoir des bons drilles blanchers-chamoiseurs', *Annales historiques de la Révolution française*, 6 (1929) 588–99.

40 On such practices, see the descriptions in N.T.L. Des Essarts, *Dictionnaire universel de police* (Paris, 1786–90).

41 *AC Troyes*. Fonds Boutiot, AA 41.

42 *AC Troyes*. FF supplément (21–7–1786).

43 *AD Gironde*. 12B 280; C 3708.

44 *AC Nantes*. FF 69 (28 and 30–4–1750).

45 *AD Rhône*. BP 3303 (14–5–1764); *AC Lyon*. 701.414.

46 *AD Gironde*. 12B 356 (30–7–1777).

47 *AD Gironde*. 12B 385 (14–8–1788).

48 *AC Bordeaux*. HH 70 (Catalogue des maitres menuisiers, sculpteurs et ebenistes de la ville et faubourg de Bordeaux, 1788).

49 *AN* F[7] 4236.

50 One of them said, 'Messieurs voulez-vous nous rendre la canne et nous arranger? Nous serons amis comme nous l'avons jamais été.' The gesture was met by an invitation to fight. 'Les devoirans ont demandé comment. Les gaveaux ont repondu à coups de poing. Les devoirans ont dit, Messieurs on se fouillera, et ceux qui auront des couteaux ou bastons on le désarmera.' *AD Aube*. 1B 1133 (15–3–1773).

51 See for example *AD loire Atlantique* B 8729[II] (7–11–1782); *AD Yonne* 1B 579 (11–6–1760); *AC Marseille* FF 342[a] (6–9–1736).

52 'Il est ébeniste, qui est d'une communauté différente de celle des menuisiers. C'est pourquoy tous les compagnons menuisiers veulent mal à luy.' *AD Gironde*. 12B 266 (3–6–1737).

53 'Qu'il n'est d'aucun devoir, ny ayant pas de compagnon de leur état.' *AD Gironde*. 12B 355 (13–8–1776). A journeyman farrier arrested in Troyes in 1786 also stated 'qu'il est du devoir entre les compagnons maréchaux seulement' (*AC Troyes*. FF *supplément*, 10–8–1786). A group of shoemakers making their way to the quayside in Bordeaux in the same year '(pour) faire leurs adieux à un compagnon qui partait', encountered two journeymen stonecutters. 'Taupe,' said one of them, in the ritual greeting used by the *compagnonnages*. One of the shoemakers replied 'qu'ils n'y avaient point de taupe parmy eux'. They were then asked their trade and declared that they were 'de braves garçons cordonniers'. 'Vous n'êtes point des braves mais des jeans foutres' was the predictable and provocative reply. *AD Gironde*. 12B 355 (7–10–1776).

54 *Bibliothèque nationale* MS. fr. 8084 fol. 405 (3–5–1697); *AN* Y 14 576 (20–2–1786).

55 *AC Chalon-sur-Saône*. FF 10 (11–6–1731). Shoemakers in Le Havre met regularly at the *Banneau de la Ville* and petitioned the municipality for recognition of their society in 1790. *AC Le Havre*. FF 50; HH 39. Shoemakers in Grenoble embarked on legal proceedings against their masters in 1788. *AC Grenoble*. FF 66 fol. 397.

56 He said, 'que son nom était "Je me fouts de cela." C'est mon nom que je porte dans mon tour de France.' *AC Nantes* HH 169 (8–7–1762). Journeymen wigmakers also had their own associations, meeting regularly in Lyon, for example, and celebrating the feast of St Louis, 'jour auquel les garçons perruquiers ont quelques rétributions'. In 1772 one of them complained to the municipal authorities that his former master had accused him of the theft of some hair. 'Cette calomnie,' he stated, '(lui) a fait un tort considérable ... puisqu'étant sur le point d'être nommé syndic dans la derniére assemblée de ses

confrères, sa nomination a été suspendue jusquà ce qu'il soit purgé de l'imputation.' *AD Rhône.* BP 3304 (5–6–1764); *AD Rhône.* BP 3389 (2–7–1772).

57 'Pour lui proposer et ses camarades, réunis dans la chambrée dont il faisait membre, de se joindre aux ouvriers chapeliers et autres.' *AD Rhône.* BP 3539 3539 (5–8–1790).

58 'Il n'en existe aucune (association) de cette espèce dans cette ville', the municipal authorities reported in 1783. 'Il y a, à la vérité, comme dans toutes les villes de la Flandre des estaminets qui ne sont ouverts à d'autres particuliers qu'à ceux qui en font les frais.' *AC Lille.* AG 38 (2). (I am grateful to Jean-Pierre Hirsch for this reference.)

59 On Rouen, see M. Sonenscher, 'Weavers, wage-rates and the measurement of work in eighteenth-century Rouen', *Textile History* (17, 7–18, 1986); on Amiens, see Pierre Deyon, *Amiens, capitale provincial* (Paris, 1969); on Troyes, see P. Colommès, *Les Ouvriers textiles de la région troyenne* (Troyes, 1948); on Nîmes, see M. Sonenscher, 'Royalists and patriots: Nîmes and its Sénéchaussée in the late 18th Century' (unpublished Ph.D thesis, University of Warwick, 1978) and *AC Marseille* FF 391 (14–1–1781).

60 Garrioch and Sonenscher, *'Compagnonnages'*.

61 'Le statut que les garçons ouvriers appellent devoir ne se fait pas dans la ville de Paris.' *AD Gironde.* C 1814.

62 'Ill n'y a jamais eu des ces sortes de compagnons à Bordeaux qu'à present; qu'ils se tiennent ordinairement dans la Bourgogne et dans la Champagne et autres lieux.' *AD Gironde.* 13B 212 (7–12–1754).

63 'Estant un compagnon du devoir, tous les autres compagnons qui se nomment gavau l'ont sollicité de venir avec eux pour essayer de battre aux champs, n'en voulant point souffrir dans la ville.' *AC Troyes.* FF supplément (5–8–1748).

64 *AD Gironde.* C 1814.

65 'Lorsqu'il est sage, qu'il travaille bien, qu'il paye sa dépence et qu'il ne fait tort à personne,' *AD Gironde.* 13B 212 (7–12–1754).

66 'C'est être amy ensemble, de se faire plaisir mutuellement,' *AD Gironde.* 12B 318 (15–5–1761).

67 He said, 'qu'il est gaveaux, de ceux qui sont libres de travailler où bon leur semble'. 'Que c'est d'être libre de travailler et d'aller travailler où il se peut trouver, sans être obligé de donner aucun argent.' *AD Gironde.* 12B 266 (3–6–1737). The term *gavot* has a certain ambiguity. A journeyman joiner explained to the *jurats* of Bordeaux in 1762, 'qu'il est censé gaveau, n'etant pas du devoir et que tout compagnon qui n'est pas du devoir est censé gaveau'. Another joiner, arrested after a fight between members of different rites in the same city stated, 'qu'il est gavau et que par consequent il ne fait pas de devoir'. *AD Gironde.* 12B 321 (31–8–1762); *AD Gironde.* 12B 339 (26–9–1770).

68 *AD Gironde* 12B 339 (26–9–1770).

69 Its best-known member was, of course, Agricol Perdiguier himself. See his *Mémoires d'un compagnon*, ed., Alain Faure (Paris, 1977).

70 *AC Mâcon* HH 11 (piece 18). (I have modernised the orthography of the names of the towns.)

71 *Devoirants* and *gavots* who were locksmiths frequented different *cabarets* on the rue Ecorcheboeuf; among the joiners the *gavots* met at the *Pomme de Paix* also on the rue Ecorcheboeuf, while the *devoirants* met, *au Purgatoire*, on the adjacent rue Ferrandière.

72 Their *capitaine*, a 22-year-old native of a village in Provence, explained that, 'en sa qualité de capitaine il est à la tête des autres compagnons. C'est luy qui préside aux délibérations qu'ils font, qui fait ranger les comptes, et apaise les difficultés qui peuvent naître entre les compagnons et les maîtres et entres les compagnons les uns avec les autres, qui fait dire la messe tous les premiers dimanches de chaque mois et présente le pain bénit, qui a soin de receuiller et faire payer les amendes imposées aux compagnons lorsqu'ils s'écartent de leurs devoirs et enfin qui a soin de fournir aux besoins des compagnons non du devoir qui passent en cette ville et qui n'ont pas d'argent, et qui entretient une correspondence avec les autres compagnons non du devoir des différentes villes.' *AD Rhône.* BP 3307 (3–11–1764).

73 Some discussion of the terms can be found in Michelle Perrot, *Les Ouvriers en Grève* (Paris, 1974). What follows is, in a limited way, a reworking of an unpublished paper on 'The meaning of skill among French artisans in the eighteenth century' presented to seminars at the Middlesex Polytechnic and the European University Institute in Florence. I am grateful for the critical comments made on that paper.

74 For one series of remarks, see the comments made by a number of journeymen locksmiths during a dispute in the trade in 1746 cited in Garrioch and Sonenscher, '*Compagnonnages*'.

75 'Ne sachant que vouloit dire ce langage,' he said, 'qu'il ne sçavoit pas ce que c'est que de gavot.' The other said, 'qu'ils venoient de Paris parce que l'on les avoit mandé, et qu'il n'y avoit que des apprentifs qu'on embauchoit, et qu'il ne connoissoit pas les règles des compagnons, que s'ils étoient jaloux de l'ouvrage qu'ils faisoient, ils n'avoient qu'à le faire eux mêmes.' *AD Yonne.* 1B 579 (11–6–1760).

76 'Ayant moi-même fait le tour de France à pied, j'ai eu occasion de connoître les compagnons charpentiers du devoir et j'ai admiré la fraternité qui règne entre eux et les secours mutuels qu'ils se donnent réciproquement,' he wrote. 'Un compagnon du devoir est celui qui a fait preuve de sa probité devant ses camarades et de son savoir faire. Pour y parvenir, il subi nombre d'examens pratiques sur l'art du trait, de charpente et sur la construction des ouvrages les plus difficiles en ce genre ... Un compagnon qu'on nomme renard au contraire est un yndividu qui n'a point voyagé et qui ne sçai point absolument son métier ... Ces compagnons renards vu leur ignorance travaillent pour 20 à 24 sous par jour tandis que les autres en ont 30. Il n'y a qu'à Nantes où est le refuge des compagnons renards ... Dans touttes les autres ville on ne les souffre point ... Faittes interroger des compagnons renards sur l'art du trait de charpente; vous verrez leur ignorance; ou bien faittes leur faire une édifice; vous verrez qu'ils n'en viendront jamais à bout.' *AC Nantes.* I² Carton 3, d.4 (4–8–1791).

77 There is, for example, no trace of this pejorative image of the *gavots* in Perdiguier's autobiography. He was, of course, a *gavot* himself.

78 'L'almant de Becair [i.e. Becker, a master cabinet maker] dispute au français de Lange [a master joiner] qu'ils ne sont pas sy adroit que les almans pour ce qui à de delicat à faire dans la menuiserie, de manière que la dispute enflammé et excitée par le boisson, ils sont sorti du cabaret pour abattre.' *AC Troyes.* FF *supplément* (24–6–1788). Other witnesses of the incident describe 'l'almant' as 'l'italien'.

79 *AN* Y 13750 (6–4–1745).

80 *AC Chalon-sur-Saône.* FF 39 (9–9–1775).

81 *AC Bordeaux.* HH 101 (23–2–1774).

82 On the famous battle of Tournus, see Coornaert, *Compagnonnages*, pp. 80, 401–12.

83 'Les compagnons serruriers allemands ne sont ny du devoir ny du non-devoir,' he stated. 'S'il n'a pas voulu travailler avec eux c'est que parlant une langue étrangère (et) ne pouvant pas les entendre … il croyoit que ces étrangers se moquoient de luy.' *AD Rhône.* BP 3307 (3–11–1764).

84 'S'il ne tenoit qu'à moi,' Faroux admitted having said, '(il) n'aurait pas d'ouvriers de long tems.' *AC Troyes.* FF *supplément* (16–6–1784).

85 Sewell, *Work and Revolution*, cited above (note 5).

86 *Ibid.* pp. 55, 54, 57–58.

87 For an excellent survey of the early history of the corporations and a long overdue warning against conflating every type of association formed by arti-sans with the corporations, see Bernard Chevalier, 'Corporations, conflits politiques et paix sociale en France aux xivè et xvè siècles', *Revue historique*, 268 (1982) 17–44. On public finance see the classic study by John Bosher, *French Finances, 1770–1795* (London, 1970). There is a need for a proper study of the corporate contribution to public revenue, particularly in the latter half of the seventeenth century.

88 For a full discussion of the aims of such regulation and an administrative history of one such trade, see J. K. J. Thomson, *Clermont-de-Lodève, 1633–1789* (London, 1982).

89 See above, pp. 38–41, 43.

90 Bernard Lepetit, 'La croissance urbaine dans la France pré-industrielle: quelques méthodes d'analyse', *Bulletin de l'Institut d'Histoire économique et sociale de l'Université de Paris* 1, 7 (1978) 1–19 (9). For a stimulating dis-cussion of urban society in early modern Europe, see Jan de Vries, *European Urbanization* (London, 1984).

91 *AC Anduze* CC 60.

92 See Sonenscher, *Hatters*.

93 See Pierre Verlet, *L'Art du meuble à Paris au XVIIIè siècle* (Paris, 1968); Svend Eriksen, *Louis Delanois, menuisier en sièges, 1731–1792* (Paris, 1968).

94 'Les jours de festes il va exactement aux offices, les matins à la congrégation des Jesuites … et l'après midi il va exactement aux vespres et au sermon … et ensuitte il se rettire chez luy où il travaille à dessigner.' *AD Gironde.* 13B 212 (25–11–1754).

95 'Leur motif de cette assemblée n'avoit d'autre object que de se divertir et de s'instruire les uns aux autres sur les ouvrages de leur métier.' *AD Gironde.* 12B 356 (30–6–1777).

96 The book, 'étoit de quelque ouvrier peu instruit et dans le besoin.' The jour-neyman retorted 'qu'il "n'avoit point de talent, qu'il n'était qu'un faiseur d'images, incapable d'éxécuter le moindre profil"'. *AN* Y 11024[a] (30–5–1782).

97 J-J. Vernier *Cahiers de doléances du bailliage de Troyes et du bailliage de Bar-sur-Seine pour les Etats généraux de 1789* (Troyes, 1909) p. 156; Lynn Hunt, *Revolution and Urban Politics: Troyes and Reims, 1786–1790* (Stan-ford, 1978); population figures can be found in Daniel Roche, *Le Siècle des lumières en Province* (Paris, 1978), vol. II, 355–77; *Bibliothèque de l'Arsé-*

nal 8° J 4684; *AC Bordeaux* HH 70; *Bibliothèque historique de la ville de Paris* Z 214; *AN* F^{12} 780. A fuller discussion of the distribution of the trades will be presented in a forthcoming study of 'Work and wages in eighteenth-century France'.

98 Thus in Rouen, in the late eighteenth century, only 5% of the journeymen tailors who registered to find work were natives of the city, while over 50% of journeymen who married in Rouen had been born there. The difference is a rough indication of the scale of temporary out-migration. See M. Sonenscher, 'Journeymen's migrations and workshop organisation in eighteenth-century France', in Steven L. Kaplan and Cynthia J. Koepp, eds., *Work in France* (Ithaca, NY, 1986), pp. 74–96.

99 The figures have been calculated from *AD Seine-Maritime.* 5E 654.

100 *AD Seine-Maritime.* 5E 658.

101 *AD Yonne.* 1B 551 (10–6–1786).

102 A fuller discussion of these calculations (based upon a smaller sample, but reaching the same conclusions) can be found in Sonenscher, 'Journeymen's migrations' and, in detail, in my forthcoming study of 'Work and wages in eighteenth-century France'.

103 For a fuller discussion of the question, see M. Sonenscher, 'Work and wages in eighteenth-century Paris', in Maxine Berg, Pat Hudson and Michael Sonenscher, eds., *Manufacture in Town and Country before the Factory* (London, 1983).

104 'Il n'y a qu'une petite partie des maîtres qui occupent des compagnons non du devoir, parce que la brutalité de ces maîtres a rebuté les compagnons.' *AD Yonne.* 1B 551 (10–6–1786).

105 For a detailed example see the discussion of the tailoring trade in Rouen, forthcoming in my 'Work and wages'.

106 'Pour avoir quasé le meuble du père; pour avoir frapé un compagnon; pour avoir raportés les afair des compagnon; pour n'avoir pas aporté le billet d'argent; pour avoir travaillé deux fois de la même boutique; pour avoir tiré son pistollet dans sa chambre; pour avoir mis une bouteille à la récepesion dans sa poche; pour avoir anbauché un aspiran sans la permission du premier compagnon; pour ne pas avoir aporté d'argent à son tour; pour avoir manqué l'assemblée; pour avoir abandoné les afair des compagnon.' *AD Gironde.* C 3708.

107 See Garrioch and Sonenscher, '*Compagnonnages*'.

108 Réné de Lespinasse, *Les Métiers et corporations de la ville de Paris*, III (Paris, 1897), p. 350.

109 *Ibid.* II (Paris, 1892), p. 391.

110 *Ibid.* III, p. 292. See too Sonenscher, *Hatters*.

111 See Sonenscher, *Hatters*, p. 138.

112 'Estant deguisés, ayant des coefures de femme sur la teste, contrefaisant les juges, procureurs et huissiers au grand scandale du public.' *AD Rhône.* 134B (Justice d'Ecully, 29–4–1776). The journeymen were *compagnons du devoir*.

113 See Colin Jones, 'The welfare of the French foot-soldier', *History*, 214 (1980) 193–213.

114 Andre Corvisier, *L'Armée française de la fin du XVIIè siècle au ministère de Choiseul: le soldat*, 2 vols. (Paris, 1964).

115 Colin Jones and Michael Sonenscher, 'The social functions of the hospital in

eighteenth-century France: the case of the Hôtel-Dieu of Nîmes', *French Historical Studies*, XIII (1983) 172–214.

116 AN E 2515 ff. 623–24 (31–5–1775). For a fuller discussion of this process see M. Sonenscher, 'Weavers, wage-rates and the measurement of work in eighteenth-century Rouen', *Textile History*, 17 (1986) 7–18; and 'Journeymen, the courts and the French trades, 1781–1791', *Past and Present*, 114 (1987).

3 WOMEN'S WORK, MECHANISATION AND THE EARLY PHASES OF INDUSTRIALISATION IN ENGLAND

I am grateful to Patrick Joyce for suggestions on the revision of this paper, and to Ludmilla Jordanova for her criticism of an early version. The 1985 Warwick Workshops on Proto-industrial Communities provided stimulating discussions of eighteenth-century industrial work. Claudia Goldin's 'The economic status of women in the early Republic: some quantitative evidence', *Journal of Interdisciplinary History*, 16:3 (1986), which was published after this volume went to press, raises some similar points to mine for the case of early industrial Philadelphia.

1 Heidi Hartmann, 'The unhappy marriage of Marxism and Feminism: towards a more progressive union', Lydia Sargent, ed., *Women and Revolution* (Boston, South End Press, 1981); Sheila Rowbottom, 'The trouble with patriarchy', *New Statesman* (21–8 December 1979); Sally Alexander and Barbara Taylor, 'In defence of patriarchy', in R. Samuel, ed., *People's History and Socialist Theory* (London, Routledge, 1981).

2 Michele Barrett, *Women's Oppression Today* (London, Verso Books, 1980); Jane Humphries, 'Class struggle and the persistence of the working class family', *Cambridge Journal of Economics*, 1:3 (1977); Sally Alexander, 'Women, class and sexual difference', *History Workshop Journal*, 17 (Spring 1984); Catherine Hall, 'The early formation of Victorian domestic ideology', in S. Burman, ed., *Fit Work for Women* (London, Croom Helm, 1979).

3 See T. H. Aston and C. H. E. Philpin, eds., *The Brenner Debate* (Cambridge University Press, 1985).

4 Michele Barrett and Mary McIntosh, *The Anti-Social Family* (London, Verso Books), p. 79; David Levine, 'Industrialisation and the proletarian family in England', *Past and Present*, 107 (May 1985); Louise Tilly and Joan Scott, *Women, Work and Family* (New York, Holt, Reinhart and Winston, 1978); Joanna Brenner and Maria Ramos, 'Rethinking women's oppression', *New Left Review*, 144 (March–April 1984).

5 See Tilly and Scott, *Women, Work and Family*, ch. 6.

6 See David Levine, 'Industrialisation and the proletarian family'.

7 See Barrett, *Women's Oppression Today*, and Brenner and Ramos, 'Rethinking women's oppression'.

8 The early discussion centred on Eli Zaretsky, *Capitalism, The Family and Personal Life* (New York, Harper and Row, 1976). Also see Hartmann, 'The unhappy marriage'.

9 Maureen Mackintosh, 'Gender and economics: the sexual division of labour and the subordination of women' in K. Young, C. Wolkowitz and R. McCullagh, *Of Marriage and the Market* (London, CSE Books, 1981).

10 I. Pinchbeck, *Women Workers and the Industrial Revolution* (1930 and London, Virago, 1981) and E. Richards, 'Women in the British economy', *History*, 53 (1974).

11 For a discussion of these positions see Joan Thirsk, 'Forward', in Mary Prior, ed., *Women in English Society* (London, Methuen, 1985) and M. Berg, 'Introduction', *The Age of Manufactures, 1700–1820* (London, Fontana, 1985).

12 Dorothy George, *England in Transition* (Harmondsworth, Penguin, 1931), p. 99.

13 Pinchbeck, *Women Workers*, p. 126.

14 Alice Clark, *Working Life of Women in the Seventeenth Century* (1919 and London, Virago, 1982).

15 See N. McKendrick, 'Home demand and economic growth: a new view of women and children in the industrial revolution', in N. McKendrick, ed., *Historical Perspectives* (Cambridge University Press, 1974); Richards, 'Women in the British economy'; R. Masch, 'Women in an age of transition 1485–1714', in B. Kanner, ed., *Women in England from Anglo Saxon Times to the Present: Interpretive Bibliographical Essays* (Hampden Conn., Anchor Books, 1979); M. Roberts, 'Sickles and scythes: women's work and men's work at harvest time', *History Workshop Journal*, 7 (1979); K. Snell, 'Agricultural seasonal unemployment, the standard of living, and women's work in the south and the east 1690–1860', *Economic History Review*, 2nd series, 34 (1981); K. Snell, *Annals of the Labouring Poor* (Cambridge University Press, 1985) ch. 6. Also see Mary Prior, 'Women and the urban economy: Oxford 1500–1800', in Prior, *Women in English Society*.

16 Olwen Hufton, 'Survey articles, women in history I. Early modern Europe', *Past and Present*, 101 (1983) 132.

17 For a survey of this debate see ch. 3, in Berg, *Age of Manufactures*, and Leslie Clarkson, 'Proto-industrialisation: the first phase of industrialisation?'

18 See David Levine, 'The demographic implications of rural industrialisation: a family reconstitution study of Shepsted, Leicestershire, 1600–1851'; Hans Medick, 'The proto-industrial family economy'. Both reprinted in P. Thane and A. Sutcliffe, eds., *Essays in Social History*, vol. II (Oxford University Press, 1986).

19 Snell, *Annals*, ch. 1, and R. Du Plessis and M. C. Howell, 'Reconsidering the early modern urban economy: the cases of Leiden and Lille', *Past and Present*, 99 (1982).

20 George, *England in Transition*, pp. 132–33. Compare R. Gray, 'The languages of factory reform in Britain, 1830–1860', in this volume.

21 Levine, 'Industrialisation and the proletarian family', p. 197

22 Peter Lindert, 'English occupations 1670–1811', *Journal of Economic History*, 40:4 (December 1980) 702–5, and 'Revising England's social tables, 1688–1812', *Explorations in Economic History*, 19 (1982).

23 Lindert, 'English occupations', p. 701; E. A. Wrigley, 'Urban growth and agricultural change: England and the Continent in the early modern period', *Journal of Interdisciplinary History*, 15:4 (Spring 1985) 698 n.11. Lindert reckons that for his finer occupational groupings (fewer than 40,000) the

true numbers could be one-third to three times his estimates. Estimates for shoemakers, carpenters etc. were 'little more than guesses'. And for categories with over 100,000 persons (agriculture, commerce, manufacturing etc.) the true value could be three-fifths to five-thirds the estimates. Lindert's tables have also been seriously doubted by Wrigley, who finds numbers in agriculture seriously underestimated.

24 Levine, 'Industrialisation'.
25 *Ibid.*
26 Adrian Randall, 'The West Country woollen industry during the Industrial Revolution' (unpublished Ph.D. thesis, University of Birmingham, 1979), vol. II, p. 249. Numbers needed to produce twelve broadcloths:

	1781–96
Men	167
Women	186
Children	306
	659

27 See A. J. Durie, 'The Scottish linen industry 1707–1775, with particular reference to the early history of the British linen company' (unpublished Ph.D., University of Edinburgh, 1973), p. 159; Brenda Collins, 'Proto-industrialisation and pre-famine emigration', *Social History*, 7:2 (1982) 132–34.
28 Adam Smith, *The Wealth of Nations* (1776 and Oxford University Press, 1976), vol. IV, vii, p. 644.
29 N. K. Rothstein, 'The silk industry in London, 1702–1766' (unpublished MA thesis, University of London, 1961), ch. 2.
30 See J. Lown, 'Gender and class during industrialisation: a study of the Halstead silk industry in Essex 1825–1900' (unpublished Ph.D. thesis, University of Essex, 1984), ch. 2.
31 G. F. R. Spencely, 'The English pillow lace industry 1845–80: a rural industry in competition with machinery', *Business History*, 70 (1970).
32 J. D. Chambers, 'The rural domestic industries during the period of transition to the factory system', *Second International Congress of Economic History*, Aix-en-Provence, 2 (1962).
33 E. G. Nelson, 'The English framework-knitting industry', *Journal of Economics and Business History*, 2:3 (1930).
34 See Select Committee on the Employment of Children in Factories, PP 1816, (397) iii, pp. 211–19, 374, 378. Also see F. Collier, 'An early factory community', *Economic History Review*, 2 (1930).
35 N. F. R. Crafts, *British Economic Growth during the Industrial Revolution* (Oxford, 1985), p. 22.
36 Osamu Saito, 'Who worked when: life time profiles of labour force participation in Cardington and Corfe Castle in the late 18th and mid 19th century', *Local Population Studies* (Spring 1979).
37 *Ibid.* pp. 15–16.
38 J. M. Martin, 'Village traders and the emergence of a proletariat in south Warwickshire 1750–1851', *Agricultural History Review* (1985).
39 Snell, *Annals*, ch. 6, p. 331.

40 Du Plessis and Howell, 'Reconsidering the early modern urban economy'; N. Zemon Davis, 'Women in the crafts in sixteenth century Lyons', *Feminist Studies*, 8 (1982).
41 Barbara Taylor, *Eve and the New Jerusalem* (London, Virago, 1983).
42 See Diana Hutton, 'Women in fourteenth century Shrewsbury', in Lindsey Charles and Lorna Duffin, *Women and Work in Pre-Industrial England* (London, Croom Helm, 1985); Sue Wright, 'Charmaids, housewyfes and hucksters: the employment of women in Tudor and Stuart Salisbury,' in Charles and Duffin, *Women and Work*, p. 116.
43 Michael Roberts, 'Images of work and gender', in Charles and Duffin, *Women and Work*, p. 140.
44 Wendy Thwaites, 'Women in the market place: Oxfordshire 1690–1800', *Midland History*, 9.
45 Mary Prior, 'Women and the urban economy: Oxford 1500–1800', in Prior, *Women in English Society*.
46 See K. E. Lacey, 'Women and work in fourteenth and fifteenth century London', in Charles and Duffin, *Women and Work*, pp. 55–57.
47 Lown, 'Gender and class', pp. 92–118.
48 Deborah Lantz, 'The role of apprenticeship in the education of eighteenth century women', unpublished paper in Warwick Working Papers in Social History – Workshops on Proto-industrial Communities, 1986.
49 Lown, 'Gender and class', p. 100.
50 Roberts, 'Images', p. 143.
51 Prior, 'Women in the urban economy', p. 109.
52 Brenner and Ramos, 'Rethinking women's oppression', p. 52.
53 Christopher Middleton, 'Women's labour and the transition to pre-industrial capitalism', in Charles and Duffin, *Women and Work*, pp. 198–200.
54 See Berg, *Age of Manufactures*, p. 173.
55 J. H. Clapham, *An Economic History of Modern Britain*, 3 vols. (Cambridge University Press, 1938), vol. I, p. 183.
56 E. L. Jones, 'Constraints on economic growth in southern England 1650–1850', *Proceedings of the Third International Congress of Economic History* (Munich, 1965).
57 A. Randall, 'Worker resistance to machinery – the case of the English woollen industry', in Warwick Working Papers in Social History – Workshops on Proto-industrial Communities, 1986.
58 Frederick Eden, *The State of the Poor*, 5 vols. (1797 and London, Printed by J. Davis for B. and H. White, 1966), II, p. 385, III, pp. 739, 814, 876; Chambers, 'Rural domestic industries', p. 438.
59 Cited in Durie, 'Scottish linen industry', p. 159.
60 Randall, 'Labour and the Industrial Revolution', vol. II, p. 253.
61 Cited in J. L. and B. Hammond, *The Skilled Labourer 1760–1832* (1919 and New York, Longman, Green and Co., 1970), p. 149.
62 Randall, 'Labour and the Industrial Revolution', p. 253.
63 C. Aspin and S. Chapman, *James Hargreaves and the Spinning Jenny* (Preston, Helmshore Local History Society, 1964), p. 57.
64 William Reddy, *The Rise of Market Culture* (Cambridge University Press, 1985), ch. 2.
65 Pinchbeck, *Women Workers*, pp. 150–51.

66 Randall, 'West Country woollen industry', vol. I.

67 W. Scott-Taggart, 'Crompton's invention and subsequent development of the mule', *Journal of the Textile Institute*, 18 (1927) 28; H. Catling, 'The development of the spinning mule', *Textile History*, 9 (1978) 43; E. Baines, *A History of the Cotton Manufacture in Great Britain* (1835 and London, H. Fisher, R. Fisher and P. Jackson, 1966).

68 Lown, 'Gender and class', pp. 123, 144–59.

69 G. B. Hertz, 'The English silk industry in the 18th century', *English Historical Review*, 24 (1909).

70 Dorothy George, *London Life in the Eighteenth Century* (London, K. Paul, Trench, Trubner, 1925), pp. 184–86.

71 Lown, 'Gender and class', pp. 109–18.

72 Select Committee on Apprentices, PP 1812–13.

73 Daryl Hafter, 'The programmed brocade loom and the decline of the drawgirl', in M. M. Trescott, ed., *Dynamos and Virgos Revisited: Women and Technological Change in History* (Metuchen, NJ, Scarecrow Press, 1979), p. 56.

74 S. Timmins, ed., *The Resources ... of Birmingham and the Midland Hardware District* (London, R. Hardwicke, 1866), pp. 179–89.

75 Randall, 'West Country woollen industry', vol. II, pp. 263, 306.

76 Select Committee on the Woollen Manufacture, PP 1806, testimonies of John Platt, W. Howard, Stephen Smith.

77 A. P. Wadsworth and J. De L. Mann, *The Cotton Trade and Industrial Lancashire, 1600–1780* (Manchester University Press, 1931), pp. 285, 325, 323, 336.

78 N. Murray, 'A social history of the Scottish handloom weavers 1790–1850' (unpublished D.Phil. thesis, University of Strathclyde, 1976), pp. 55–62; M. Berg, 'The introduction and diffusion of the power loom (unpublished MA dissertation, University of Sussex, 1972).

79 See testimonies of wide range of clothiers in Select Committee on Woollen Manufacture.

80 Randall 'West Country woollen industry'.

81 S. D. Chapman and S. Chassagne, *European Textile Printers in the Eighteenth Century: a Study of Peel and Oberkampf* (London, Heinemann Educational, Pasold Fund, 1981), pp. 95–96, 194.

82 Cynthia Cockburn, 'Caught in the wheels: the high cost of being a female cog in the male machinery of engineering', in D. Mackenzie and J. Wajeman, *The Social Shaping of Technology* (Milton Keynes, Open University Publications, 1985), p. 55.

83 This point about the association of technology with war was made by Cynthia Cockburn. Also see Carlo Cipolla, *Guns, Sails and Empires* (London, Collins, 1965), for a development of the argument.

84 E. Hopkins, 'Working hours and conditions during the Industrial Revolution: a reappraisal', *Economic History Review*, 35 (1982).

85 Edward Fitzmaurice, *Life of William Earl of Shelbourne*, vol. I, 1737–1766 (London, Macmillan and Co., 1875), p. 404.

86 Cited in Roy Porter, *English Society in the Eighteenth Century* (Harmondsworth, Penguin, 1982), pp. 213–14.

87 D. C. Eversley, 'Industry and trade, 1500–1800', *Victoria History of the Counties of England: Warwickshire*, vol. VII (London, Constable and Co., 1965), pp. 110–11.

88 See Berg, *Age of Manufactures*, ch. 13.
89 W. Hutton, *A History of Birmingham to the End of the Year 1780* (Birmingham, Pearson and Rolleson, 1781).
90 Berg, *Age of Manufactures*, p. 313.
91 C. Heward, 'Home, school and work: changes in growing up in the Birmingham jewellery quarter, 1815–1881' (unpublished MA thesis, University of Warwick, 1982).
92 These arguments are developed in pp. 164–67 of my book, *Age of Manufactures*.
93 An exemplary study is G. M. Sider, 'Christmas mumming and the New Year in Outport Newfoundland', *Past and Present*, 71 (1976) 102–25.
94 Snell, *Annals*, ch. 7.
95 Reddy, *Rise of Market Culture*. Also see Reddy 'The textile trade and the language of the crowd at Rouen 1752–1851', *Past and Present*, 74 (1977) 62–89.
96 See debate between D. E. Williams 'Morals, markets and the English crowd in 1766', *Past and Present*, 104 (1984) and A. Charlesworth and A. J. Randall, 'Morals, markets and the English crowd – a comment', *Past and Present* (forthcoming). Also see A. J. Randall 'The industrial moral economy of the Gloucestershire weavers in the eighteenth century', in John Rule, ed., *Labour and Trade Unionism in Eighteenth Century England* (London, Longman, forthcoming).
97 Olivia Harris, 'Households and their boundaries', *History Workshop Journal*, 13 (Spring 1982) 146–49.
98 These points were raised by David Washbrook in his talk, 'Markets and custom in 18th century South India', in a session on 'Market custom and moral economy', Warwick Workshop on Proto-industrial Communities III, Custom Culture and Community, July 1985.
99 See M. Harrison, 'Chayanov and the economics of the Russian peasantry', *Journal of Peasant Studies*, 2 (July 1975).
100 For analysis and research in this mould see J. Baker Miller, 'Ties to others', in M. Evans, ed., *The Woman Question* (London, Fontana, 1982); M. P. Ryans, 'The power of women's network', in J. L. Newton *et al.*, *Sex and Class in Women's History* (London, Routledge, 1983); E. Ross, 'Survival networks: women's neighbourhood and sharing in London before World War I', *History Workshop Journal*, 15 (Spring 1983); R. Whipp and M. Grieco, 'Family and the workplace', *Warwick Economic Papers*, 239 (1983).
101 See Sian Moore, 'Women's politics within the industrial community: Bradford, West Yorkshire, 1780–1845', Warwick Working Papers in Social History – Workshops on Proto-industrial Communities, 1986.
102 Hans Medick, 'Plebeian culture in the transition to capitalism', in R. Samuel and G. Stedman Jones, *Culture, Ideology and Politics* (London, Routledge, 1982), p. 92.
103 M. Douglas and B. Isherwood, *The World of Goods: Towards an Anthropology of Consumption* (1978 and Harmondsworth, Penguin, 1980), pp. 11, 202.
104 Ross, 'Survival networks', pp. 11, 14.
105 Joan Thirsk, *Economic Policy and Projects: The Development of Consumer Society in Early Modern England* (Oxford University Press, 1978), pp. 22–23.

106 N. McKendrick, 'Home demand, and economic growth', p. 197.
107 L. Weatherill, 'Consumer behaviour, the ownership of goods and early industrialisation', paper to Warwick Workshop on Proto-industrial Communities, Custom, Culture and Community, 1985, to be published in *Continuity and Change* (1986).
108 Adam Smith, *Wealth of Nations*, vol. I, p. 49.
109 See Ruth Pearson, 'The greening of women's labour in the Third and the First World', in S. Allen, *The Experience of Unemployment* (London, Macmillan and Co., 1986) and her 'Homework, outwork, subcontracting: women's work in historical and international perspective', University of East Anglia Working Paper, 1986.
110 *Aris's Gazette*, Advertisements of trade announcements, 1750–1796.
111 *Ibid.*

4 THE PROPERTY OF SKILL IN THE PERIOD OF MANUFACTURE

1 K. Marx, *Capital* (London, Everyman, 1930), vol. I, ch. 12, 'Division of labour and manufacture'.
2 Marx, *Capital*, vol. I, p. 389.
3 Adam Smith, *Wealth of Nations*, ed. E. Cannan (London, 1904), vol. I, pp. 74–75.
4 There is a considerable literature on working rhythms in pre-industrial manufacture. The seminal article is: E. P. Thompson, 'Time, work-discipline and industrial capitalism', *Past and Present*, 38 (1967) 56–97. For a discussion see J. G. Rule. *The Experience of Labour in Eighteenth Century Industry* (London, Croom Helm, 1981), pp. 52–57.
5 Marx, *Capital*, p. 420.
6 For the details of apprenticeship see Rule, *Experience of Labour*, ch. 4.
7 PP 1802/3, VII, Minutes of evidence before the Committee on the Laws relating to the Woollen Trade, pp. 30, 57.
8 *Ibid.* pp. 141, 166–67.
9 Marx, *Capital*, p. 389.
10 'General Ludd's triumph', reprinted in J. L. and B. Hammond, *The Skilled Labourer*, ed. J. G. Rule (London, Longman, 1979), p. 212.
11 Marx, *Capital*, p. 390.
12 For a fuller discussion of the usages of 'artisan' see J. G. Rule, 'The frontier of skill: artisan defences in the eighteenth century', paper presented to the Anglo-American conference on the social world of Britain and America, 1600–1820, Williamsburg, 1985.
13 Smith, *Wealth of Nations*, Vol. I, pp. 73–74.
14 L. D. Schwarz, 'Income distribution and social structure in London in the late eighteenth century', *Economic History Review*, 32 (1979) 256–57.
15 *Commons Journals*, 23 (12 April, 1738) 176–77.
16 S. and B. Webb, *The History of Trade Unionism* (London, Longman, 1911), pp. 35–36.
17 Rule, *Experience of Labour*, pp. 34, 156–58. See also several references to hatters' unions in C. R. Dobson, *Masters and Journeymen. A Prehistory of Industrial Relations 1717–1800* (London, Croom Helm, 1980).
18 E. Howe, ed., *The London Compositor: Documents Relating to Wages,*

Working Conditions and Customs of the London Printing Trade (Oxford University Press, 1947), p. 143.

19 *Commons Journals*, 36, 18 Feb. 1777, p. 193.

20 Rule, *Experience of Labour*, p. 182.

21 *Ibid.* pp. 30–31.

22 There is a tendency to write as if artisans were a small elite fraction of the manufacturing labour force. There is no way of measuring their numbers, but even a passing acquaintance with the literature is sufficient to show that of male workers engaged in the production of manufactured goods they formed a very high proportion.

23 For a fuller discussion in a comparative perspective see J. G. Rule, 'Artisan attitudes: a comparative survey of skilled labour and proletarianisation before 1848', *Bulletin of the Society for the Study of Labour History*, 50 (1985) 22–31.

24 P. Linebaugh, 'Labour history without the labour process: a note on John Gast and his times', *Social History*, 7:3 (1982) 327.

25 R. St George, 'The decentralisation of skill in New England society, 1620–1820', paper presented to the Anglo-American conference on the social world of Britain and America, 1600–1820, Williamsburg 1985, pp. 33–34.

26 *Gorgon*, 28 Nov. 1818.

27 A. Aspinall, *The Early English Trade Unions* (London, Batchworth, 1949), doc. 317, p. 311.

28 PP 1817, IV, Report from Committee on the Petitions of the watchmakers of Coventry, minutes, p. 47.

29 Quoted in E. P. Thompson, 'English trade unionism and other labour movements before 1790', *Bulletin of the Society for the Study of Labour History*, 17 (1968) 23.

30 Howe, *London Compositor*, p. 129.

31 J. L. and B. Hammond, *The Town Labourer*, ed. J. Lovell (London, Longman, 1978), p. 205.

32 Quoted in M. A. Shepherd, 'The origins and incidence of the term Labour Aristocracy', *Bulletin of the Society for the Study of Labour History*, 37 (1978) 52.

33 Quoted Rule, *Experience of Labour*, p. 107.

34 *Ibid.* p. 113.

35 J. R. Burn, *Justice of the Peace*, 1776 edn quoted in Rule, *Experience of Labour*, pp. 107–8.

36 *Ibid.* p. 106.

37 Alice Clark, *The Working Life of Women in the Seventeenth Century* (London, Virago, 1982), pp. 297–98; S. Alexander, 'Women's work in nineteenth-century London', in J. Mitchell and A. Oakley, eds., *The Rights and Wrongs of Women* (Harmondsworth, Penguin, 1976), p. 78; Maxine Berg, *The Age of Manufactures*, 1700–1820 (London, Fontana, 1985), ch. 6.

38 S. Alexander, 'Women, class and sexual difference', *History Workshop Journal*, 17 (1984) 136–37.

39 P. Joyce, 'Labour, capital and compromise: a response to Richard Price', *Social History*, 9:1 (1984) 75.

40 Berg, *Age of Manufactures*, p. 151.

41 See the examples contained in Aspinall, *Early Trade Unions*.

42 A. Somerville, *The Autobiography of a Working Man* (1848 and repr. London, McGibbon and Kee, 1967), pp. 96–99.

43 M. Sonenscher, 'The sans-culottes of the year II: rethinking the language of labour in pre-revolutionary France', *Social History*, 9:3 (1984) 323–24, and 'Work and wages in Paris in the eighteenth century', in M. Berg, P. Hudson and M. Sonenscher, eds., *Manufacture in Town and Country before the Industrial Revolution* (Cambridge University Press, 1983), pp. 160–61. G. J. Holyoake, *Sixty Years of an Agitator's Life* (sixth impression, 1906), p. 23.

44 Quoted in A. Plummer, *The London Weaver's Company* (London, Routledge and Kegan Paul, 1972), p. 326.

45 Book of prices, copy in the Modern Records Centre, University of Warwick.

46 See note 8 above.

47 Rule, *Experience of Labour*, p. 58. Eight hats was thought a fair day's labour. M. D. George, *London Life in the Eighteenth Century* (Harmondsworth, Penguin, 1966), p. 210. The required amount of work was known as the 'log' and, according to a working tailor in 1810 was 'considerably too much for any but a clever and very quick hand, but then, as it was fixed by the workmen themselves, there was neither room for complaining of the masters, nor any good end to be answered by grumbling to the men'.

48 *Autobiography of Joseph Gutteridge*, reprinted in V. E. Chancellor, ed., *Master and Artisan in Victorian England* (London, Evelyn, Adams and Mackay, 1969), pp. 97–98.

49 Rule, *Experience of Labour*, pp. 196–97.

50 Thomas Paine, *The Rights of Man* (1791 and New York, Dolphin Books, 1961), p. 312.

51 H. T. Dickinson, *Liberty and Property. Political Ideology in Eighteenth-Century Britain* (London, Weidenfeld and Nicolson, 1977), pp. 268–69.

52 For a useful discussion of this issue see: A. Black, *Guilds and Civil Society in European Political Thought from the Twelfth Century to the Present* (London, Methuen, 1983), especially ch. 14.

53 PP 1817, Select Committee on the Petitions of the Coventry Watchmakers, VI, p. 18.

54 L. Colley, 'The apotheosis of George III: loyalty and the British nation 1760–1820', *Past and Present*, 102 (1984) 96–97.

55 D. Vincent, *Bread, Knowledge, and Freedom. A Study of Working Class Autobiography* (London, Methuen, 1982) p. 67; S. and B. Webb, *Industrial Democracy* (London, Longman, 1914), p. 455; PP 1812/13, IV, Report from Committee on the Apprentice Laws, pp. 35, 44, 56. See R. St George, 'Fathers, sons, and identity: wood-working artisans in south-eastern New England, 1620–1700', in I. M. G. Quimby, ed., *The Craftsman in Early America* (New York, 1984), pp. 89–125. The question of inheritance of artisan skills has not yet been so significantly explored for England, but see M. B. Rowlands, *Masters and Men in the West Midland Metalware Trades before the Industrial Revolution* (Manchester University Press), pp. 39–40. For an example of trade union restrictions on the number of sons allowed to be admitted see the 1812 rules of the woolcombers reprinted in Aspinall, *Early Trade Unions*, as document 126.

56 For examples of 'customary' rates see Rule, *Experience of Labour*, p. 61. For wage assessment in Gloucestershire see W. E. Minchinton, 'The petitions of the weavers and clothiers of Gloucestershire in 1756', *Trans. Bristol and*

Gloucestershire Arch. Society, 70 (1951) 126–41. The tramping system is well described in E. J. Hobsbawm, 'The tramping artisan', in his *Labouring Men* (London, Weidenfeld and Nicolson, 1977), pp. 34–63. Printed books of prices could be surprisingly lengthy and detailed; that of the London cabinetmakers for 1788 is 143 pages.

57 See the preface to the 1788 book of prices; Rule, *Experience of Labour*, p. 88.

58 *Ibid.* pp. 199–200.

59 *Ibid.* pp. 195–97.

60 C. Behagg, 'Secrecy, ritual and folk violence: the opacity of the workplace in the first half of the nineteenth century', in R. Storch, ed., *Popular Culture and Custom in Nineteenth-Century England* (London, Croom Helm, 1982), pp. 154–79.

61 Benjamin Franklin, *Autobiography* (London, 1903), pp. 56–58.

62 Behagg, 'Secrecy, ritual and folk violence'; Report of Select Committee on Petitions of the Coventry Watchmakers, p. 73.

63 W. H. Sewell, *Work and Revolution in France* (Cambridge University Press, 1980), p. 1.

64 I. Prothero, *Artisans and Politics in Early Nineteenth-Century London: Gast and his Times* (Folkestone, Dawson 1979), p. 337.

65 *Communist Manifesto*, Penguin edn, p. 44.

66 Prothero, *Artisans and Politics*, pp. 26–27.

67 See my introduction to the 1979 edition of the Hammonds' *Skilled Labourer*, pp. xiii–xiv, and Henry Mayhew, *The Unknown Mayhew*, ed. E. P. Thompson and E. Yeo (Harmondsworth, Penguin, 1973), pp. 290, 400–2.

68 P. Joyce, *Work, Society and Politics. The Culture of the Factory in Later Victorian England* (London, Methuen, 1980), p. 62.

69 Rule, *Experience of Labour*, pp. 204–6; Linebaugh, 'Labour history without the labour process', p. 323; George, *London Life*, pp. 308–10.

70 E. J. Hobsbawm, 'The labour aristocracy in nineteenth-century Britain', in his *Labouring Men*, p. 273.

71 M. Sanderson, 'Literacy and the Industrial Revolution', *Past and Present*, 56 (1972) 75–104.

72 Samuel Bamford, *Early Days* (London, Cass, 1967), pp. 42–3.

73 W. Hutton, *History of Birmingham* (London, 1781), pp. 130–9.

74 For a recent summary see the excellent pamphlet by Robert Gray, *The Aristocracy of Labour in Nineteenth-Century Britain c. 1850–1914* (London, Macmillan, 1981).

75 E. P. Thompson, 'Eighteenth-century English society: class struggle without class', *Social History*, 3:2 (1978) 154.

76 G. Stedman Jones, 'England's first proletariat', *New Left Review*, 90 (1975) 60.

77 See J. G. Rule, 'Artisan attitudes', pp. 24–5 for a description in a comparative context.

78 Stedman Jones, 'England's first proletariat', p. 49; see also: Joyce, 'Labour, capital and compromise', p. 71.

79 Prothero, *Artisans and Politics*, p. 336.

80 See especially the writings of A. E. Musson, for example his pamphlet, *British Trade Unions 1800–1875* (London, Macmillan, 1972), pp. 11, 19, 29–35.

81 C. Behagg, 'Custom, class, and change: the trade societies of Birmingham', *Social History*, 4:3 (1979) 456.
82 See the comment of the cotton weavers' committee of 1811 when they realised the futility of seeking a minimum wage from parliament: 'This committee are utterly at a loss to conceive on what fair grounds legislative interference can be improper under circumstances so necessitous', quoted in Rule, 'Introduction' to the *Skilled Labourer*, p. xviii. The importance of political repression for the growth of class consciousness is a main theme of E. P. Thompson's, *Making of the English Working Class*.
83 The reassertion of separate craft autonomy was an evident feature of unionism in the building industry after the collapse of its Owenite phase.
84 On the problem of 'boundaries' especially gender-related in Owenism see the challenging analysis in Barbara Taylor, *Eve and the New Jerusalem* (London, Virago, 1983).

5 'L'OUVRIÈRE! MOT IMPIE, SORDIDE . . .': WOMEN WORKERS IN THE DISCOURSE OF FRENCH POLITICAL ECONOMY, 1840–1860

An earlier version of this chapter was delivered at the conference on 'The City as Social Crucible', at the University of Texas, Austin, in April 1986. I wish to thank members of the conference, and especially Eric Hobsbawm, for their useful comments. Discussions with Ian Burney and Mary Lou Roberts were extremely helpful for formulating some of the interpretations. I am also grateful to members of the seminar on 'Cultural Constructions of Gender' at Brown University's Pembroke Center for Teaching and Research on Women during 1982–5, and especially Denise Riley and Elizabeth Weed. Donald Scott was my most important critic at every stage.

1 *The Second Empire: Art in France under Napoleon III* (Philadelphia, Philadelphia Museum of Art, 1978), p. 310.
2 *The Second Empire*, pp. 309–10.
3 Claire G. Moses, *French Feminism in the Nineteenth Century* (Albany, NY, State University of New York Press, 1984), pp. 151–72.
4 Denise Riley, '"The Free Mothers": pronatalism and working women in industry at the end of the last war in Britain', *History Workshop Journal*, 11 (Spring 1981) 110.
5 On the regulation of prostitution see Alain Corbin, *Les Filles de noce: misère sexuelle et prostitution aux 19e et 20e siècles* (Paris, Aubier, 1978); and Jill Harsin, *Policing Prostitution in Nineteenth-Century Paris* (Princeton, NJ, Princeton University Press, 1985).
6 Chamber of Commerce of Paris, *Statistique de l'industrie à Paris, 1847–48* (2 vols., Paris, 1851), vol. I, p. 11. See also J. W. Scott, 'Statistical representations of work: the politics of the Chamber of Commerce's statistique de l'industrie à Paris, 1847–48', in S. L. Kaplan and C. J. Koepp, eds., *Work in France: Representations, Meaning, Organization and Practice* (Ithaca, NY, Cornell University Press, 1986), pp. 335–63.
7 A. Parent-Duchâtelet, *De la prostitution dans la ville de Paris* (2 vols., Paris, 1836; third edn, 1857), vol. I, pp. 103–4, cited in Harsin, *Policing Prostitution*, p. 123.

8 Parent-Duchâtelet, *De la prostitution*, cited in Therèse Moreau, *Le Sang de l'histoire: Michelet, l'histoire, et l'idée de la femme aux XIXe siècle* (Paris, Flammarion, 1982), p. 77. Moreau points out that the editors of the third edition of Parent's work insisted that a taste for luxury was the sole cause of prostitution.

9 *Statistique*, vol. II, p. 277.

10 *Statistique*, vol. II, p. 252.

11 Charles Dunoyer, 'De la concurrence', *Le Journal des économistes*, 1er série, 1 (1842) 135. (*Le Journal des économistes* hereafter cited as *JE*.)

12 Interestingly, there was almost no reference to servants in these discussions, although they were surely a problem in urban settings. Olwen Hufton, writing on discussions of urban prostitution in eighteenth century Europe notes a similar phenomenon: 'the seduced servant has a very secondary role in such data as we possess'. Olwen Hufton, 'The fallen woman and the limits of philanthropy in the early modern metropolis: a comparative approach' (unpublished paper, presented at the Davis Center, Princeton University, April 1986), p. 38. The omission of servants from these discussions clearly merits further explanation.

13 Jean-Baptiste Say, *Traité de l'économie politique* (6th edn, 2 vols., Paris, 141), p. 324. See also, J. Garnier, 'Étude sur la répartition de la richesse: profits et salaires', *JE*, 1er série, 18 (1847) 209; and Vée (Maire du 5e arrondissement de Paris), 'Du paupérisme dans la ville de Paris', *JE*, 1er série, 10 (1845) 224–71.

14 Say, *Traité*, pp. 372–74.

15 Say, *Traité*, p. 372.

16 Say, *Traité*, p. 372.

17 Say, *Traité*, pp. 593–94.

18 Say, *Traité*, p. 599.

19 See Wally Seccombe, 'Patriarchy stabilized: the construction of the male breadwinner wage norm in nineteenth-century Britain,' *Social History*, 11 (January 1986) 53–76, for a discussion of concepts of the wage in English working class discourse. Seccombe's exclusive focus on 'the proletariat' tends to underplay the importance of political economy's theories in setting in place the wage system. Similarly, Jeanne Boydston begins with Marx for a theoretical discussion of housework in relation to wages, when she might have looked first at the political economists to whom Marx directed his critique, but within whose framework he wrote. J. Boydston, 'To earn her daily bread: housework and antebellum working-class subsistence', *Radical History Review*, 35 (1983) 7–25.

20 *L'Atelier*, 30 December 1842, p. 31.

21 Eugène Buret, *De la misère des classes laborieuses en France et en Angleterre* (2 vols., Paris, 1840), vol. I, p. 287, cited in Moreau, *Le Sang*, p. 74.

22 'Prostitution is only a *specific* expression of the *general* prostitution of the *labourer*, and since it is a relationship in which not the prostitute alone, but also the one who prostitutes, fall – and the latter's abomination is still greater – the capitalist, etc., also comes under this head.' K. Marx, *Economic and Philosophic Manuscripts of 1844* (Moscow, Foreign Languages Publishing House, 1959), note 1, pp. 99–100. See also Marx's various discussions of women's work and prostitution which cite and comment on the 1840s writings of French political economists, pp. 31–34.

23 Moreau, *Le Sang*, p. 240.

24 Giovanna Procacci, 'Le Gouvernement de la misère: la question social entre les deux révolutions, 1789–1848' (unpublished thèse de 3e cycle, Université de Paris VIII, 1983). These are Procacci's characterisations of the representation of misery by political economists. I share much of her analysis of the ways in which misery was identified as an object of study, marginal to sound order and thus in need of regulation. But I think she misses the chance to probe her subject further by neglecting the gendered representation of misery that was developed. Misery was depicted as feminine and that entailed important implications, both for the analysis of the state of the working classes *and* for the position and status of women. How that feminine representation worked is the focus of this paper.

25 Hufton reminds us that urban iconography frequently represents the city as a whore, 'The fallen woman', p. 2.

26 Jules Michelet, *La Femme* (Paris, Flammarion, 1981), p. 91.

27 Achille de Colmont, 'De l'amélioration de la situation sociale des ouvriers', *JE*, 1er série, 20 (1848) 195.

28 G. Procacci, 'Social economy and the government of poverty', *Ideology and Consciousness*, 4 (1979) 62. See also, Louis Reybaud, 'Introduction', *JE*, 1er série, 1 (1842) 9.

29 Jacques Donzelot, *La Police des familles* (Paris, Editions de Minuit, 1978).

30 Theodore Fix, 'Situation des classes ouvrières', *JE*, 1er série, 10 (1844) 39. See also Joseph Garnier, 'Études sur la repartition de la richesse', p. 210.

31 See A. Blaise, 'Cour d'économie politique du Collège de France', *JE*, 1er série, 1 (1842) 206, for an argument against the prevailing tendency to include moral science within political economy.

32 These views cited in J.-B. Say, *Cours complet d'économie politique* (2 vols., Paris, 1840), p. 180.

33 de Colmont, 'De l'amélioration', p. 257.

34 Dunoyer, 'De la concurrence', p. 32.

35 'Chronique économique', *JE*, 2e série, 34 (1862) 324–25. The question of women and printing requires further investigation for it comes up again and again in these years, not only among political economists, but also among feminists and trade unionists.

36 Say, *Cours complet*, p. 548, and Julie-Victoire Daubié, 'Quel moyens de subsistance ont les femmes', *JE*, 2e série, 34 (1862), 361–62. (I have cited Daubié's articles and not her book in this essay because the book, when published in 1866, was a much expanded version of her initial essay. It seemed more useful to use the articles for the purposes of this paper both because of when they were written and where they were published.)

37 T. Fix uses this analogy in 'Situation', pp. 9–10.

38 William Sewell, *Work and Revolution in France: The Language of Labor from the Old Regime to 1848* (New York, Cambridge University Press, 1980), pp. 223–32.

39 *Ibid.* p. 227.

40 *Ibid.* p. 229.

41 *Ibid.* pp. 224–25. See also William Reddy, *The Rise of Market Culture: The Textile Trade and French Society, 1750–1900* (New York, Cambridge University Press, 1984), pp. 138–84.

42 Fix, 'Situation', p. 31.
43 'il est pire moralement dans les grandes manufactures, où les hommes et les femmes travaillent dans les mêmes ateliers, sortent aux mêmes heures, ce qui fait que les moeurs sont plus dissolues qu'ailleurs...', 'Enquête: de la condition des femmes', *L'Atelier*, 30 December 1842, pp. 31–32.
44 Terme and Monfalcon, *Histoire des enfants trouvés* (Paris, 1840), p. 16, cited in Rachel Fuchs, *Abandoned Children: Foundlings and Child Welfare in Nineteenth-Century France* (Albany, NY, State University of New York Press, 1984), p. 39.
45 H. Baudrillart, 'De l'enseignement de l'économie politique', *JE*, 2e série, 38 (1862) 180–81.
46 Jules Simon, *L'Ouvrière* (2nd edn, Paris, Hachette, 1861), p. ii.
47 J. Daubié, 'Travail manuel des femmes', *JE*, 2e série, 39 (1863) 97–8.
48 Simon, *L'Ouvrière*, p. i.
49 Daubié, 'Travail manuel', p. 99.
50 Michelet, *La Femme*, p. 54.
51 Simon, *L'Ouvrière*, p. v.
52 *Ibid.* p. v.
53 *Ibid.* p. 42.
54 *Ibid.* p. 46.
55 *Ibid.* p. 71.
56 *Ibid.* p. 273.
57 *Ibid.* p. 87.
58 *Ibid.* p. 83.
59 *Ibid.* p. 88.
60 See, for example, the writings of Alphonse Esquiros, *Les Vierges martyres* (Paris, 1846), p. 177: 'Les soucis de la maternité sont en effect les seuls travaux naturels de la femme; les autres la déforment...'
61 H. Dussard, 'Compte rendu de *l'Ouvrière*', *JE*, 2e série, 30 (1861) 94.
62 Simon, *L'Ouvrière*, p. 273.
63 *Ibid.* p. 168.
64 *Ibid.* p. 45.
65 Daubié, 'Quels moyens de subsistance', p. 365.
66 Daubié, 'Travail manuel', p. 94.
67 Daubié, 'Quel moyens de subsistance', p. 378.
68 Daubié, 'Travail manuel', p. 83.
69 *Ibid.* p. 80.
70 *Ibid.* p. 96.
71 *Ibid.* p. 84.
72 Daubié, 'Travail manuel', *JE*, 2e série, 38 (163) 203.
73 *Ibid.* p. 210.
74 It seems crucial for feminist critiques of conceptions of the wage to begin not with Marx, but with political economy. On this question see Harold Benenson, 'Victorian sexual ideology and Marx's theory of the working class', *International Labor and Working Class History*, 25 (Spring 1984) 1–23. See also Rosalind Petchesky, 'Dissolving the hyphen: a report on Marxist-feminist groups 1–5', in H. Eisenstein, ed., *Capitalist Patriarchy and the Case for Socialist Feminism* (New York, Longman, 1981), pp. 376–77.

6 THE LANGUAGES OF FACTORY REFORM IN BRITAIN, *c.* 1830–1860

1 See, e.g., M. Berg, *The Age of Manufactures, 1700–1820* (London, Fontana, 1985); P. Hudson, 'Proto-industrialisation: the case of the West Riding', *History Workshop Journal*, 12 (1981); R. Samuel, 'The workshop of the world: steam power and hand technology in mid-Victorian Britain', *History Workshop Journal*, 3 (1977).

2 See I. J. Prothero, *Artisans and Politics: John Gast and his Times* (London, Dawson, 1979); E. P. Thompson, *The Making of the English Working Class* (Harmondsworth, Pelican edn, 1968).

3 For the notion of 'logic of process' see E. P. Thompson, *The Poverty of Theory and Other Essays* (London, Merlin Press, 1978), pp. 143–46.

4 See especially B. L. Hutchins and A. Harrison, *A History of Factory Legislation*, 3rd edn (London, Cass, 1926); U. R. Q. Henriques, *Before the Welfare State* (London, Longman, 1979), chs. 4, 5; M. W. Thomas, *The Early Factory Legislation* (Leigh-on-Sea, Thames Bank Publishing Co., 1948); J. T. Ward, *The Factory Movement* (London, Macmillan, 1962).

5 P. Corrigan and D. Sayer, *The Great Arch* (Oxford, Blackwell, 1985), ch. 6; R. Johnson, 'Educating the educators: "experts" and the state, 1833–39', in A. P. Donajgrodzki, ed., *Social Control in Nineteenth Century Britain* (London, Croom Helm, 1977); P. Richards, 'State formation and class struggle', in P. Corrigan, ed., *Capitalism, State Formation and Marxist Theory* (London, Quartet, 1980).

6 P. Bartrip, 'British government inspection, 1832–1875: some observations', *Hist. Journal*, 25 (1982); W. G. Carson, 'The conventionalisation of factory crime', *International Journal for the Sociology of Law*, 7 (1979).

7 S. Alexander, 'Women's work in nineteenth-century London', in J. Mitchell and A. Oakley, eds., *The Rights and Wrongs of Women* (Harmondsworth, Pelican, 1978); Berg, *Age of Manufactures*; A. Humphries, 'Protective legislation, the capitalist state and working class men', *Feminist Review*, 7 (1981); A. V. John, ed., *Unequal Opportunities: Women's Employment in England, 1800–1918* (Oxford, Blackwell, 1986).

8 G. Stedman Jones, *Languages of Class* (Cambridge University Press, 1983); M. Sonenscher, 'The sans-culottes of the year II', *Social History*, 9 (1984).

9 A. Gramsci, *Selections from the Prison Notebooks*, ed. and trans. Q. Hoare and G. Nowell Smith (London, Lawrence and Wishart, 1971), p. 327.

10 See Thompson, *Poverty of Theory*, esp. pp. 262–95; and cf. R. Williams, *Marxism and Literature* (Oxford University Press, 1977).

11 M. Berg, *The Machinery Question and the Making of Political Economy* (Cambridge University Press, 1980), pt v.

12 See R. Williams, *The Country and the City* (St Albans, Paladin, 1975); Thompson, *Making of the Working Class*, pp. 377–84 has some valuable comments on the nature of paternalist feeling.

13 For Oastler see C. Driver, *Tory Radical: The Life of Richard Oastler* (New York, Oxford University Press, 1946).

14 *Ibid.* ch. 4.

15 Samuel G. Fenton, Ms diary, 22 Jan. 1829: Leeds Reference Library.

16 R. Oastler, *A Letter to Mr. Holland Hoole* (1832): Oastler Collection, Goldsmiths Library, University of London (hereafter OC).

17 'Yorkshire Slavery', *Leeds Mercury*, 16 Oct. 1830, quoted Driver, *Tory Radical*, p. 43.

18 *Speech of Michael Thomas Sadler, Esq., on Moving the Second Reading of the Factories Regulation Bill* (1832), pp. 6–7: OC.

19 Oastler, *A Letter*, p. 9.

20 D. Gregory, *Regional Transformation and Industrial Revolution* (London and Basingstoke, Macmillan, 1982); Hudson, 'Proto-industrialisation'; D. T. Jenkins, *The West Riding Wool Textile Industry, 1770–1835* (Edington, Pasold Research Fund, 1975).

21 Cf. R. G. Wilson, *Gentlemen Merchants* (Manchester University Press, 1971).

22 For attitudes of professional men see *The Journal of Dr. John Simpson of Bradford* (Bradford, City of Bradford Metropolitan Council, 1981); this seems to capture the air of bored condescension with which 'average' professional men participated in local affairs. (Simpson loathed Bradford, but was nevertheless a member of various local committees.) It is regrettable that the diary (for 1825) does not extend to the period of factory agitation.

23 William Duncombe, MP, at York county meeting, 24 April 1832, in *The Justice Humanity and Policy of Restricting the Hours of Children and Young Persons in the Mills and Factories of the United Kingdom* (1833), p. 36: OC. This volume reprints a number of speeches etc. in support of Sadler's Bill, and provides a useful cross-section of the arguments and rhetorics employed.

24 Samuel Smith, *ibid.*, p. 39.

25 Quoted in Driver, *Tory Radical*, p. 232.

26 G. Crabtree, *A Brief Description of a Tour through Calder Dale* (1833), p. 17: OC; see also Thompson, *Making of the Working Class*.

27 *Poor Man's Advocate*, 3 March 1832.

28 *A Few Arguments in favour of Mr. Sadler's Bill ... and against Oppression in general, by a member of the Huddersfield Political Union* (1833), pp. 4–5: OC.

29 Select Committee on Labour of Children in Factories, PP 1831–2, xv, q.1587: hereafter Select Committee 1832.

30 John Hanson, speech at Halifax, in *Justice Humanity...*, p. 71.

31 Names from Crabtree traced in Factory Commission, Supplementary Report, PP 1834, xx, 1: hereafter Supplementary Report; E. Gaskell, *The Life of Charlotte Brontë* (Harmondsworth, Penguin, 1975), p. 67; this account of Keighley and Haworth also seems appliable to Calderdale.

32 Names from *Poor Man's Advocate* compared with V. A. C. Gatrell, 'Labour, power and the size of firms in Lancashire cotton', *Economic History Review*, 30 (1977), p. 100; of fifteen firms outside Manchester named in the *Poor Man's Advocate*, only two could be traced in the Supplementary Report, and these both had less than 50 hp. For Doherty's activities see R. G. Kirby and A. E. Musson, *Voice of the People: John Doherty, 1798–1854* (Manchester University Press, 1975), ch. 10.

33 *The Voice of the West Riding*, 13 July 1833.

34 Cf. Gregory, *Regional Transformation*, pp. 129–32.

35 Select Committee 1832, q. 1230, qq. 167–8.

36 'The justice of exposing tyrannical employers', reprinted as prospectus for *The Poor Man's Advocate* (1832–33): bound copies in Goldsmiths Library.

37 See, e.g., *Poor Man's Advocate*, 17 March 1832.

38 J. Scott, 'Men and women in the Parisian garment trades: discussions of family and work in the 1830s and 1840s', in P. Thane *et al.*, eds., *The Power of the Past* (Cambridge University Press, 1984).

39 W. R. Greg, *An Enquiry into the State of the Manufacturing Population and the Causes and Cures of the Evils Therein Existing* (1831), pp. 16–17: OC.

40 Oastler, *A Letter*, p. 29.

41 *The Commissioners' Vade Mecum Whilst Engaged in Collecting Evidence for the Factory Masters* (1833), pp. 6–7: OC.

42 Prothero, *Artisans and Politics*.

43 Berg, *Age of Manufactures*, chs. 6 and 7.

44 'Justice of exposing tyrannical employers'.

45 Supplementary Report, C.1 pt II, no. 77; see also nos. 78, 218, 279; cf. Select Committee 1832, qq. 431–586.

46 E. Baines, *Baines's Account of the Woollen Manufacture of England*, ed. K. G. Ponting (New York, A. Kelley, 1970), p. 75.

47 *A Conversation between George Hadfield and Charles Comber*: OC broadsides.

48 See Select Committee 1832, qq. 3666–71, 3378–87, 4064–94. Carol Bradley drew my attention to this issue.

49 Crabtree, *Brief Description*, p. 8; cf. James Everett, *Memoirs of the Life, Character and Ministry of William Dawson* (1842), pp. 370–75; Select Committee 1832, qq. 4057–4142 (A. Wildman, Keighley, Methodist Sunday School teacher).

50 William Dawson, in *Justice, Humanity*..., pp. 9–11.

51 Select Committee 1832, q. 2338 (J. Goodyear, Huddersfield).

52 See esp. Stedman Jones, *Languages of Class*, chs. 1, 3. I offer some criticisms in my 'The deconstruction of the English working class', *Social History*, 11 (1986).

53 Crabtree, *Brief Description*, p. 9.

54 *Ibid.* p. 15.

55 *To the Factory Masters in Cragg Dale who have 'challenged' Richard Oastler without publishing their Names* (July 1833); *An Appeal to the Public by the Factory Masters in Cragg Valley* (July 1833): OC broadsides.

56 *To the Factory Masters*...

57 W. G. Carson, 'Symbolic and instrumental dimensions of early factory legislation', in R. Hood, ed., *Crime, Criminology and Public Policy* (London, Heinemann, 1974), p. 135.

58 Handwritten notes on reverse of copy of 1833 Factory Bill: OC broadsides.

59 Henry Ashworth, Supplementary Report, D.1, no. 223; Fernleys and Wilson, Stockport, *ibid.*, D.1, no. 237.

60 *Ibid.* C.1, no. 23.

61 *Voice of the West Riding*, 20 July 1833.

62 Select Committee 1832, e.g., q. 1186 (W. Kershaw, Gomersal).

63 H. M. Clokie and J. W. Robinson, *Royal Commissions of Inquiry* (Stanford and London, Stanford University Press, 1937).

64 J. P. Kay, *The Moral and Physical Condition of the Working Classes Employed in the Cotton Manufacture in Manchester* (1832), p. 5: OC.

65 Factory Commission, First Report, PP 1833, XX, p. 44: hereafter First Report.

66 R. Oastler, *Speech delivered ... Huddersfield ... June 18 1833* (1833): OC;

W. Hanna, *Memoirs of the Life and Writings of Thomas Chalmers*, vol. III (1851), p. 366: I am indebted for this reference to Ena Ainsworth.

67 Carson, 'Symbolic dimensions'; 'Conventionalisation of factory crime'.

68 Carson, 'Symbolic dimensions', p. 129; for Wibsey Moor see 'Alfred', *The History of the Factory Movement*, 2 vols. (1857), vol. II, ch. 3.

69 R. Oastler, *The Unjust Judge, or the Sign of the Judge's Skin* (1836); Driver, *Tory Radical*, pp. 326–30.

70 E. Hodder, *The Seventh Earl of Shaftesbury*, 2 vols. (1886), vol. I, p. 163; and for Ashley's view of Oastler see *ibid.* p. 214.

71 See esp. A. Howe, *The Cotton Masters, 1830–60* (Oxford, Clarendon Press, 1984); P. Joyce, *Work, Society and Politics* (Brighton, Harvester Press, 1980).

72 V. A. C. Gatrell, 'Incorporation and the pursuit of Liberal hegemony in Manchester, 1790–1839', in D. Fraser, ed., *Municipal Reform and the Industrial City* (Leicester University Press, 1982); J. Seed, 'Unitarianism, political economy and the antinomies of liberal culture in Manchester, 1830–50', *Social History*, 7 (1982).

73 Gatrell, 'Liberal hegemony'.

74 See, e.g., the views of Kennedy reported in *A French Sociologist Looks at Britain: Gustave d'Eichthal and British Society in 1828*, ed. B. M. Ratcliffe and W. H. Chaloner (Manchester University Press, 1977), pp. 98–99.

75 C. Hall, 'Middle-class women and work in the early nineteenth century', paper presented at conference on 'The Politics of Work', history of work group, History Workshop Centre for Social History, October 1985.

76 Howe, *Cotton Masters*; Joyce, *Work, Society and Politics*; M. Sanderson, 'Education and the factory in industrial Lancashire, 1780–1840', *Economic History Review*, 20 (1967).

77 Hall, 'Middle-class women'; P. Spencer, *Hannah Greg (née Lightbody), 1766–1828* (Styal, Quarry Bank Mill Trust, 1982) for an example of such activities.

78 For Hoole see Gatrell, 'Liberal hegemony', p. 44.

79 Joyce, *Work, Society and Politics*, p. 11; three of the manufacturers Joyce mentions appear as fairly emphatic supporters of factory legislation, though not necessarily a ten hours bill, in the factory commissioners' questionnaire discussed below (tables 1, 2).

80 Supplementary Report, c.1, no. 54.

81 Select Committee 1832, qq. 3003 ff.

82 See S. Dentith, 'Political economy, fiction and the language of practical ideology', *Social History*, 8 (1983); Seed, 'Unitarianism'.

83 Howe, *Cotton Masters*, pp. 182–83.

84 H. Hoole, *A Letter the Right Honourable Lord Viscount Althorp ... in Defence of the Cotton Factories of Lancashire* (1832), p. 10: OC.

85 Driver, *Tory Radical*, chs. 5 and 6.

86 Kay, *Moral and Physical Condition*, preface.

87 Greg, *Enquiry*, p. 39.

88 *Ibid.* pp. 28–29.

89 'Alfred', *History*, devotes a chapter to Greg and Kay, see vol. I, ch. 11.

90 Greg, *Enquiry*; Kay, *Moral and Physical Condition*, annotated copies in OC.

91 *Ten Hours Advocate*, 21 Nov. 1846.

92 Driver, *Tory Radical*, pp. 85–86.

93 Kay, *Moral and Physical Condition*, preface.

94 T. S. Ashton, *Economic and Social Investigations in Manchester* (London, P. S. King, 1934); the papers of the Society are in the Archives Department, Manchester Central Library.

95 First Report, E. 4, evidence of W. R. Greg; Supplementary Report, D. 1, no. 117.

96 Manchester Statistical Society, *An Analysis of the Evidence taken before the Factory Commissioners* (1834), p. 31.

97 Howe, *Cotton Masters*, p. 181; cf. Gatrell, 'Labour, power and size of firms'; R. Lloyd Jones and A. A. Le Roux, 'The size of firms in the cotton industry', *Economic History Review*, 33 (1980).

98 First Report, evidence of Houldsworth, Greg, Ashton, Ashworth; Supplementary Report, D. 1, no. 218 (Hoole).

99 See D. T. Jenkins, 'The validity of the factory returns, 1833–50', *Textile History*, 4 (1973).

100 The most relevant questions are no. 37, about 'the probable effects of a still further reduction of the working hours', and no. 79, which invites 'any further observations'; in the supplementary questionnaire issued to most of the Yorkshire respondents no. 27 simply asks for 'any remarks you may be desirous of making'.

101 Supplementary Report, D. 1, no. 223.

102 *Ibid.* D. 1, no. 174 (Houldsworth).

103 Resolutions of a meeting of manufacturers at Blackburn, 17 April 1826; and, e.g., Clegg to Fielden 8 June 1836, 15 Jan. 1839: Fielden papers, John Rylands Library, Manchester, uncatalogued at time of use.

104 Supplementary Report, D. 1, no. 163.

105 *Ibid.* C. 1, no. 142 (E. Firth, Heckmondwike, blanket manufacture, 20 hp steam).

106 *A Letter to Sir John Cam Hobhouse ... on the Factories Bill* (1832), pp. 12, 16: OC (the author appears to be a worsted spinner).

107 *Ibid.*

108 Supplementary Report, C. 1, nos. 45, 52 (both Bradford worsted manufacturers).

109 *Ibid.* C. 1, nos. 271, 279.

110 Carson, 'Symbolic dimensions', p. 135.

111 Sanderson, 'Education and the factory', pp. 274–75.

112 Howe, *Cotton Masters*, pp. 178–93.

113 Draft speech, dated 5 July 1833: Marshall Papers, Brotherton Library, University of Leeds, MS 200, 17.4 (iii).

114 R. Boyson, *The Ashworth Cotton Enterprise* (Oxford University Press, 1970), ch. 9.

115 'Observations on Mr. Heathcote's letter and the proceedings of Horner': Ashworth Papers, Lancs. RO.

116 See Joyce, *Work, Society and Politics*; Howe, *Cotton Masters*, ch. 8.

117 I am indebted to Carol Bradley for discussion of her work in progress and sight of an unpublished paper which bears on this point.

118 Richards, 'State formation'.

119 W. R. Lee, 'Robert Baker: the first doctor in the Factory Department', *British Journal of Industrial Medicine*, 21 (1964); B. Martin, 'Leonard Horner:

a portrait of an inspector of factories', *International Review of Social History*, 14 (1969); Thomas, *Early Factory Legislation*.

120 Bartrip, 'British goverment inspection'.

121 Quoted Thomas, *Early Factory Legislation*, p. 94.

122 Select Committee on the Act for the Regulation of Mills and Factories, PP 1840, x, qq. 8471–3: hereafter Select Committee 1840.

123 L. Horner, *On the Employment of Children in Factories* (1840), p. 4.

124 *Ibid.* p. 16.

125 *Ibid.*

126 Select Committee 1840, 'Report'.

127 *Ibid.*

128 Thomas, *Early Factory Legislation*, ch. 12 for a detailed discussion.

129 Select Committee 1840, qq. 4425, 4879–85, 9224–44; cf. J. Fielden, *The Curse of the Factory System* (1836), pp. 32–40.

130 Select Committee 1840, 'Report'.

131 *Ibid.*

132 See, e.g., W. Cooke Taylor, *Notes of a Tour in the Manufacturing Districts* 2nd edn (1842); J. Ginswick, ed., *Labour and the Poor in England and Wales, 1849–51: Letters to the Morning Chronicle*, vol. 1 (London and Totowa, NJ, Frank Cass, 1983); B. Disraeli, *Coningsby* (Harmondsworth, Penguin, 1983), Book IV, chs. 1–3; I. Kovacevic, *Fact into Fiction: English Literature and the Industrial Scene, 1750–1850* (Leicester and Belgrade, Leicester University Press/University of Belgrade, 1975).

133 Cooke Taylor, *Notes of a Tour*, pp. 23–24; Ginswick, *Labour and the Poor*, p. 36; Disraeli (191) makes metaphoric play with Millbank's pride in his fruit.

134 Letter from L. Horner, in N. W. Senior, *Letters on the Factory Act* (1837), p. 34.

135 *Ten Hours Advocate*, 28 Nov. 1846; cf. above, note 53.

136 Ashworth Papers: memo on Manners' visit.

137 Cooke Taylor, *Notes of a Tour*, p. 19.

138 'Alfred', *History*, vol. II, pp. 51–52; P. Grant, *The Ten Hours Bill* (1866), pp. 52–54. 'Alfred' devotes about 260 of some 566 pages to the three years from the *Leeds Mercury* letters to the 1833 Act, and the remaining pages to the years before 1830 and from 1833 to 1847.

139 *Ten Hours Advocate*, 14 Nov. 1846.

140 *Ibid.* 3 Oct. 1846.

141 Grant, *Ten Hours Bill*, p. 63.

142 Hodder, *Seventh Earl*, vol. I, p. 346.

143 Select Committee 1840, q. 8315.

144 *Ibid.* qq. 38, 319–20, 38, 350, 8384.

145 'Alfred', *History*, vol. I, p. 118.

146 Grant, *Ten Hours Bill*, p. 54.

147 *Ibid.* p. 5.

148 *The Autobiography of Thomas Wood, 1822–1880* (1956), in J. Burnett, ed., *Useful Toil* (London, Allen Lane, 1974), p. 306: Wood started at the mill aged eight, c. 1830.

149 W. R. Croft, *The History of the Factory Movement, or Oastler and His Times* (Huddersfield, 1888), preface.

150 F. Peel, *The Risings of the Luddites, Chartists and Plug-drawers* (London,

Frank Cass, 1968; reprint of 3rd edn 1895); see also B. Wilson, *The Struggles of an Old Chartist*, in D. Vincent, ed., *Testaments of Radicalism* (London, Europa Publications, 1977).

151 Croft, *History of the Factory Movement*, p. 99.

152 *Memoirs of Eminent Men of Leeds* (1868), pp. 54–61.

153 Driver, *Tory Radical*, p. 520.

154 Forster to Balme, 7 Dec. 1867: Balme Collection, Bradford Central Library; see also Joyce, *Work, Society and Politics*, pp. 322–26.

155 E. Akroyd, 'On the relations betwixt employers and employed under the factory system', *National Association for the Promotion of Social Science Trans.*, 1 (1857) 527; for the Akroyds see R. Bretton, 'Colonel Edward Akroyd', *Trans. Halifax Antiq. Soc.* (1948–49); K. Tiller, 'Working class organisations and attitudes in three industrial towns' (unpublished Ph.D thesis, University of Birmingham, 1975), pp. 47–49, 57, 400–1.

156 E. Akroyd, 'On factory education and its extension', *National Association for Promotion of Social Science Trans.*, 1 (1857) 159–63.

157 See, e.g., R. Baker, *The Factory Acts Made Easy* (1851); *'It's Nobbut' and 'Nivver Heed': a lecture given by Robert Baker, esq.* (2nd edn 1860).

158 Baker, *Factory Acts*, pp. 10–11, 34.

159 Rickards to John Brigg and Co., post-marked 22 May 1859: Keighley Library, Box of ephemera marked 'Factory Act'; I am much indebted to Mr I. Dewhirst for showing me this item.

160 J. Hodgson, *Textile Manufacture and Other Industries in Keighley* (1879), p. 179.

161 Select Committee 1840, q. 4425.

162 *Ibid.* q. 8480.

163 Carson, 'Conventionalisation of factory crime'; A. E. Peacock, 'The successful prosecution of the factory acts, 1835–55', *Economic History Review*, 37 (1984); P. Bartrip, 'Success or failure? the prosecution of the early factory acts'; C. Nardinelli, 'The successful prosecution of the factory acts: a suggested explanation'; A. E. Peacock, 'Factory act prosecutions: a hidden consensus', all in *Economic History Review*, 38 (1985).

164 Bretton, 'Colonel Edward Akroyd', p. 68; Hodgson, *Textile Manufacture*, p. 42.

165 Hodgson, *Textile Manufacture*, p. 174.

166 Cooke Taylor, *Notes of a Tour*, p. 32; J. C. Holley, 'The two family economies of industrialism: factory workers in Victorian Scotland', *Journal of Family History* (Spring 1981), pp. 63–4.

167 Akroyd, 'Factory education', p. 157.

168 'Alfred', *History*; Croft, *History of the Factory Movement*; Grant, *Ten Hours Bill*.

169 'Alfred', *History*, pp. 299–300.

170 *Ibid.*

171 Fielden, *The Curse*, p. 17.

7 TIME TO WORK, TIME TO LIVE: SOME ASPECTS OF WORK AND THE REFORMATION OF CLASS IN BRITAIN 1850–1880

This chapter draws on research for a Ph.D. thesis at Birmingham University ('Skilled workers on Tyneside, 1850–1880' [forthcoming]), supervised by Dorothy Thompson. For their encouragement and help at various times, I am also extremely grateful to Cora Kaplan, Patrick Joyce, Olivia Harris, and Ellen Ross. Brief versions were given as talks to the History Workshop 1983 and the 'Politics of Work' conference at the History Workshop Centre in 1985; I learned from the participants at both.

1 Raymond Williams, *Towards 2000* (London, Chatto and Windus/The Hogarth Press, 1983), p. 168.
2 Historians have recently displayed renewed awareness of the uneven development of capitalist industrialisation in Britain: David Cannadine, 'The past and the present in the English industrial revolution 1880–1980', *Past and Present*, 103 (1984), surveys changing views.
3 See R. Q. Gray, *The Aristocracy of Labour in Nineteenth Century Britain, c. 1850–1900* (London, Macmillan, 1981), and, for a restatement of the thesis by its major proponent, E. J. Hobsbawm, *Worlds of Labour* (London, Weidenfeld and Nicolson, 1984), chs. 11–14.
4 For an introduction see N. R. Elliott, 'Tyneside, a study in the development of an industrial seaport', *Tijdschrift voor econ. en soc. geografie*, 53 (1962).
5 P. Westmacott and J. F. Spencer, 'On the engineering manufactures of the district' in W. G. Armstrong *et al.*, eds., *The Industrial Resources of the Tyne, Wear and Tees* (British Association, 1863), pp. 266–67; S. Pollard, 'The economic history of British shipbuilding, 1870–1914' (unpublished Ph.D. thesis University of London, 1950), Table A.3, p. 555. Further details for Tyneside are in K. McClelland, 'Skilled workers on Tyneside, 1850–1880' (unpublished Ph.D. thesis, University of Birmingham, forthcoming).
6 W. Richardson, 'Introduction' to *Visit of the British Association to Newcastle-upon-Tyne* (1889), p. xiii; although see *Newcastle Courant*, 13 December 1861, for some forms of employment largely hidden from the census.
7 See Charles More, *Skill and the English Working Class, 1870–1914* (London, Croom Helm, 1980), for a discussion of the nature of skill.
8 These estimates are based on figures in Parliamentary Papers 1886 [C. 4797] XXIII. Royal Commission on Depression, 3rd Report, Appendix A.IV (i and iv), pp. 298–9, (John Price of Palmer's); H. H. Creed and W. Williams, *Handicraftsmen and Capitalists* (Birmingham, 1867), pp. 112–17 (Avonside engine works, Bristol); evidence from Sir Edward Harland to the Webbs Trade Union Collection, A.XV (1), p. 11.
9 See Gray, *Aristocracy of Labour*, for discussion; for one of the many instances of this view, see the anonymous review of *Essays on Reform* in *The Saturday Review*, 6 April 1867.
10 *Newcastle Chronicle*, 21 September 1861.
11 PP 1871 [C452], XXV. First Report of the Commissioners into Friendly and Benefit Building Societies, qq. 6424–5 (T. E. Priest).
12 Iorwerth Prothero, *Artisans and Politics in Early Nineteenth-Century London* (Folkestone, Dawson, 1979), pp. 4–5.
13 See esp. Raphael Samuel, 'Workshop of the world: steam power and hand technology in mid-Victorian Britain', *History Workshop Journal*, 3 (1977).
14 E.g.: 'The labourers in question are not "unskilled" men, many of them have been 13 years at the business, and having frequently to instruct an apprentice or unskilled 'wright [i.e. shipwright] when they are called upon to assist.' *Newcastle Weekly Chronicle*, 13 May 1871.

15 *Newcastle Chronicle*, 5 and 26 May 1854; J. Grantham, *Iron Shipbuilding* (London, 1858), p. 36.

16 For a general survey of engineering see Keith Burgess, *The Origins of British Industrial Relations* (London, Croom Helm, 1975), ch. 1; for shipbuilding, Keith McClelland and Alastair Reid, 'Wood, iron and steel: technology, labour and trade union organisation in the shipbuilding industry, 1840–1914', in R. Harrison and J. Zeitlin, eds., *Divisions of Labour* (Brighton, Harvester Press, 1985).

17 M. A. Bienefeld, *Working Hours in British Industry: An Economic History* (London, George Allen and Unwin, 1972), ch. 3 charts the formal changes; for the notion of the 'normal day' see esp. S. and B. Webb, *Industrial Democracy* (London, 1898), part II, ch. 6.

18 E. J. Harland, 'Shipbuilding in Belfast – its origins and progress' in Samuel Smiles, *Men of Invention and Industry* (London, 1884), pp. 292–93; 'Rules and regulations to be observed by the workmen in the employ of Robt. Stephenson & Co.' (1838) reprinted in J. E. Mortimer, *History of the Boilermakers' Society, vol. I, 1834–1906* (London, George Allen and Unwin, 1973), facing p. 32; cf. the similar rules of Hawthorn's, also for 1838, in J. F. Clarke, *Power on Land and Sea* (Newcastle, Hawthorn Leslie (Engineers) Ltd, n.d. [1979]), p. 5.

19 For a survey of general trends see the brief discussion in R. C. O. Matthews, C. H. Feinstein and J. C. Odling-Smee, *British Economic Growth 1856–1973* (Oxford, Clarendon Press, 1982), ch. 2; the difficulties of measuring productivity in engineering are discussed in R. Floud, *The British Machine Tool Industry, 1850–1914* (Cambridge University Press, 1976), pp. 194 ff.

20 PP 1867–68 [3980–V], XXXIX, Royal Commission on Trade Unions etc., 9th Report, q. 18077; *Transactions of the Institution of Naval Architects* (1899), p. 121; both cited in S. Pollard and P. Robertson, *The British Shipbuilding Industry, 1870–1914* (Cambridge, Mass., Harvard University Press, 1979), p. 163.

21 John Burnett, *Nine Hours Movement. A History of the Engineers' Strikes in Newcastle and Gateshead* (Newcastle upon Tyne, 1872), p. 6.

22 Alasdair Clayre, *Work and Play: Ideas and Experience of Work and Leisure* (London, Weidenfeld and Nicolson, 1974), is an interesting survey.

23 *The Principles of Political Economy* (1825), p. 7 cited in S. Wolin, *Politics and Vision* (London, George Allen and Unwin, 1961), p. 320.

24 See, *inter alia*, Thomas Carlyle, *Past and Present* (London, 1843), Book III, ch. 11.

25 *Newcastle Chronicle*, 5 May 1854.

26 *Newcastle Chronicle*, 24 August 1861.

27 See also Patrick Joyce, *Work, Society and Politics. The Culture of the Factory in Later Victorian England* (Brighton, Harvester, 1980), for much of relevance to this theme.

28 *Newcastle Weekly Chronicle*, 13 September 1873.

29 United Society of Boiler Makers and Iron Shipbuilders (hereafter Boilermakers), *Annual Report*, 1878, p. vi. 1877, p. vii. I must thank the Society for permission to consult their records.

30 Boilermakers, *Annual Report*, 1881, p. xiii.

31 PP 1893–94 [C6894 – VII], XXXII. Royal Commission on Labour, 3rd

Report, q. 20683; for fluctuations in the industry see McClelland and Reid, 'Wood, iron and steel', pp. 156–58 and Pollard and Robertson, *Shipbuilding*, ch. 2.

32 Noel Thompson, *The People's Science. The Popular Political Economy of Exploitation and Crisis 1816–34* (Cambridge University Press, 1984), p. 219.

33 Thompson, *People's Science*, pp. 221–25.

34 Cited in Bernard Semmel, *The Rise of Free Trade Imperialism* (Cambridge University Press, 1970), p. 130.

35 G. W. Norman, speech at a banquet of the Political Economy Club, London 1876, cited in Semmel, *Free Trade Imperialism*, p. 203.

36 See among others, Simon Dentith, 'Political economy, fiction and the language of practical ideology in nineteenth-century England', *Social History*, 8 (1983) 183–99; Boyd Hilton, *Corn, Cash, Commerce* (Oxford University Press, 1977), pp. 308–13.

37 John Stuart Mill, 'On the definition of political economy; and on the method of investigation proper to it' (1836) in *Collected Works*, vol. IV (London, Routledge and Kegan Paul, 1967), p. 321.

38 Friendly Society of Iron Founders, (hereafter FSIF), *Annual Report*, 1870, pp. v–vi; *The Chain Makers' Journal and Trades' Circular*, 11 (April 1859), 81.

39 *Northern Daily Express*, 12 January 1858; *Newcastle Weekly Chronicle*, 1 December 1866.

40 See e.g., *Chainmakers' Journal*, 11 (April 1859) 81–82; for John Stuart Mill's definition of capital, *The Principles of Political Economy* (7th edn, 1871, ed. W. J. Ashley, London, 1909), p. 54.

41 Burnett, *Nine Hours Movement*, p. 13.

42 Gareth Stedman Jones, 'Rethinking Chartism' in *Languages of Class* (Cambridge University Press, 1983), p. 156.

43 A view expressed earlier in the century by, e.g., William Thompson: see Thompson, *People's Science*, pp. 26–29.

44 *Chainmakers' Journal*, 11 (April 1859), 82.

45 Burnett, *Nine Hours Movement*, p. 16.

46 R. V. Clements, 'British trade unions and popular political economy, 1850–1875', *Economic History Review*, 14 (1961–62), 93–104; W. H. Fraser, *Trade Unions and Society. The Struggle for Acceptance 1850–1880* (London, George Allen and Unwin, 1974), ch. 7. By and large these are critical of the Webbs: for their views see esp. *Industrial Democracy*, part II, ch. 13.

47 FSIF, *Annual Report (Auxiliary Fund)*, 1867, p. 120; similar views may be found in, e.g., FSIF, *Annual Report*, 1879, p. 136 and *Chainmakers' Journal*, 2 (August 1858), 10.

48 *Chainmakers' Journal*, 3 (September 1858), 17.

49 *Newcastle Chronicle*, 28 December 1861.

50 Boilermakers, *Annual Report*, 1880, p. viii.

51 See esp. Richard Price, *Masters, Unions and Men* (Cambridge University Press, 1980), pp. 58ff.

52 *Rules and Regulations of the Newcastle-on-Tyne Branch of the Typographical Association* (Newcastle, 1877), p. 3; see also e.g., the Preface to the rules of the Amalgamated Society of Engineers (1851, revised 1864) repr. in PP

1868–69 [4123–1], XXXI, vol. 2. Royal Commission on Trade Unions, 11th Report, Appendix, p. 246.

53 Cited in Webb, *Industrial Democracy*, p. 564.

54 See *Industrial Democracy*, esp. part II, ch. 11; John Rule in this volume.

55 FSIF, *Annual Report*, 1868, p. vi.

56 E. J. Hobsbawm, 'Artisans and labour aristocrats?' in *Worlds of Labour*, pp. 262–64; *Newcastle Weekly Chronicle* (Supplement), 10 June 1865. This was common too when the trades participated in the reform demonstrations of 1866–67.

57 Boilermakers, *Monthly Report*, October 1873, p. 8.

58 ASE Rules in Royal Commission on Trade Unions, rule 14 (1); More, *Skill*, part 2 discusses apprenticeship; see also, among others, Webb, *Industrial Democracy*, part II, ch. 10 (a).

59 E.g., for the design department at Armstrong's see PP 1887 [C5116], XIV. Select Committee on Manufacturing Departments of the Army, qq. 8891–8899; for the development of science in shipbuilding, Pollard and Robertson, *Shipbuilding*, pp. 130–37.

60 PP 1893–94 [C6894–VII], XXXII. Royal Commission on Labour, 3rd Report [Group A], q. 21592 (Alexander Wilkie). Alfred Williams, *Life in a Railway Factory* (1915; repr. Gloucester, Alan Sutton, 1984), contains much evidence on the lack of interest in or knowledge of one shop by that of another.

61 From a description of the patternmaker's craft in *Metal*, 1882, cited in W. Mosses, *History of the United Pattern Makers' Association 1872–1922* (London, United Patternmakers' Association, 1922), p. 65.

62 'A journeyman engineer' [Thomas Wright], 'On the inner life of workshops' in *Some Habits and Customs of the Working Classes* (London, 1867), p. 84.

63 Charles Manby Smith, *The Working Man's Way in the World* (1853; repr. London, Printing Historical Society, 1967), p. 15; John Burnett, ed., *Useful Toil* (Harmondsworth, Penguin, 1977), p. 332.

64 Burnett, *Useful Toil*, pp. 308–9; John Dunlop, *The Philosophy of Artificial and Compulsory Drinking Usage* (6th edn, London, 1839), pp. 14, 176 and 185 and *passim*.

65 *Newcastle Chronicle*, 5 and 8 November 1858, 2 November 1861.

66 Dunlop, *Drinking Usage*, pp. 83–84, 177.

67 Christopher Thomson, *The Autobiography of an Artisan* (London, 1847), pp. 72–73; see also Brian Harrison and Patricia Hollis, eds., *Robert Lowery. Radical and Chartist* (London, Europa, 1979), pp. 82–83 for 'immorality' among Newcastle tailoring apprentices in the 1830s. (Harrison and Hollis also quote the passage from Thomson.)

68 Burnett, *Useful Toil*, p. 350; see also Thomas Jordan, a miner, who recalled that he used to be taken as a child down the mine by his father but could not admit to being afraid for he would have been called 'queer'; in Burnett, p. 103.

69 'A Working Man', *Working Men and Women* (London, 1879), p. 110.

70 E. P. Thompson, 'The grid of inheritance: a comment' in J. Goody, J. Thirsk and E. P. Thompson, eds., *Family and Inheritance* (Cambridge University Press, 1976), p. 359.

71 Interview with J. Maddison, General Secretary of the FSIF: Webb TU Collection, A.XIX, pp. 237–38; Boilermakers, *Annual Report*, 1884, p. v; PP 1897 (334), X. Select Committee on Government Contracts, q. 2,728. For

attempts to measure the extent of patrimony see G. Crossick, *An Artisan Elite in Victorian Society* (London, Croom Helm, 1978), pp. 113–18; Roger Penn, *Skilled Workers in the Class Structure* (Cambridge University Press, 1984), chs. 10–12; More, *Skill*, pp. 65–68.

72 Boilermakers, *Monthly Report*, October 1873, p. 9.

73 FSIF, *Annual Report*, 1879, pp. 136–37; *Chainmakers' Journal*, 1 (July 1858) 2; Boilermakers, *Trade Report*, September 1860; Boilermakers, *Annual Report*, 1873, p. viii; Boilermakers, *Annual Report*, 1876, pp. xi–xii.

74 For some helpful discussion about the extent and nature of 'compromise' and 'reciprocity' between capital and labour in this period see Richard Price, 'The labour process and labour history', *Social History*, 8 (1983) 57–75 and the subsequent exchanges between Price and Patrick Joyce, *Social History*, 9 (1984), 67–76, 217–31.

75 *Chainmakers' Journal*, 6 (November 1858), 42.

76 Fraser, *Trade Unions*, surveys the general position; McClelland, 'Skilled workers on Tyneside' includes a discussion of the extent of trade unionism on Tyneside.

77 FSIF, *Annual Report*, 1880, p. 122.

78 See Price, *Masters, Unions and Men* for building.

79 Douglas Reid, 'The decline of St. Monday 1766–1876', *Past and Present*, 71 (1976).

80 Wright, 'Inner life of workshops', pp. 84–85.

81 Harry Pollitt, *Serving My Time* (London, Lawrence and Wishart, 1940), pp. 59–60.

82 Boilermakers, *Monthly Report*, April 1881, p. 13; see also, e.g., *Trade Report*, April 1868; *Monthly Report*, February 1876, p. 6; note also Dudley Baxter's comment that drinking habits were one important cause of loss of working time in 'many well-paid trades': *National Income* (London, 1868), pp. 46–47.

83 I. L. Bell, *The Iron Trade of the United Kingdom* in PP 1886 [C4715], XXI. Royal Commission on the Depression, 2nd Report, Part I, Appendix A (1), p. 342; *Chainmakers' Journal*, 15 (August 1859), 121–22; PP 1847 (678) X. Select Committee on Navigation Laws, 5th Report, q. 8055.

84 E. J. Hobsbawm, 'Custom, wages and work-load in nineteenth-century industry' in *Labouring Men* (London, Weidenfeld and Nicolson, 1964).

85 Hobsbawm, 'Custom', p. 357.

86 Boilermakers, *Annual Report*, 1882, p. xiii.

87 PP 1867–68 [3980–1], XXXIX. Royal Commission on Trade Unions, 5th Report, q. 8745.

88 Hobsbawm, 'Custom', p. 348; for general discussions of the notion of the 'family wage' see Michele Barrett and Mary McIntosh, 'The "family wage": some problems for socialists and feminists', *Capital and Class*, 9 (1980) 51–72 and Wally Seecombe, 'Patriarchy stabilized: the construction of the male breadwinner wage norm in nineteenth-century Britain', *Social History*, 11 (1986) 53–76.

89 Thomas Pringle, *The Shipwrights' Trades' Unions of the Wear and Tyne* (1860) cited in P. H. Rathbone, 'An account of shipwrights' trades' societies' in National Association for the Promotion of Social Science, *Report on Trades' Societies and Strikes* (London, 1860), p. 507; Boilermakers, *Monthly Report*, January 1886, p. 11.

90 By 1894 a little over 70% of all trade unions either insisted on piece-work or had come to recognise it: Webb, *Industrial Democracy*, pp. 286–87. In 1876 one commentator even thought that 90% of British manufactures were paid in piece-work: Frederic Hill, *Piece-work as Compared with Time-work* (London, 1876), p. 8.

91 Boilermakers, *Monthly Report*, January 1880, pp. 8–9; Royal Commission on Trade Unions, 11th Report, vol. 2, Appendix D, pp. 82–83 (Daniel Guile, FSIF); FSIF, *Annual Report*, 1876, p. 123; Royal Commission on Trade Unions, 5th report, q. 8689 (Daniel Guile); Boilermakers, *Annual Report*, 1875, pp. xii–xiii. Similar objections were raised to overtime.

92 Boilermakers, *Annual Report*, 1882, pp. xiii–xiv.

93 K. McClelland, 'A politics of the labour aristocracy? Skilled workers and Radical politics on Tyneside, c.1850–1874', *Bulletin of the Society for the Study of Labour History*, 40 (1980) 8–9. (Abstract of paper.)

94 Boilermakers, *Monthly Report*, June 1885, pp. 8–9.

95 Royal Commission on Trade Unions, 11th Report, vol. 2, Appendix D, pp. 78–79; Royal Commission on Trade Unions, 5th Report, q. 8745.

96 Boilermakers, *Trade Report*, February 1863; *Newcastle Chronicle*, 14 February 1863; Mortimer, *History*, pp. 62–3.

97 Boilermakers, *Trade Report*, October 1859.

98 E. P. Thompson and E. Yeo, eds. *The Unknown Mayhew* (London, Merlin Press, 1971), pp. 405–6; Boilermakers, *Monthly Report*, February 1873, pp. 4–5; McClelland and Reid, 'Wood, iron and steel', pp. 167–68 and *passim*.

99 For the 1871 strike and its impact see, among others, Burnett, *Nine Hours Movement*; E. Allen *et al.*, *The North-east Engineers' Strikes of 1871* (Newcastle, Frank Graham, 1971); S. and B. Webb, *History of Trade Unionism* (London, 1920), pp. 316 ff. and 352–57; a fuller analysis of the strike and its background is in McClelland, 'Skilled workers on Tyneside'.

100 'Modern domestic service', *Edinburgh Review*, 115 (1862), 414–15; William Tayler, a footman writing in 1837, in Burnett, *Useful Toil*, p. 185; see also the comments of John Robinson, a butler, writing in the 1890s: Burnett, p. 209.

101 'A Working Man', *Working Men and Women*, ch. 10, 'The unskilled labourer'.

102 Minutes of the Newcastle Branch of the Provincial Typographical Association (in Tyne and Wear County Record Office, 807/2–3), entries for 25 April 1874, 24 April 1877, 29 April 1876.

103 cf. Hobsbawm, 'The labour aristocracy in nineteenth-century Britain' in *Labouring Men*, esp. p. 275.

104 D. C. Cummings, *An Historical Survey of the Boiler Makers' Society* (Newcastle, 1905), pp. 60–65; caulkers were later accepted as a distinct trade and admitted to the Society in 1877.

105 Burnett, *Nine Hours Movement*, pp. 10, 14.

106 Boilermakers, *Monthly Report*, January 1874; for the relations between platers and helpers see McClelland and Reid, 'Wood, iron and steel', pp. 166, 169, 171–72 and references cited there.

107 J. Lynch, 'Skilled and unskilled labour in the shipbuilding trade', *Report of the Industrial Remuneration Conference* (London, 1885), pp. 114–18.

108 FSIF, 1871, cited in Webb TU Collection, A.XIX, p. 222. See also, e.g., Boil-

ermakers, *Monthly Report*, December 1882: 'The Society wanted to make the members as respectable a class of men as existed in the country.'

109 Cited in Maxine Berg, *The Machinery Question and the Making of Political Economy 1815–1848* (Cambridge University Press, 1980), pp. 328–29.

110 Allen Clarke, *The Effects of the Factory System* (London, 1899), p. 145.

111 Hippolyte Taine, *Notes on England*, trans. E. Hyams (London, Thames and Hudson, 1957), p. 225; Thomas Wright, 'Inner life of workshops', pp. 96–97.

112 Clarke, *Factory System*, p. 72.

113 W. A. Abram, 'Social condition and political prospect of the Lancashire workmen', *Fortnightly Review*, new series, 4 (1868), 432.

114 *Newcastle Weekly Chronicle*, 24 February 1866.

115 *Chainmakers' Journal*, 6 (November 1858), 42.

116 *Jarrow Chronicle*, 10 June 1871; on the need for more recreational time see also the comments of Peter Bailey on the ten hours and later movements in his *Leisure and Class in Victorian England* (London, Routledge and Kegan Paul, 1978), pp. 13, 49–50, 80–81; see also, for another e.g., the Birmingham policemen's strike of 1871: Carolyn Steedman, *Policing the Victorian Community* (London, Routledge and Kegan Paul, 1984), p. 135.

117 FSIF 1871, cited in Webb TU Collection, A.XIX, p. 222.

118 Catherine Hall, 'The early formation of Victorian domestic ideology' in Sandra Burman, ed., *Fit work for women* (London, George Allen and Unwin, 1979).

119 Boilermakers, *Annual Report*, 1883, p. xiii.

120 PP 1872 (242) IX. Select Committee on Habitual Drunkards, q. 2,526 (J. Hurman); PP 1877 (271) XI. Select Committee (House of Lords) Intemperance, 2nd Report, qq. 3,173, 3,182, 3,454 (Capt. S. J. Nicholls, Chief Constable of Newcastle).

121 Boilermakers, *Monthly Report*, July 1879, pp. 10–11; Mrs. C. Liddell, *A Shepherd of the Sheep* (London, 1916), p. 44.

122 Nicholls, evidence to Select Committee on Intemperance, q. 3292.

123 Two excellent surveys of recreation are Bailey, *Leisure and Class* and Hugh Cunningham, *Leisure in the Industrial Revolution* (London, Croom Helm, 1980).

124 Peter Bailey, '"Will the real Bill Banks please stand up?" Towards a role analysis of mid-Victorian working-class respectability', *Journal of Social History*, 12 (1979), 336–53 discusses the context-bound nuances of 're-spectability'.

125 For example E. S. Beesly wrote that the 'best workmen' wanted a diminution of hours so that the workman may 'educate himself, ... enjoy himself, and above all ... see more of his family': 'The social future of the working class', *Fortnightly Review*, new series, 5 (1869), 359.

126 Liddell, *Shepherd*, pp. 41–42. For an analysis of the housing problem in Newcastle and Gateshead in the 1850s and beyond see M. J. Daunton, *House and Home in the Victorian City* (London, Edward Arnold, 1983), ch. 2; the evidence concerning the extent to which the housing of skilled workers on Tyneside was substantially better than that of the unskilled is ambiguous: it cannot be discussed here.

127 See, among others, 'An artisan at his club', *Newcastle Weekly Chronicle*, 20 February 1869, a fascinating journalist's account of the pattern of a man's evenings; unfortunately it is too lengthy to be quoted here.

128 Ellen Ross, '"Not the sort that would sit on the doorstep": respectability in pre-world war 1 London neighbourhoods', *International Labor and Working Class History*, 27 (1985), 39–59.

129 Pollitt, *Serving My Time*, Preface and ch. 1; T. H. S. Escott, *England: its People, Polity and Pursuits* (2 vols., London, 1879), vol. 1, p. 399.

8 'A TIME FOR EVERY PURPOSE': AN ESSAY ON TIME AND WORK

I am grateful for helpful discussions with Peter Clark, Linda Hantrais, Patrick Joyce and Nicole Samuel. I am indebted to Carole Ann Meredith for her invaluable insights into time.

1 J. Ditton, 'The problem of time: styles of time management, and schemes of time-manipulation amongst machine-paced workers', University of Durham, Department of Sociology and Social Administration, Working Papers in Sociology No. 2 (1971), p. 51 n. 36. See also Association for Social Studies of Time, Second Conference, Cambridge, 13 April 1985, Conference Report, *passim*.

2 Flinn and Smout, for example, in 1974 felt that there was little which had added to Thompson's view on time and work in spite of Hexter's treatment of Braudel two years earlier: see notes 15 and 27 below.

3 G. Simmel, *Essays on Interpretation in Social Science*, translated and edited by G. Oakes (Manchester University Press, 1981), p. 127.

4 *Ibid.* pp. 128, 132–34.

5 *Ibid.* pp. 138–41.

6 E. Hobsbawm, 'Looking forward: history and the future', *New Left Review*, 125 (Jan.–Feb. 1981), 4, 14, 16.

7 C. Tilly, *As Sociology Meets History* (New York, Academic Press, 1981), pp. xiii, 7, 46.

8 *Ibid.* p. 6.

9 K. Nield and J. Blackman, Editorial, *Social History*, 10 (1985), 7.

10 T. Radford, 'The clockwork of history', *The Guardian*, 19 Jan. 1984, p. 18; D. S. Landes, *Revolution in Time: Clocks and the Making of the Modern World* (Cambridge, Mass., Harvard University Press, 1983).

11 S. Kern, *The Culture of Time and Space* (London, Weidenfeld and Nicolson, 1983); A. Burgess, 'Clock-watching', *The Observer*, 15 Jan. 1984, p. 49.

12 A. Mayr, 'The music of times and tides', paper presented to ASSET, Second Conference, Cambridge, 1985, p. 1.

13 For an introductory overview of the Annales school see C. Charney, 'Braudel: last of the French giants', *The Times Higher Education Supplement*, 13 Sept. 1985, p. 10.

14 See note 5.

15 F. Braudel, *On History*, translated by S. Matthews (London, Weidenfeld and Nicolson, 1980), pp. 3–14. See also, J. Hexter, 'Fernand Braudel and the mode Braudellian', *Journal of Modern History*, 13 (1972), 1–23.

16 Braudel, *On History*, pp. 3–4.

17 Charney, 'Braudel', p. 10; Braudel, *On History*, pp. 26–27, 32; E. Le Roy Ladurie, *The Territory of the Historian*, translated by B. and S. Reynolds

(Brighton, Harvester Press, 1979), ch. 7, 'The "event" and the "long term" in social history: the case of the Chouan uprising', pp. 111–28.

18 E. Durkheim and M. Mauss, *Primitive Classification*, trans. R. Needham (Chicago, Cohen and West, 1969); H. Bergson, *Introduction à la metaphysique* (Paris, Press Universitaires de France, 1903).

19 For an insightful review of early work on time in anthropology and sociology see P. Clark, 'The multiplicity of time reckoning systems in modern western industrial organizations', paper presented to the 34th Conference of the Society for Applied Anthropology, 1974; M. Mauss, 'Essai sur les variations saisonnieres des societes Eskimoux', *L'Année sociologique*, 9 (1904); E. Evans-Pritchard, *The Nuer* (Oxford University Press, 1940); C. Lévi-Strauss, *Structural Anthropology* (London, Basic Books, 1969).

20 P. A. Sorokin, *Sociocultural Causality, Space and Time* (Duke University Press, 1943); G. Gurvitch, *The Spectrum of Social Time* (Dordrecht, Reidel, 1964).

21 Mauss, 'Essai', p. 127; Z. Zerubavel, *Hidden Rhythms—Schedules and Calendars in Social Life* (University of Chicago Press, 1981).

22 W. Grossin, 'The multiplicity of different times', paper presented to the ESRC Seminar on Time, the Family and Leisure within the Franco–British Perspective, 13–16 March 1985. See also his, *Les Temps de la vie quotidienne* (Paris, 1974).

23 P. Laslett, 'Social structural time', paper presented to ASSET, Second Conference, Cambridge 1985, pp. 1–3.

24 S. Toulmin and J. Goodfield, *The Discovery of Time* (London, Hutchinson, 1965); Ditton, 'Problem of time', p. 13.

25 G. Mead, 'An essay on time' in A. Strauss, ed., *George Herbert Mead on Social Psychology* (University of Chicago Press, 1965), p. 331; Ditton, 'Problem of time', p. 13; Burgess, 'Clock-watching', p. 49; D. Chambers, 'The constraints of working hours on leisure life styles', mimeo, Department of Behavioural and Communication Studies, Polytechnic of Wales, 1985, p. 2.

26 Clark, 'Time reckoning systems', p. 1.

27 E. P. Thompson, 'Time, work-discipline and industrial capitalism', *Past and Present*, 38 (1967), 56–97. See also the reprint in M. W. Flinn and T. C. Smout, *Essays in Social History* (London, Clarendon Press, 1974), pp. 39–77, used here for citation purposes.

28 Evans-Pritchard, *The Nuer*; P. Bourdieu, 'The attitude of the Algerian peasant towards time', in J. Pitt-Rivers, ed., *Mediterranean Countrymen* (Paris, Mouton, 1963), pp. 55–72.

29 Thompson, 'Time, work-discipline', p. 40.

30 *Ibid.* p. 43.

31 *Ibid.* p. 53.

32 *Ibid.* pp. 58–64.

33 *Ibid.* pp. 64, 66.

34 D. Reid, 'The decline of Saint Monday 1766–1876', *Past and Present*, 71 (1976), 76–101.

35 M. Bienefeld, *Working Hours in British Industry: An Economic History* (London, Weidenfeld and Nicolson, 1972), pp. 1–7, 177–78, 222–26.

36 See for example the approach and sources used in The Trade Union Research Unit, *Working Time in Britain* (London, The Trade Union Research Unit, 1981).

37 Rowntree and Co. Ltd, the cocoa works, York, Factory rules, 7th edition, 1957, section G. 'timekeeping'. C. Sharp, _The Economics of Time_ (Oxford, Martin Robertson, 1981), p. 7; W. Cottrell, 'Of time and the railroader', in D. W. Minar and S. Greer, eds., _A Concept of Community_ (London, Butterworths, 1969), pp. 142–51.

38 R. Bendix, _Work and Authority in Industry_ (New York, Wiley, 1956); J. A. Merkle, _Management and Ideology_ (London, University of California Press, 1980), pp. 209, 220.

39 R. Samuel, ed., _Miners, Quarrymen and Saltworkers_ (London, Routledge and Kegan Paul, 1977), pp. xi, xii–xiii.

40 K. Marx, _Capital_, edited by F. Engels and translated by S. Moore and E. Aveling (vol. I, 3rd German edn, London, Allen and Unwin, 1938 (1867)), p. 482; D. Montgomery, _Workers Control in America_ (Cambridge University Press, 1979), p. 104; H. Gutman, _Work, Culture and Society in Industrializing America_ (New York, Knopf, 1976), pp. 38–55.

41 J. Zeitlin, 'Social theory and the history of work', _Social History_, 8 (1983), 365, 370–1.

42 Thompson, 'Time, work-discipline', p. 55; D. Gregory, _Regional Transformation and Industrial Revolution. A Geography of the Yorkshire Woollen Industry_ (London, Macmillan, 1982), p. 187.

43 A. L. Stinchcombe, 'Social structure and organisation', in J. G. March, ed., _Handbook of Organizations_ (Chicago, Rand McNally, 1965).

44 P. H. Grinyer and J. C. Spender, _Turnaround: Management Recipes for Strategies of Success_ (London, Associated Business Press, 1979).

45 C. Sabel, _Work and Politics_ (Cambridge University Press, 1982); C. Sabel and J. Zeitlin, 'Historical alternatives to mass production: politics, markets and technology in nineteenth-century industrialization', _Past and Present_, 108 (1985), 133–76.

46 C. Freeman, 'Long waves and innovation', paper presented to Technology Policy Unit, Aston University, March 1983; H. Ramsay, 'Participation: the pattern and its significance', in T. Nichols, ed., _Capital and Labour_ (Glasgow, Athlone Press, 1980).

47 C. Calhoun, 'Community: towards a variable conceptualization for comparative research, _Social History_, 5 (1980), 105–27; A. Macfarlane, 'History, anthropology and the study of communities', _Social History_, 5 (1977), 631–52.

48 R. Whipp, 'Labour markets and communities: an historical view', _Sociological Review_, 33 (1985), 767–90.

49 Gregory, _Regional Transformation_, pp. 86–87; P. Joyce, _Work, Society and Politics. The Culture of the Factory in Later Victorian England_ (Brighton, Harvester Press, 1980); D. Massey, _Spatial Divisions of Labour. Social Structures and the Geography of Production_ (London, Macmillan, 1984), pp. 12–66.

50 M. Berg, _The Age of Manufactures_ (London, Fontana, 1985), ch. 7, 'Custom and community in domestic manufacture and the trades'; J. Benson, _Penny Capitalism_ (Dublin, Gill and Macmillan, 1983).

51 T. Hareven, _Family Time and Industrial Time. The Relationship Between the Family and Work in a New England Industrial Community_ (Cambridge University Press, 1982), pp. xi–8, 359–63. See also M. Anderson, 'The emergence of the modern life cycle in Britain,' _Social History_, 10 (1985), 69–88.

52 G. Simmel, *Conflict* (London, Free Press of Glencoe, 1955), p. 58 ff.; N. Rosenberg, *The American System of Manufacture* (Edinburgh University Press, 1969).

53 Gregory, *Regional Transformation*, p. 86; S. Webb and A. Freeman, *The Seasonal Trades* (London, Constable, 1912); S. Hill, *The Dockers. Class and Tradition in London* (London, Heinemann, 1976), p. 49.

54 S. Clegg, 'Organisational democracy, power and participation', in F. Heller and C. Crouch, eds., *International Year Book of Organisational Democracy* (London, Wiley, 1983), vol. I, p. 7; Merkle, *Management and Ideology*, p. 209. S. Pollard, *The Genesis of Modern Management* (London, Edward Arnold, 1965), p. 250.

55 Zeitlin, 'Social theory', pp. 365, 371; D. Roy, '"Banana time", job satisfaction and informal interaction', *Human Organization*, 18 (1960), 158–68; Gregory, *Regional Transformation*, p. 82; A. Williams, *Life in a Railway Factory* (London, Duckworth, 1915 (1909)), pp. 42, 56, 249; J. Hassard, 'Continuous duty to 42 hours: the struggle for a normal working day in British fire fighting, 1833–1979', mimeo, Department of Business Administration and Accountancy, UWIST, 1984, pp. 3, 28.

56 M. Grieco, 'Standardised hospital design and work organisation in the health sector', mimeo, Work Organization Research Centre, Aston University, April 1985.

57 K. McClelland, 'Time to work, time to live: some aspects of work and the reformation of the working class in Britain', paper presented to the History Workshop, Social History Centre, History of Work seminar, Ruskin College, Oxford, 19 October 1985; P. Joyce, 'Work', in F. M. L. Thompson, ed., *The Cambridge Social History of Great Britain, 1750–1950* (forthcoming).

58 *The Times Imperial and Foreign Trade Supplement* (August 1917), p. i. See also R. Whipp, 'Potbank and union: a study of work and trade unionism in the pottery industry, 1900–1924' (unpublished Ph.D. thesis, Warwick University, 1983), ch. 1, 'The pottery industry', pp. 1–55.

59 G. W. and F. A. Rhead, *Stafforshire Pots and Potters* (London, Hutchinson, 1906), p. 27; J. C. Wedgwood, *Staffordshire Pottery and its History* (London, Sampson, Law, Marston, n.d.), pp. 204–5.

60 *The Stafforshire Advertiser*, 26 May 1906, p. 6; D. J. Machin, 'The economics of technical change in the British pottery industry' (unpublished MA thesis, Keele University, 1973), p. 63.

61 *The Times Imperial and Foreign Trade Supplement* (1917), section XII.

62 *The Pottery Gazette*, 1 Feb. 1906, letter of W. T.; 25 Jan., p. 181 and 1 May, p. 585 (1908); 1 Sept. 1918, p. 723.

63 Whipp, 'Potbank and union', pp. 34–8. See especially the monthly reports of *The Labour Gazette* on 'The pottery industry', e.g. July 1902.

64 R. Whipp, '"The art of good management": managerial control of work in the British pottery industry, 1900–1925', *International Review of Social History*, 29 (1984), 360–63.

65 *The Times Supplement*, August 1917, 'Sanitary ware'. Cf. sanitary's performance in the *Labour Gazette* with B. Mitchell and P. Deane, *Abstract of British Historical Statistics* (Cambridge University Press, 1962), 'Houses built – Gt. Britain 1856–1956', p. 239.

66 National Council of the Pottery Industry, *Notes on Whiteware Alkaline Casting Slip* (Hanley, National Council of the Pottery Industry, 1925), p. 3;

J. Gray, proprietor of Brittania works, *Pottery Gazette*, 1 April 1921, p. 643.

67 Whipp, 'Art of good management', pp. 370–71.

68 Accountant's Report to the 1924 Wage Inquiry, p. 8, Ceramic and Allied Trade Union (CATU), Hanley; Department of Commerce, Miscellaneous Series No. 21, *The Pottery Industry* (Washington, Government Printing Office, 1915), p. 395; Letter of R. Stirrat to Sam Clowes, union organiser, dated 1920.

69 *Report of a Conference of Operatives and Manufacturers on the Pottery Industry* (Darlington, North of England Newspaper Co. Ltd., 1917), manufacturers' submission, section III; C. J. Noke and H. J. Plant, *Common Commodities and Industries. Pottery* (London, Sir Isaac Pitman, 1924); *The Staffordshire Sentinel*, 14 Jan. 1918, p. 9.

70 Whipp, 'Potbank and union', pp. 58–66.

71 Machin, 'Economics of technical change', p. 77; National Society of Pottery Workers, *Reconstruction in the Pottery Industry* (Manchester, National Society of Pottery Workers, 1945), p. 3; Letter of C. Sedgly to S. Clowes, March 1919; Interview with E. Ellis; Letter of J. Lovatt to Outram and Co., 23 May 1913 (CATU); Evidence of HMI Redgrave to *The Departmental Committee on the Truck Acts* (1906), Report, p. 778.

72 Interview with W. Bell; *Pottery Gazette*, 1 May 1922, p. 780 and G. Tuckwell comments 1 Nov. 1911, p. 1,246; *The Times*, 27 Sept. 1898, p. 5.

73 HMI Factory Reports (London 1913), p. 86. D. Mycock evidence to *The Departmental Committee on the Employment of Women and Young Persons to the Two-Shift System* (1920), Cmd. 1038, q. 1881; Letter of Keeling and Co. to J. Lovatt, 24 April 1914, CATU; Gregory, *Regional Transformation*, pp. 86–87; M. Godelier, 'Work and its representations: a research proposal', *History Workshop Journal*, 19 (1980), 167; J. H. Clapham, *An Economic History of Modern Britain*, vol. 3, *Machines and National Rivalries 1887–1914* (Cambridge University Press, 1938), p. 189.

74 M. Grieco and R. Whipp, 'Women and the workplace: gender and control in the labour process', in D. Knights, ed., *Studies of Gender and Technology in the Labour Process* (London, Gower, 1986), pp. 115–37.

75 See National Society of Pottery Workers, survey of members, 1924, CATU; *Pottery Gazette*, 1 Oct. 1911, p. 1155; 1 August 1916; p. 849, 1 July 1918, p. 562 and 1 Oct. 1919, p. 1109; R. Whipp, 'The stamp of futility: the Staffordshire potters 1880–1905', in R. Harrison and J. Zeitlin, eds., *Divisions of Labour. Skilled Workers and Technological Change in Nineteenth Century England* (Brighton, Harvester Press, 1985), p. 119.

76 Whipp, 'Potbank and union', pp. 244–57, especially 256, and 270; *The Staffordshire Advertizer*, 14 July, p. 5 and 6 Oct., p. 5 (1906).

77 C. R. Walker and R. H. Guest, *The Man on the Assembly Line* (Cambridge, Mass, Harvard University Press, 1952; republished New York, 1979); H. Beynon, *Working for Ford* (Harmondsworth, Penguin, 1973).

78 R. H. Guest, 'Organisational democracy and the quality of work life: the man on the assembly line in Crouch and Heller', *Organisational Democracy*, p. 139.

79 TASS, *A Policy for the British Motor Vehicle Industry* (London, TASS, n.d.), p. 9.

80 H. A. Turner, G. Clack and G. Roberts, *Labour Relations in the Motor*

Industry. A Study of Industrial Unrest and an International Comparison (London, Allen and Unwin, 1967), pp. 40–43, 88.

81 S. Tolliday, 'Trade unions and collective bargaining in the British motor industry 1896–1970', mimeo, King's College Research Centre, Cambridge University, June 1984.

82 W. Lewchuk, 'The British motor vehicle industry 1896–1982', mimeo, McMaster University, 1983.

83 J. P. Bardou, J. J. Chanaron, P. Fridenson and J. M. Laux, *The Automobile Revolution. The Impact of an Industry* (Chapel Hill, University of Carolina Press, 1982), pp. 247 ff.

84 G. Bloomfield, *The World Automotive Industry* (London, David and Charles, 1978), p. 39; F. G. Woollard, 'Some notes on British methods of continuous production', *Proceedings of the Institute of Automobile Engineers*, 19 (1924–5), 451–53, 465; 'Engine assembly. The system and layout employed by the Austin motor company limited', *Automobile Engineer*, 37 (1947), 90–97.

85 R. Whipp and P. Clark, *Innovation in the Auto Industry. Production, Process and Work Organisation* (London, Frances Pinter, 1985), ch. 3, the Rover Company.

86 J. Foreman-Peck, 'Exit, voice and loyalty as responses to decline: the Rover company in the inter-war years', *Business History*, 23 (1981), 191–207.

87 Whipp and Clark, *Innovation*, ch. 3, III 'Wilks and the P series'.

88 Interview with S. King, *Motor*, 26 June 1974; J. Ensor, *The Motor Industry* (London, Longman, 1971), pp. 12, 23.

89 Interview with senior design engineer. See also R. Whipp, 'Management, design and industrial relations in the British automobile industry: the SDI project', *Industrial Relations Journal*, 17 (1986); *Stock Exchange Gazette*, 19 Oct. 1964.

90 Interview with senior project engineer.

91 See Whipp and Clark, *Innovation*, ch. 3, 'The Rover company', sections II, III and IV.

92 'Car assembly. The layout of the Meteor works of the Rover company limited, Solihull', *Automobile Engineer*, Sept. 1946, pp. 2–13.

93 Analysis of company executive register 1945–1968, Rover archive, British Motor Industry Heritage Trust, Studley, Warwickshire; Interview with Rover IR director.

94 *Rover News*, April 1973, pp. 2 ff.; H. B. Light, *The Rover Story*, ch. 24, Rover archive; Interview with track supervisor; Rover board minutes, 2 June 1960, Rover archive. See Whipp and Clark, *Innovation*, 'The SDI project: commissioning and operation', section II.

95 Light, *The Rover Story*, ch. 24.

96 Interview with P6 paint rectifier shop steward: *A Workers' Enquiry into the Motor Industry* (London, Institute for Workers' Control, n.d.), p. 13 – compare S. Tolliday, 'High tide and after. Coventry engineering workers and shopfloor bargaining 1945–80', in W. Lancaster and A. Mason, eds., *Life and Labour in a Twentieth Century City: The Experience of Coventry* (forthcoming).

97 Interviews with senior shop steward, p. 3 and final assembly steward, p. 2.

98 Whipp and Clark, *Innovation*, pp. 129–30.

99 See Urwick Orr Report to Rover Co. Ltd, 28 Oct. 1970, *passim*, Rover com-

pany directors' minutes, 8 and 9 November 1968; Interviews with senior P6 shop steward and P6 final trim worker.

100 Austin-Rover Group, 'The right product', mimeo 1984; *Automotive News*, 16 Jan. 1984, pp. 5–7; R. Kaplinsky, 'Electronics-based automation technologies and the onset of systemofacture', *World Development* (forthcoming).

101 R. Pahl, 'Time and the social relations of everyday tasks', paper presented to Anglo-French seminar on family and time.

102 N. Thrift, 'On the determination of social action in time and space', *Environment and Planning D: Society and Space*, 1 (1983), 23–57; H. F. Moorhouse, 'Labouring', *Bulletin of the Society for the Study of Labour History*, 49 (1984) 72–74; Godelier, 'Representations of work'. Further avenues for exploration include the relation of time and gender, see A. M. Daune-Richard, 'Travail professionel et travail domestique: étude exploratoire sur le travail et ses representations au Sein des Lignees Feminines', Petite collection CEFUP, Aix-en-Provence University.

103 G. Greene, *The Tenth Man* (London, Bodley Head, 1985), p. 35.

9 The 'WORK' ETHIC AND 'LEISURE' ACTIVITY: THE HOT ROD IN POST-WAR AMERICA

1 The following were all influential: C. Walker and R. Guest, *The Man on The Assembly Line* (Cambridge, Mass., Harvard University Press, 1952); E. Chinoy, *Automobile Workers and the American Dream* (Garden City, NY, Doubleday, 1955); R. Blauner, *Alienation and Freedom* (University of Chicago Press, 1964). They are often much more sophisticated in tone than a continuing genre of exposés of the 'nature' of car 'work'. See, for example, H. Beynon, *Working For Ford* (London, Allen Lane, 1973), and S. Kamata, *Japan in The Passing Lane* (London, Allen and Unwin, 1983).

2 Sparked off by: H. Braverman, *Labor and Monopoly Capital* (New York, Monthly Review Press, 1974). Braverman expressly ignored the subjective perception of 'work', a convenient device which has served his myriad followers well in prolonging the 'labour process debate'.

3 A. Kornhauser, *The Mental Health of the American Worker* (London, 1965).

4 *Ibid.* p. 7.

5 *Ibid.* p. 199.

6 M. Rose, *Re-Working The Work Ethic* (London, Batsford, 1985); R. E. Pahl, *Divisions of Labour* (Oxford, Blackwell, 1984); H. F. Moorhouse, 'American automobiles and workers' dreams', in K. Thompson, ed., *Work, Employment and Unemployment* (Milton Keynes, Open University Press, 1984).

7 Rose, *Re-Working*, p. 19.

8 *Ibid.* p. 105.

9 Pahl, *Divisions*, p. 336.

10 *Ibid.* p. 329. Thus I do not think I could fit the work on hot rods I discuss in the text into Pahl's 'Preliminary typology of work' on his p. 125.

11 Pahl, *Divisions*, p. 106 fn.

12 D. Rodgers, *The Work Ethic in Industrial America 1850–1920* (London, University of Chicago Press, 1978), p. 14.

13 See the neglected book by K. Kusterer, *Know How on the Job* (Colorado, Westview, 1978).

14 R. Sennett and J. Cobb, *The Hidden Injuries of Class* (Cambridge University Press, 1972), though I doubt that most workers do 'suffer' in the way this book suggests. Rather 'sacrifice' *does* provide purpose.

15 And see the interesting hypotheses about the cognitive style intrinsic to automobile production in P. Berger *et al.*, *The Homeless Mind* (London, Penguin, 1974) pp. 32–43.

16 See the extended discussion of this, and its effects in dividing workers on gender lines, in C. Cockburn, *Brothers* (London, Pluto, 1983).

17 *Fortune*, 36:5 (November 1947).

18 M. Dubofsky *et al.*, *The United States in the Twentieth Century* (London, Prentice Hall, 1978), p. 427.

19 R. P. Smith, *Consumer Demands for Cars in the U.S.A.* (Cambridge University Press, 1975), Appendix A, Table 3.

20 J. Bernard, 'Teenage culture: an overview', *The Annals of the American Academy of Political and Social Science*, vol. 338 (November 1961), p. 4.

21 The position of *Hot Rod* and the NHRA (National Hot Rod Association) at the centre of the subculture has meant that their version of its history tends to be that which prevails in the few accounts which are available. As well as items indicated below, introductions to the hot-rod culture are contained in J. Storer, 'Coach-building in customizing', in S. Murray, ed., *Petersens Creative Customizing* (Los Angeles, Petersen, 1978), pp. 4–13; W. Parks, *Drag Racing: Yesterday and Today* (New York, Trident, 1966); R. Denny, *The Astonished Muse* (University of Chicago Press, 1957), ch. 7; R. Boyle, *Sport: Mirror of American Life* (Boston, Little Brown, 1963), ch. 4; L. Levine, *Ford: The Dust and the Glory* (London, Collier-Macmillan, 1968), ch. 16. E. Lawrence, 'Gow jobs', *Colliers*, July 26 1941 and 'Hot rods', *Life*, 5 November 1945, are early mass-media accounts.

22 See the typology set out by G. Balsley, 'The hot rod culture', *American Quarterly*, 2:1 (Spring 1950).

23 E. Jaderquist, *The New How to Build Hot Rods* (New York, Arco, 6th printing 1977), p. 33.

24 F. Horsley, *Hot Rod It – and Run For Fun* (Englewood Cliffs, Prentice Hall, 1957), p. 151.

25 *Hot Rods* interventions in the subculture are discussed in detail in: H. F. Moorhouse, 'Organising the hot rods', *British Journal of Sports History*, 3:1 (May 1986), and H. F. Moorhouse, 'Racing for a sign: defining the "hot rod" 1945–1960', *Journal of Popular Culture* (forthcoming).

26 *Hot Rod* (afterwards *HR*) 1:10 (1948); 3:5 (1950), 2:1 and 2 (1958).

27 S. Alexander, 'All over in 6 seconds', *Road and Track*, August 1974, pp. 73–78.

28 Pahl, *Divisions*, p. 102 fn notes the development in Britain of DIY magazines from 1959 onwards but does *not* investigate the ideologies they promoted.

29 *HR* 1:2 (1948).

30 *Ibid.* 1:4 (1948).

31 *Ibid.* 2:3 (1949).

32 *Ibid.* 2:12 (1949).

33 *Ibid.* 4:6 (1951).

34 *Ibid.* 6:12 (1953).

35 *Ibid.* 2:3 (1949).
36 *Ibid.* 4:9 (1957).
37 *Ibid.* 7:2 (1954).
38 *Ibid.* 4:7 (1951).
39 *Ibid.* 4:9 (1951).
40 *Ibid.* 4:9 (1951).
41 *Ibid.* 6:5 (1953).
42 *Ibid.* 7:1 (1954).
43 *Ibid.* 3:2 (1950).
44 *Ibid.* 1:11 (1948).
45 *Ibid.* 11:2 (1959); J. P. Viken, 'The sport of drag racing and the search for satisfaction, meaning and self' (unpublished Ph.D. thesis, University of Minnesota, 1978), pp. 80–81 notes that the hot rodders he observed were better at mending cars than 'professional' mechanics at the local garage.
46 *HR* 4:3 (1951).
47 Balsley, 'Hot rod culture', reprinted in *HR* 4:7 (1951).
48 *HR* 5:8 (1952).
49 I discuss how *Hot Rod* worked on the term 'hot rod' to try to encompass more and more of the 'motor-minded' in H. F. Moorhouse, 'Racing for a sign'.
50 C. W. Mills, *White Collar* (New York, Oxford University Press, 1951), chs. 10–11; T. Burns, 'The study of consumer behaviour', *Archives Européenes de sociologie*, 7 (1966). See my discussion in H. F. Moorhouse, 'American automobiles and workers' dreams', in K. Thompson, ed., *Work, Employment and Unemployment* (Milton Keynes, Open University Press, 1984); S. Ewen, *Captains of Consciousness* (New York, McGraw Hill, 1976) sees the roots of 'consumer culture' in the 1920s but the flowering as a post-war phenomenon.
51 *HR* 3: 8 (1950).
52 *HR* 4:5 (1951).
53 H. Felsen, *Hot Rod* (New York, Dutton, 1950) is the novel. TV and radio shows include 'Dragnet', 'Life with Riley', 'Public Defender', and 'The Bob Cummings Show'. In all of these, according to *Hot Rod*, the shows' central characters were made to appreciate the serious nature of the hot rod enterprise.
54 'The drag racing rage', *Life*, April 29 1957, p. 78.
55 Of course, one of the assumptions in much of the literature about 'work' as paid labour is to assume that every skilled worker was actually a good or competent craftsman. This is one of the ways in which social analysis has presented an idealised view of 'work' in the past.
56 *HR* 5:3 (1952).
57 *Ibid.* 6:5 (1953).
58 *Ibid.* 8:1 (1955).
59 *Ibid.* 4:9 (1951).
60 D. Garlits and B. Yates, *King of the Dragsters* (London, Chilton, 1967), pp. 18–19.
61 B. Ottum, 'Is there life after hot rodding?', *Sports Illustrated* (March 1981), pp. 40–41.
62 Exemplified in the title and text of T. Madigan, *The Loner: The Story of a Drag Racer* (Englewood Cliffs, Prentice Hall, 1974).

63 H. Higdon, *Six Seconds to Glory: Don Prudhommes Greatest Drag Race* (New York, Putnams, 1975), p. 95.
64 Close to that 'Reader's Digest philosophy' which Mills, *White Collar*, p. 283, regarded as important in post-war America. Serious study of the 'stars' of any unpaid activity is virtually non-existent.
65 *HR* 3:10 (1950).
66 See an example: 'Losinski, what are your secrets?' in *HR* 6:12 (1953).
67 By 1960 Petersen, the owner of *Hot Rod* could appear on the front page of the *Wall Street Journal* in a series about 'the new millionaires and how they made their fortunes', serving, perhaps, as an inspiration to the entrepreneurial elite. This story, though, does not really emphasise his 'work', but cleverness in spotting gaps in the market and, indeed, his 'high-living'. 'Road to riches', *Wall Street Journal*, 22 July 1960.

Index

Abram, W. A., 205
Académie des Sciences Morales et
Politiques, 121, 129
agricultural workers, 70, 202; female, 67, 68
Akroyd, Edward, 175, 176, 177
Alexander, Sally, 107, 108
'Alfred' (Samuel Kydd), history of factory movement, 172
Allen, John, 183
Althorp, Viscount (John Charles, 3rd Earl Spencer), 154, 155, 156, 166, 173
Amalgamated Society of Engineers (ASE), 191, 196, 201, 202
Amiens, confraternities of journeymen in, 47
Amsterdam seamstresses, 93
Anduze, France, occupations in, 54
Anglicans, 157, 158
Annales school, 211, 213, 215
Anthony, P. D., *The Ideology of Work*, 4
anthropology, anthropologists, 213; and meanings of work, 2–10, 13, 18; and relationship between time and work, 214–15, 217, 235
Anti-Corn Law League, 145
apprentices, apprenticeship, 50, 71, 85, 110, 181, 190–4, 233; female, 67, 73, 75; patrimonial system, 111, 194; repeal of statutory (1814), 105, 107, 111; and restriction of entry to trade, 100–1, 102, 105–6, 108
Aris's Gazette, notices relating to women's employment (1752–90), 86–7, 98
aristocracy of labour, 11, 18, 106, 116, 180
Arkwright, Richard, 78
Armitage, William, 174
arms manufacture, gun trade, 84, 87, 222
Armstrong's engineering and ordnance works, Tyneside, 181, 184

artisans, skilled workers, 13, 15, 16, 18, 99–118, 148, 150–2, 180–209; control of labour process, 100, 109–10, 112, 115, 117, 151–2, 183; definition of, 102, 181–2; independence of, 29, 107, 110, 113, 153, 202, 203; relations with employers, 109–10, 195–6, 200; role in labour movement, 113–14; 118, 143; separation from common labourer, 99, 101, 108, 109, 115, 202–3; solidarity, mutuality, 113, 116; values of, 104, 108–9, 114, 151; *see also* French journeymen; master artisans; skill
Ashley, Lord (Anthony Cooper, 7th Earl of Shaftesbury), 154, 156, 162, 167, 172, 178; Select Committee (1840), 168, 169, 170, 176
Ashton, Thomas, 163, 170
Ashworth, Henry, 163, 164, 167, 170, 171
Atelier, L', 125
Audiganne, Armand, 129, 132
automobile industry: American, 230, 231, 237, 251, 254; British, 211, 229–36; *see also* car workers
Auvernat (French journeyman), 51–2
Auxerre, France, 50, 55, 57, 58

Bailey, P., 24
Baker, Robert, 175
Bamford, Samuel, 116
Bardou, J. P., 231
Bedaux time-and-payment system, 223, 233
Behagg, C., 18, 113, 118
Bendix, R., 218
Benson, J., 221
Benthamism, 145, 155, 156, 160, 167, 172
Berg, Maxine, 107, 221, 235
Bergson, H., 214
Bienefeld, M., 217, 223
Birley, Richard, 176